3-82

Charles S. Peirce

Charles S. Peirce

From Pragmatism to Pragmaticism

by Karl-Otto Apel

Translated by John Michael Krois

University of Massachusetts Press   Amherst, 1981

Introduction and Author's Preface to the English translation
Copyright © 1981 by The University of Massachusetts Press

English translation and Translator's Preface
Copyright © 1981 by John Michael Krois

Originally published in German under the title
Der Denkweg von Charles S. Peirce:
Eine Einführung in den amerikanischen Pragmatismus,
by Karl-Otto Apel, copyright © 1967, 1970 by
Suhrkamp Verlag, Frankfurt am Main

The publisher gratefully acknowledges the support of the
National Endowment for the Humanities toward the publication
of this book.

Contents

Author's Preface
to the English Translation

With the English translation of this book—a book conceived fifteen years ago in the framework of my German edition of Peirce's writings—I am presented with an occasion to recollect about the course of my thought. How did I actually come to the conception expressed in this book on Peirce, and what role has my occupation with his philosophy played for me since its publication? A brief answer to these questions could be of interest to English-speaking readers of a book on Peirce written from a German perspective. In addition, it can also contribute to the clarification of certain, specific aspects of the following presentation of Peirce's thought.

I do not want to conceal the fact that my perspective has undergone certain shifts in the course of my studies of Peirce. In the beginning, my concern was merely with presenting the founder of American Pragmatism to a German audience. For me, this project stood in the context of an attempt to reconstruct the history of philosophy in a way that would confront the different, future-directed philosophies that serve today to actually mediate theory and practice. The philosophies involved were on one hand, Pragmatism and Existentialism, which provide the complementarity system that constitutes Western ideology, and on the other hand, Marxism, which, in an orthodox version, provides the integration system that defines ideology in the East. The concepts "complementarity" and "integration" refer in this context to the particular relationship between public and private life and the relationship between scientific rationality and ethics.

This early background conception for an introduction to American Pragmatism in fact still formed the outer framework of the Peirce book, as is indicated on the first and last pages. Yet in the course of

my Peirce studies, that is, as I entered more deeply into Peirce's philosophy, this historical conception receded into the background. I recognized more and more that Peirce was a much less appropriate choice
than William James or John Dewey would have been as the prototype
of American Pragmatism in an ideal comparison with the other two
philosophies of the mediation of theory and practice. As a matter of
fact, for the comparison with Existentialism, William James's thought
(such as in *The Will to Believe*) is particularly interesting, and for the
comparison with Marxism, John Dewey's philosophy. But what role
can Peirce play in a comparison with those philosophies that are presently really effective in the world?

Is Peirce, as the founder of the "pragmatic maxim" for the clarification of meaning and of the principle of "Fallibilism," merely a forerunner of today's "philosophy of science" as it has developed under
the name of "Logical Empiricism" or under Popperianism? This view,
as far as I can see, was the most influential interpretation of Peirce
besides the one according to which he was primarily to be regarded
as the forerunner of James and Dewey. A further, interesting retrospective approach to Peirce saw him as an American Neo-Kantian, a
view expressed, for example, by Jürgen von Kempski and Murray G.
Murphey in their monographs. They granted Peirce great originality,
but credited it to his fundamental misunderstanding of Kant.

All of these retrospective views of Peirce were helpful to me,
especially the last one.[1] But I could not accept any of them as a satisfactory perspective for interpretation. In particular, a critical analysis
of the last of these perspectives showed that Peirce was an independent thinker of the greatest systematic interest to the contemporary
philosophical situation. Peirce's decade-long attempt to critically reconstruct Kant's *Critique of Pure Reason* is, to be sure, anything but
historical or philological, but it does not end with a misunderstanding
of Kant. Nor do I think that it ends, as representatives of a modern,
realistic metaphysics contend, in a restoration of a pre-Kantian type
of ontological, cosmological speculation. The methodological primacy
of the epistemological question of the "grounds of the validity" of
cognition over metaphysics is upheld in Peirce's philosophy to the
end. But this is connected with a semiotic, transcendental-pragmatic
transformation of the logic of cognition into a logic of inquiry.

---

1. On this, see my essay "From Kant to Peirce: the Semiotic Transformation
of Transcendental Logic," in *Proceedings of the Third International Kant Congress*, 1970, ed. Lewis White Beck (Dordrecht: Reidel, 1972), pp. 90–104; reprinted
in *Kant's Theory of Knowledge*, ed. Lewis White Beck (Dordrecht: Reidel, 1974),
pp. 23–37; and in Karl-Otto Apel, *Towards a Transformation of Philosophy*,
trans. Glyn Adey and David Frisby (London, Boston, and Henley: Routledge &
Kegan Paul, 1980), pp. 77–92.

The characteristic innovation of Peirce's logic of inquiry cannot be regarded as a return to metaphysical Realism or Idealism, but rather as a meaning-critical postulate in the framework of a semiotic transformation of Kant's "transcendental logic." This occurs when Peirce replaces the concept of "incognizable things in themselves" with the concept of the "infinitely cognizable," the concept of the "transcendental subject" of cognition with the concept of the "indefinite community" as the subject of the "ultimate opinion," and, finally, the transcendental deduction of the a priori "principles" of knowledge through the transcendental deduction of the long range validity of the three modes of inference that make cognition possible.

Difficulties do arise, however, with Peirce's doctrine of the three fundamental categories, insofar as he attempts to found these after 1900, evidently, upon the two *presemiotic* disciplines of mathematics— the mathematical logic of relations—and phenomenology or phaneroscopy. Here I admit that I have attempted to think beyond Peirce by using Peirce's own ideas against him and holding to the primacy of his semiotic transformation of the logic of cognition as the foundation of philosophy. Here, by the way, the interesting task arises of comparing Peirce's semiotic transformation of Kant with Ernst Cassirer's "Neo-Kantianism" in his *Philosophy of Symbolic Forms*.

With these remarks I wish to indicate that Peirce finally became important for me primarily as an ally in the systematic undertaking of a "transformation of (transcendental) philosophy." This involves, for one thing, using a transcendental semiotic or transcendental pragmatics to overcome what I call the "abstractive fallacy" in the semantics proposed in the logic of science by Carnap, Tarski, and, implicitly, Popper. In place of an "epistemology without a knowing subject" (Popper) or a dyadic semantics, which declares the "pragmatic dimension" of sign interpretation to be exclusively a theme for the empirical sciences, there should be an attempt to give a foundation that, despite the necessary methodological abstraction, recognizes and takes into account the fundamental importance of the subject dimension in the triadic sign relation as the condition of the possibility of valid, objective knowledge.[2] This results in an overcoming of the "methodological solipsism" that begins by assuming the autarchy of the knowing subject (a postulate upheld from Descartes to Husserl), and

2. On this, see my essays "Zur Idee einer transzendentalen Sprachpragmatik," in *Aspekte und Probleme der Sprachphilosophie*, ed. Josef Simon (Freiburg: Alber, 1974), 283–326; "Der semiotische Pragmatismus von C. S. Peirce und die 'Abstractive Fallacy' in den Grundlagen der Kantschen Erkenntnistheorie und der Carnapschen Wissenschaftslogik," in *bewußt sein*, Festschrift für G. Funke, ed. A. J. Bucher, H. Drüe, and Thomas Seebohm (Bonn: Bouvier Verlag, 1975), pp. 49–58; and "Transcendental Semiotics and the Paradigms of First Philosophy," *Philosophic Exchange*, 2, no. 4 (1978), 3–22.

conceives the knowing subject itself a priori as a member of an "unlimited communication community," an insight based upon transcendental reflection on validity claims.

Here, in the investigation of subjective and intersubjective communication and interpretation presuppositions of science, the interests
of a semiotically transformed transcendental philosophy meet with
the interests of hermeneutic philosophy. Such philosophy should, I
think, not conceive of the topics which the *Geisteswissenschaften* seek
to "understand" as methodologically in competition with the topics of
sciences that seek to provide nomological "explanations," but rather
as subjective and intersubjective conditions of the latter.[3] The subject
matter is the historical dimension of our understanding of the world,
the dimension that makes possible the existence of an interpretation
community as a collective knowing subject. Here too the instruments
provided by Peirce's semiotic seem to be helpful, but not in the form
of the behavioristic reconstruction that they were given by Charles
W. Morris.[4] Rather, I am thinking of the form that Josiah Royce gave
to semiotic in his late work, which was developed in response to
Peirce's thought, where Royce developed a philosophy of the historical interpretation community.[5]

Finally, I believe that transcendental semiotic, or transcendental
pragmatics, with its insight that the thinking (and by this I mean
"arguing") subject must necessarily conceive of itself as a member of
a communication community, can serve as the basis for a final foundation of ethics. This insight provides a decoding of what Kant referred
to as the "Faktum der Vernunft" (*factum* of reason), to which the
recognition of a basic ethical norm is supposed to belong, for it shows
that this recognition is in fact the unconditioned duty to reach a consensus about norms through argumentation.[6] This fundamental meta-

3. See my essays "The A priori of Communication and the Foundation of
the Humanities," *Man and World*, 5, no. 1 (1972), 3–37; "Types of Social Science
in the Light of Human Interests of Knowledge," *Social Research*, 44, no. 3 (1977),
425–70; reprinted in *Philosophical Disputes in the Social Sciences*, ed. St. Brown
(Harvester Press, 1979); *Die Erklären: Verstehen Kontroverse in Transzendental-
Pragmatischer Hinsicht* (Frankfurt: Suhrkamp, 1979); "The 'Erklären: Verstehen'
Controversy in the Philosophy of the Human and Natural Sciences," in *Chroni-
cles of the International Institute of Philosophy*, vol. 2, forthcoming.

4. See my critical introduction to the German edition of Morris's *Signs,
Language and Behavior* [*Zeichen, Sprache und Verhalten*] (Düsseldorf: Schwann,
1973), 9–66.

5. For a discussion of this, see my essay "Scientism or transcendental Pragmatics? On the question of the interpretation of signs in the semiotics of pragmatism," in *Towards a Transformation of Philosophy*, pp. 93–135.

6. See my essays "The A priori of the communication community and the
foundations of ethics," in *Towards a Transformation of Philosophy*, pp. 225–
300; "Sprechakt-theorie und transzendentale Sprachpragmatik zur Frage ethischer

norm of ethics seems to me to be implicit in an a priori of argumentation that cannot be circumvented, just as there is a theoretical basic norm that calls for us to redeem truth claims in the discourse of an unlimited community of argumentation.[7]

Of course, the last mentioned perspectives go beyond Peirce; and probably they will seem to Peirce's pragmatic and neo-pragmatic followers today, who think along the lines of Dewey or Quine, to be superfluous "transcendentalism." Yet this much seems to me undeniable: the conception of a transcendental semiotic that I have sketched here can find a great reservoir of untapped viewpoints and arguments in Peirce's extensive body of writings. If I were to stand once again before the task of interpreting Peirce's philosophy, then I would, from the very outset, take his semiotic as the general focal point and would incorporate the corresponding parts of his work to a much greater extent than I did in the present book.

Finally, I have the pleasant task of thanking all those who have contributed to the publication of this English translation. First of all, I want to thank the translator, John Michael Krois. I thank as well Howard Gold and James Liszka, from whom the initiative for this edition came, and Richard Martin, editor at the University of Massachusetts Press, for his continued support. Last but not least, I thank Prof. Richard Bernstein for his appreciative introduction.

University of Frankfurt   Karl-Otto Apel
West Germany

Normen," in *Sprachpragmatik und Philosophie*, ed. Karl-Otto Apel (Frankfurt: Suhrkamp, 1976), pp. 10–173; "The Problem of Philosophical Fundamental Grounding in the Light of a Transcendental Pragmatic of Language," *Man and World*, 8, no. 3 (1975), 239–75; and "Warum transzendentale Sprachpragmatik?" in *Prinzip Freiheit*, ed. H. M. Baumgartner (Freiburg: Alber, 1979), pp. 13–43.

7. See my essays "C. S. Peirce and the Post-Tarskian Problem of an Adequate Explication of the Meaning of Truth," *The Monist*, 63, no. 3 (1980), 386–407 and "C. S. Peirce's and Jürgen Habermas' Consensus Theory of Truth," *Transactions of the Charles S. Peirce Society*, in press.

Translator's Preface

Karl-Otto Apel's work on Peirce, which is translated here, originally appeared as the two-part introduction to his two-volume edition of Peirce's writings in German translation. The first volume was published in 1967 and the second appeared in 1970. Professor Apel combined his extensive introductions to these volumes to create a self-contained, developmental study that was published in 1975 as *Der Denkweg von Charles S. Peirce*. It was decided to retitle this English translation in a way that makes the developmental nature of the study explicit, because there is no English term that easily captures the sense of *Denkweg* in the original German title.

In this translation I have tried for an accurate rendering of the argument. I have usually been more literal than free in my choice of modes of expression. Whenever I was faced with a decision between an idiomatic or a more accurate translation I have chosen the latter; if the result is not always a typical English sentence, it is because the original sentence is itself academic, rather than popular German. In keeping with English usage I have frequently divided Apel's very long sentences into shorter ones.

There are a number of technical terms in this study that require special attention. Since this is a book by a German philosopher about an American thinker, many of the key terms are simply translated back into the original idiom. I have followed standard vocabulary where possible in English translations of German philosophical terms. One exception to this is that when Apel uses *Aufhebung* in the Hegelian sense of the term I have preferred to leave it in the original. I see no advantage in rendering it as "sublation," as is sometimes done in Hegel translations. It was also necessary to diverge from the common practice of following Norman Kemp Smith's translation of

Anschauung as "intuition."[1] Apel uses *Anschauung* in its literal sense
of looking at something, having a view of something. It would lead to
great confusion to translate *Anschauung* as "intuition" because for
Peirce the English word "intuition" has the special sense of immediate
insight. For Peirce, intuition means: "a premiss not itself a conclusion"
(5.213). Because of this I have chosen formulations such as "vision"
or "perception," which more accurately reflect the sense in which Apel
uses the word *Anschauung*.

A closely related term that occurs often in Apel's book, and is
used frequently in German philosophy generally, is *spekulativ*. This
German form of the Latin noun *speculatio* does not carry the stigma
attached to the English word "speculative," which is associated with
forming illusory ideas and idle dreams about things beyond possible
experience or practical bearing. In German *spekulativ* is simply used
to mean "theoretical" in the sense of a philosophical theory. Peirce
also used the term in this way, and distinguished it from the pejora-
tive interpretation by writing: " 'Speculative' is merely the Latin form
corresponding to the Greek word 'theoretical,' and is here intended to
signify that the study is of the *purely* scientific kind, not a practical
science, still less an art."[2] The reader should keep this usage in mind
when the term occurs in this book.

Another case of a misleading standard translation, at least in a
work dealing with Peirce, is the practice of translating *Vorstellung* as
"representation." Since Apel himself discusses this problem in the
book, I only want to indicate that I use the word "representation" as
the translation of the cognate term *Repräsentation*, while the word
Vorstellung is translated as "notion" or another mentalistic term in
order to avoid confusing the semiotic mode of speaking with a discussion expressed in terms of consciousness.[3] The philosophical importance and nature of this distinction is one aspect of the difference between the critique of meaning and the critique of knowledge that Apel
discusses at length in this book.

Urteil is translated as "judgment," and *Aussage* is given as
"proposition." These are generally accepted equivalents.

The phrase *immer schon*, "always already," has a particular significance in German hermeneutics. Writers in that field use this phrase
to call attention to the "hermeneutical circle" in our understanding of

---

1. See *Immanuel Kant's Critique of Pure Reason*, trans. Norman Kemp Smith
(New York: St. Martin's Press, 1965), esp. pp. 65–66.

2. Charles Sanders Peirce, "Ideas, Stray or Stolen, about Scientific Writing.
No. 1," *Philosophy and Rhetoric* 11 (1978): 152.

3. On the usual translation of *Vorstellung* as "representation" see *Immanuel
Kant's Critique of Pure Reason*, esp. p. 314.

the world.[4] According to writers in hermeneutics, any investigation must begin with some context of established interpretations. Peirce too explored this problem of the beginning point of philosophical interpretation at length; beliefs always precede doubt, and we can only begin an inquiry from where we begin it, with the attitudes and prejudices that we bring with us. This situation is unavoidable because, as sign interpreters, we are always in a community of interpretation. These themes in Peirce are among those that make his thought so interesting to contemporary German philosophers. The term "always already" is not a phrase that occurs naturally in English, yet I have retained this literal translation of *immer schon*. When this phrase occurs in the text it indicates that the specific philosophical problem of preinterpretation has been raised.

Finally, some explanation is necessary of the terms in this book that were either coined by Apel or play an important role in his own thought. These terms are: *Sinnkritik*, *Verständigung*, and *Kommunikationsgemeinschaft*. *Sinnkritik* (translated as "critique of meaning") and its adjectival form *sinnkritisch* (translated as "meaning-critical") play an important role in Apel's interpretation of Peirce. For Apel, *Sinnkritik* designates reflection on the preconditions of the understanding of meaning and, hence, of argument. Apel coined this term to distinguish between contemporary philosophizing and the earlier philosophical concern with *Erkenntniskritik*, critique of knowledge.[5] The difference between these two methods of analysis represents for him a shift or transformation in philosophy generally, from an older phase in which philosophers sought to investigate knowledge by reference to "consciousness," to a new phase in which meaning is thought to be more fundamental than "knowledge." In this new phase of philosophy attention is directed to language and other types of signs, rather than to "ideas" or "minds," which from this new point of view appear to be constructs that depend upon the more basic phenomenon of meaning. Habermas adopts the term *Sinnkritik* in his examination of Peirce in *Knowledge and Human Interests* (*Erkenntnis und Interesse*). The English translation of Habermas's book uses the

---

4. On the "hermeneutical circle" see Martin Heidegger, *Sein und Zeit* (Tübingen: Max Niemeyer, 1972), §32; Cf. Hans-Georg Gadamer, *Wahrheit und Methode* (Tübingen: J. C. B. Mohr [Paul Siebeck], 1975), 2, Chap. 2, Sec. 1, pp. 250–90.

5. For an early discussion of this term and its significance for Apel in defining the field of contemporary philosophy, see "Wittgenstein und Heidegger: Die Frage nach dem Sinn von Sein und der Sinnlosigkeitsverdacht gegen alle Metaphysik," reprinted in Karl-Otto Apel, *Transformation der Philosophie*, 2 vols. (Frankfurt am Main: Suhrkamp, 1973), 1: 225–75.

expression "critique of meaning" for *Sinnkritik*, and I have kept the same translation here.[6]

The term *Verständigung* presents difficulties because there is no English that reflects all the important senses of this word. *Verständigung* means: (1) the process of grasping or understanding a meaning at all, (2) notifying or telling somebody something, and (3) coming to mutual understanding or agreement. By contrast, the German *Verstehen* only expresses the first of these three meanings and I have translated it as "understanding." For *Verständigung* I have followed Apel's own practice in his English articles of using the phrase "communicative understanding,"[7] but have inserted the German in brackets where necessary. *Verständigung* is one of the central ideas in Apel's "communicative ethics," and the reader seeking further clarification of *Verständigung* should consult his writings on that subject.[8]

The term *Kommunikationsgemeinschaft* is given here as "communication community." For a full discussion of that term, the reader should turn to the essay "The *A Priori* of the Communication Community and the Foundations of Ethics."[9]

Professor Apel's book was written with a German audience in mind. This is one reason why it should provide a new perspective on Peirce for English-speaking readers. It places Peirce's ideas in a context that is different from the familiar territory of American Peirce scholarship. But it also poses the problem that the author presumes familiarity on the reader's part with certain philosophical trends— Hegelianism, existentialism, Neo-Marxism, and hermeneutics—which might only be known in varying degrees by the readers of this translation. I have added footnotes in some places to clarify passages that seem to presuppose a particular awareness of some such trend or problem in German thought, but have kept this practice to a minimum in order not to increase the already large number of references. Such notes are indicated by "—Trans." References have been given in their complete form in keeping with American documentation practice.

I wish to thank Howard Gold and James Liszka for suggesting

6. Jürgen Habermas, *Knowledge and Human Interests*, trans. Jeremy J. Shapiro (Boston: Beacon Press, 1971), Chap. 6, "The Self-Reflection of the Natural Sciences: The Pragmatist Critique of Meaning."

7. See Karl-Otto Apel, "Types of Social Science in the Light of Human Interests of Knowledge," *Social Research* 44 (1977), 425–70.

8. See esp. Karl-Otto Apel, "Sprechakttheorie und transzendentale Sprachpragmatik zur Frage ethischer Normen" in *Sprachpragmatik und Philosophie*, ed. Karl-Otto Apel (Frankfurt am Main: Suhrkamp, 1976), pp. 10–173. On *Verständigung* see pp. 135–44.

9. Karl-Otto Apel, *Towards a transformation of philosophy*, trans. Glyn Adey and David Frisby (London, Boston, Henley: Routledge and Kegan Paul, 1980), pp. 225–300.

that I undertake this project and for all their efforts in arranging the details of publication. Each has also read a version of the translation in manuscript and given helpful advice. Professor Richard Bernstein, who kindly consented to write an introduction, has also read a draft of the manuscript and given me the benefit of his criticisms. Special thanks are due to Mr. Richard Martin, editor at the University of Massachusetts Press, whose patience and friendly help have made the book's preparation easier for me. Finally, I want to express my particular gratitude to Professor Apel with whom I have discussed all the key terms of this translation and who has made many valuable suggestions on the manuscript.

University of Trier   John Michael Krois
West Germany

Introduction

Charles Sanders Peirce is considered by many to be America's most original and greatest philosopher, but outside the philosophic community his name and work are still barely known. Even among philosophers, Peirce is more honored as the founder of the pragmatic movement than he is seriously studied and discussed. The story of the vicissitudes of Peirce's influence is a fascinating one. It is commonly believed that during his lifetime (September 10, 1839–April 19, 1914), Peirce was intellectually isolated and without any significant influence or recognition. It is certainly true that Peirce, who placed so much emphasis on a critical community of inquirers, lacked such a community where his bold conjectures could be challenged, criticized, and refined. But we must not forget that the leading American philosophers of the time, including William James, Josiah Royce, and John Dewey, not only recognized Peirce's genius, but were all deeply influenced by him in their philosophic work. It was primarily through William James's popular essays on pragmatism that Peirce was acknowledged to be the founder of the pragmatic movement. Peirce was sufficiently uneasy about the nominalistic and subjectivistic tendencies in James's version of pragmatism that he was eventually led to reformulate his own conception of pragmatism, which he labeled "pragmaticism"—a name "which is ugly enough to be safe from kidnappers." Peirce pleaded with James to engage in the serious study of logic that Peirce took to be the backbone of his own philosophy. Although he failed to persuade James, he did succeed with Royce whose later writings reveal Peirce's significant impact. This is especially evident in the way Royce appropriated and modified Peirce's ideal of an unlimited community of inquirers into the general and central conception of a community of interpreters. Although John Dewey was a graduate student at Johns Hopkins during Peirce's brief period on the faculty, he was not among the circle of young logicians that Peirce attracted. It was only after Dewey moved away from his early idealistic leanings that he came to appreciate the full power of Peirce's thought. Dewey's own philosophic development shows a growing appropriation of Peirce's conception of inquiry as an on-going self-corrective process rooted in an open critical community. He sought to apply these theses to a theory of the democratic community.

Despite this recognition by America's leading philosophers, when Harvard University secured Peirce's voluminous unpublished writings after his death, there was still skepticism about the real merits of his work. The task of editing the papers was turned over to a young instructor and a graduate student, Charles Hartshorne and Paul Weiss. Lacking any editorial experience, they confronted the complex and monumental task of editing Peirce's scrambled drafts and scribblings. Fortunately, they had the perspicacity to recognize the scope and importance of Peirce's work. It is primarily through their efforts in editing the first six volumes of the *Collected Papers* that Peirce became known to a wider circle of thinkers than his close friends.

When the first six volumes of the *Collected Papers* were published between 1931 and 1935—a collection that represents a small fragment of Peirce's writings—initially only a few hundred copies were sold. (A new chronological and much more comprehensive collection of Peirce's writings is now being prepared for publication.) The influence of the pragmatic movement had begun to wane among American professional philosophers. In the late thirties and forties, there was an increasing interest in logical positivism, logical empiricism, and the philosophy of science. After the Second World War, new currents and interests were adopted from the style of linguistic philosophy practiced in Oxford. The ahistorical—indeed the antihistorical—bias of logical empiricism and linguistic philosophy was taken over by many leading American philosophers. There was an implicit dogma that it is one task "to do" philosophy—to solve or dissolve philosophic problems and puzzles—and quite a different task to study the history of philosophy, even the recent history. As a result, Peirce's work, along with that of the other "classic" American philosophers, seemed to fall into oblivion. At best it was considered to be a subject appropriate for those concerned with American intellectual history.

Ever since the publication of the *Collected Papers*, there has been a dedicated group of Peirce scholars who have labored to make the richness of Peirce's thought accessible to a larger philosophic audience, but in the main their work has been marginal to what many philosophers have taken to be the pressing philosophic problems of the day. There are deep ironies in this neglect of Peirce, because many of the issues and insights that have emerged in recent philosophy of science, language, and action were not only anticipated by Peirce, but were explored by him with depth and originality. This has sometimes been acknowledged by philosophers like Sir Karl Popper, W. V. O. Quine, Wilfrid Sellars, and Hilary Putnam. But however much we can now recognize continuity and convergence, it would be difficult to maintain that this recognition has been the result of careful examination of Peirce's philosophy. It is almost as if many contemporary philosophers have had to rediscover and work out for themselves what Peirce had already discovered in his reflections on inquiry, science, language, and conduct.

When we turn to the almost total lack of attention to Peirce's work by British and European philosophers, the story is even bleaker. There was a brief flurry of engagement with pragmatism at the turn of the century, but it was primarily James's pragmatism that was discussed and severely criticized. Pragmatism was judged (or rather misjudged) to be diffuse, weak, and antiintellectual—little more than an ideological expression of the vulgar aspects of American materialism and the "typical" American impatience with theory. Even those philosophers—such as Bergson, Husserl, and Wittgenstein—who were impressed with William James's *Principles of Psychology* were ignorant of Peirce's original philosophy. A great exception was the brilliant young British philosopher, F. P. Ramsey, who was closely associated with Russell and Wittgenstein. One can only speculate about what influence Peirce's work might have had on the course of British philosophy if Ramsey had not died at such a young age.

A philosopher's thought lives when it is critically encountered, when there is a shared concern about the problems and questions with which he or she is struggling and those recognized to be central to ongoing philosophic discussion. By this criterion, it would seem that Peirce's philosophy has not been a vital part of the living conversation of the larger philosophic community. Or so it would have seemed until recently. For in the past few decades a remarkable change has taken place. Peirce's originality and his almost uncanny anticipation of those problems and issues that are *now* taken to be at the heart of philosophy are being fully recognized. His work is being interpreted in fresh and novel ways. This new interest in Peirce has been stimulated by the philosophic and linguistic concerns of many European thinkers. One of the pervasive characteristics of contemporary philosophy has been the linguistic turn—the diverse ways in which the study of language has been taken to be absolutely central to philosophy. This is not only characteristic of Anglo-American philosophy, but is also true of such continental movements as hermeneutics and semiotics. A century ago, Peirce projected and began to outline a theory of signs—a comprehensive semiotics. It was Peirce who declared that man not only uses signs but that he himself *is* a sign. It is this dimension of Peirce's thought—his project of developing a theory of signs that would encompass all modes of signification—that is now receiving such widespread attention and investigation.

Retrospectively, we can see how Peirce's philosophic inquiries span issues that have become central to both Anglo-American and Continental philosophy. As a practicing experimental scientist and one of the most creative logicians of his time, Peirce forcefully argued that the dominant conception of the nature of science that had been shaped by the empiricist and rationalist tradition was grossly inadequate. It distorted the true experimental spirit of scientific inquiry. He sought to get at the roots of this distortion, which he took to be the Cartesianism that had infected so much modern thought with its obsession with foundationalism and indubitability. He elaborated a new image of scientific inquiry that emphasized the essential fallibility of all scientific inquiry, and how it can be understood without indubitable foundations. He sought to exorcise the subjectivism of the Cartesian framework and replace it with a proper understanding of the intersubjective and communal dimensions of scientific inquiry. His "image of science"—and indeed all inquiry—focused on inquiry as a continuous self-corrective activity governed by the norms of a critical community of inquirers. Furthermore, Peirce was one of the first to argue that the study of the history of science was essential for a proper philosophical understanding of science. It has become increasingly evident that Peirce helped initiate a revolution in our thinking about the nature and context of scientific inquiry that has been elaborated and refined in the work of philosophers like Quine, Sellars, Putnam, Kuhn, Popper, and Toulmin (despite the many important differences among them).

But Peirce was not just a philosopher of science and a logician. If we are to gain a genuine understanding of scientific inquiry, then it is necessary to probe metaphysical and cosmological issues. Meaning and truth in science must be examined from a more general theory of language and signification. In his late work, the general theory of signs—semiotics—plays an increasingly dominant role. In this respect there is continuity between Peirce's project of a universal and comprehensive theory of signification and these themes as they have been elaborated in the contemporary philosophic movements of hermeneutics and semiotics. It is precisely because Peirce sought to weave together themes that are central to Anglo-American philosophy and Continental philosophy that so many thinkers are turning to him for guidance in developing a genuine dialectical synthesis. One cannot help noting the irony that many Anglo-American thinkers are coming to recognize the power, suggestiveness, and fertility of Peirce's thought because of the critical attention that he is now receiving from European thinkers. It may come as a surprise that one of the most thoughtful, sophisticated, and illuminating studies of Peirce has been written by a German philosopher, Karl-Otto Apel.

To appreciate the context in which this book was written and its significance, it is necessary to have some understanding of the historical situation of German philosophy during the period following the Second World War. After the trauma and grotesque break with tradition during the Nazi years, there was an urgent sense of the need to reestablish continuity with the flourishing of German philosophy that began with Kant and lasted through the first part of the twentieth century. At the same time there was the desire to be self-critical, to probe not only the strengths of this tradition but its weaknesses and inadequacies. The self-containment and isolation of German philosophy was shattered. German thinkers were open to different philosophic movements in order to learn from them and in order to critically evaluate their own tradition. There has also been a sense of the need to work toward a systematic perspective that would address the pressing theoretical and practical problems of our time.

Karl-Otto Apel has been one of the leading German philosophers to emerge during this fertile period. His own philosophic work exhibits the threefold concern that has shaped German philosophy during this post-Second World War period—to rethink and to recover what is still "living" in the tradition of German philosophy, which since Kant has emphasized human freedom, rationality, and self-reflection; to engage in a critical encounter with different philosophic movements, especially analytic philosophy and pragmatism; and to develop a transformation of philosophy that would overcome scientism, relativism, and historicism, and that would point the way for a unified rational basis for both theoretical and practical discourse.

Apel began his philosophic career schooled in the tradition of hermeneutics that has been given a universal and ontological significance in the work of Heidegger and Gadamer, but he also has had a deep interest in analytic philosophy. He has argued that when we grasp the internal dialectic of both analytic philosophy (as exhibited in the work of the early and late Wittgenstein) as well as the way in which hermeneutics has developed, we discover that both these movements have undergone a transformation that reveals a convergence (as well as tensions and differences). Apel has been arguing that a transformation has been taking place that brings analytic and Continental philosophers closer together. When we understand what is valid and reject what is misguided in both these movements, we can see how they point to the need for elaborating a "transcendental pragmatics" that uncovers the a priori structure of all human communications. It is in this attempt to develop a universal transcendental pragmatics that the work of Peirce has become so central for Apel. He argues that the type of "communication community" that is suggested as a regulative ideal by Peirce opens the way to elaborating a transcendental pragmatics that is rich enough to encompass science and ethics, theoretical and practical discourse. The very expression "transcendental pragmatics" indicates Apel's deliberate attempt to find a dialectical synthesis of Anglo-American and Continental philosophy. Many philosophers working in these different traditions might normally think that "pragmatics" and "transcendental philosophy" are not only radically distinct but are incompatible with each other. The very idea of a "transcendental pragmatics" might seem to be a category mistake. Apel is, of course, aware of this widespread bias. It is the very challenge that he seeks to confront. I have stressed the genesis of Apel's interest in Peirce, and the central role that Peirce plays in Apel's systematic investigations, because it is important to realize that Apel's interest in Peirce is motivated primarily as a result of philosophic concerns. Frequently the best and most illuminating commentaries of a given philosopher are those in which a genuine dialogue is taking place, where a philosopher is being questioned for the illumination that his or her work sheds on philosophical issues. Apel's study of Peirce is this type of living an exciting conversation.

The book was originally written to serve as an introduction to the German translation of selections from Peirce's writings. Apel's immediate task was to provide a proper context within which readers unfamiliar with Peirce could understand his work, and at the same time to provide a coherent interpretation of the development of Peirce's thought. But quite apart from Apel's original intentions, his study stands as one of the best introductions to Peirce in any language. It is much more than an introduction to Peirce. It is a penetrating scholarly interpretation that addresses many problems that have been discussed by Peirce scholars. The task of understanding and interpreting Peirce poses tangled difficulties. Peirce never wrote a single systematic treatise that sums up his position, or even stands as a centerpiece of his philosophy. Furthermore, Peirce's writings are so varied—ranging over all human knowledge and experience—that they pose a challenge to any interpreter to detect an underlying coherence and unity of thought. Despite Peirce's interest in system and architectonic, his writings present the appearance of being fragmentary, and at times even seem to be incompatible with each other. The problem that any interpreter of Peirce faces is how to make sense of, how to see the thematic unity of what appears to be so disparate and even chaotic. Apel's solution to his problem of interpretation is to analyze Peirce's thought from a developmental perspective. The stages of this development follow Peirce's chronological career. But Apel's primary intention is to recover and reconstruct what were the primary problems that Peirce was addressing at each stage of his development, to indicate the ways in which Peirce sought to solve these problems, and to show how they led to a new set of issues that needed to be analyzed.

In each of the four stages of development that Apel discriminates, he claims that there is a central set of articles or lectures that reveals the distinctive character of Peirce's interests. He carefully analyzes these papers in order to justify his interpretation of Peirce. A philosophic drama unfolds where one gains not only a deepening insight into Peirce's development, but into the main problems of contemporary philosophy.

The first period that Apel analyzes spans the years from 1855 to 1871, from Peirce's earliest reflections on philosophy until the founding of the Metaphysical Club in Cambridge. (The Metaphysical Club consisted of a group of thinkers from different disciplines including William James and Chauncey Wright who met to discuss philosophic issues.) Apel—who calls Peirce the "Kant of America"—stresses the importance of Peirce's early critical study of Kant. It is clear that Kant was a major influence on Peirce, but it is also clear that Peirce felt that Kant's solution to the problems he uncovered was inadequate. One of the larger themes that emerges in Apel's study is Kant's prevailing influence throughout Peirce's development. He argues that we can read Peirce as bringing about a semiotic transformation of Kant's transcendental philosophy—a transformation that moves from the analysis of consciousness and self-consciousness to the intersubjectivity of linguistic communication. In this first stage of his development, Peirce focused on criticizing the concept of the thing-in-itself, and pursuing the ramifications of this critique, especially as it pertains to developing a new list of categories. The dominant theme of this first stage of development is the movement from the critique of knowledge to the critique of meaning. Many of the issues that were to preoccupy Peirce throughout his life are already suggested in this first stage, as Peirce began to elaborate what Apel calls a "meaning critical realism."

The second stage lasted from the discussions of the Metaphysical Club until the time of Peirce's dismissal from Johns Hopkins in 1884 (the only regular academic position that he ever held). Apel sees this as the "classic period" of American pragmaticism. It is the time when pragmatism was influenced by the work of Chauncey Wright and Alexander Bain. This was a time when Peirce seemed to move much closer to the main emphases of the empiricist tradition, or more accurately, when he attempted to incorporate what he took to be valid in the empiricist tradition. When James popularized pragmatism in the last decade of the nineteenth century, it was the pragmatic doctrines of this period that he had in mind. But throughout this period Peirce continued his serious study of the new logic. At Johns Hopkins he exerted a strong influence on a small group of logicians and mathematicians who were becoming aware of the revolutionary developments in logic that were occurring during the nineteenth century. As Apel shows, even during this period, Peirce was already wary of attempts to assimilate pragmatism to the type of nominalism and subjectivism that Peirce took to be the disease of modern philosophy. Peirce was already developing arguments against the limitations of empiricism that anticipate many of the critiques of logical empiricism and positivism.

The major shift in Peirce's philosophy, as Apel unfolds his philosophic narrative, takes place during the third stage of his development—a period that corresponds to Peirce's "retirement" to Milford, Pennsylvania. It is characterized by a growing and bold speculation about cosmological, metaphysical, and evolutionary problems. During this period the systematic and architectonic aspirations of Peirce's philosophy come into prominence. Peirce's "meaning critical realism" is placed within a wider context that seeks to come to grips with the spontaneity, novelty, and continuity that is evidence throughout the cosmos. During this stage too, in an age before quantum physics, Peirce attacked the type of mechanistic determinism and belief in causal necessity that was so entrenched during his time. He elaborated an evolutionary interpretation of the cosmos and our place within it that wove together the subtle interplay of novelty and continuity.

The final stage that Apel discusses begins in 1902 and lasts until Peirce's death in 1914. This was the time when James's pragmatism was enjoying enormous popularity, and when Peirce felt the need not only to dissociate himself from James but to reformulate what he took to be the essentials of his own *pragmaticism*. It is also a time when Peirce returned to many of the themes introduced by his "meaning critical realism" now informed and mediated by his metaphysical and cosmological speculations. It is during this period that we find the richest development of the theory of signs and the central place that semiotics plays in all philosophy. It is in this final stage that Apel locates the basis for a transcendental pragmatics. Apel seeks to carry on Peirce's project and move beyond it by revealing the a priori structure for all human communication. Apel argues that while Peirce provides the guidelines for such a transcendental pragmatics, he did not succeed in showing the underlying unity between theoretical and practical reason. Apel even suggests that such an extension of Peirce's line of inquiry enables us to sketch the basis of a theory of communicative ethics.

Apel's study of Peirce's development and his attempt to justify his interpretations during each period with the careful analysis of the relevant texts go a long way to making sense of the totality of Peirce's thought and to showing its underlying thematic coherence. Of course, many of his interpretations are controversial and will surely generate discussion among scholars of Peirce. But they are well thought out and supported with arguments and the analysis of texts. Apel always pays close attention to Peirce's texts and problems, but his informed discussions of contemporary analytic philosophy, semiotics, and hermeneutics help to place Peirce in perspective.

This impressive introduction to Peirce serves as an excellent guide through the thorny and tangled paths of Peirce's philosophy. It will also stimulate scholars of Peirce who have emphasized different aspects of Peirce's thought, and may take exception to some of Apel's forcefully argued interpretations. But perhaps its greatest contribution is that it offers to anyone seriously interested in the primary philosophic issues of our time the opportunity to discover the multifarious ways in which Peirce's thought is relevant and illuminating. Apel eminently succeeds in helping to bring Peirce back into the living conversation of philosophy.

Richard J. Bernstein

I

The Philosophical Background
of the Rise of Pragmatism
in the Thought
of Charles Sanders Peirce

1
Peirce and the
Contemporary Function of Pragmatism

Despite the exaggeration and simplification that is involved in the revelation of any complex truth, it can be said that in the world of so-called industrial society there are exactly three philosophies that really function. By this I do not mean just that they are advocated, but that they in fact mediate between theory and practice in life. These philosophies are Marxism, Existentialism, and Pragmatism.[1] These share in this function simply because they were the first to have taken up as a topic of thought the great problem of humanity thrust into an unfinished world, the mediation of theory and praxis with regard to an uncertain future. Each in its own way has recognized that in a world that is not a finished cosmos, in a life that, as Kierkegaard says, "must be lived in terms of the future," and in a social situation that can be changed, philosophy cannot be self-contained. As a theoretical study, philosophy cannot put the praxis of life aside, as if it could first recognize the essence of things through pure, disinterested contemplation and then orient praxis to its theory. Nor can philosophy act as though the laws of the unfinished world could be determined a priori or as though history, which is open to the future, could be disengaged in reflection that would no longer be practically embedded. I do not want to attempt to give a further characterization of the new self-conception of these three philosophies of the mediation of theory and praxis. The unity of their point of departure, which can be understood historically as a response to Kant's primacy of practical reason and to Hegel's completion of theoretical metaphysics as the metaphysics of history, is lost all too quickly.

Instead of attempting to develop the theoretical tenets of these different, very complex philosophies from this starting point in nineteenth-century thought, I want to direct a brief look at their function in the contemporary world. That is, I want to consider the fact that these three philosophies share the task of mediating between theory and praxis in modern industrial society.

To begin with, we could consider the following geographic distribution of thought: Marxism controls communist Eurasia, Pragmatism dominates in the Anglo-Saxon countries and in Scandinavia, and Existentialism predominates in the rest of Europe and extends to the Latin American countries. Although such a statement would certainly not be wrong, let me propose another division that I think is more instructive.

Orthodox Marxism-Leninism, under the administration of which the proletarian revolution was carried out, and which is presently leading the "development of Socialism" during the phase of the "dictatorship of the proletariat," had to install itself, as far as we can tell today, as the dogmatic administrator of the mediation of theory and praxis. It must be postulated through the medium of the "party line," a pervasive "unity of theory and praxis" for all areas of collective life, which also extends deeply into private life. This must be upheld, at least as an institutional fiction, if not brought about de facto by force. Only in this way, according to its presuppositions, can there be attained solidarity of action among all members of society and, thereby, man's control over history (the "realm of freedom"). This mediation of theory and practice can only function insofar as the individual readily sees his private life from the perspective of the solidarity of action in the collective. Insofar as someone excludes his private life from the collective—even if only covertly—it automatically comes under the regulation of the existential mediation of theory and practice, whereby public concerns (politics, economic institutions, science, technology) become accessible to pragmatic criteria of judgment and regulation.[2]

With this, we have already formulated the principle of the distribution of work according to which the mediation of theory and praxis in fact appears to function in the "Western world," that is, where the conditions for the operation of a parliamentary democracy are actually present. Here we can speak of a unified mediation of theory and praxis only to the extent that public interests happen to be indistinguishable from private interest, as in strict scientific research. In all other areas of life the situations that are to be dealt with through the "intelligent mediation of ends and means" (Dewey) are normally distinguished from those "border situations" (Jaspers) in which the fact of "my own death" (Heidegger) is itself sufficient to demand a risky decision regarding some absolute "project [Worumwillen]." However, to the extent that cases diverge from such "border situations," public and private interests cannot be made to coincide with each other without the use of force. Out of this fact results a division of labor between Pragmatism and Existentialism which appears to me to be characteristic of the philosophical mediation of theory and praxis in the Western world.

This should not be taken to imply that, according to the principle just presented, people explicitly advocate one or the other of these two complementary philosophies at different times, so that a politician, for example, recognizes Existentialism in his private life, but declares himself for Pragmatism in public life. The politician may maintain any kind of world view, like any member of a pluralistic society. But as a politician in a parliamentary democracy, he must act in public life as if he were a pragmatist and in private life as if he were an existentialist. That is to say, the world view that he personally more or less consciously adopts can be brought into play as an absolute truth in his private life only at his own existential risk, even though it may originally be a dogma with concrete content, claiming both private and public validity. In his public function as a politician he can bring up his world view for discussion only within a party, filtered through the process of opinion formation, which itself already obeys pragmatic rules. But this means, however, that he can suggest it as a hypothesis among other hypotheses for testing within the community, for instance, as a presupposition of positive law or political legislation.

This shows, as John Dewey rightly saw, that in its objective structure, a democratic society is a community of self-responsible experimenters in which everyone basically trusts the others to present plausible—that is, testable—hypotheses, but in which nobody believes the others to possess the absolute truth.

This objective structure of social life, which Karl Popper with some justification has contrasted, under the term "open society," with the implicit presuppositions of the older metaphysics and the actual, political tendencies of dialectical "historicism," determines the rules for the philosophical mediation between theory and praxis in Western public life.[3] It thereby automatically relegates the metaphysical-theological orientation towards life to the sphere of rules for private decisions of the kind that Existentialism since Kierkegaard has analyzed.

This functional complementarity between the pragmatic and existentialist mediation of philosophical theory and life praxis is itself objective and seems to me to characterize the social reality of philosophy in Western society.[4] But things are different in various geographical areas of the West, as far as the conscious recognition of this reality is concerned.

In Anglo-Saxon countries the official philosophy is not alone in its inclination to regard as superfluous any supplementation of the pragmatically formulated mediation of theory and praxis, either by an existentialist life orientation or by a—where possible undogmatized—dialectical philosophy of history. In middle Europe, on the other hand, and above all in Germany, there is a general resistance, based upon a mixture of humanist piety towards traditional metaphysics and an obstinate wish to ignore the new Anglo-Saxon philosophy, to recognizing the pragmatic rules of daily life, politics, economics, science, and technology as philosophically relevant and to taking seriously as philosophy those philosophies that have analyzed this reality.[5]

As far as official Anglo-Saxon philosophy's aversion to taking seriously the themes of existential philosophy and Marxism is concerned, it is not upheld by the classic authors of Pragmatism. In his essay *The Will to Believe,* William James introduced Kierkegaard's central concern—the individual's subjective interest in fundamentally unprovable and therefore existentially relevant truth—into the context of the community of scientific experimenters, proposing such truth as the limit of this community.[6] For this reason, it is good to understand his version of Pragmatism in terms of this theme and not of the metaphor of "business life," which is easily misunderstood by those who are unfamiliar with the American idiom. John Dewey, however, who sought primarily to expand the social-political and ethical-pedagogical implications of pragmatic "Instrumentalism," developed—as Marx did—a critique of ideology in the manner of "Historical Materialism" as part of his naturalistic transformation of his earlier Hegelianism. He sympathetically followed the Russian "experiment" at a Marxist reconstruction of society as long as it seemed to him to be compatible with the idea of a democratic experimental community. That the existential structure of borderline situations we have postulated also in fact exists in Anglo-Saxon countries and makes itself felt there can perhaps be seen most clearly in the worldwide "existentialization" of protestant theology. This, in fact, is an expression of the only possible, open, and socially acceptable understanding of religious belief in a world of science and democratic tolerance.

The present study, however, was written with the opposite task in mind: that of introducing the "prosaic" world of Pragmatism to the German reader, a reader who tends, insofar as he is concerned with philosophy, to be instead existentially or idealistically and dialectically inclined. This study accompanied the first German publication of texts by a thinker who has been practically unknown in Germany, even among the few German authors who have seriously examined American Pragmatism.[7] And yet Charles Sanders Peirce (1839–1914), with whom we are concerned here, is more than the "founder of Pragmatism," as William James referred to him in 1898. He is, beyond this,

certainly the greatest American thinker of all. Peirce deeply influenced not only James and Dewey, but also the great idealist and systematic thinker Josiah Royce, the Kantian logician C. I. Lewis, and
George Herbert Mead and Charles Morris, the founders of a quasi-
behavioristic social science and semiotic. Peirce was also one of the
pioneers in mathematical logic in the nineteenth century. His "logic
of relations" further developed the initial ideas of Boole and De Morgan and created the basis for Ernst Schröder's "algebra of relations."[8]

One reason it took so long for Peirce to become known in the
philosophical world is the external fact that his numerous essays,
scattered throughout different journals, and his far more numerous
works not published during his lifetime, became available in a systematically ordered form only between 1931 and 1935, and again in
1958 with the publication of the *Collected Papers*.[9] However, this external reason for Peirce's late fame is itself merely an expression of a
deeper problem in the evolution of Peirce's reputation: Pragmatism's
other two classical figures overshadowed him despite all their references to their forerunner. Peirce's original writings were little known
during his lifetime, not only because of their inaccessibility or because
of the circumstance that Peirce's academic career, which began with
so much promise in 1879 at Johns Hopkins University, had already
ended forever in 1883.[10] They were also only rarely acceptable and
interesting to his contemporaries because of their analytic subtlety,
their illustrations—understandable only to the expert—from the history of the exact sciences, their excursus on the history of philosophy
(especially on the history of terminology), and their continual references to the author's research on logic in the strict sense. The only ex-
ceptions here are Peirce's essays "The Fixation of Belief" from 1877
and "How to Make Our Ideas Clear" from 1878, both of which were
quite well known even during Peirce's lifetime. But to Peirce's contemporaries, the basic ideas found in these two birth certificates of
Pragmatism seemed to find definitive expression and an illustration of
their importance for life only in William James's vivid and lively lectures and classes.

While Peirce later often criticized James's characteristic, subjectivistic, and psychological interpretation of Pragmatism,[11] this short-
coming seemed finally to be eliminated in John Dewey's more sociological reception. During his lifetime Peirce rebuked Dewey for a lack
of logical subtlety.[12] Logical subtlety, however, did not belong to the
demands of the philosophical spirit of the times in 1900. The most
profound transformation in Anglo-Saxon philosophy in the twentieth
century took place in regard to this very point. The harvest of mathematical logic sown by Peirce himself, nearly as unrecognized as his
German contemporary Gottlob Frege, was evident after the appear-

ance of *Principia Mathematica* by Bertrand Russell and Alfred North Whitehead.[13] After its conversion into what is known as "analytic philosophy," which began with Russell, G. E. Moore, and Wittgenstein, symbolic logic transformed the style of academic philosophy in England and North America. This change of style itself was suited to allowing the previously unpopular aspects of Peirce's philosophy to appear in a positive light. Moreover, Peirce's writings appeared, like Leibniz's, to be split up into *Opuscula* which seemed to meet exactly Moore's watchword of philosophizing "piecemeal and by fragments." In addition, the *Collected Papers* appeared at the time when the "Vienna Circle," inspired by Russell and Wittgenstein, emigrated to America and began there to unfold an important influence which continues today.[14]

Peirce's logically rigorous Pragmatism had to appear more relevant and important to this logical Empiricism than the often unclear and popularly expressed Pragmatism of the psychologist James or that of the politically and pedagogically engaged Dewey. In Peirce the neopositivists could find already formulated all of their key problems and, as it seemed at first, even the solutions, such as the semantic approach to philosophizing (linguistic analysis), the problem of the criteria of the meaning of sentences, and the solution to this problem through the so-called principle of verification.

But the prima facie relationship between Peirce and neopositivism proved to be very problematic upon closer examination. Regardless, Peirce's importance grew to the extent that logical Empiricism was confronted with its wearisome aporias, and analytic philosophy moved beyond it altogether towards pragmatic or pragmatoidal positions.[15]

Hence, the "Logical Semantics" created by Carnap was forced to recognize the importance of the pragmatic dimension of signs that Charles Morris introduced into the discussion, consciously going back to Peirce.[16] The discussion of the principle of verification led to the insight, long anticipated by Peirce, that it is impossible to reduce the meaning of general concepts to sense data (or to reduce scientific propositions to so-called protocol sentences), and that we must be satisfied with the "prognostic relevance" of theoretical concepts (or, respectively, of whole theories). Karl Popper's discoveries that general propositions are not completely verifiable, but are completely falsifiable, and that the so-called protocol of experience, consisting of statements which contain general concepts, itself presents the problem of verification demanding a new protocol ad infinitum, amount in fact to the rediscovery of Peircean insights.[17] Carnap's discovery of the problem of so-called dispositional concepts points in the same direction and, once again, to Peirce.[18]

Peirce's central insight into what is termed the "reductive fallacy" in radical positivism stands out in all of these difficulties. It also had to limit the claims made for the "Behaviorism" that was being developed at that time, especially in the United States, and incorporated into the program of the "unity of science." Here again the forerunner, Peirce, to whom the behaviorists and semibehaviorists (e.g., G. H. Mead and Charles Morris) liked to appeal, had taken account from the very start the impossibility of reducing meaning, meaning-intention, or the understanding of meaning to concrete behavior.[19] This was because, as we will consider more closely later, Peirce not only developed a philosophy of possible experimental verification and the "experimental community of investigators" that it presupposes, but also previously presented a philosophy of the "interpretation" of opinions and the "community of interpretation" that this presupposes within the community of experimenters.[20]

Peirce's pragmatic semiotic uses the social interrelationship between the regulation of behavior and possible experience to interpret the problem of understanding meaning. At the same time it also attempts to lay anew the foundations of the philosophy of language in a "speculative grammar" and "speculative rhetoric." Interest in Peirce's semiotic naturally increased after "analytic philosophy," in the wake of the late Wittgenstein, turned to the analysis of ordinary language—specifically, to "language games" as public, institutionally regulated units of language usage, behavior praxis, and possible experience.[21] The appreciation which Moore shared with the late Wittgenstein for common-sense criteria of what is meaningful and true within each pragmatic horizon of meaning was also a point of contact with the theme of Common-sensism that extends from Reid and Hamilton to Peirce. But the Common-sensism upheld by the late Wittgenstein, like his Pragmatism, is much more extreme and one-sided than Peirce's because Wittgenstein in fact recognizes no further goal for philosophy than the diagnosis and therapy of empty cases of the pragmatic function of language. He thereby appears to view everyday linguistic usage as a sacrosanct criterion.

But Peirce's Common-sensism is "Critical Common-sensism." While Peirce confronts empty speculation with the proven practicality and even "instinctual" basis of common sense, he also appeals to another, opposing criterion for the regulation of scientific languages (the "ethics of terminology") and scientific progress. Instead of being guided by the provisional validity of common sense and temporarily undoubted scientific opinions, he conceives these as subject to regulative principles as Kant defined them.[22] As a result, Peirce's Critical Common-sensism already offered a way to bridge the themes of the logical construction of exact languages (Carnap) and the 'logic of science (Carnap, Popper, Hempel, et al.), on the one hand, and the so-called linguistic schools of analytic philosophy (Oxford and Cambridge), on the other, themes which today are still often felt to be mutually exclusive.

The above-mentioned relationships between Peirce and "analytic philosophy" point to the deeper reasons why the founder of Pragmatism, who was also its logician, became truly recognized in the Anglo-Saxon world only after Pragmatism's psychologist, James, and its social pedagogue, Dewey, had become known. The order in which interest focused on these thinkers reflects the fact that only after modern logical Positivism's attempt both to restrict and to renew the ideal of pure *theoria* had resulted in an aporia did it become completely clear that the mediation of theory and praxis today is not only the key problem of speculative philosophy, but also that of empirical science.

Charles S. Peirce, who, unlike James and Dewey, was professionally a practicing scientist (geodesist, astronomer, chemist),[23] proved to be a congenial interpreter of the problem of the technical-operational investigation of the meaning of the basic concepts of physics, a problem which came to public consciousness only in the twentieth century. The "semantic revolution" that, as Phillip Frank stressed, took place with Einstein's demand for a definition of "simultaneity" that would incorporate instructions for possible measurements of the simultaneity of events, led logically, considering the expanding foundational crisis of modern physics, to the demand for a "semantically consistent system" of physics. This system would identify and justify the material conditions for the operational realization of its concepts (e.g., "natural constants" like the speed of light, Planck's quantum of action, and elementary length).[24] This "semantic revolution" corresponds, it seems to me, much more precisely to Peirce's "logic of inquiry" (to its postulated synthesis of logically convergent theory construction and the operational clarification of meaning in experiment) than, for example, to the suggestions of Ernst Mach, to which Einstein sometimes refers, or to the program of logical Positivism which was referred to at times in the "Copenhagen Interpretation" of quantum theory.[25] In fact, I believe that the comparison of Peirce's conceptions with the results of the "logic of exact science" that first came to a broader development in the twentieth century shows that a species of Pragmatism also has the last word in the interpretation of the experimental mediation of theory and praxis in science and preserves the acceptable aspects of Positivism.[26]

In order to avoid giving existing prejudices too much latitude, it is important to stress from the start that Peirce's kind of Pragmatism has nothing to do with that concept of Pragmatism—and particularly its concept of truth—which the earlier German discussion of Pragmatism drew from William James's lectures.[27] This should not be taken to imply that there are no points of contact between Peirce and James or that the latter only misunderstood Peirce. Actually, James and Dewey are indebted to Peirce, often in a nearly word-for-word fashion, for nearly all the new patterns of thought in their philosophy. But they took these patterns from the "architectonic" context of Peirce's philosophy and gave them a new and in each case different accent. Their kind of Pragmatism became popular and is doubtless somewhat closer to the typical view of Pragmatism found in Germany than is Peirce's, but their kind still remains far removed from his. To make this point clearer it will be helpful to discuss briefly the relationship between American Pragmatism and Nietzsche's Pragmatism.

In Hermann Noack's book on the philosophy of Western Europe the following—from the German perspective very characteristic—reference to American Pragmatism is presented in the framework of an "Evaluation of Nietzsche's Work and Influence": "Nietzsche agrees here [namely, in the view that the "supposed 'truth' " in the end consists "only" in "certain views and concepts meeting the need or demand to preserve life, i.e. that they are only correct in the sense of their utility"] to a large extent with the so-called 'Pragmatism,' which is especially widespread in the Anglo-Saxon countries. According to this doctrine, founded by Charles S. Peirce (1839–1914) and William James (1842–1910) and upheld in England by F. C. S. Schiller (1864–1937), all of our concepts, judgements, and beliefs are only rules for our actions (*Pragma*) which possess as much truth as they have value for our life."[28] Noack amplifies this characterization immediately through a reference to Hans Vaihinger's *Philosophy of "As If,"* for which "the uppermost leading concepts of all scientific and philosophical knowledge are only 'constructions' which can be recognized as such but still are nonetheless indispensable for the theoretical and practical management of life."[29]

In the context of this introduction it is important to note that what Noack describes here is what Max Scheler termed "honest Pragmatism."[30] As Scheler knew, it is something untypical of the Anglo-Saxon countries in particular. The naïvety—or even dishonesty?—which Scheler hereby implies can be left aside. This much at any rate is clear: this skeptical-sounding "Pragmatism" that discredits the meaning of "truth" with terms like "so-called," "as if," "only," and "nothing other than," rather than explicating it through reference to possible praxis, can probably be conceived of at all only in the context of the problem of nihilism which came to a head with Nietzsche. It has its equally definitive as well as hyperbolic formulation in Nietzsche's notorious "definition" that "Truth is the kind of error without which a certain species of life could not live. The value for life is ultimately decisive."[31]

Nothing could be further from Peirce's thought than such a conception of truth. He would have understood it historically as being, like every kind of "as if" philosophy, the final outcome of "Nominalism" and would have exposed it, with the help of his semantic Pragmatism, as a meaningless pseudo-insight.[32] Moreover, he would have linked the whole style of thought which made possible this witty, nihilistic, romantic, literary "Pragmatism" with the disintegration of logic in middle Europe that he had recognized early in his career.

But the Pragmatism of "as if" truth also has hardly anything to do with Dewey's Instrumentalism, or even with James's psychological-existential defense of the "Will to Believe," even though a couple of James's incautious formulations seem to fit into the context of Nietzsche's Pragmatism. American Pragmatism has none of the two-faced character that is visible in Nietzsche's definition of truth; it does not annihilate itself in the conflict which Nietzsche himself provoked between a biological reduction of truth and the simultaneous unmasking of this truth as a "lie" or "fiction" on the basis of the covertly upheld concept of purely contemplative truth. Pragmatism does not uphold either one of Nietzsche's concepts of truth. Instead, it seeks to establish through the critique of meaning what truth can mean in the context of possible—Peirce would say conceivably possible—practically relevant situations in experience. In the attempt to answer this question neither James nor Dewey, it seems to me, was able, in contrast to Peirce, to avoid fully the "reductive fallacy" in the sense of psychologism or social Darwinism. Peirce was prevented from slipping into contemporary "Naturalism" by his Kantianism. He always adhered to Kantianism in the form of a reinterpretation of the concept of "regulative principles to which nothing empirical can correspond," in terms of a realist theory of universals, a reinterpretation which also protected him, on the other hand, from the Fictionalism of the Kantian Hans Vaihinger.[33]

Peirce's Kantianism, with its realist view of universals, brings us to the last aspect of Peirce's importance today. This aspect, which was also the last to be recognized in all its ramifications, seems strange at first glance. As Pragmatism is usually understood, it always seems to enter into things as *ultima ratio* when Positivism or even Kantianism is conclusively shown to contain a nominalistic critique of metaphysics in its basic propositions. Kant's transcendental philosophy of the a priori conditions for the possibility of experience seems then to disintegrate into a conventionalism about de facto "presuppositions" that are only a priori relative to a specific experience which is assumed to be given. Positivism converges with this conventionalistic dissolution of Kantianism when we realize that Positivism cannot reduce laws of nature to sense data, that is, that there are conventions concealed even in protocol sentences as sentences and that these conventions have validity only thanks to their proven, practical effectiveness.

Peirce's Pragmatism appears at first to reflect this characteristic tendency of modern epistemology. He understands Kant's transcendental "presuppositions," first according to the model of "postulates" of practical reason and, second, as mere hypothetical and provisional "conventions." He also replaces the positivist's demand for a reduction of concepts and theories to the data of experience with the demand that they be borne out by the data of experience. Yet the pragmatic theory of validity, which explicitly includes the "Fallibilism" of all human beliefs (all synthetic judgments), should not terminate, according to Peirce, in the victory of conventionalistic Nominalism. Rather, it should agree with a properly conceived realist theory of universals. The decisive feature of the critique of meaning that enters here, and that led Peirce as a young man to regard Nominalism as the πρῶτον ψεῦδος of modern philosophy, is that conventionalist Nominalism (under which Vaihinger's Fictionalism would have to be included) makes sense only when—as a foil to human conventions—we presuppose the existence of incognizable things-in-themselves. According to Peirce, however, this presupposition characteristic of all Nominalism, which Kant had unreflectively brought into play, is itself a superfluous fiction, belonging to that bad metaphysics which the "pragmatic maxim" exposes as meaningless. We cannot postulate something incognizable as a presupposition of knowledge, since all cognition itself has the character of hypothetical postulation. In other words, Peirce accepts Kantianism insofar as it entails the restriction of the validity of all concepts to possible experience, and calls this "Pragmatism" (5.525).[34] Peirce's rejection of incognizable things-in-themselves (5.452), owing to just this very critical restriction, leads him to the possibility—in fact the unavoidability—of a realist metaphysics, a metaphysics whose hypothetical postulates must all be fallible, but whose general concepts must be able to prove their objective validity "in the long run." This is because we cannot conceive the "real" to be anything other than that which is "cognizable" (5.275). By starting with a critique of meaning Peirce makes room for a sweeping evolutionary metaphysics in the vein of Hegel and Schelling.[35]

The founder of Pragmatism, who anticipated the task of the neopositivistic "logic of inquiry" in so many detailed ways, was in reality quite old-fashioned regarding the strategic tendency of his work as a whole, that is, if we apply the criteria of "analytic philosophy." Peirce's philosophizing "piecemeal and by fragments," which some *moderni* want to count as a point in his favor, came about quite against his will. After the publication of the *Collected Papers* it was no longer possible to overlook that it is all held together by a systematization or, as Peirce himself said, by an "architectonic" in Kant's sense. This is perhaps the most ambitious attempt at an all-encompassing synthesis that the history of philosophy has seen since Hegel.

Although Peirce's Common-sensism and pragmatic maxim anticipated the central themes of clarifying our thoughts and criticizing meaning, as they are found in the philosophy of linguistic analysis and, more precisely, in the late Wittgenstein, Peirce does not draw the conclusion—to the disappointment of many *moderni*—that metaphysics as a science is impossible and that the task of philosophy is to ward off this pragmatically empty language game.[36] To be sure, the clarification and critique of meaning with the pragmatic maxim are supposed in a radical way to expose meaningless, ontological formulations of questions; this was later done by Wittgenstein and Neopositivism. Yet, as Peirce explicitly emphasizes, use of this maxim does not itself present solutions to philosophical problems, but is only a methodological presupposition, both a purgative and a thread of Ariadne, for a metaphysics that is hypothetical, inductive, and verifiable "in the long run."

At the time when William James, with reference to Peirce, proclaimed "Pragmatism" an independent philosophy, Peirce found that in order to provide a foundation for his metaphysics, he had to place the pragmatic maxim in the context of a normative logic of science. This in turn presupposed the normative disciplines of ethics and aesthetics, on the one hand, and a phenomenological doctrine of categories, on the other.[37] The metaphysics itself, on which Peirce worked primarily in the last decade of the nineteenth century, was a vision of an unending cosmic evolution in which reason in the form of habits was incorporated and concretized at first incompletely in natural laws and then finally completely in the history of the "unlimited community" of investigators and deliberate agents. As such, this metaphysics had to meet three postulates. First, as "Tychism" it should allow room for chance to play a role that would be removed only in the ideal limiting case of the complete embodiment of reason in the habits of the community. Second, as "Synechism" it should show the reality of universals (the objective validity in the long run of inductive generalizations) to be identical with "continuity" in evolution. Third, as "Agapism" it should provide a foundation for the attraction of "evolutionary love" through the *summum bonum* or, put in aesthetic terms, of the "harmonic order."

Peirce's complete system stood under the guidance of the "architectonic" which was given its final form shortly after 1900. As Murphey states, "Its foundation was to have been mathematics and formal logic which would supply a priori the possible formal categories of thought, while the content of these categories would come from phenomenology. Upon this base would be built the normative theory of inquiry, which would supply the aim and methods of investigation in all areas of knowledge. Then should have come the metaphysics."[38] In an unpublished manuscript from circa 1890 that was intended for a book (the unfinished "A Guess at the Riddle"), Peirce characterized the task which he set for himself as follows: "The undertaking which this volume inaugurates is to make a philosophy like that of Aristotle, that is to say, to outline a theory so comprehensive that, for a long time to come, the entire work of human reason, in philosophy of every school and kind, in mathematics, in psychology, in physical science, in history, in sociology, and in whatever other department there may be, shall appear as the filling up of its details" (1.1).

2

The Problem of an Introduction
to Peirce's Work as a Whole:
The Four Periods
of the Development of His Thought

There are a number of different ways to attain a view of Peirce's systematic thought as a whole. These must be reconstructed with effort from a large quantity of disparate fragments. The neopositivists, who are interested solely in the "logic of experimental science" and in the pragmatic maxim as a principle for the radical criticism of metaphysics, tend to ignore Peirce as a systematic thinker and to select from the mass of fragments only those with interesting and fruitful contributions to the philosophy of science and semiotics.[1] Orthodox Kantians tend to evaluate Peirce as an original neo-Kantian who on the whole, however, fell back into a view which Kant's critical stance had overcome and who hence, because of his misunderstanding of Kant, was forced to go back to a speculative, idealistic, and dogmatically rationalistic kind of metaphysics.[2] Neorealists, on the other hand, see only a false step in modern philosophy's turn to transcendental Subjectivism and Idealism of the Kantian variety. Hence, they tend to minimize the importance of Pragmatism's basic relationship to the critique of meaning, which Peirce himself traced back to Kant and Berkeley. They claim Peirce as a forerunner of Whitehead, who, by deepening Thomas Reid's philosophy of common sense, overcame the presuppositions that Kant shared with Hume and Berkeley and so cleared the way for a realistic metaphysics.[3] All of these perspectives have provided valuable insights into Peirce's original contribution to philosophy, a fact that becomes especially clear when the books written in the light of these views are compared with the interpretation of Peirce prominent at the beginning of the century, when he was regarded as a forerunner of James and Dewey. The same can be said for the numerous, often excellent, studies that analyze only single aspects or problems in Peirce's works, according to the motto "piecemeal and by fragments."[4]

The perspective of this study is limited by its having been written to serve as an introduction to Peirce's Pragmatism in connection with the publication of a German edition of selections from Peirce's writings. Its point of departure is the view that the "methodological principle" of Pragmatism offers the key to the whole of Peirce's philosophy. It does this even though Pragmatism refers to no completed "world view,"[5] but rather to the positive solution of philosophical problems, and must itself be supplemented by other principles.[6] This means, however, that I interpret Peirce's Pragmatism from the outset in the light of the implications which Peirce later explicitly put forth in the concept of "Pragmaticism," in opposition to psychological and nominalistic versions of Pragmatism.[7]

It cannot be denied that these implications—that is, the realist view of universals, Critical Common-sensism, the doctrine of the categories, the semiotic of interpretation, normative logic, and synechistic metaphysics—are present only insufficiently in the two essays of 1877 and 1878 that became famous as the birth certificates of Pragmatism and that William James referred to in 1898 in the public proclamation of "Pragmatism."[8] Indeed, there emerged in these two essays psychologistic, naturalistic, and nominalistic tendencies that Peirce was later again and again obliged to correct.[9] On the other hand, it is possible to show that nearly all the specifically Peircean implications of Pragmatism that later forced him to distance himself from his "followers" were at least implicit in the writings from 1867–69 and in the Berkeley review of 1871, where a first version of the pragmatic maxim was formulated. According to the latest historical research and the texts themselves, it seems that Peirce was led to a temporary inclination towards the nominalistic-empirical tradition through the meetings of the so-called Metaphysical Club in Cambridge (from winter 1871 to the end of 1872). Prior to that time and afterwards he was more strongly influenced by Kant and Duns Scotus and, for a time, also by Hegel, the Hegelian Royce, and Schelling.

This view only appears to contradict the widespread understanding found in American secondary literature, according to which the true birthplace of Pragmatism, and hence of independent American philosophy, was the Metaphysical Club of 1871–72, in which Peirce and William James were impregnated with positivistic theories of verification and Darwinian doctrines by Chauncey Wright, as well as with Alexander Bain's proto-pragmatic belief-doubt psychology by Nicholas St. John Green.[10] In fact, the theories Peirce published in

1877–78 without using the designation "Pragmatism," theories to which James referred in 1898 as the first documents of Pragmatism, were first presented by Peirce in 1872 in the Metaphysical Club. In addition, according to Peirce himself, he first used the term "Pragmatism," taken from Kant, to signify his own teaching in 1871 in this club which he had founded. But the recognition of these facts does not contradict the equally clear, demonstrable fact that Peirce had upheld a far more rationalistic philosophy prior to the time of the Metaphysical Club and that he had by 1871 already conceived the essential foundations of Pragmatism, in the framework of the early "theory of cognition and reality," in his critical study of medieval and modern philosophy, especially Kant and Berkeley.[11] Here I shall unite these basic doctrines under the term "meaning-critical Realism."

The time of the Metaphysical Club in fact forms an important juncture in the history of American philosophy, but it represents an ambivalent period in Peirce's development, during which two different tendencies of thought become entangled. The one leads from Bain, Green, and Chauncey Wright over Peirce's foundation of Pragmatism (1871–78) to James and Dewey. The other leads from the meaning-critical Realism of the early Peirce over the period of the birth of Pragmatism, which stood under heavy empiricist-nominalist influence in the club discussions, to the consolidation of Peirce's philosophy in "Pragmaticism." The accompanying graphic illustration indicates what the situation was like. This diagram can be quite precisely verified in

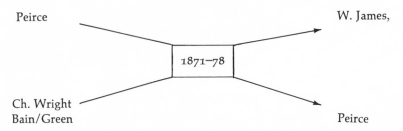

the further development of Peirce's philosophy. For it is not the case that Peirce again took up a tendency of the period from 1868 to 1871 only under the influence of the publication of James's *Pragmatism*. In reality this reconsideration had already taken place in the last decade of the nineteenth century while Peirce was wrestling with the problems of a teleological, synechistic metaphysics. James's *Pragmatism* brought sudden fame to Peirce, who since 1887 had been living in isolation, largely forgotten, in Milford, Pennsylvania. Its publication forced Peirce to explicitly formulate his own position, which he was encouraged to present in lectures and essays. He did this in the years that followed under the very delicate circumstances of his personal situation. Although he had to be thankful to his "followers," and in the face of his increasingly difficult financial situation could not shove aside the fame of being the founder of Pragmatism, he could not be untrue to his whole philosophical conception, which had led him in a completely different direction from that of his old, ever-helpful friend William James.[12] Peirce found the solution to this conflict in 1905 in the adoption of the name "Pragmaticism" for his doctrine.

We can derive a division of the development of Peirce's philosophy into four periods from the above characterization of the development of his thought. These four periods are also distinctly discernible in the history of his publications: a series of essays in a particular journal is found in the middle of each. In addition, the four periods correspond to the decisive turns of events in Peirce's life.[13]

The first period (from 1855 to 1871) embraces Peirce's early years, from the beginning of his study of Kant, undertaken when he was sixteen years old, to the temporary conclusion of his critical study of the philosophical tradition. Besides a series of five essays on formal logic and the doctrine of the categories in the *Proceedings of the American Academy of Arts and Sciences* in 1867, publications falling into this period include three essays on the theory of cognition in the *Journal of Speculative Philosophy* in 1868–69 and the Berkeley review in the *North American Review* in 1871, where the pragmatic maxim for making meanings clear is anticipated. I have chosen to unite this first period under the heading "From the Critique of Knowledge to the Critique of Meaning."

The second period (from 1871 to 1883) encompasses the time of Peirce's public success, from the founding of the Metaphysical Club in Cambridge to the tragic turn of his life, which is signified by his dismissal from his teaching post at Johns Hopkins University.[14] Numerous geodetic and astronomic investigations, expeditions, and participation in congresses in the service of the United States Coast Survey, and the *Photometric Researches*[15] at the Harvard Observatory, fall into this period, as well as the series of six "Illustrations of the Logic of Science" in *Popular Science Monthly* in 1877–78. The first two articles in this series, "The Fixation of Belief" and "How to Make Our Ideas Clear," are considered the birth certificates of "Pragmatism." The fruits of Peirce's teaching at Johns Hopkins from 1879 to 1883 appeared in 1883 in the volume *Studies in Logic*, which contains works by Peirce and his students of mathematical logic.[16] This period may be termed the classic epoch of the development of Pragmatism and "American philosophy."

The third period (from 1883 to 1893 or 1902) spans the time in which Peirce—particularly after moving to Milford, Pennsylvania— worked alone on studies in logic and metaphysics and, circa 1901–2, achieved the final architectonic of his philosophical system. The central philosophical publication of this period is the series of six essays on metaphysics in *The Monist* between 1891 and 1893, in which the aspects of evolutionary cosmology, "Tychism," "Synechism," and "Agapism," are presented. During this period Peirce also made repeated attempts to put a large philosophical work up for subscription, all of which failed (the last attempt was his application to the Carnegie Foundation, which was unsuccessful because his work dealt with "logic" and not with "natural science").[17] As a result, Peirce was forced after his discharge from the Coast Survey in 1891 to earn his income through miscellaneous work for journals and dictionaries.

The fourth period (from 1898 or 1902 to 1914) embraces the time in which Pragmatism was discussed internationally, following William James's "California Address," which gave Peirce a last chance to win an audience for his philosophy. This period ends in 1914 with the death of the philosopher, who had been supported by a fund from his friends since 1906 and who had suffered from cancer since 1909. At the center of this period stand, first, the difficult but significant ("architectonic") Harvard lectures of 1903 on Pragmatism, in which Peirce made the first attempt to connect all aspects of his "system" of 1901–2 with the concept of Pragmatism, and second, the series of three essays on Pragmatism in *The Monist in* 1905–6, as well as numerous additions to this series that remained unpublished in his lifetime. Here Peirce attained the completion of *his* conception of Pragmatism.

The periods that I have just sketched clearly reveal a major distinction between the second and third periods. I have taken this into account by separating the text into two parts. The first deals with the development of Pragmatism, the second with the further development of Peirce's philosophy from Pragmatism to Pragmaticism. In what follows I turn to the philosophical background of the development of Pragmatism in Peirce and so, first, to the period of his thought that led him in his critical examination of the Western philosophical tradition away from the "critique of knowledge" to the "critique of meaning."

The First Period: Peirce and the Tradition, or, From the Critique of Knowledge to the Critique of Meaning

A. Peirce's Criticism of the Tradition and His Alternative: A Preview

It cannot be said of Peirce—as of some of today's representatives of formal logic and the "logic of exact science"—that he had no sense of history, no consciousness of the fact that all thought is mediated through tradition. The opposite is true. From the beginning of his Kant studies in 1855, Peirce formulated his systematic thought in a continuous dialogue with the great Western tradition of thought. His need to take proper account of history went so far that, as early as in his works of 1868, he introduced the terms that he planned to use—for example, "intuition," "hypothesis," and "contemplation"—with long excurses on the history of terminology. Later, in the propagation of the "Ethics of Terminology," Peirce's concern was not just the logical clarity of definitions, but reflection on precisely his own starting point in the history of philosophical language.[1] Of course, his historical studies were never directed merely to the historical interpretation and presentation of the past. They were rather primarily interwoven in a continuous way with his own creative work on such problems. But this did not hinder him from also attaining innovative, historical insights into particular areas and getting them down on paper. He was probably the most learned authority on the history of logic in the nineteenth century, a man who thoroughly knew not only the ancient and medieval texts, but beyond that, nearly all the documents of the logic of his time, excluding the works of Gottlob Frege. This knowledge and the circumstance that he was himself decisively involved in the new attempt to found logic in the spirit of mathematics made him probably the first person to see clearly the importance of scholasticism as a flowering age of logic and logically disciplined philosophy, and enabled him to perceive the decline of logic since Humanism, especially in the psychologistic nineteenth century.[2] His sympathetic empathy for the historical life situation of the Middle Ages reminds the reader occasionally of Herder or even of Novalis, even though he tended to embed this evaluation in a dialectical scheme of development in the manner of Hegel or Comte.[3] Additionally, Peirce was qualified particularly well as an authority and pioneer in research on the history of the exact sciences, again because of the personal union of the historian with the practicing specialist.

In the present context we are concerned not with special historical insights or scholarly authority, but with the young Peirce's central argument with the philosophical tradition, which between 1867 and 1871 already allowed him to attain something like a new way out of the dilemma of the conflicting positions of the nineteenth century. It would not be false to say that Peirce's foundation of American philosophy is a synthesis of English and German philosophy or, to be more precise, of Kant and Hume. It is a new mediation between rationalism and empiricism which once again establishes—as Kant did before—a new position between these two that sees through a "dogmatism" and disavows it for the future. But this characterization does not do justice to Peirce's pre-pragmatic, far-reaching critical reading of the history of philosophy. Peirce does not confine himself here between Hume and Kant, but rather calls into question basic presuppositions shared by both Hume and Kant, presuppositions of the entire modern period of philosophy. He does this, inspired by his knowledge of the history of logic, while orienting himself to the Aristotelian Middle Ages and, simultaneously, retaining certain basic presuppositions of the modern critique of knowledge.

It is very difficult to get satisfactory information from the pre-pragmatic Peirce about his own philosophical position. He appears to use contradictory terms for it, like "Phenomenalism" and "Idealism," on one hand, and "Realism" on the other. As historical predecessors he refers—almost in the same breath—to Duns Scotus and Kant (e.g., 8.15) and, with reservations, to Berkeley (8.30). But Peirce gives us a secure point of reference for interpreting him in his negative characterization of a term which he uses as a kind of foil to his own intentions. This is his very broad and, indeed, unusual concept of "Nominalism," which signalizes practically every thinker since Ockham (later, even Duns Scotus would be too nominalistic for him). Peirce's complaint concerning the Nominalism of the modern epoch is not that it refuses to recognize the existence of general concepts in *abstracto* (put scholastically, *ante res*). Platonism of this kind, which Peirce re-

jects, is not the position that he sees as the aim of a properly understood realistic view of universals, such as was already found in Duns
Scotus. Peirce later reaffirms Nominalism's anti-Platonist critique by
denying the "existence" but not the "reality" of universals. Actual
present existence belongs only to individual things that we can indicate *hic et nunc*.[4] Nor does Peirce criticize (moderate) Nominalism for
linking the recognition of universals in principle with the possibility
of representation through signs (for thought in general) and the denial
of the existence of universals *in rebus* independent of this possible
context.   .

The view that the recognition of universals is bound to the possibility of the world's being represented by signs in a community of
thinking beings is actually a central presupposition of Peirce's philosophy, which he no doubt owes to the great semiotic tradition of British Nominalism since Ockham, Bacon, and Hobbes. This is the lineage
of what Murphey[5] has called the "semiotic Phenomenalism" or "Idealism" of the young Peirce.[6] From this arises his new foundation of
semiotic as semiotic logic with the subordinate disciplines of "speculative grammar," "critical logic" (like "semantics"), and "speculative
rhetoric" (a theory of interpretation and the community of interpretation which finally also includes the pragmatic theory of meaning).
What Peirce criticizes Nominalism for is simply this: that it is incapable of reconciling the dependence of universals in principle upon possible representation of the world through signs with the objective
nature of universals, that is, their virtual reality in individual things,
independently of what an individual here and now or a limited community at a particular time might think about these things. To put it
in a more radical way, Peirce accuses Nominalism of having a bad
metaphysics, one containing the nonsensical presupposition that there
could or even must be things-in-themselves which are not representable in signs—which are, that is, unknowable. This presupposition is
nonsensical for Peirce because, as a meaningful hypothesis, it must *itself* apply the function of sign representation to things-in-themselves.

Peirce combines this objection with criticism of the *medium quod*
concept of knowledge, which he traces back to Augustine (8.261), according to which we know not the things in the outer world themselves, but only their effects in consciousness, and we therefore must
assume that cognition as such necessarily shuts us off somehow from
the things-in-themselves. This concept of knowledge, which has been
predominant since the late Middle Ages, implies, for one thing, the
view that consciousness is a container ("receptacle") which has "natural signs" (Ockham) of things as its contents. These signs are confronted in introspective thought, while the existence of the things outside, the so-called outside world, attains a fundamentally problematic

status (from Descartes to Kant). Here, too, Peirce does not deny all the accomplishments of critical epistemological analysis since Ockham. He accepts the model of causal affection of the senses through the things in the outside world and the idea that we infer the existence and nature of things in the outside world from "natural signs" (the "impressions" in consciousness). But he does not identify the affection of the senses in these "impressions" with cognition, which in this case would have to be primarily "introspective," "intuitive," and without any connection to the use of signs. Instead, he identifies knowledge with hypothetical inference of things in the outer world. This takes place on the basis of circumstances that can be investigated in a purely physical-physiological manner (nerve excitations in the encounter with "brute facts") and on the basis of the sign quality of psychic data which itself is not yet cognition (the "feelings" in which the results of the nerve excitations are given purely qualitatively in the manner of an emotional disposition). For Peirce, knowledge consists neither of being affected by things in themselves nor of intuition of given data, but rather of the bringing about ("mediation") of a consistent opinion about the real; or, to be more precise, the "representation" of outer states of affairs. These indicate their "existence" to us in the physical-physiologically researchable confrontation of the subject with the object and leave behind in the confused manifold of feeling-like data those qualitative expressive signs or likenesses ("icons") of their particular nature which, by the discovery of a predicate in the form of an interpreting symbol ("interpretant"), are reduced in a hypothetical inference (the "conception" of something as something) to the unity of a consistent proposition about an external fact.

This semiotic transformation of the modern concept of knowledge, based on the idea of hypothetical inference, replaces the *medium quod* concept of knowledge, so to speak, with a *medium quo* view of knowledge and makes possible Peirce's "metaphysical" and "transcendental" deduction of his fundamental categories. This transformation consists in bringing out abstractly the three elementary concepts that are contained in the function of cognition as sign representation and that are hence required if a synthesis of the manifold of sense data in a consistent opinion is to be attained. Here we are concerned with two concepts that were already brought out in the characterization of cognition as a sign function: (1) "quality" (or "expression" of the particular nature of things through the "iconic" similarity of feelings), and (2) "relation" or the real confrontation of the subject with existing objects or "brute facts" (which in language has its equivalent in so-called indices), and "representation" of real facts by the "mediation" of an indication of existence and the qualitative iconic expres-

sion of the (possible) particular nature of things in a "hypothesis."
This hypothesis is an abductive inference which results in the symbolic predicative formulation of a synthesis (of "something" as "something"). Later, after Peirce had formulated the deduction of the categories in terms of the logic of relations,[7] he understood "quality,"
which in itself is free of relations, as an illustration of the formal category of "Firstness," the two-place relation of the encounter between
subject and object as an illustration of the formal category of "Secondness," and the three-place relation of "representation" (designation of something as something for an interpreting consciousness) as
an illustration of "Thirdness." According to Peirce's logic of relations—as well as his earlier semiotic deduction of illustrations for the
three categories—there can be no further fundamental categories because all other elementary concepts can be traced back to these three.
On the other hand, only the complete consideration of all three fundamental categories offers the warrant for an architechtonically and
phenomenologically complete philosophical system, while every attempt to eliminate one of the three amounts to a "reductive fallacy"
(cf. 5.79–81).

The individual phases or aspects characterizing Peirce's criticisms
of the main representatives of the history of philosophy since Duns
Scotus are already present or at least suggested in the foregoing sketch
of the way in which Peirce went beyond modern philosophy's basic
starting point, which he recognized early to be nominalistic.[8] The
British nominalists from Ockham to John Stuart Mill are subject to
this criticism to the extent that they exhibit a sensualistic-intuitionistic
concept of knowledge, which equates the psychic conditions of cognition (the "sense data"), or even the physical and physiological conditions of the realization of "sense data" (the causal affection of the
senses through external things in themselves), with cognition itself.
To Peirce it is indicative of an important step forward in the history
of philosophy that Berkeley (and after him David Hume and John
Stuart Mill) dispense with the presupposition of unknowable causes
of sense experience and seek instead to express the so-called potency
of things in the external world to affect our senses through concepts of
possible sensory experience. But this turn away from unknown causes
to results that are expected in experience, which pointed the way for
the development of Pragmatism, itself suffers from the confusion of
equating "cognition" (i.e., for Peirce, the hypothesis of the substantially real as that reality which would be revealed in the lawful context of possible qualitative experience) with the particular factual sensations themselves. In this way Berkeley leaves out the material
substance of things and does not understand that their reality lies in
the function of "explaining the constant conjunction between acci-

dents." This function of "exciting ideas with such regularity that we can know what to expect" (8.31) must be left to God, since Berkeley lacks a correctly understood hypothesis of substance. Moreover, because Berkeley identifies the reality of things with their actually being experienced (at least with their being thought of by God), he does not understand that "the coherence of an idea with experience in general does not depend at all upon its being actually present to the mind all the time. . . . That *an object's independence of our* [actual] *thought about it* is constituted by [precisely] its connection with experience in general, he has never conceived" (8.30).[9] As a whole, the British tradition of nominalistic Empiricism—to which James's version of Pragmatism always belonged—deserves recognition, according to Peirce, for having always striven for simple and clear solutions to problems, in line with Ockham's principle of economy, and for having repeatedly directed our attention to the convincing character of the immediate indication of facts existing *hic et nunc* in sense perception. (The latter tendency of British philosophy can be clearly seen even prior to Ockham's Nominalism in Duns Scotus's concept of *haecceitas*. Peirce later declared this concept to be the principle of individuation as it was pragmatically explicated through the function of "indices" in language.) In the light of his doctrine of categories, however, Peirce had to reject reductions of Thirdness ("mediation," "thought," "law," "habit," "continuity," "normative science," "final cause") to Firstness (e.g., "ideas" as "sense data") or Secondness (e.g., "impressions" as "hard facts," de facto actions or "behavior") as an unacceptable application of Ockham's razor.

The opposite extreme to British Nominalism in the light of Peirce's doctrine of categories is the philosophy of Hegel, with which Peirce demonstrably concerned himself for the first time in 1868, in conjunction with a controversy with the Hegelian Harris, the editor of the *Journal of Speculative Philosophy*.[10] Although Peirce rejected Hegel's dialectical logic more or less vigorously his whole life long, he always felt attracted to the program of an "objective logic" of "continuity" in nature and history and later made reference to the "three stages of thought" in Hegel as equivalences of his three fundamental categories. But he accuses Hegel of wanting to overcome the irrationality of the first and the contingency of the second categories through the third category and therefore of not doing justice to the "outward clash," the confrontation with "brute facts," or to the element of indefinite possibility in the future ("chance" as an aspect of Firstness).[11] For two reasons, Peirce sees Hegel as even belonging essentially to the history of Nominalism. First, when Hegel, in contrast to the British sensationalists, allows the validity of general concepts to triumph completely over the immediate particular nature and *hic et nunc* of sense perception, he does not thereby prove their validity *in rebus;* instead he absolutizes the arbitrary action of subjectivity, which has a nominalistic origin.[12] Platonism and Nominalism generally stand for Peirce in a secret alliance. Second, in a completely other regard, Hegel is a nominalist for Peirce because he—in secret agreement with the British nominalists—conceives as the object of philosophy only the world of completed facts, the past, and not the real possibilities of things, *esse in futuro.*[13] In his criticism of Nominalism Peirce agrees with Hegel on one point, perhaps the most important one, in the conviction that the assumption of incognizable things-in-themselves (in other words, the attempt to limit the power of knowledge through knowledge a priori) is nonsensical. Here, doubtless, lies the most important theme of the pre-pragmatic Peirce's criticism of Nominalism. This criticism indicates that Peirce was concerned not only or even primarily with the problem of universals as it was formulated by the scholastics, but rather with the removal of some deeply hidden nonsense in the very presuppositions of modern philosophy itself.

B. The "Meaning-Critical" Approach and the New "Theory of Reality" in the Writings of 1868–69 and 1871

The meaningless presupposition in the modern theory of knowledge lies, according to Peirce, in the implicit assumption at work in Ockham, Descartes, Locke, and Kant that cognition is blocked off from the things actually to be known by its own causal mechanism and so has primarily to do with the effects of things in the *receptaculum* of consciousness, while the external things remain incognizable as "things-in-themselves."[14] In opposition to this view, which purports to be based on the criticism of knowledge, Peirce begins with a criticism of meaning, and here lies his truly original thought, one that most likely stemmed from his earlier semiotic transformation of the concept of knowledge.

On that view we cannot conceive things except in relationship to possible cognition, but this means primarily with reference to the possibility of forming a meaningful, semantically consistent, and true opinion about them. Even those who speak about incognizable things-in-themselves bear witness to the fact that this is so, for they lay claim to having formed a semantically consistent and true opinion about things as things-in-themselves. The essence of knowledge lies for Peirce in this formation of opinion ("representation," "belief") through conscious or unconscious inference. In 1866–67, in conjunction with his semiotic transformation of the concept of knowledge,

Peirce had interpreted Kant's "transcendental synthesis of apperception" as a "reduction of the manifold of sense data to the unity of
consistency" by a hypothesis.[15] But when the essence of knowledge
lies in the formation of a semantically consistent opinion and not primarily in a unified, perceptually schematizable representation (*Vorstellung*) of the world,[16] then it is no longer possible to oppose the ability
to think of an incognizable world in itself to the ability to imagine
things in a spatial, temporal world of appearances as Kant had done.[17]
The restriction in the critique of knowledge of the applicability of
categories and general concepts to possible experience then becomes
the meaning-critical restriction of the meaning of something like reality in general to possible knowledge, that is, to cogniz*ability*.

But with the meaning-critical definition of the real as the cognizable, Peirce already had at his disposal the means for doing justice in
a new way to one motive, although not the most decisive one, for
Kant's distinction between "noumena" and "phenomena."[18] One reason why the thing-in-itself in Kant might be taken to be indispensable
is that in this concept the things themselves, which are what they are
regardless of what we might think about them, are distinguished from
the various human aspects of things that are discovered under different finite conditions. This is a distinction that could be viewed as essential and constitutive for man's "excentric" consciousness of the
"world," in contrast to the centristic domination of animals by their
environment.[19] But Peirce is able to do justice to this question precisely through the distinction between the—infinitely—cogniz*able*
and that which is in fact known at some time or other. Peirce formulates this position in the first essay of 1868: ". . . ignorance and
error can only be conceived as correlative to a real knowledge and
truth, which latter are of the nature of cognitions. Over against any
cognition, there is an unknown but knowable reality; but over against
all possible cognition, there is only the self-contradictory. In short,
cognizability (in its widest sense) and *being* are not merely metaphysically the same, but are synonymous terms" (5.257).

In the second essay from 1868 Peirce repeats the thesis—"We
have no conception of the absolutely incognizable" (5.265)—and reconfirms the meaning-critical starting point of his argumentation—
". . . since the meaning of a word is the conception it conveys, the
absolutely incognizable has no meaning because no conception at-
taches to it. It is, therefore, a meaningless word; and, consequently,
whatever is meant by any term as 'the real' is cognizable in some degree, and so is of the nature of a cognition, in the objective sense of
the term" (5.310).

The last part of this sentence betrays some uncertainty about this
new position. In fact, Peirce appears at first to understand it as a vari-

ety of Berkeleian Idealism, since, in the first 1868 essay, he says: "If I think 'white,' I will not go so far as Berkeley and say that I think of a person seeing, but I will say that what I think is of the nature of a cognition" (5.257).

And when Peirce returns to this problem in the second 1868 essay he seems to understand his own position to be idealistic in the broadest sense of the term, for he introduces it in the context of a historical reflection in the following way: "That upon Cartesian principles [Peirce means, on the basis of the presupposition that we are certain only about the contents of our own consciousness, and the existence of things outside consciousness is problematic; their causal affection of consciousness, through which they are supposed to be known by means of their effects, can be explained only by claiming divine assistance] the very realities of things can never be known in the least, most competent persons must long ago have been convinced. Hence the breaking forth of idealism, which is essentially anti-Cartesian, in every direction, whether among empiricists (Berkeley, Hume), or among noologists (Hegel, Fichte)" (5.310). And in conjunction with this Peirce continues: "The principle now brought under discussion [that the concept of the incognizable is meaningless] is directly idealistic" (5.310).

From the passages just quoted, we can see that Peirce's aim is definitely not to reduce reality, as Berkeley does, to being known in a subjectivist-idealistic fashion. In what follows Peirce in fact attempts to formulate a position that does justice both to Idealism and to Realism. He says, ". . . there is no thing which is in-itself in the sense of not being relative to the mind, though things which are relative to the mind doubtless are, apart from that relation" (5.311).

Peirce later gives meaning to this difficult sentence in the light of his doctrine of categories. He associates the sheer existence of real things, independently of their relationship to our minds, with the experience of resistance to our will in the "outward clash,"[20] as well as with the "indicative" function of language, such as in the expression "this here," which cannot be used as a "symbol" independently of a situation (Secondness), while reality is seen as something that can be meaningfully intended (represented in symbols) and is related to possible knowledge (Thirdness). In the present context of 1868, Peirce is concerned with defining the conceivable, that is, representable, meaning of reality, and this can be sought only in regard to understanding in general, that is, to "cognizability." From here Peirce attains his characteristic definition of the reality of the real, a definition which, as we shall see, provides the framework for semantic Pragmatism and needs only to be filled out through the pragmatic maxim. The first formulation of this definition is introduced in the following manner:

And what do we mean by the real? It is a conception which we must first have had when we discovered that there was an unreal, an illusion; that is, when we first corrected ourselves. Now the distinction for which alone this fact logically called, was between an *ens* relative to private inward determinations, to the negations belonging to idiosyncrasy, and an *ens* such as would stand in the long run. The real, then, is that which, sooner or later, information and reasoning would finally result in, and which is therefore independent of the vagaries of me and you.[21]

This definition of reality through the idea of the "ultimate opinion" or the "ideal perfection of knowledge" (5.356), which first appears in the second of the 1868 essays, is extended in all of Peirce's following works.[22] In these it becomes increasingly clear that it is not an idealistic theory, but rather indicates a new path that avoids both Idealism and dogmatic metaphysical Realism. I believe that this starting point should be designated "meaning-critical Realism." That this new "theory of reality" is not idealistic is apparent, it seems to me, in the further development of this view that Peirce began in 1868. In a way, this development represents a concretization of the idea of "consciousness in general" in the direction of a "postulate of practical reason," in Kant's sense. Peirce then adds the following comment to his definition of "reality": "Thus, the very origin of the conception of reality [namely, from the difference between my idiosyncrasy and that which proves to hold as an opinion "in the long run"] shows that this conception essentially involves the notion of a COMMUNITY, without definite limits, and capable of a definite increase of knowledge."[23]

In 1871 Peirce clarifies this thought further in the following way: ". . . the catholic consent[24] which constitutes the truth is by no means to be limited to men in this earthly life or to the human race, but extends to the whole communion of minds to which we belong, including some probably whose senses are very different from ours, so that in that consent no predication of a sensible quality can enter, except as an admission that so certain sorts of senses are affected" (8.13).

This characterization of the "indefinite community" makes two things clearly evident. First, we are dealing here with an embodiment of *reason* itself as an ideal normative principle in Kant's sense. It must accomplish what no finite consciousness can attain in its factual cognition and what no finite community which could die out or be destroyed by a catastrophe is able to offer. It must be equal to the task of unlimited possible progress in the cognition of the unending, cognizable real.[25] Second, we see distinctly from Peirce's characterization that the "indefinite community" is an *embodiment* of reason, that it is not a "consciousness in general" or a "realm of spirits" but rather an unending community of beings that possess some kinds of senses and are able to communicate in signs.

Later, in the pragmatist period, Peirce would more closely describe the method of cognition which this community has to utilize, beyond the logically correct use of signs, so that it is able to be the carrier of the advance of knowledge, an advance which is supposed to have a chance to reach the "ultimate opinion" about the real in general and in totality. The community proves then to be one of experimenting investigators who are in a position to undertake interventions into nature (e.g., measurements). But this pragmatist "community of experimenters" is only a further concretization of the presupposition of a real community which was introduced in 1868 as the condition for a possible definition of reality by means of the notion of cognizability. The community that Peirce presupposes must also be real[26] as a "community of interpretation" (and hence as the condition of the possibility of the so-called *Geisteswissenschaften*), and it proves to be so—as the pragmatic analysis will show—by the fact that it converts its understanding of symbols into real operative rules of behavior or habits. The significance of this introduction of a real entity as the condition for a possible definition of meaning (and hence for the critique of meaning that has to replace the critique of knowledge) becomes apparent when we consider that the "material conditions of knowledge" which physics today has to consider in the operational definition of its basic concepts, along the lines of Peirce's pragmatic maxim,[27] are also nothing more than the "real presuppositions" of the definition of meaning. They are closer to and more like the presupposition of the real community in Peirce's definition of reality[28] than the presupposition of "consciousness in general" in Kant's critique of reason.[29] Here lies the difference between the transcendental philosophy of "pure consciousness" and a philosophy which recognizes, besides the a priori of reflection (where, of course, mind, or as Peirce says, Thirdness, has the last word), also the a priori of engaged cognition or mediation through real praxis. Marxism, Existentialism, Pragmatism, and in a certain sense even the Life-philosophies of Dilthey, Nietzsche, and Bergson discovered the problem of the operative mediation of theoretical meaning through real praxis and thereby went beyond the bounds of the philosophy of consciousness in both its empiricist and its noological forms. The resulting threat of neglect to the a priori of reflection, which Erich Heintel has termed "forgetfulness of *logos*" (in opposition to Heidegger's accusation of "forgetfulness of being"),[30] can hardly be blamed on Peirce.

But to return to the definition of reality as Peirce conceived it in the pre-pragmatic context of the critique of meaning, the presupposition of the real community belonging to this definition shows that the "theory of reality" may not be interpreted idealistically,[31] rather, this theory is from the outset conceived to be realist in regard to universals. This turn of thought follows immediately (in 1868 and 1871) upon the rejection in the critique of meaning of the concept of absolute incognizable things-in-themselves; along with this rejection, it marks the transition to the criticism of Nominalism in the narrow sense. Peirce perceives the supposedly incognizable things-in-themselves as singular initial triggers of the knowing process interpreted as an unendingly mediated inferential process of hypothesis formation. That is, they represent an "ideal limit" to knowledge; knowledge as such always ensues through general, that is, vague, concepts, and so conceptual knowledge can approach only infinitely the individual thing conceived as something completely determinate.[32] But since the individual thing as the ideal limit of knowledge can be conceived only in general concepts, then thought in vague, abstract concepts must also be capable of being true. In other words, philosophical knowledge itself cannot argue against the possible objective validity of its concepts. It must "trust itself to be capable of reaching truth," as Hegel says. But with this the realist view of universals is already affirmed for Peirce.

Peirce formulates this thought as follows:

But it follows that since no cognition of ours is absolutely determinate, generals must have a real existence. Now this scholastic realism is usually set down as a belief in metaphysical fictions. But, in fact, a realist is simply one who knows no more recondite reality than that which is represented in a true representation. Since, therefore, the word "man" is true of something, that which "man" means is real. The nominalist must admit that man is truly applicable to something; but he believes that there is beneath this a thing in itself, an incognizable reality. His is the metaphysical figment. [5.312]

In 1871 Peirce repeats the same point in the following way:

It is plain that this view of reality [namely, that one which defines the "external" reality of things, insofar as it is independent of actual opinions about it, by means of its cognizability in the ideal final opinion of the unlimited community of researchers] is inevitably realistic [regarding the theory of universals]; because general conceptions enter into all judgements, and therefore into true opinions. . . . It is perfectly true that all white things share whiteness in them, for that is only saying, in another form of words, that all white things are white; but since it is true that real things possess whiteness, whiteness is real. It is a real which only exists by virtue of the act of thought knowing it, but that thought is not an arbitrary or accidental one dependent on any idiosyncrasies, but one which will hold in the final opinion. [8.14]

Up until now I have intentionally referred only to those—fundamental—arguments of Peirce's realist theory of universals that are understandable without any discussion of the medieval controversy about universals. This should not be taken to imply that reference to this controversy and Peirce's positive appeal to Duns Scotus are completely irrelevant for Peirce's position. But this much can be established by abstractly considering those arguments which are immediately connected with Peirce's definition of reality, namely, that Peirce's realist view of universals follows primarily from his meaning-critical Realism, which, as we have already seen, is a way of overcoming the Nominalism that mediates modern Idealism's critique of knowledge. The controversy that actually gave birth to Peirce's meaning-critical Realism, including the renewal of the realist view of universals, was his original interpretation of Kant, that is, his meaning-critical reinterpretation of the restriction of all concept formation in the sense of the "transcendental analytic." Peirce confirms this to be the case right after the last-cited apology for the realist view of universals, when he notes:

This theory [that the reality of universals cannot be conceived to be independent from the activity of thought] involves a phenomenalism. But it is the phenomenalism of Kant, and not that of Hume. Indeed, what Kant called his Copernican step was precisely the passage from the nominalistic to the realistic view of reality. It was the essence of his philosophy to regard the real object as determined by the mind. That was nothing else than to consider every conception and intuition which enters necessarily into the experience of an object, and which is not transitory and accidental, as having objective reality. In short, it was to regard the reality as the normal product of mental action, and not as the incognizable cause of it. [8.15]

This noteworthy passage shows in two places that Peirce has not yet taken possession of his new position with complete awareness. In this formulation, meaning-critical Realism still carries the outer shell, so to speak, of traditional Idealism. The first passage, where Peirce calls his position a "phenomenalism" in Kant's sense, is easiest to explain. What he wants to express here is not something like a wish to make a distinction between "phenomena" and "noumena," as Kant does. This is distinctly seen in the text following, where he says:

The realist will hold that the very same objects which are immediately present in our minds in experience *really exist just as they are experienced* [emphasis added] out of the mind; that is he will maintain a doctrine of immediate perception. He will not, therefore, sunder existence out of the mind and being in the mind as two wholly improportionable modes. When a thing is in such relation to the individual mind that that mind cognizes it, it is in the mind; and its being so in the mind will not in the least diminish its external existence. For he does not think of the mind as receptacle, which if a thing is in, it ceases to be out of.[33]

This is probably the first exposure of what Wittgenstein later called *metaphorischer Schein*. By pointing it out here in the schematism of the so-called critical theory of knowledge,[34] Peirce removes all suspicion that he could be a phenomenalist in the traditional sense of the term. But what does Peirce mean then by the concept "phenomenalism" in Kant's sense? In the text referred to just now, Peirce distinguishes himself from the Phenomenalism of Berkeley and Hume by stressing that the meaning of the "belief in external realities," to which he adheres, lies simply in the view that this real "is independent of what phenomenon is immediately present" (8.13). This gives rise to the statement that "phenomenalism" in Kant's sense is that meaning-critical theory which understands reality "in terms of possible experience," that is, Kant's "empirical realism" without the background of incognizable things-in-themselves. The late Peirce was to confirm this with all the clarity that one could ask for in an essay from about 1905, unpublished during his lifetime, entitled "Pragmatism":

Kant (whom I *more* than admire) is nothing but a somewhat confused pragmatist. A real is anything that is not affected by men's cognitions *about it;* which is a verbal definition, not a doctrine. An external object is anything that is not affected by any cognitions, whether about it or not, of the man to whom it is external. Exaggerate this, in the usual philosophical fashion, and you have the conception of what is not affected by any cognitions at all. Take the converse of this definition and you have the notion of what does not affect cognition, and in this indirect manner you get a hypothetically abstract notion of what the *Ding an sich* would be. In this sense, we also have a notion of sky-blue demonstration; but in half a dozen ways the *Ding an sich* has been proved to be nonsensical; and here is another way. It has been shown that in the formal analysis of a proposition, after all that words can convey has been thrown into the predicate, there remains a subject that is indescribable and that only can be pointed at or otherwise indicated, unless a way, of finding what is referred to, be prescribed.[35] The *Ding an sich,* however, can neither be indicated nor found. Consequently, no proposition can refer to it, nothing true or false can be predicated of it. Therefore, all references to it must be thrown out as meaningless surplusage. But when that is done, we see clearly that Kant regards Space, Time, and his Categories just as everybody else does, and never doubts or has doubted their objectivity. His limitation of them to possible experience is pragmatism in the general sense; and the pragmatist, as fully as Kant, recognizes the mental ingredient in these concepts. Only (trained by Kant to define), he defines more definitely, and somewhat otherwise, than Kant did, just how much of this ingredient comes from the mind of the individual in whose experience the cognition occurs. The kind of Common-sensism which thus criticizes the Critical Philosophy and recognizes its own affilia-

tion to Kant has surely a certain claim to call itself Critical Common-
sensism. [5.525]

What Peirce here calls "Critical Common-sensism" is—at least
in the present regard—the meaning-critical approach of his first period, which he explicitly integrated into the "Pragmatism" of his late
works. Peirce also calls it "Pragmatism in the general sense" and
thereby quite appropriately designates that preliminary phase of Pragmatism which had been worked out in the first period's meaning-
critical approach, in contrast to the special Pragmatism of the second
period. The talk about the "mental ingredient" in the universal concepts that Kant calls categories brings us back to the second passage
in the 1871 text in which, as I said, Peirce has not yet completely
taken possession of his position. There he interprets and accepts
Kantianism as that theory which teaches us "to regard the reality as
the normal product of mental action, and not as the incognizable
cause of it."

The turn away from the causes of cognition in the past to the
goals of cognition in the future which points the way for Pragmatism
is brought out well in this formulation, but at the price, so it seems,
of an absolute Idealism: an identification of cognition with the production of reality in contradiction to Critical Common-sensism. After
seeing through the metaphor of "consciousness as a container," Peirce
seems to have fallen victim to the metaphor of cognition as a manu-
facture. It cannot be denied that he formulates his famous definition
of reality "in terms of the ultimate opinion" in several places in a way
that is in line with Idealism. He does this, for example, in the 1869
essay entitled "Grounds of Validity of the Laws of Logic," where he
speaks about the "ideal perfection of knowledge by which we have
seen that reality is constituted" (5.356), and as late as 1893 in a (no
doubt) passing comment that is obviously to serve as a brief formulation. There he says, ". . . the real is the idea in which the community
ultimately settles down."[36] However, in the authoritative and carefully
prepared definition of "truth" and "reality" on the basis of the pragmatic maxim, in "How to Make Our Ideas Clear" (1878), he says,
"The opinion which is fated to be ultimately agreed to by all who investigate, is what we mean by the truth, and the object represented
in this opinion is the real."[37] And in a controversy with the Hegelian
Josiah Royce ("our American Plato"), who attempted to subsume
Pragmatism under absolute Idealism, Peirce stresses "that the essence
of the realist's opinion is that it is one thing to be and another thing
to be represented."[38] Earlier he had borrowed from Royce himself the
argument that the identification of the real with the final opinion
would lead to a regressus ad infinitum: ". . . if the non-ego to which

the inquirer seeks to make his ideas confirm is merely an idea in the future, that future idea must have for its object an idea in the future to it, and so on *ad infinitum*" (8.104). From this Peirce explicitly concludes: "There is no escaping the admission that the mould to which we endeavor to shape our opinions, cannot itself be of the nature of an opinion" (8.104).

In fact, the real, in the sense of the 1878 definition, as that which would be the object of the final definitive opinion about it, must encompass not only whatever a knowing subject can meet with at any time as something independent of himself and yet "knowable" *hic et nunc*, but also the real development of knowledge in the process of inquiry by the "indefinite community."[39] When we consider that according to Peirce the real embodiment of the results of cognition consists in the establishment of habits of action (as the pragmatic verification of universals), then we can easily come to the conclusion that the object of the "ultimate opinion" is to be identified with the achievement of the full order of all "habits" that completes the imperfect lawfulness of nature. This conclusion is confirmed in the metaphysics of the late Peirce. But at the same time it is interpreted in the sense of an "objective idealism" which understands these habits not "from below" as laws of nature, but rather, like Schelling, "from above," so that laws of nature are taken as petrified habits. In addition, Peirce characterizes the goal of this development as *"concrete reasonableness."*[40]

Let us return, after this look ahead at the consequences of Peirce's definition of reality,[41] to the meaning-critical approach of the first period of Peirce's thought. It should be clear by now that it is to this position, which Peirce preferred to understand as an interpretation, rather than as a refutation, of Kant, that we are to look for the origin of Pragmatism as a principle for the criticism of meaning. It is tempting to see an adequate answer to Kant in this meaning-critical Realism that would lead us directly to modern philosophy, bypassing speculative Idealism and Neo-Kantianism. Such modern philosophy is everywhere concerned to trace such metaphysical constructions, which cannot be reconciled with the "common sense" of language usage, back to some hidden meaninglessness that is inspired by *metaphorischer Schein* and not by the proper use of linguistic means.[42] However, if we desire to evaluate Peirce's critical approach to Kant in the sense indicated, it is not possible to overlook the main reason for Kant's distinction between "phenomena" and "noumena."[43] Kant saw himself forced to make this distinction because without it he did not believe he could answer the question how synthetic judgments are a priori possible. To be more exact, the answer that he gave to this question—namely, that the understanding prescribes the law to nature—can claim to be valid for things as they appear to us in time and space, but not for things as they are in themselves.

Now it surely can be said of Peirce that he took the transcendental question in its most elementary form very seriously. The problem of going from logic to the categories (Kant's metaphysical deduction) did not hold his careful attention just from around 1860 to 1867—that is, until the completion of the "New List of Categories"—but later on as well, when he attempted a derivation of the categories from the logic of relations.[44] In addition, there is an analogy in Peirce's thought to the transcendental deduction, as I have already mentioned.[45] And in the acceptance of Kant's "phenomenalism" that I quoted above, Peirce in fact laid claim to the "Copernican revolution" for himself. How can this be brought into agreement with the elimination of the distinction between "noumena" and "phenomena?" It would be easy to assume that Peirce never correctly understood Kant.[46]

I do not want to attempt to refute this suspicion directly, considering the circumstance that the greatest independent thinkers do not tend to understand their predecessors as professional historians of philosophy do. I want to put the question in a different way: Can an answer to the question how the "transcendental deduction," where possible in a modified form, and the denial of incognizable things-in-themselves are to be united be gained from Peirce's writings, especially the writings of his early period, where he engages in his criticism of Kant?

It seems to me to be possible and worth the effort to reconstruct a positive answer in reference to Peirce's earlier writings. Such a reconstruction is, in my view, also the best conceivable introduction to the young Peirce's "theory of cognition." This was prepared for from about 1860, then worked out in the three essays of 1868–69 (especially in the little-considered third one), and finally carried over in 1872 into Pragmatism in its "theory of inquiry."

C. Fallibilism and Transcendental Deduction: The New Theory of Knowledge

a. The New Theory of Knowledge as an Alternative to Kant's Critique of Reason. Kant seems to place before all those who have understood him the following alternative: either admit the existence of unknowable things-in-themselves or give up founding the objective validity of science. This is because the objective validity of science rests on the necessity of its "principles." The necessity of synthetic knowledge, however, can be explained only when the conditions for the possibility of experience are also the conditions for the possibility of the objects of experience. If this is to be understood as conformity with things-in-themselves, then it is just a coincidental fact which itself cannot be scientifically founded, but can only be accepted as a matter of belief in a dogmatic metaphysics. Therefore, the distinction between "phenomena" and "noumena" is a presupposition of a critical philosophy which can found the validity of science. The only alternative is David Hume's skepticism. The answer that Peirce has to offer in this problematic situation can be summed up in a preliminary way in the term which designates an aspect of his later "Pragmaticism" as "Critical Common-sensism": the term "Fallibilism." What are we to understand by this in the present context?

It means something like this: between Hume's skepticism and Kant's claim to be able to explain the necessity of scientific propositions on the basis of their transcendental-logical conditions there is a third way.[47] It consists in admitting the hypothetical and, hence, fallibilistic character of all scientific *propositions*, but in proving in a transcendental deduction the necessary validity of the *inferential procedure* through which science's synthetic propositions are attained. The Kantian distinction between "phenomena" and "noumena" is thereby again replaced, as it was in the theory of reality, by the distinction between what is in fact known and the infinity of what can be known. Only cogniz*ability*, which is derived from the meaning-critical definition of reality, can also prove to be necessary in the logic of cognition.

But as far as all actual cognitions are concerned, the fact is that, as "hypotheses" which reduce the manifold of sense data to a consistent opinion, they transcend experience even though—insofar as they are meaningful at all—they are subject to "inductive" verification through experience. Hypothesis and experience are no longer mutually exclusive for Peirce, who instead replaces the Kantian alternative of synthetic a priori propositions and synthetic a posteriori propositions with the fruitful circle of the correlative presuppositions of hypothesis (abductive inference) and experimental confirmation (inductive inferential procedure).[48] Even the most fundamental, practically indubitable, general premises presupposed in these inferences—such as, for instance, that there are real things, that they affect our senses, and the like—hold only a priori relative to the cognitions for which they are presupposed. However, as truth claims they are "fallible," like the entire corpus of knowledge to which the finite human being can attain, and therefore they are subject to confirmation by experience.

The only completely a priori and transcendentally necessary presupposition for Peirce is the validity of the synthetic process of inference "in the long run." Peirce again strictly follows Kant in this modification of the transcendental deduction by demonstrating, in opposition to John Stuart Mill, that the validity of inductive and abductive inference procedures cannot be empirically founded, that is, traced to metaphysically chance facts.

With this "abbreviation"[49] of transcendental philosophy we attain a view of how the understanding can, so to speak, prescribe the law to nature in the long run, without hindering nature's ability to determine on its own behalf the content of all conceivable synthetic propositions, by means of the outer force of experience. Expressed in terms of Peirce's categories, Thirdness (synthetic mediation of the data of experience through inference procedures) and Secondness (the self-indication of existing things in sense experience, which corresponds to the indexical function of language) pervade and complement one another. With this, however, there is no longer any reason, because of the objective validity of science, to limit it to knowledge of mere appearances. The reason for this limitation stood only as long as philosophy, led by the platonic ἐπιστήμη concept of science, held apodictically certain cognitions to be the only alternative to absolute skepticism.[50] Peirce calls this phase of the history that of the "a priori method" of the "fixation of belief."[51] It follows the "method of authority" and is replaced by the "method of science." It should be noted here that Peirce's "method of science," as it is founded in his logic of inquiry, is not identical with the Positivism conceived by Comte and Mill, not even when Positivism is supplemented by the recognition of formal deductive logic and mathematics, as in logical Positivism. Peirce recognizes not only facts and deductive logic, but also synthesis a priori, which is the basis of the logic of induction and hypothesis formation and which by means of such a logic makes possible an *ars inveniendi*. He is thereby able once again, like Kant, to mediate between Rationalism and Empiricism, between German and British philosophy.

By means of the texts, I want next to elucidate briefly the genesis of Peirce's "theory of knowledge" in the pre-pragmatic phase.[52]

b. Peirce's Early Kant Studies (ca. 1860–67). Kant's "transcendental synthesis of apperception" was the starting point of the theory of knowledge for Peirce, but he interpreted it as early as 1861 as an inference. Every cognition demands an operation of the understanding which unifies the manifold of sense data; "an operation upon data resulting in cognition is an inference."[53]

At that time Peirce still thought of deductive inference in terms of the mode of "Barbara," even though he already used the term "hypothesis," and he therefore had to think of knowledge as an axiomatic system, the final universal premises of which are already contained in the mind. It is significant that he did not at that time adopt Kant's proof of the validity of synthetic a priori judgments for these final "primal truths," but rather referred to them as presuppositions whose truth must be believed. Leaving aside here whether he was correct, Peirce saw a circle in Kant's transcendental solution, since it "says that the results of metaphysics are worthless, unless the study of consciousness produces a warrant for the authority of consciousness. But the authority of consciousness [itself] must be valid within the consciousness or else no science, not even psychological transcendentalism, is valid. . . ."[54]

From this criticism of Kant's "transcendentalism" Peirce arrived at that point characteristic of all Pragmatism (as well as Existentialism and Marxism), of calling into question the separation of theoretical and practical reason. In Peirce's criticism of Kant this meant that he had to consider the belief in postulates which Kant wanted to reserve for practical reason as already required within the theory of knowledge: "Faith is not peculiar to or more needed in one province of thought than in another. For every premiss we require faith and no where else is there any room for it. This is overlooked by Kant and others who drew a distinction between *faith* and *knowledge*."[55]

This passage from 1861 sheds light on a criticism of Kant that Peirce was to hint at in an 1893 footnote illustrating the "a priori method" in the "Fixation of Belief":

When he [Kant] comes to the ideas of God, Freedom, and Immortality, . . . he subjects these ideas to a different kind of examination [i.e., different from the categories], and finally admits them upon grounds which appear to the seminarists more or less suspicious, but which in the eyes of laboratorists are infinitely stronger than the grounds upon which he has accepted space, time, and causality. . . . Had Kant merely said, I shall adopt for the present the belief that the three angles of a triangle are equal to two right angles because nobody but brother Lambert and some Italian has ever called it in question, his attitude would be well enough. But on the contrary, he and those who today represent his school distinctly maintain the proposition is *proved*, and the Lambertists *refuted*, by what comes merely to general disinclination to think with them.[56]

Despite Peirce's rejection of the transcendental foundation of the truth of synthetic a priori judgments, he continued to hold to the possibility of a "metaphysical" and "transcendental" deduction of categories as the simple concepts of an ontological logic. I have already briefly described the results of the painstaking efforts that finally, in the "New List of Categories" (1867), led him to derive the three fundamental categories from the function of sign representation as the unity of all forms of synthesizing sense data for a consciousness.[57] We must now consider the inferential character of sign representation more closely. As early as 1861 Peirce saw an inference at work in the synthesis of apperception (see the beginning of this section), and so it is understandable that the function of sign representation, which he analyzed in 1867, was for him both the unity of all forms of judgments and the unity of all forms of inference. The judgment is, as a semiotic transition from the antecedent (subject) to the consequent (predicate), simply an implicit inference.[58]

It seems that Perice was brought by the study of Duns Scotus to understand the forms of judgments, also, in terms of their function in inference.[59] In a fragment from 1865 he wrote: "It is necessary to reduce all our actions to logical processes so that to do anything is but to take another step in the chain of inference. Thus only can we effect that complete reciprocity between Thought and its Object which it was Kant's Copernican step to announce."[60]

In his essays in 1868–69 Peirce sought to provide the proof which he had called for then, that all human actions have the character of logical inferences. Later, in his Pragmatism, he would also bring real actions of human beings into this interpretation, and finally, primarily in the third period, he would seek to conceive natural processes, insofar as they proceed according to laws, as unconscious inferences.[61] But for the time being, around 1868, the proposed program led him to his first great discovery in the field of logic: the distinction among "deduction," "induction," and "hypothesis" (later also termed "abduction" or "retroduction"). Peirce was to give an account of this in a lecture manuscript from 1903: "I endeavored to formulate the process [i.e., of induction] syllogistically; and I found that it would be defined as the *inference* of the major premiss of a syllogism from its minor premiss and conclusion. . . . With this hint as to the nature of induction, I at once remarked that if this be so there ought to be a form of inference which infers the Minor premiss from the major and the conclusion. Moreover, Aristotle was the last of men to fail to see this. I looked along further and found that . . . Aristotle opens the 25th [chapter of the second book of the *Prior Analytics*] with a description of the inference of the minor premiss from the major and the conclusion."[62]

Peirce could subsequently take the three forms of inference which he distinguished as deduction, hypothesis, and induction to be the explicated forms of analytic, synthetic, and what Kant calls synthetic a priori judgments, whereby the synthetic general judgments naturally forfeit their a priori character.[63] With this, Peirce found himself in possession of the answer to the question "How are synthetic judgments possible?" which in 1869 he explicitly put before the Kantian question of the possibility of synthetic a priori judgments, taking the former to be the more fundamental (5.348).

In particular, the hypothesis or so-called abductive inference has a key function in Peirce's "theory of cognition" and is important for understanding the pragmatic maxim in his theory of inquiry. A hypothesis for Peirce is not only each "explanation" of an event on the basis of a presupposed general law and an antecedent condition,[64] but—as I have already indicated in different ways—every synthetic unified interpretation of a manifold of sense data in a judgment of experience. Here too we have, according to Peirce, implicitly (or, in psychological terms, unconsciously) an "explanation" of the sense data as the result of postulating a fact hypothetically under the presupposition of a general law. This is the reason why every judgment of experience, if it is meaningful, must be capable of being inductively tested by reference to consequences confirmable through sense perception that can be deductively derived from it. This test, which the pragmatic maxim recommends as a thought experiment, establishes—with the help of deductive and inductive inferences—whether a judgment of experience is an acceptable "hypothesis" that actually "explains" certain phenomena, that is, reduces them to the unity of a semantically consistent opinion about the real.

Peirce recognizes early the close relationship between the problem of the primary interpretation of sense data in a hypothesis and the problem of the constitution of objects in language.[65] An early draft of the "New List of Categories" says that "to conceive is to collect under a supposition, to make a hypothesis, and therefore cannot dispense with the use of words."[66] The problem posed here is presented more radically in the Harvard lectures on the "Logic of Science" from 1866–67:

Names are commonly assigned, in our day, as synonyms for longer and more inconvenient names. . . . But it is plain that in the early youth of language, and of each man, many names must be adopted which have no equivalents at all. Now I maintain that *such* adoption of names is a hypothetic process. Before a name connoting certain characters is invented, those characters cannot be thought of, in themselves, at all.[67] The object is thought through these characters, and is thus thought as determined in a certain mode; but to think it as one of the things which have these characters in common, or to think of the things which have these characters in common as being in any other [way] determined or undetermined is to possess a term which connotes these characters.[68]

The logical problem that Peirce sees here consists in the fact that for the primary interpretation of something "as something" the requisite name[69] cannot be found through deduction, as in conventional subsumption, since in that case we presuppose a general premise which already contains the comprehensive term. Peirce has in mind this solution: because the only thing that is given to us as a premise for the interpretive hypothesis is the confused impression "This thing is so," there must also take place both an inductive inference yielding the major premise "Whatever should have this name would be thus" and a hypothetical inference, which already vaguely presupposes the inductive inference, "This thing is one of those which have this name."

Murphey, who discusses this interesting passage, calls the argumentation a *petitio principii*, but notes that Peirce defends it with the argument that induction and hypothesis are not forms of demonstration.[70] Here, it seems to me, we have in fact touched upon the point of "synthetic inferences" in Peirce's "logic of discovery."[71] The problem of beginning a "hermeneutic synthesis" (Heidegger's term), which is obviously the concern here, has not by coincidence been characterized in the German tradition of hermeneutics as the "circle in understanding."[72]

Peirce is already concerned in the 1866–67 plan of his "logic of science" with a limiting of his theory of hypothesis, a case in which it is impossible in principle to bring the postulated process of inference under the control of consciousness. This limiting case is found in the "judgment of sensation." According to Peirce, an inference must also be made in a color sensation. For "colour [meaning a certain color perception] can only arise from the relative states of the nerve at different times."[73] Or as it says in another fragment: ". . . the simplest colour is almost as complicated as a piece of music. Colour depends upon the *relations* between different parts of the impression; and, therefore, the differences between colours are the differences between colours harmonies; and to see this difference we must have the elementary impressions whose relation makes the harmony. So that colour is not an impression, but an inference."[74]

But since the conclusion postulated here takes place, at least on an elementary level,[75] without any intellectual insight, but rather on the basis of an anthropological-biological constitution, Peirce speaks of a "constitutional nominal hypothesis," in contrast to an "*intellectual* hypothesis."[76]

The limiting case of the interpretation of the world through hypotheses or abductive inferences would later acquire decisive significance for Peirce because it is adapted to mediate the rationalistic thesis that all knowledge is mediated through previous knowledge, an idea implicit in the conception of knowledge as inference, and the empiricist demand for "immediate perception of the outer world." For Peirce, "perceptual judgments" provide the first premises presupposed by all empirical science, as well as the final verifiable consequences of theories. Peirce was not to supply a definitive solution to this problem, however, until his 1903 lectures on Pragmatism.[77] In the 1868 essays, to which we turn now, he first worked out the rationalistic side of his theory of knowledge and took to its logical conclusion the thesis that there is no "intuition," that is, no knowledge that is not mediated through previous knowledge.

c. *The First Essay on the Theory of Knowledge (1868).* In the first 1868 essay ("Questions concerning Certain Faculties Claimed for Man"), Peirce discusses seven questions in the manner of a scholastic treatise, according to the *sic et non* method.[78] There, the thesis that there is no "intuition" is conjoined with the special theses that (2) there is no "intuitive self-consciousness" (he means consciousness of the individual self), (4) there is no "faculty of introspection," (5) we cannot think "without signs," and (6) a sign for "something absolutely incognizable" has no meaning. It is characteristic of the refined logical acumen with which he defends these theses that he introduces the main thesis, that there is no "cognition" which "is not determined by a previous cognition" (7), in such a way that he first discusses whether we can decide through intuitive cognition if a cognition is intuitive (1) or, rather, if we can intuitively decide "between the subjective elements of different kinds of knowledge" (3). From his numerous and always exceptionally acute observations I can bring out here only those which are the most important of his conclusions and are characteristic of his philosophy as a whole.

Among these is the calling into question of the subjectivistic criterion of evidence to consciousness, a conclusion fundamental to his later Pragmatism. For Peirce, the point here lies in the fact that a human being who calls upon this subjective criterion of evidence thereby excludes himself from the possibility of exhausting the positive criteria of evidence in outer experience (see 5.214). In other words, a belief always arises out of an exhaustion of the positive criteria of evidence, and the subjective (reflective) criterion of evidence that Descartes postulated does not add anything to the belief which has already come about in this way. This last consideration acquired decisive importance for Peirce's critique of Descartes.[79] Peirce equates the Cartesian reference to the subjective criterion of evidence as an *"internal authority"* with the medieval practice of referring to authorities (5.215). In doing so he prepares the way for his later doctrine of the different methods (or periods) of the "fixation of belief," which contrasts the outer authority of writings in the Middle Ages to the "inner authority" of the "a priori method" and this, in turn, to the (once again) outer authority of experimental evidence.

A further result that always remained valid for Peirce is the thesis that our private self-consciousness is the result of a complex variety of inferences; among these, outer experience and, not the least, a shared world are needed even by the child. That this self-consciousness is more certain than everything else does not contradict his thesis, as Peirce demonstrates in a little showpiece of logical acuteness (see 5.237). The specific metaphysical point of Peirce's theory of self-consciousness is found in the fact that, for Peirce, the negative experiences of ignorance and error are what force the idea of a private self-consciousness upon us: "Ignorance and error are all that distinguish our private selves from the absolute *ego* or pure apperception."[80] Here we have a glimpse at the religious and moral background of the methodological conception of the "community of investigators" which has the mission of "embodying" the absolute ego or "pure apperception" in the unending process of inquiry and of eliminating "idiosyncrasies" by establishing those habits which go along with this process.[81]

In his discussion of whether we can intuitively distinguish between the subjective elements in knowledge, Peirce calls attention for the first time to the difference between Bain's definition of a belief as "that judgment from which a man will act" and the mere feeling of the certainty of a belief. He does this with the behavioristic-sounding comment: "If belief is taken in the active sense [i.e., in Bain's sense], it may be discovered by the observation of external facts and by inference from the sensation of conviction which usually accompanies it" (5.242). This means that it is possible to verify that somebody has a belief by inferring the ways of behaving that are to be expected in such a case. However, it is not possible to determine that someone has a belief solely by means of external observation. Peirce left it to others in the twentieth century to set forth theses of that kind.

Peirce's rejection of introspective intuition lead him to the conclusion that thought can recognize itself only in the signs through which it communicates: "The only thought, then, which can possibly be cognized is thought in signs. But thought which cannot be cognized does not exist. All thought, therefore, must necessarily be in signs" (5.251).[82] But this thesis also entails for Peirce the conclusion that there cannot be any intuitive cognition whatsoever. All thought has its reality in signs, not in an instantaneous vision devoid of relations. Its reality is in the interpretation of a thought sign by means of a thought in the time that follows. This thought itself must then be a sign for another thought, and so on ad infinitum (5.253).

In the final paragraphs of the second essay from 1868 Peirce works out further details of the idea that the semiotic process of interpretation continues infinitely, both backwards and forwards in direction (see 5.313–17). Here, in the context of the discussion of the "reality of mind," Peirce makes it clear that the signs that communicate the thought process between individuals are not just restricted to language or written signs, but also include all of the data of outer and inner experience itself. Indeed, Peirce goes so far as to conceive man himself as a "thought sign." The individual contents of human consciousness, feelings in the broadest sense of the word, are sign vehicles, just as are the material elements of the outer world. In the context of the inferential process of thought, which extends beyond the individual, human beings play the role of material qualities of thought signs.[83] Peirce contrasts this belief with the usual egocentric conception of the self as will. The will, taken as the brute force of private arbitrariness, falls under the category of Secondness and definitely cannot guarantee man an identity with himself. He can only find this insofar as he incorporates himself literally, his organism and his language in the broad sense, into the process of thought and lets himself be used as a sign. In this way he receives his self-identity, the identity of the Kantian "I think," from the consistency of this trans-individual process of thought.[84]

In this highly speculative context Peirce attains some fundamental insights into the relationship between man and language. By conceiving the content of the meaning of words in an analogy with the intellectual content of the man-sign, Peirce discerns that both gain from the accumulation of information and, moreover, that the information in man increases the meaning of his words, while the storage of information in words intellectually enriches man without, in a way, any effort on man's own part. As man's creation, words "might turn round and say: 'You mean nothing which we have not taught you, and then only so far as you address some word as the interpretant of your thought'" (5.313).

We have already shown in the discussion of Peirce's "theory of reality" that a philosophy which conceives knowledge to be representation by signs (the formation of a true opinion about the real) must reject as meaningless the concept of the absolutely incognizable and as a whole must therefore become a critique of meaning.[85] A consequence of this view, namely, that the individual thing can be conceived only as the ideal limiting case of cognition, has also been mentioned.[86] The chief problem that Peirce has to solve in the first essay from 1868 consists in showing how to reconcile the idea that every cognition is mediated by endless inferences based upon previous cognitions with the idea of beginning each cognition in time by an affection of the individual objects of empirical knowledge. This problem can also be formulated in terms of Peirce's doctrine of categories.[87] Put in that way, the affection of the senses by the individual thing is a natural event in time and space which falls under the category of Secondness. As such it can never explain cognition, since cognition is "mediation" (Thirdness) and can never be reduced to a natural event.[88]

Peirce used a mathematical comparison to explicate the solution to this problem (5.263). He compared cognition of the external world to the immersion of a triangle, point first, into water. The consciousness of insight characteristic of knowledge corresponds to the horizontal line that the water level makes on the immersed triangle. Tracing cognition back to previous cognitions would be comparable to slowly pulling the triangle out of the water. The lines made across the triangle would become shorter and shorter. This accords with a fact emphasized repeatedly by Peirce: cognitions that provide the basis for inferring a cognition tend to be much less conscious and evident than the cognition that they bring about. Finally, with the slow removal of the triangle, we have the case in which we no longer are capable of recognizing the line cutting across it, and yet the mathematician knows that as long as the triangle is immersed in the water at all an infinite number of such lines are nevertheless possible between the water level and the point of the triangle. According to Peirce, this situation corresponds to the fact that all of our cognitive processes below a certain level are lost in the unconscious, and yet we must assume inferential processes below that level. For example, the synthetic inference processes that are the basis for our acquisition of a knowledge of three-dimensional space are conscious to us just as little as are those by which we acquire knowledge of a surface or even a line (without the blind spot on the retina making itself noticeable).[89]

However, the point of the comparison is that the triangle can nonetheless be submerged into water at a certain time. This natural event (Secondness) corresponds to the natural event of the impetus to cognition in sensory cognition. According to Peirce, this matter of fact (Secondness) only appears to contradict the postulate (Thirdness) of the infinitely mediated character of every cognition as thought (Thirdness). The elimination of this apparent contradiction is for Peirce like the resolution of Zeno's paradox of Achilles and the turtle.[90] That is, in the present context, a temporal process like cognition, which has a beginning (affection of the senses) and an end (temporary level of knowledge), takes place in a stretch of time as a continuum in which every part itself contains parts. Now Peirce is evidently of the opinion that cognition as thought (Thirdness), not as the empirical object of psychological and physiological inquiry (Secondness), can be conceived of on the model of a continuum as something infinitely mediated. In his later logic and metaphysics of continuity, which he worked on especially in the last decade of the nineteenth century and considered to be his most important philosophical achievement, Peirce also applied this conception to the evolutionary lawfulness of nature understood from the standpoint of thought. This transformed the problem of the compatibility of the actual affection of the senses and the infinite mediation of thought into the problem of the compatibility of contingent facticity (Second-ness) and, finally, normatively defined lawfulness (Thirdness).

d. The Second Essay on the Theory of Knowledge (1868). In the second 1868 essay Peirce draws several consequences from four of the previously asserted incapacities of man. We have already con-sidered the consequences of the incapacity to think without signs (3), as well as those of the incapacity to conceive of the absolutely in-cognizable (4).[91] These are principle aspects of the meaning-critical "theory of reality" with which this introduction to Peirce began. All that remains are the consequences of incapacities for "introspection" (1) and "intuition" (2).

Peirce places value on the fact that the epistemological theses which he defended in the foregoing "Quaestiones" cannot lay claim to absolute certainty. Such a thing is not possible in Peirce's falli-bilistic philosophy. Hence, it is all the more important to show the plausibility of these theses by pointing out their consequences (5.264). As a consequence of the first two negative principles about the nature of human cognition Peirce derives the positive thesis that we must "reduce all mental action to the formula of valid reasoning."[92] He does not mean a process substantiated by internal observation, which would be inconsistent with his rejection of introspection as a criterion for making decisions in the theory of knowledge. Rather, he holds that "something . . . takes place within the organism which is equiv-alent to the syllogistic process" (5.268). In order to explicate the in-ferential process he is referring to, Peirce introduces the doctrine of the three forms of inference that we met with above, the apodictic form of deduction and the two forms of synthetic or probable infer-ence: induction and hypothesis.[93] He believes that he is thereby equipped to meet the main criticism that can be made against his logi-cal conception of human intellectual activity, namely, reference to the fact that there is such a thing as erroneous thinking (5.280). In what follows he attempts to offer proof that all conceivable cases of errone-ous thought can be traced back to operations that, to be sure, are weak in the sense of belonging to the nondemonstrative logic of syn-thetic inferences, and yet are fundamentally valid (5.280–82).

In the following section, which deals with the consequences of the semiotic conception of the process of thought, another important argument can be found to contribute to the proof that all human thought can be traced to inferences. As an expert on British psycho-logical theories of knowledge as formulated by Berkeley, Hartley, and Hume, Peirce had to come to grips with the thesis, seemingly contrary to his own view, that all logical inference and especially the synthetic inference that is supposed to lead to the expansion of knowledge can be reduced to the psychological laws of the association of sense impressions, laws that might even be regarded as physiological (see 5.295–307).[94] Peirce takes pains now to show that the so-called laws of association must, on the contrary, be traced back to the three forms of inference. In accordance with his categorial architectonic he therefore subsumes association by resemblance under hypothesis and subsumes association by contiguity in space and time under induction. His essential argument in doing this is his thesis that we do not think by means of remembered images, but rather always in abstract quasi-concepts that must be understood in terms of judgments, no matter how inexplicit they may be.

This line of argument is closely related for Peirce to his realist conception of universals, because the task here is to show that man is not limited, as Berkeley and Hume claim, to thinking of completely determined objects, so that, for example, the thought of a triangle "must be of one, each of whose angles is of a certain number of degrees, minutes, and seconds" (5.299). On the contrary, thought is primarily in vague abstractions. This should not be taken to imply that Peirce does not know that the objects are completely determinate; it implies only that for him "the nominalists . . . confound thinking a triangle without thinking that it is either equilateral, isosceles, or scalene, and thinking a triangle without thinking whether it is equilateral, isosceles, or scalene" (5.301).

One of the most essential consequences—for Peirce's whole philosophy—of his reinterpretation of the nominalistic psychology of association according to logic and the realist theory of universals is the new concept of habit that emerges in the process. Hume reduces the laws of nature, or, rather, the logical operations by which they are inferred, to mere habits, that is, to actual habits formed by association in the sense of the Peircean category of Secondness. Peirce, on the other hand, understands habits in a way similar to Hegel, as the means by which the thoughts are transmitted: as the embodiment of "mind" or Thirdness.[95] Without recognizing this it is hopeless to try to understand the pragmatic maxim of the theory of meaning as Peirce comprehends it.[96]

e. The Third Essay on the Theory of Knowledge (1869) and a Supplement on the Transcendental Deduction of the Validity of Synthetic Inferences (1878). The third essay, from 1869, deals specifically with the question that the editor of the *Journal of Speculative Philosophy,* the Hegelian W. T. Harris, had requested Peirce to answer, but that Peirce believed he could answer only in a series of three articles, the question of the "Grounds of the Validity of the Laws of Logic."[97]

After Peirce had in the first two essays traced the essence of cognition, that is, synthetic inference, to the inferences found in hypothesis and induction, he set about answering the quasi-Kantian question of the conditions of the possibility of valid synthetic judgments. On this Peirce himself says: "According to Kant, the central question of philosophy is 'How are synthetical judgments *a priori* possible?' But antecedently to this comes the question how synthetical judgments in general, and still more generally, how synthetical reasoning is possible at all. . . . That is the lock upon the door of philosophy" (5.348).

Peirce's new general philosophical perspective, which we have already pointed out, led him to modify the Kantian question and, accordingly, also to gain a new view of the transcendental deduction of the objective validity of science. For Kant, too, the question how synthetic judgments are possible was prior to the question how synthetic judgments a priori are possible. But Kant saw the ground of the possibility of synthetic judgments, that is, of the objectively valid "judgments of experience," as distinguished from mere "judgments of perception," in the existence of synthetic judgments a priori. For this reason the point of his answer to the question how synthetic a priori judgments are possible resided in the thesis that they are possible only as a formulation of the conditions for the possibility of our experience, not as a formulation of any insights into the essence of things-in-themselves. For Peirce, however, the question of the grounds of the validity of experience is, from the outset, not identical with the question of the possibility of synthetic judgments a priori, because he has a different concept of the validity of science's synthetic judgments.

For Peirce, the synthetic judgments in science do not have to be necessarily true in order to be "objectively" valid. Their objective validity can be based instead on the validity in the long run of the logical method by which they are acquired. This is the reason why particular judgments owe their validity not just to laws given a priori for possible experience (Thirdness), but also to the momentary standing of experience gained from interaction with the reality of nature in itself (Secondness). In other words, the Fallibilism which Peirce upholds regarding the truth of all scientific propositions implies the systematic possibility of a return from Kantian Phenomenalism to a metaphysical Realism. This presupposes that it is possible at the same time to prove the necessary truth of science in the long run. The problem of a transcendental deduction of the objective validity of science is therefore now posed in terms of the synthetic process of inference that it uses. But since the only concern here, under the assumption that all particular judgments are fallible, can be to prove the validity of synthetic inferences in the long run, the problem of transcendental deduction is transformed for Peirce into the problem of the foundation of induction. He was to reconfirm this explicitly many times. Hence, a footnote to the first essay from 1868 states:

In fact, it is the particular function of induction to produce universal and necessary propositions. Kant points out, indeed, that the universality and necessity of scientific inductions are but the analogues of philosophic universality and necessity; and this is true, in so far as it is never allowable to accept a scientific conclusion without a certain indefinite drawback. But this is owing to the insufficiency in the number of the instances; and whenever instances may be in as large numbers as we please, *ad infinitum*, a truly universal and necessary proposition is inferable. [5.223 n]

After arriving at this ad infinitum progression as the consequence of the Kantian remark that the generality of induction (which Peirce takes to be possible) is analogous to the generality of synthetic a priori judgments (which he does not seriously believe to be possible), he turns to Kant's "highest principle." This is supposed to explain the possibility of synthetic a priori judgments and serves here in an analogous way in the context of the transcendental deduction of the validity of induction. Peirce's text continues: "As for Kant's second principle, that the truth of universal and necessary propositions is dependent upon the conditions of general experience, it is no more nor less than the principle of Induction" (5.233 n). How can this approach to a transcendental foundation of the validity of induction be made plausible? Peirce's brief illustration in the 1868 footnote is more extensively explicated in the last section of the 1878 essay entitled "The Probability of Induction." He gives there the following example: "I take from a bag a handful of beans; they are all purple, and I infer that all the beans in the bag are purple. How can I do that? Why, upon the principle that whatever is universally true of my experience (which is here the appearance of these different beans) is involved in the condition of experience. The condition of this special experience is that all these beans were taken from that bag" (2.691; see also 2.690 and 2.692).

Where is the Kantian point in this foundation of the validity of induction? Like Hume and, in particular, like John Venn in his *Logic of Chance*, Peirce begins with the view that we cannot find the slightest reason among facts for holding that "when we sample a bag of beans . . . the fact of some beans being purple involves the necessity or even the probability of other beans being so."[98] In an exact analogy to Kant's answer to Hume on the problem of causality Peirce now introduces the Kantian principle into his solution to the problem of the validity of probable inferences: "But synthetic inference is founded upon a classification of facts, not according to their characters, but according to the manner of obtaining them. Its rule is, that a number of facts obtained in a given way will in general more or less resemble other facts obtained in the same way; or, *experiences whose conditions are the same will have the same general characters*" (2.692).

The conclusion of the last sentence, where Peirce seeks to express the analogy to Kant's "uppermost principle," actually ought to read: "will (in general) have the same general characters." Otherwise, it would be possible to get the idea that Peirce's foundation for induction itself presupposes a deterministic principle of causality. What it actually presupposes is that we not only infer according to a certain (synthetic) logical principle, but also "acquire experiences [*Erfahrungen machen*]"[99] according to this principle in our experimental interventions into the world, in this case taking samples at random. The foundation of induction on the presupposition of the preconditions for experience, however, always includes the use of the procedure in the long run. Peirce expresses this idea in this way: ". . . in the case of analytic inference we know the probability of our conclusion (if the premises are true), but in the case of synthetic inferences we only know the degree of trustworthiness of our proceeding" (2.693).[100]

The actual basis of the validity of induction does not lie for Peirce, however, in any kind of factual preconditions for experience, but rather in the definition of the real necessitated by the critique of meaning. According to this definition the real is that which is cognizable "in the long run," and that means, in other words, cognizable in general concepts by an inductive procedure. By provisionally proceeding "ad infinitum" to the goal of the final opinion of the community postulated in the "cognizability" of the real, Peirce is able to establish the "highest point," which enables him to give a transcendental deduction of the objective validity of induction and, hence, of science. "Though a synthetic inference cannot by any means be reduced to deduction, yet that the rule of induction will hold good in the long run may be deduced from the principle that reality is only the object of the final opinion to which sufficient investigation would lead" (2.693). Here we can easily recognize that the function of the constitution of objective validity which accrues for Kant to the "transcendental synthesis of apperception" must belong for Peirce to what Kant called a "regulative principle" of inquiry, "to which nothing empirical can correspond." This regulative principle cannot, of course, then be understood in the way Kant conceived such principles, as "as if" fictions. No matter how necessary Kant conceived these fictions to be, such a view would rob Peirce's fallibilistic Realism of its only support.

In the 1869 essay entitled "The Grounds of the Validity of the Laws of Logic" Peirce unfolds the transcendental deduction of the objectivity of inductive logic in a way more differentiated than that sketched above. With this he also presents the transcendental deduction of synthetic logic generally, since it also depends on this validity in general or "in the long run."[101] Here I will be able to characterize only the general course of Peirce's thought.

To begin with, Peirce does not think it possible to base the validity of induction on the fact of regularity in the universe, as the empiricists, especially John Stuart Mill, sought to do (5.342–45). First of all, the universe contains at least as many irregularities as regularities; secondly, if the empirical constitution of the universe is supposed to be the ground of the validity of induction, then we should be able to think of a universe in which inductive inferences would not be valid. In a series of very incisive observations, Peirce shows that this is not possible. The positive proof of the validity of induction falls into two parts for him. First, he shows that the general validity to which every inductive inference lays claim "depends simply upon there being such a state of things that any general terms are possible" (5.349). But that this is so results from the meaning-critical definition of reality, that is, from the realist theory of universals that is implicit in it. This meaning-critical presupposition that universal concepts as such must be valid, or else we could not have a meaningful concept of reality, does not mean, however, that some specific inductive inference is valid. The question therefore remains "why men are not fated always to light upon those inductions which are highly deceptive" (5.351). Peirce believes that he can now also deduce the answer to this question from the meaning-critical definition of reality. But that means that it is deduced, as in the previously quoted argument from 1878, from the circumstance presupposed in the definition that there must be an ideal final opinion about this reality, an opinion that can be attained in a sufficiently long series of inferences.

According to Peirce there is, however, yet another, final, presupposition involved in this transcendental deduction of the validity of induction, namely, that a real world exists at all. But he does not attempt to provide a proof of reality.[102] Rather, he shows that everyone who wants to deny reality, as well as everyone who wants to prove it, already presupposes it—presupposes, that is, existence of the real.[103] Here, to my mind, we have one of the earliest documents of philosophizing at the level of the critique of meaning, represented in the twentieth century particularly by Wittgenstein. Such philosophizing no longer believes it possible to take up a position outside the world in order then to prove the world's existence.[104]

In his fallibilistic theory of knowledge Peirce replaces the "constitutive" (in Kant's sense) principle of the unity, to be obtained here and now, of the object of knowledge with the postulate of the infinitely distant "ultimate opinion" or, rather, the validity of knowledge in the long run. By doing this he introduces into the context of the foundation of the logic of cognition all those famous questions that Kant had reserved for practical reason. The question "What can I know?" can no longer be separated from the questions "What should I do?" or "What may I hope?" as it was for Kant. Although Peirce was a follower of Thomas Reid's variety of Common-sensism and very early revealed a tendency to mediate problems of theoretical and practical reason correlatively,[105] he became fully conscious of the ethical, existential, and religious presuppositions of the logical, methodological procedure he recommended to mankind only after he had completed his transcendental deduction of the validity of knowledge. Since the result of every particular inference in science is always provisional, fallible, and so is not guaranteed to be knowledge, Peirce can only promise that "by faithfully adhering to that mode of inference, we shall, on the whole, approximate to the truth" (5.354). However, he asks, what about the individual human being who has no chance of living to see the previously determined end of the process of inquiry, the "ultimate opinion," and who opposes the common interest in the unending process of knowledge to "a transcendent personal interest infinitely outweighing all others," such as an interest in a final religious belief that can give his life a basis?

Here Peirce clearly raises Kierkegaard's central question. Even today, it is this existential interest that provides the reason why, in nontotalitarian societies, the philosophy of the private mediation of theory and praxis cannot be made to coincide with their public mediation.[106] Peirce's answer, however, is religious Scientism. His view is anti-Kierkegaardian and existential-infinitist: "Logic rigidly requires, before all else, that no determinate fact, nothing which can happen to a man's self, should be of more consequence to him than everything else. He who would not sacrifice his own soul to save the whole world is illogical in all his inferences, collectively. So the social principle is rooted intrinsically in logic" (5.354).

In what follows Peirce tries to limit the appeal character of this statement. The theoretician in him once again gains the upper hand and seeks only to establish that logicality (in the sense of his theory of knowledge) in fact implies the "complete self-identification of one's own interests with those of the community" (5.356). Peirce is fully aware of the fact that he cannot counter the risks of subjective belief with some kind of proof that the community of investigators will attain the truth in the long run. What he believes he can prove (deduce) in his philosophy is simply this: first, we have always already conceived reality as that which would be known (meaning-critical Realism) as the ideal final opinion of an unlimited community of investigators; and, second, as a result of this, there must be a real possibility of achieving the goal of knowledge that becomes a necessity if the conditions of a sufficiently long, undisturbed process of inquiry are actually given. But here Peirce recognizes the risk in his "logical Socialism": "There cannot be a scintilla of evidence to show that at some time all living beings shall not be annihilated at once, and that forever after there shall be throughout the universe any intelligence whatever."[107] This is where the existential character of his Infinitism becomes evident. The goal of the process of inquiry is itself concerned with a "transcendent" interest "infinitely outweighing all others": "This infinite hope which we all have . . . is something so august and momentous, that all reasoning in reference to it is a trifling impertinence. . . . We are in the condition of a man in a life and death struggle; if he have not sufficient strength, it is wholly indifferent to him how he acts, so that the only assumption upon which he can act rationally is the hope of success" (5.357).

In the arguments I have quoted just now, in which Peirce defends his "principle of hope," it should be possible to find the kernel of that existential Pragmatism which William James presented in 1897 in *The Will to Believe*.[108] James's arrival at the thesis that belief in the truth of certain convictions can in some cases aid in making these convictions true, and his illustration of this idea with the example of the mountain climber who has to determine (and that means to decide) if he can jump over a cleft in the rocks before him or not, can be seen as a consequence of the Peircean principle of hope. However, James shows a tendency to bring to the fore the irrational aspects implicit in Peirce's Scientism in a way that favors the finite individual who sees the fate of his soul independently of society and its scientific progress, in particular in the right to religious belief. Here James doubtless represents the aim of privately oriented Existentialism in the context of American Pragmatism.

Peirce himself, who energetically renewed his support of logical Socialism in 1878 (see 2.652–55), was to admit in 1898 in a mood of sarcastic resignation (in what must of course be recognized as a popular lecture that was forced upon him: "Philosophy and the Conduct of Life," the first part of his lectures "Detached Ideas on Vitally Important Topics") that man naturally acts quite differently in "vital matters" than in science: "We must act in such matters; and the principle upon which we are willing to act is a *belief*" (1.636). Here Peirce uses the word "belief" expressly in James's sense, and that means, according to his own words, in a sense that has no meaning for science (1.635). Earlier, however, in the first of the famous Pragmatism articles from 1877–78, Peirce introduced the concept in just such a fashion, so that the "method of science" should appear to be the only method of the "fixation of belief" that is also ultimately acceptable in praxis. Let us consider now how Peirce arrived at this conception.

4

The Second Period: The Genesis
of Meaning-Critical Pragmatism (1871–78)

A. From the Berkeley Review to the Birth of Pragmatism
in the Metaphysical Club (1871–72)

It should be clear from the preceding exposition that our search for the new starting point brought to the history of philosophy by Peirce's philosophy should not begin with those essays from 1877–78 that James later made famous as the "birth certificates" of Pragmatism. Moreover, as I have indicated several times, Pragmatism's basic approach is itself already implicit in the correlative presuppositional relationship among "hypothesis" ("abduction"), "deduction" (of the consequences of a hypothesis), and "induction" (examination of the generality of the consequences of the hypothesis by checking the sensory data). Peirce had in fact already rather distinctly formulated the point that he later, for clarification, termed the "pragmatic maxim" before the discussions in the Metaphysical Club (winter 1871 to winter 1872).[1] He did this, for example, in a passage in the 1869 essay (5.331), but the point is particularly unmistakable in the Berkeley review of 1871.

In this large review Peirce comes to terms with the British tradition. He also gives the most complete exposition of his meaning-critical Realism (on universals) and introduces the pragmatic maxim as an alternative to Berkeley's (and Mill's) principle of verification as the criterion of meaningful statements.[2] What he objects to in this criterion of meaning is that it elevates to the criterion of the possible existence of entities such as matter the psychologically relevant capacity to form a sensory idea, instead of the logic of hypothesis formation. Such a principle of verification, as Peirce emphasizes, makes complicated theory construction in mathematics and natural science impossible. In order to show that general or what Berkeley called "abstract" concepts are also quite capable of being tested in reference to possible experience, Peirce suggests a modification of Berkeley's criticism (a criticism also upheld by Hume, Comte, and Mill) of meaningless linguistic signs. Peirce suggests that "a better rule for avoiding the deceits of language is this: Do things [the entities posited in language] fulfil the same function practically? Then let them be signified by the same word. Do they not? Then let them be distinguished" (8.33). And now Peirce applies this new pragmatic point of view to the concept of the "general idea" criticized by Empiricism: "If I have learned a formula in gibberish which in any way jogs my memory so as to enable me in each single case to act as though I had a general idea, what possible utility is there in distinguishing between such a gibberish and formula and an idea? Why use the term *a general idea* in such a sense as to separate things which, for all experiential purposes, are the same?" (8.33).

Here Peirce introduces a new criterion for the meaning of a general idea which no longer makes this meaning dependent upon the possibility of forming an idea, as does Sensationalism. Instead, for this criterion meaning depends upon the possible regulation of behavior "in each single case." If we can expect such a regulation, then even a gibberish expression can prove to be a meaningful symbol for a general idea, the possibility of which radical Empiricism denies.

In the foregoing text Peirce shows that the meaning of a "capacity" that we attribute to things lies in the regularity of expected future events (8.12). Several paragraphs later he emphasizes Duns Scotus's doctrine that the general concept as a *species intelligibilis* does not have to exist *actualiter* in consciousness, but rather only *habitualiter* (8.18). In 1868 Peirce already interpreted the "habits" of Hume's associationist psychology as the results of inductive inferences.[3] Here it seemed to Peirce obvious to combine the regularity expected of the behavior of things interpreted in some way and the habitual regulation of human behavior by means of the concept that man obtains of a thing, so as to form a single doctrine about the possible clarification of concepts. In this way the essence of things could be explicated by the conditional framework of certain behavioral preconditions and, assuming these, by experiences that are to be expected with regularity. Peirce in fact arrived at such a solution immediately after writing the Berkeley review and presented it in 1871 in the Metaphysical Club, which he himself, presumably, had founded. Peirce's name for this solution was "Pragmatism," a title that he derived from Kant.[4] But other participants in the Metaphysical Club offered new, stimulating suggestions that entered into this Pragmatism of 1871–72 and led to a reformulation of the "theory of cognition" (1868), resulting in a new "theory of inquiry." Let us take a brief look at these suggestions.

In a recollection written in 1906 (or on a more recent view, in 1907-8) Peirce called the philosopher Chauncey Wright (d. 1875), who was "famous at that time," the "boxing master" of the club.[5] Peirce was in contact with Wright for a long time, at least from the appearance of John Stuart Mill's *Examination of Sir William Hamilton's Philosophy* (London, 1865). In an 1865 review of Mill's sensational, polemic book Wright gave his own analysis of "belief" and "doubt," "knowledge" and "ignorance," "in terms of motives to action." Max Fisch says that "this analysis is a nearer approach to that in Peirce's pragmatic essays of 1877-78 than anything so far in Peirce's own writings."[6] Wright's particular aim was to work out the "method of science," especially its ability to be productive, and this meant for him also its independence from the speculative point of view of metaphysics.[7] Wright described the method of science in the following way:

The objective method is verification by sensuous tests, tests of sensible experience,—a deduction from theory of consequences, of which we may have sensible experiences if they be true. The subjective method, on the other hand, appeals to the tests of internal evidence. . . . While ideal or transcendental elements are admitted into scientific researches, though in themselves insusceptible of simple verification, they must still show credentials from the senses, either by affording from themselves consequences capable of sensuous verification, or by yielding such consequences in conjunction with ideas which by themselves are verifiable.[8]

Wright is here proved to be a very progressive forerunner of modern Neopositivism, and his distinction between objective and subjective evidence probably contributed in an important way to Peirce's Descartes critique of 1869. While the older version of Positivism was chiefly directed to the genetic derivation of ideas from sense perception, Wright shifted the emphasis, sometimes in a frankly instrumentalistic way, to the modern concern for what we can do with ideas. According to Wright: "Nothing justifies the development of abstract principles in science but their utility in enlarging our concrete knowledge of nature. The ideas on which mathematical mechanics and the calculus are founded, the morphological ideas of Natural History, and the theories of Chemistry are such working ideas,—finders, not merely summaries of truth."[9] Here a tendency becomes visible that leads from Wright via Peirce and James directly to Dewey.

Wright's approach to the critique of metaphysics in his concept of "closed questions" also sounds very modern. It is echoed not only in Peirce, but in Wittgenstein, Carnap, and Popper as well. Wright defined this concept in this way: "A question is closed when we have a knowledge precluding the possibility of evidence to the contrary, or where we are ignorant beyond the possibility of enlightenment. An ontological knowledge of the supernatural, or even of the natural—that is, a knowledge of anything existing by itself and independently of its effects on us—is, according to the experiential philosophy, a closed question."[10]

Wright combined his version of Positivism with evolutionistic ideas which he took directly from Darwin, rather than from Spencer, whom he took to be a semimetaphysician with little acquaintance with research. In his essay "The Evolution of Self-Consciousness," Wright sought to trace the continuity between animal instinct and human intelligence and to explain the different epochs or methods of thought "in terms of adaptive behavior."

He found support in this undertaking in the "belief-doubt" theory of the Scottish philosopher Alexander Bain (1818–1903), which was also known to the other members of the Metaphysical Club.[11] According to Peirce's later testimony (5.12), this theory was propagated primarily by the jurist Nicolas St. John Green, whom Peirce therefore designated the "grandfather of Pragmatism" (5.12). Bain first presented his belief-doubt theory in his book *The Emotions and the Will* (1859). There we find that famous formula which Peirce reported to be so essential for Pragmatism: "Belief is essentially related to Action, that is, volition. . . . Preparedness to act upon what we affirm is admitted on all hands to be the sole, the genuine, the unmistakable criterion of belief. . . ."[12]

In fact, Bain came even closer to the specifically Peircean, conditional version of Pragmatism, as in the following formulation: "Belief is an attitude or disposition of preparedness to act."[13] This proximity is also evident in Bain's example that our belief in a report about Africa is explicated by the statement that "*if* we went to Africa we *would* do certain things in consequence of the information."[14] As a behavioral disposition, Bain's "belief" resulted, like Peirce's "habit," from "induction," but with Bain, as with Hume, this amounted to a process of association that is also found among animals: ". . . belief is a primitive disposition to follow out any sequence that has been once experienced, and to expect the result."[15]

Bain designated "doubt" as the opposite of "belief." He characterized these opposite states of mind as follows. Belief is "the name for a serene, satisfying, and happy tone of mind," whereas doubt as a state of mind "is one of discomfort in most cases, and sometimes of the most aggravated human wretchedness."[16] Man is therefore inclined by nature to avoid doubt and to achieve a state of belief. Belief is our natural state. We have a primordial trust in the continuance of present states of affairs and in the continuing effectiveness of our manner of behavior. But experience disappoints us and so doubt arises, enduring until the emergence of a new belief, that is, a new, secure behavioral disposition that is equal to the situation.

It can be said that in the first of his Pragmatism articles, "The Fixation of Belief," Peirce took over this belief-doubt theory almost in its entirety, whereas in the second article, "How to Make Our Ideas Clear," he sought to combine Chauncey Wright's principle of verification in some way with Bain's interpretation of belief as a conditional, behavioral disposition. If we consider just this synthesis of these two complexes of ideas against the background of the theory of evolution, then we have nearly all the necessary ingredients of popular Pragmatism as it was later set forth by James—but not those of Peirce's Pragmatism, which he later preferred to name "Pragmaticism." Whoever is interested in Peirce must take seriously his intention, described above, to synthesize the impulses provided by modern British philosophy with the conception that he had developed from 1867 to 1871 under the inspiration of Kant and Duns Scotus, as well as Thomas Reid, Hamilton, and Whewell.[17] Peirce never wanted to progagate Pragmatism as a self-sufficient philosophy. For him it was a methodological principle in the framework of his "logic of science" or "theory of inquiry," on which he had worked since 1865.[18] In the "Logic of 1873," the remaining manuscripts of which were published in 1958 in the seventh volume of the *Collected Papers* (7.313–61), Peirce sought to complete the large synthesis of his previous philosophy with the methodological principle of Pragmatism. These remaining preliminary sketches reveal an architectonic coherence that is hardly noticeable in the popular series of articles published in 1877–78. What is most of all lacking in the essays from 1877–78 is the doctrine of categories and the semiotic framework that Peirce had intended from the beginning to provide for Pragmatism as a theory of meaning.[19] It was not until 1903 or, rather, 1906 that Peirce repeated his attempt to integrate Pragmatism into his complete semiotic system, and these attempts remained unpublished.[20] In several passages, such as in the famous diamond example, the manuscripts from 1873 offer better examinations of the problem of the pragmatic maxim than does the famous article from 1878, as I will show later.[21] However, let us next observe the new conception of the process of cognition that Peirce's philosophy owed to the stimulation offered by the Metaphysical Club.

B. The New Theory of Inquiry (1872–73 and 1877–78)

If we review the essays from 1868–69 as a whole we get the impression that the empirical element of our encounter with experience, or, rather, the verification of statements, has not yet really been given its due in Peirce's theory of cognition. In the terminology of his theory of categories, we could say that Firstness (the qualitative givenness of the world) and Secondness (the confrontation with brute facts) are unimportant in comparison with the function of Thirdness ("thought," "reasoning," "representation"), for example, the function of inference in the unending process of sign interpretation. In the theory of cognition from 1868 the concept of truth seems to be essentially a rationalistic theory of coherence. At least it is not yet explicitly clear that or how the "consistency" of a hypothesis that is supposed to reduce sense data to the unity of an opinion is capable of confirmation, not just with regard to its premises, but with regard to sense data itself.

A second characteristic feature of the 1868 theory of cognition is also involved. Knowledge is conceived here basically as the process of inference transcending individuals. It is bound, to be sure, to signs and a communication community, and Peirce is very intent on the fact that knowledge has a beginning in time by means of the affection of the senses, despite its infinite mediation as a process of inference. Yet knowledge does not seem actually to have a function in life. Knowledge does not seem to have anything to do with the concrete situation in which man has to react here and now or with the goals that he must attain in order to remain alive. For knowledge as a process extending forwards and backwards to infinity, life appears to be only the sign material through which it attains its own specific aim, the achievement of the "ultimate opinion" in which the real is adequately represented.

Here the belief-doubt theory propagated in the club chiefly by Green must, with its biological background, have given the logically oriented Peirce a decisive impulse to renew the basis of his theory of knowledge. This theory was able all at once to embed cognition, from its most primitive early forms to the process of scientific research, in the context of life. "Doubt" as the irritation of a secure form of behavior and "belief" as the reinstitution of security in behavior constitute a *terminus post quem* and a *terminus ante quem* of the cognition process in time. In a way, they stake out in each case a finite functional unity in the infinite process of cognition. With this arises the new problem of the relationship between the function in life of knowledge as it is limited by concrete doubts and respective new beliefs and the infinite function of knowledge as it is defined by the regulative principle of the "ultimate opinion" and, more deeply, by the cognizability of the real. But we must recognize that although Peirce did not at first satisfactorily resolve the problematic tension that results from this relationship, he left it open until he was able later to mediate between these poles in his Critical Common-sensism.

This exemplifies an essential difference between Peirce's philosophy and all the other varieties of Pragmatism, which begin by sacrificing regulative ideal principles in favor of cognition's function in life.

A new point of view concerning the problem of the method of cognition evidently arises for Peirce from this tension between the unending task of seeking for truth and the finite function of cognition in life: the formation of a fixed belief. In the meaning-critical postulate of the "ultimate opinion" as the representation of the real, it is naturally assumed that there can be only *one* normatively justified method of inquiry that is "predestined" to achieve this ideal goal. This assumption is confirmed repeatedly in Peirce's writings from the first period of his thought. But if we consider the fixation of belief from the standpoint of the life function of stabilizing behavior, then our eyes are opened to the variety of methods which help man to attain this "pragmatic" goal and by which, in fact, he has achieved it in the course of history. This observation presents us with yet a further question. Is there, among these many methods, really a single one that is capable of doing justice to both the finite function of cognition in life and the unending task of the search for truth? Moreover, is there a real developmental tendency in history that allows the function of knowledge in life, that is, the stabilization of belief as a disposition to behave, to converge finally with the task of the search for truth? These questions outline the horizon of the problems posed for the new theory of inquiry that Peirce developed in 1872–73 and published for the first time in 1877 in "The Fixation of Belief."

a. "The Fixation of Belief" (1877). "The Fixation of Belief," the first essay from the *Popular Science Monthly* series, is symptomatic of the pragmatic turn in the new theory of inquiry, and Murray Murphey has with some justification termed it "one of the most curious and least satisfactory [papers] that Peirce ever wrote."[22] But it may with equal justification be counted among the most interesting and historically fruitful of Peirce's philosophical works. Both evaluations derive from the tension, previously noted, between the two opposing motives that are to be met with in the essay. The problem in question leads directly to the discussion of truth later brought about by William James. In the first part of the essay, where Peirce defines the goal of inquiry with reference to the newly introduced Bainian belief-doubt theory, he writes: "With the doubt, therefore, the struggle [for new certainty] begins, and with the cessation of doubt it ends. Hence, the sole object of inquiry is the settlement of opinion" (5.375)." Peirce then expands: ". . . as soon as a firm belief is reached we are entirely satisfied, whether the belief be true or false. . . . The most that can be maintained is, that we seek for a belief that we shall *think* to be true. But we think each one of our beliefs to be true, and, indeed, it is a mere tautology to say so" (5.375).

This passage seems to point towards the theory of truth upheld later by William James and John Dewey, according to which the true is supposed to be identical with what is "satisfying" to us, that is, with that which is fruitful and helpful in a given situation, that which mediates between means and ends, and so on. But near the end of the essay, where Peirce introduces the objective "method of science" as the definitive method of inquiry, he says: ". . . the method must be such that the ultimate conclusion of every man shall be the same" (5.384). In the footnote from 1903 he adds: "Or would be the same if inquiry were sufficiently persisted in" (5.384 n). He continues:

Such is the method of science. Its fundamental hypothesis, restated in more familiar language, is this: There are Real things, whose characters are entirely independent of our opinions about them; those Reals affect our senses according to regular laws, and, though our sensations are as different as are our relations to the objects, yet, by taking advantage of the laws of perception, we can ascertain by reasoning how things really and truly are; and any man, if he have sufficient experience and he reason enough about it, will be led to the one True conclusion. [5.384]

That definition of truth accords exactly with the meaning-critical definition of reality from 1868 and 1871 and is explicitly repeated in this corresponding fashion in the following essay, "How to Make Our Ideas Clear" (1878), where it is inferred, as a definition, from the pragmatic maxim (5.407). This definition of truth had been proposed in 1871 as the meaning-critical equivalent and positive supplement to the traditional definition of the real as that which is independent of our actual opinions (8.12). In 1878 it is characterized in the same way as the pragmatic *Aufhebung* of the abstract definition of the real (5.406). Obviously, it has hardly anything to do with what is usually, following James, called the "pragmatic definition of truth," since it is free from the outset, because of its normative, ideal character, of any "reduction" to actual opinions or practical consequences. It not only stands in complete harmony with the absolutistic intention of the traditional correspondence concept of truth, it also reveals the methodological direction of that idea of truth which would like to eliminate a priori all relativism from particular sensory experiences and, hence, from particular verifications. Peirce's definition fulfills this regulative function by means of the principle of convergence immanent in it, which opposes every conceivable kind of relativism in experience with the power of inferential thought "in the long run."[23] But how does this normative definition of truth, which goes with a rationalistic optimism, fit together with the thesis derived from the belief-doubt theory that we cannot even seek a true opinion, but rather only one that eliminates our doubts here and now and so stabilizes our behavior?

The first key to answering this question is the principle of Fallibilism that I have already mentioned several times. Peirce is convinced that the opinions that men can form here and now, even in science, can never with certainty be identified with the truth in the sense of the final opinion. For this reason he maintains that people are satisfied with a settled opinion "whether the opinion be true or false" in the sense of the normative definition. But this answer is insufficient to enable us to understand the particular, doubtlessly strange-seeming point in the passage quoted from the first part of the essay. For Peirce does not say that people attain only firm beliefs and not the truth. He claims that they seek only a firm belief that is satisfactory to them and that "the sole object of inquiry is the settlement of opinion." There seems to be a blatant contradiction here between the beginning and the conclusion of the essay.

On my view these odd-seeming statements can be interpreted from two different perspectives. First of all, we can make the critical observation that Peirce quite simply confused the result of his own disinterested description and evaluation of human behavior with the genuine intentions of human beings or, stated differently, that he forgot to trust people to recognize for themselves the distinction that he makes between what can be in fact attained (a fixed opinion) and what would be the absolute truth (the ideal final conviction of all researchers). This methodological forgetfulness of one's own critical efforts tends to be characteristic of every naturalistic exposé of human intellectual acts, that is, those led by ideals.[24] There can be hardly any doubt that Peirce succumbed in 1877 to a subtle variety of this naturalist fallacy.[25] The nature of his mistake can be studied best of all in his criticism of Descartes, which Peirce believed he could derive immediately from his definition of the goal of inquiry.

Peirce argued in the second of his 1868 essays in the following way against Descartes' methodological doubt (see 5.265). In science we cannot begin with "complete doubt" or with an "initial scepticism." This "formalism" is merely "self-deception" and can never lead to a real furtherance of knowledge. We must "begin with all the prejudices that we actually have" when we begin to study a problem and wait for the "real doubt" that arises in the course of the process of inquiry, which suggests concrete investigations. In the face of the process of inquiry which proceeds from real doubt and substantial beliefs, Cartesian doubt is "as useless a preliminary as going to the North Pole would be in order to get to Constantinople by coming down regularly upon a meridian" (5.265). Peirce takes up this argument again in the 1877 essay and tries to base it on the principle that nobody could doubt a fixed opinion, once it has been achieved, on the basis of something such as the idea of absolute truth (5.376). When all the accessible criteria of experience in some concrete question have been exhausted, then the belief that has been thereby attained, be it either true or false, is in practice indubitable, and a merely formal or methodological doubt is incapable of changing anything about this substantial belief.

The positive thrust of this criticism of Descartes hardly needs to be emphasized in the present age of existential philosophy and historical-hermeneutical thought.[26] Descartes' methodological doubt can in fact neither take the place of real, motivated doubt nor itself mobilize any concrete topic of doubt, just as the so-called subjective (reflective) criterion of evidence, which Peirce also criticizes, is unable to offer support for our concrete beliefs that goes beyond objective concrete criteria of evidence.[27] At the same time, however, Peirce forgets in arguing this way that he himself, as a fallibilist, is quite capable of having critical reservations regarding even the most proven and practically indubitable beliefs. Does this fundamental, formal, critical perspective which, according to Peirce's repeated assurances, is what constitutes the spirit of science itself, have nothing to do with Descartes' formal methodological doubt? In truth, Peirce simply forgets here to distinguish between the philosophical and the scientific levels of reflection. He is so deeply engaged in the analysis of the conditions of the concrete process of inquiry that he does not reflect on the conditions of the possibility of his own theoretical analysis of science.[28] Here we should also consider whether Descartes' radical doubt, even though it is not capable of immediately motivating concrete research as such, has not in fact generated a new total disposition in mankind at the highest level of reflection, a disposition which has created the very situation of an open community of experimenters that Peirce and Dewey praised so much, including the habitual readiness to doubt dogmas of every kind and to undertake research projects that hardly need to wait for particular outer occasions. Peirce, in fact, saw this problem in his late conception of Critical Common-sensism and attempted to reconcile the possibility of formal critical reservations concerning all beliefs with the practical indubitability of beliefs that have proven themselves sufficiently.[29]

The justified theme of Peirce's critique of formal doubt, however, lies in his rejection of the Cartesian claim to be able to attain, by means of this doubt, a *fundamentum inconcussum* from which it is possible to deduce a priori any or even all concrete empirical beliefs. If we keep this in mind, then Peirce's peculiar allegation that the goal of inquiry is not the (absolute) truth, but merely the fixation of belief, can be seen in a different light. For the fallibilist philosopher of science, who always distinguishes in a provisional way between the ideal goal of inquiry and what is actually attainable, the problem must arise of what practical, attainable goal the inquiring person can set here and now and what criteria can be decisive for him in answering the question whether the goal of research has been achieved practically. Peirce would evidently like to arrive at a definition of the goal of inquiry from the standpoint of this question, a definition which first of all is neutral in regard to the historical differentiation of methods, but which at the same time gives us the necessary latitude to understand this differentiation. He finds this anthropologically neutral definition in the very one that I have already quoted, according to which man in fact seeks to arrive at a satisfactory fixation of belief. Peirce gives an even more precise definition of the criteria of the beliefs sought after by all mankind, a definition which is neutral regarding all the different possible methods of the fixation of belief and yet at the same time makes visible the real motivation for a differentiation of these methods. It reads: "It is certainly best for us that our beliefs should be such as may truly guide our actions so as to satisfy our desires; and this reflection will make us reject every belief which does not seem to have been so formed as to insure this result" (5.375).

With this formula Peirce has not presented a theory of truth in the sense of popular Pragmatism, but rather has simply named the criterion according to which man regulates and, indeed, must regulate his beliefs long before he is in possession of a philosophical conception of truth. But this pragmatic criterion of the guidance of our actions in the sense of the satisfaction of our intentions to act also remains in effect if we are to give a normatively valid philosophical definition of truth that does not remain abstract, but serves as a regulative principle for the evaluation of beliefs. Peirce shows this in his definition of truth in terms of the pragmatic maxim, which he was to add to this text in 1903: ". . . truth is neither more nor less than that character of a proposition which consists in this, that belief in the proposition would, with sufficient experience and reflection, lead us to such conduct as would tend to satisfy the desires we should then have. To say that truth means more than this is to say that it has no meaning at all" (5.375 n).

This definition does not amount in any way to a reduction of truth to arbitrary subjective usefulness for man. First of all, Peirce limits the instrumentality of a true belief to just those practical consequences which are implied in the meaning of the belief in question if it is true. For example, the belief that I am immune to wounds is not proven true by my performing miracles of bravery while believing in my immunity. That would be a point for William James. Rather, the truth of this belief is proven if in a battle I cannot in fact be wounded. That accords with the operational criteria of scientific verification that Peirce finally had in mind. It is precisely these criteria that must have guided man's experimental behavior from time immemorial, criteria that reside in what Scheler termed "work knowledge [*Arbeitswissen*]."[30] Secondly, neither does Peirce's definition of truth imply a "reduction" of truth to the objective operational criteria of the verification of a belief. That too would be a Jamesian point. Peirce, by contrast, does not without reason formulate his definition in the complicated grammatical form of the so-called *counterfactual condicionalis*.[31] The truth of a statement does not have to prove itself in specific practical contexts, nor can it in principle exhaustively prove itself through such tests. But if certain conditions *were* fulfilled, it *would* prove to be true in a continuing tendency to satisfy our logically justified desires. A pragmatic definition of truth must, according to Peirce, accomplish at least this much. It must explicate the predicate "true" in such a way that the criteria are given by which we can recognize in practice if a statement is, probably, true.[32] By formulating such an operatively serviceable definition of truth in his 1877 paper and in his 1903 addition to it, Peirce provides a pragmatic supplement to his meaning-critical definition of reality and truth as expressed in terms of the "ultimate opinion." He thereby shows not only what the truth would finally be *idealiter*, but also how man can already recognize here and now if he is on the right methodological path to attain that absolute truth.

However, Peirce understands the definition of the goal of inquiry (taking "inquiry" in the broadest anthropological sense of the term) initiated by real doubt in such a way that it makes understandable to us not only the final development of the experimental scientific method of inquiry, but also even the prescientific attempts to arrive at a fixation of belief, which are unsatisfactory in the long run. These attempts must, according to Peirce, at least appear to be so constituted that they "would tend to satisfy" our desires. This deliberation offers him the possibility of deducing the different scientific and nonscientific methods of the fixation of belief typologically from an anthropological root and thereby of making understandable the historical development from prescientific to scientific method.

I cannot enter here into an interpretation of the derivation and characteristics of each of the four methods of the fixation of belief; I want only to point out the dialectical movement that determines the sequence of the four. The "method of tenacity," according to which the individual adheres to his opinion once it is formed despite all external influences, is in a sense the most obvious and simplest method. It works particularly well in areas where those ultimate beliefs are formed which permit little outer verification or falsification.[33] In practice, however, it turns out to be untenable because it isolates people and so is inconsistent with the social conditions of man's existence. In Peirce's words: "The social impulse is against it. . . . Unless we make ourselves hermits, we shall necessarily influence each other's opinions; so that the problem becomes how to fix belief, not in the individual merely, but in the community" (5.378).

The method that comes next both systematically and historically is the one that transfers tenacity's formula of rejecting disturbing influences to the state, taken as a large agent. This is accomplished by the "method of authority," which, at least in the chief world views, enforces a *consensus catholicus* by means of institutions like an office in charge of doctrine, an inquisition, a censor, and so on, often while cleverly accommodating people's peripheral daily experiences (see 5.380). Peirce leaves us no doubt of his respect for the great historical achievements of this method, which, as early as 1868–71, he saw represented in the age of Scholasticism and the cathedrals. He was impressed most of all by the leading idea of the *consensus catholicus* as such (see 8.12 and 8.16). Nonetheless, the method of authority fails in the long run because of two external factors that serve to mobilize internal arguments against it. The first of these is that "no institution can undertake to regulate opinions upon every subject" (5.381). This circumstance as such does not lead to any serious limitation in the function of the method of authority as long as people are prevented from communicating over too great a distance or period of time. But as soon as this communication becomes possible for even the smallest intellectual elite group, doubt will arise among this elite about the truth of the authoritative beliefs that were previously taken for granted.[34] The elite will then come to the fundamental insight that "there is no reason to rate their own views at a higher value than those of other nations and centuries" (5.381). Moreover, "they will further perceive that such doubts as these must exist in their minds with reference to every belief which seems to be determined by the caprice either of themselves or of those who originated the popular opinions" (5.382). Therefore a new methodological requirement for the fixation of belief arises. This is supposed to be no longer just a technique for creating stability; it should itself contribute a criterion which "shall also decide what proposition it is which is to be believed" (5.382). From this arises the method of dialectical discussion, speculative philosophy's method of knowing which calls upon reason as its standard.

After the previous course of Peirce's argument we should expect that the new method of dialogue and reason as the standard for all people must lead beyond the dogmatic "consensus" already attained by the method of authority to a *consensus catholicus* that is binding for all people. In his "Logic of 1873," Peirce had in fact named the third method that of "public opinion" (7.317). In 1877, however, his argument shows that the method of speculative reason leads once more to the isolation characteristic of the first method, but this time it is to the isolation of thinkers and their systems. The reason lies, according to Peirce, in the fact that the final presupposition of the speculative method is the assumption of a single principle from which all valid knowledge is supposed to be deduced a priori. But on closer consideration the final principle is subject to a criterion of aesthetic preference; it must be agreeable to reason.[35] But this presupposition is in the end incapable of confirmation or control, and so the third, or "a priori," method fails at its task.[36]

Since the a priori philosophers' rational principles settle at the most their own doubts, and since a return to dogmatic belief as produced by the method of authority is also incapable of stilling philosophical doubt once it has been aroused, a completely new method of the fixation of belief becomes necessary: "To satisfy our doubts, therefore, it is necessary that a method should be found by which our beliefs may be determined by nothing human, but by some external permanency—by something upon which our thinking has no effect. (But which, on the other hand, unceasingly tends to influence thought . . .)" (5.384, parenthetical addition from 1903).

Here Peirce is able to synthesize the categorical aspect of reality present in the outward force of sensory experience (Secondness) with his theory, developed in 1868, of the synthetic inference of the general structure of reality (Thirdness).[37] Peirce explicitly establishes this synthesis when he states: "Our external permanency would not be external, in our sense, if it was restricted in its influence to one individual. It must be something which affects, or might affect, every man. And, though these affections are necessarily as various as are individual conditions, yet the method must be such that the ultimate conclusion of every man shall be the same. (Or would be the same if inquiry were sufficiently persisted in)" (5.384, parenthetical addition from 1903).

Here Peirce arrives at his old meaning-critical, normative definition of reality or truth, and it becomes clear that he achieves a synthesis of this definition of reality in terms of its general, conceivable meaning (Thirdness) with the experimental method's demand for an external factor determining thought through the compelling evidence of experience (Secondness) by means of the principle of convergence.[38] According to this principle, inferential thought directs the compelling, but relative, evidence of experience to cognition in the long run of the real as it is in itself and for us. In doing so it interprets the data of experience and all of its subjective conditions as signs. The required fourth method of the fixation of belief therefore literally goes towards introducing nature's contribution to knowledge by methodologically and experimentally making its voice heard in the dialogue of the "unlimited community" and its unending semiotic process of inference. When this occurs, then man is on the way to the "final opinion." Moreover, a *consensus catholicus*, a satisfying fixation of belief, can also be attained here and now—under basic fallibilistic limitations—by exhausting all the available criteria in the experimental community of investigators.

It is difficult to avoid the impression that Peirce succeeded here in "apprehending his time (the age of science) in thought," an epoch that today is actual and that followed the age of great systems and, necessarily, ingenious individual thinkers in whom the absolute momentarily came to itself.

If we compare the method of science with the prescientific methods for the fixation of belief from the standpoint introduced by Peirce, then its superiority consists in the fact that it takes full account for the first time of the function of belief in life, that is, in establishing a habit of behavior that proves itself in the long run. In contrast to all the prescientific ways of proceeding, it tests all of the practical criteria for the confirmation of a belief available before belief is fixed. This recognition is the pragmatic result of the essay "The Fixation of Belief." But it is conceivable that the previous examination of the possible criteria for the confirmation of a belief as a disposition to behave might not just be necessary for its "fixation," that is, for the evaluation of the truth of an opinion, but might even be needed for the evaluation of its possible meaning. This step in thought is implicit in the sharp distinction between the question of meaning and the question of truth which has become widespread in post-Wittgensteinian thought.[39] This move also lets us easily make the transition from the first to the second, still more famous, birth certificate of Pragmatism.

b. "How to Make Our Ideas Clear" (1878). The task of the second essay from the 1877–78 series, "How to Make Our Ideas Clear," in the context of the theory of inquiry, is to supplement the meaning-critical approach to definition developed in the "theory of reality" so that it does justice to the method of science sketched in the first article of the series. That is, it has to show how the experimental criteria of scientific verification can be taken into account even in the method of definition. This task accounts for the partially parallel construction of the first two essays from the Pragmatism series. The aim of both, ultimately, is to expound the new scientific method against the background of the obsolete methods. In the second essay, which is directed to the problem of definition, the prerational methods, of course, do not play a role, since they do not operate with definitions. Hence, the second essay begins with a discussion of the traditional a priori method of definition or clarification of meaning. As in 1868 and again in 1877, Peirce begins with a polemical reference to Descartes' call for clear and distinct ideas. After having already discredited the subjective principle of evidence that for Descartes was to replace the scholastic principle of authority as the criterion of truth, Peirce now even calls it into question as a criterion of meaning: "But since, evidently, not all ideas are true, he was led to note, as the first condition of infallibility, that they must be clear. The distinction between an idea *seeming* clear and really being so, never occurred to him" (5.391). For Peirce himself the typical definition of clarity as the "unmistakability" of an idea ultimately reduces to mere familiarity with the normal use of the idea (5.389). Descartes must also have noticed, Peirce suspected, that consciousness of clear ideas does not hinder people from associating opposite opinions with them. For this reason he introduced the further criterion of "distinctness," by which he probably meant that the ideas "must sustain the test of dialectical examination . . . but that discussion must never be able to bring to light points of obscurity connected with them" (5.391). Leibniz tried to make this last point more precise and thereby returned to logic's traditional method of definition by seeking to find the distinctness of a concept in the complete analyzability of its definition.[40]

Peirce admits that the abstract analytic method of definition in traditional logic is best adapted to set in order the beliefs that we already have, and that the handbooks "are right in making familiarity with a notion the first step toward clearness of apprehension, and the defining of it the second" (5.392). But his own aim is to attain a method of definition on the basis of the principles presented in the first essay of the series, a method which achieves a grade of clarity of thought higher than the "distinctness" of the logicians since Descartes and Leibniz (5.394). In what follows Peirce recapitulates the principles of the belief-doubt theory with very sensitive psychological and phenomenological descriptions. But for the new method's approach to making meanings clear, what is essential is not the question how we arrive at fixed beliefs (i.e., the question of the pragmatic criteria of truth), but rather the question what a fixed belief is according to its function in life (i.e., the question of its pragmatic meaning). Peirce answers this question with a metaphor: "It [a belief] is the demicadence which closes a musical phrase in the symphony of our intellectual life. . . . The *final* upshot of thinking is the exercise of volition" (5.397). The essence of belief as the demi-cadence between the beginning of the process of thought and its final result can now be described by three characteristics of belief: "First, it is something that we are aware of; second, it appeases the irritation of doubt; and, third, it involves the establishment in our nature of a rule of action, or, say for short, a *habit*" (5.397).

It is easy to show that these three characteristics correspond to three different philosophical evaluations of a belief. Subjective consciousness of a belief is the starting point and basis of an introspective philosophy of self-evidence in the manner of Descartes.[41] The easing of the irritation of doubt corresponds, as a psychologically understood goal of research, to the pragmatic problem of truth dealt with in the essay "Fixation of Belief," but the establishment of a rule of action offers the starting point for the pragmatic theory of definition or clarification of meaning. In fact, Peirce adopts this point of view for his first introduction of what is referred to later as the "pragmatic maxim." He does this in the form in which he had already suggested it more spontaneously and casually in the Berkeley review: "The essence of belief is the establishment of a habit; and different beliefs are distinguished by the different modes of action to which they give rise. If beliefs do not differ in this respect, if they appease the same doubt by producing the same rule of action, then no mere differences in the manner of consciousness of them can make them different beliefs" (5.398).

If we consider this formulation of the pragmatic maxim more closely, we then have occasion to guard it against misunderstandings that would lead immediately to popular Pragmatism and the crudest kind of Behaviorism. And when we read that "different beliefs are distinguished by the different modes of action to which they give rise," we could easily conclude that we should decide whether we are confronted with different beliefs by observing and exactly describing what actions in fact result from the beliefs in question. This principle ("Ye may know them by their fruits") would in fact actually be sufficient to evaluate human beliefs in many everyday cases. It would even be fitting as a principle for the behavioristic investigation of meaning; an example from linguistics would be a case in which we are dealing with the average behavior of those who speak a language, and this behavior stands in a regular context with those utterances of meaning in question, such as, in a Wittgensteinian language game, the unity of a form of life, use of language, and interpretation of the meaning of the world.[42] But in such a case it is tacitly presupposed that the behavior to be observed is connected by a rule with the expression of meaning we are to judge and that this corresponds exactly to the normatively correct understanding of this expression of meaning. This presupposition, however, can in no way be taken for granted.

The correct understanding of utterances of meaning is precisely what becomes problematic in the critical cases in philosophy and the history of ideas. For example, if the topic of discussion is what the doctrines of a metaphysician or the founder of a religion actually mean, then an orientation towards the actual consequences of their doctrines would legitimate, among other things, precisely those empty controversies and warlike confrontations which a criterion of meaning would want to show to be baseless.

In reality, nothing is further from Peirce's mind in introducing the pragmatic maxim for the clarification of meaning than replacing the understanding of the meaning of ideas with the observation or description of their factual consequences. Rather, as a logician he assumes that the "modes of action" which are to constitute a criterion for kinds of beliefs follow according to a rule from the beliefs that correspond to the correct understanding of them. For Peirce this means a correct interpretation through inference. Here it would of course be possible to object that if the pragmatic maxim for the clarification of meaning already presupposes the correct understanding of meaning, then it cannot seek to achieve a methodological clarification of meaning with the help of the behavior that follows from a belief. In short, semantic Pragmatism, as a method for understanding, rests upon a logical circle. This argument enjoys a wide popularity, but rests in the present case, as it almost always does when it is offered in a nontrivial philosophical context, upon a confusion between a legitimate *circulus fructuosus* in synthetic logic and a *circulus vitiosus* in deductive logic, which is of course to be avoided.[43] In fact, Peirce's discovery consists precisely in recognizing the fact that understanding of the meaning of concepts or sentences can be deepened in a fundamental way by the idea of the practical consequences (including possible empirical observations) that "would" result from a correct understanding. This idea is acquired by thought experiment, not empirical observation. On my view we have here a form of the "hermeneutic circle" described by Dilthey, or, as Hegel says, of dialectical "mediation," which has assimilated the new element of the foregoing mediation of meaning understanding through future praxis.[44]

Peirce did not introduce his pragmatic maxim in the 1878 essay with the logical refinement that he later utilized when he sought to defend it in the name of "Pragmaticism" against popular simplifications. It is possible to show, however, that Pragmatism as formulated in 1878 should be interpreted only as a "normative science"—the term Peirce used explicitly in 1903. This applies as well to the second fundamental formulation, which also appears to provide a starting point for popular Pragmatism and Behaviorism. There Peirce expresses his conception of thought in this way: "To develop its meaning, we have, therefore, simply to determine what habits it produces, for what a thing means is simply what habits it involves" (5.400).

This twofold use of the word "simply" can easily suggest to the reader that a naturalistic "reduction" of meaning is being undertaken. In addition, the reader tends to interpret the "habits," which Peirce equates with the meaning of a thought, as observable facts. This is in line with Hume's or Behaviorism's use of the term, but not with Peirce's usage as *rules* of behavior in which universals are realized and to which nothing empirical can categorically correspond. It is easy to overlook Peirce's dictum that we have to "determine," not observe or describe, what forms of behavior a thought produces, or to miss seeing that the word "involves" at the end of the sentence does not mean "factually results in," but rather "would have as a logical consequence according to a rule." However, Peirce shows this logical refinement, which he would later need in order to defend his Pragmatism, in the comments immediately following his provocative formula: "Now, the identity of a habit depends on how it might lead us to act, not merely under such circumstances as are likely to arise, but such as might possibly occur, no matter how improbable they may be" (5.400).

Here Peirce clearly expresses that the habit, which for him holds, so to speak, the secret of meaning, is not a factual consequence that we can await with some probability, but rather a normative guide for possible action, whose universal regulative function can and must be anticipated by the interpreter of an idea in a thought experiment. In a footnote from 1903 Peirce once again sharpens the distinction between a habit as a counterfactual *condicionalis* and expected concrete results by adding the clause, "No matter if contrary to all previous experience" (5.400 n). Even then the habit that is implicit in a universal concept would reveal its identity as a rule, that is, as a "mediation" of the facts in the sense of Thirdness. This itself implies that the correct interpretation of ideas found in the installation of a human habit has the function of changing the actual, empirically describable world in terms of the interpreted idea. That is, as Peirce would later say, reason will be realized more and more in the form of new laws mediated through human thought.[45]

In the following text, Peirce continues to explicate the concept of a habit and for the first time suggests a synthesis of the proto-pragmatic motive of habit, derived from Bain, with the empirical principle of verification, inspired by Chauncey Wright, Berkeley, and Mill, by means of the conception of a logical conditional context in which possible actions and sense data are related to each other as possible triggers or results of actions. He writes: "What the habit is depends on *when* and *how* it causes us to act. As for the *when*, every stimulus to action is derived from perception; as for the *how*, every purpose of action is to produce some sensible result" (5.400).

Peirce gives an example that illustrates the possible relationships between sensory experience and the practical behavior regulated by habit. Faced with the dogmatic disagreement between Catholics and Protestants about the meaning of the doctrine of transubstantiation, he tries to establish first of all how we are able to gain a concept of "wine" in the framework of possible belief. In doing so he distinguishes between two forms of statements (see 5.401): first, "that this, that, or the other, is wine"; and second, "that wine possesses certain properties."

The first clause has the function of indicating that some sensory experience is the stimulus for a possible action, for example, through the "index," "this here." The action that comes into question is determined by the regulative habit that corresponds to the predicate "is wine." "This is wine" could therefore mean, among other things, "This is drinkable." The second clause then explicates the meaning of the concept "wine" through further predicates which indicate the characteristics of wine. The meaning here is that the sentence "This is wine" calls upon those who have already been animated to act through the indicative sentence "This is wine" to consider one by one the "sensible effects" of the possible action, for example, drinking. The relationship between actions and their possible ends is explicated from the beginning by a statement of a thing's qualities, expressing these as expected possible results. In this way behavior subject to control by successful action is made possible. Peirce summarizes the relationships between possible sense experience and possible actions implied in the two quoted clauses as follows: "Such beliefs are nothing but self-notations that we should, upon occasion, act in regard to such things as we believe to be wine according to the qualities which we believe wine to possess. The occasion of such action would be some sensible perception, the motive of it to produce some sensible result" (5.401).

On the basis of this pragmatic analysis, Peirce must evaluate as "senseless jargon" the dogmatic claim that something is wine, that is, that it has "all the sensible characters of wine, yet being in reality blood" (5.401). In doing this he presupposes that the substance of the wine cannot, as Catholic dogma assumes, be separated from its qualities and so be conceived as subject to a "transubstantiation." Substance cannot be completely reduced for Peirce, as it can for Berkeley, to characteristics perceivable through the senses; it "has no being at all except the being a subject of qualities. . . . But if all its qualities were to be taken away . . . it not only would not exist, but it would not have any positive definite possibility."[46] Here it becomes clear for the first time that the pragmatic method for the analysis of meaning could also be suited to providing a criterion for distinguishing between meaningful and meaningless sentences, an aspect that Peirce would later explicitly express as a principle.[47]

Immediately following the example of the possible meaning of wine, Peirce comes to the decisive formulation of the pragmatic maxim to which he was later to return again and again: "Consider what effects, that might conceivably have practical bearings, we conceive the object of our conception to have. Then, our conception of these effects is the whole of our conception of the object" (5.402).

In this formulation of the pragmatic maxim, which is neither the clearest nor the most informative, the concept of the expected, experienceable, sensory effects of an object—for example, of wine—is utilized to explicate the meaning of the object. The possible, conditional mediation of these expectations by rule-directed human behavior or by the possible initiation of goal-directed actions by the object's "sensible effects" is only suggested in an unsatisfactory way by the insertion of the clause "that might have practical bearings." What is more interesting is the fivefold use of derivations of the verb "conceive," which strikes us immediately. Peirce quite rightly refers to this striking use of words in a 1906 footnote to the pragmatic maxim, in which he seeks to counter the suspicion that he wanted in 1878 to "reduce" the intellectual purport of symbols to something that does not itself have the character of concepts, such as to sense data or concrete actions (see 5.402 n. 3). In fact, the word "conceive" and its derivations are used in all of Peirce's writings, from the time of his early Kant studies, to designate intellectual (inferential) cognition, in contrast to "sensation" (intuition) as in Nominalism and Empiricism. For Peirce, sensation can only operate in the context of the synthetic function of universal "conception" as inductive verification *hic et nunc* (Secondness within Thirdness).

In the pragmatic maxim of 1878 Peirce actually equates in the thought experiment a thing's concept and the sought-after concept of a thing's effects, and this equation corresponds implicitly to a more progressive formulation of the pragmatic maxim in terms of the analysis of sentences. This prescribes the equivalent reformulation of assertions about things and their qualities into conditional statements which refer to the sensible effects of things in regard to possible human actions. A first step towards formulating the pragmatic maxim in terms of the analysis of sentences is already found in the physically oriented, consciously popular, examples that Peirce gives following the definitive formulation of the maxim, for example: ". . . let us ask what we mean by calling a thing *hard*. Evidently that it will not be scratched by many other substances" (5.403); or again: "To say that a body is heavy means simply that, in the absence of opposing force, it will fall" (5.403).

Here the "if . . . then" structure of Pragmatism's formula for the analysis of sentences is visible, but it should be noted that Peirce does not yet introduce into the "if" statement the operations that human beings are to carry out; he specifies rather the possible causal effects of natural processes. It is a basic principle of the natural sciences since Galileo, however, that we can have objectively valid, confirmable knowledge about a natural process only if we are able to produce this process in an experiment.[48] For example, even dropping a "heavy body" is supposed to have the character of an experimental operation. But, on the other hand, the ability to produce this natural process itself presupposes theoretical knowledge of the causes and effects of the process to be produced.[49] As a result, expressing the pragmatic maxim in terms of the analysis of sentences so that it can serve as an "operative definition" in physics means that it not only must introduce possible human actions into the "if" statement of a conditional context, but also must precisely prescribe these possible "actions" as "operations," a process which implies an exact knowledge. Peirce would later give such a formulation of the pragmatic maxim, which simultaneously expressed its function as a criterion of meaning. In 1905, for example, he described the attitude of mind characteristic of the "typical experimentalist" by assuring us that "whatever assertion you may make to him, he will either understand as meaning that if a given prescription for an experiment ever can be and ever is carried out in act, an experience of a given description will result, or else he will see no sense at all in what you say" (5.411).

In the year in which Peirce wrote those lines, volume seventeen of the *Annalen der Physik* carried Albert Einstein's foundational work on the "special theory of relativity," a work which made visible the breadth of the implications in the "semantic revolution" present in the operative definitions of the basic concepts of physics. We can enter into the meaning of Peirce's Operationalism for the foundational problems of physics and mathematics after a closer examination of later documents. In the following section we shall direct a brief look at the unresolved questions in the philosophy Peirce developed as a young man, questions reflected in several problematic passages in Pragmatism's birth certificate, and questions that served as the starting point for Peirce's later "revision" of Pragmatism under the name "Pragmaticism."

C. The Unresolved Problems of the
Second Period: A Look Ahead

In "How to Make Our Ideas Clear," immediately following the pragmatic interpretation of the assertion that something is hard, Peirce
makes the astonishing statement that "There is absolutely no difference
between a hard thing and a soft thing so long as they are not brought
to the test" (5.403). With this thesis he seems to contradict the essential points of the basic conception of his philosophy as he has developed it so far.

First, he makes the distinction between the meaning of the predicates "hard" and "soft" depend upon the actual performance of an
experiment. That contradicts the use of the logical and grammatical
form of thought of a counterfactual *condicionalis* to explicate the
meaning of general concepts, which, until this time, we could regard
as the point of Peirce's theory of meaning.[50]

Second, he also in this way makes the truth of the statements
"This thing is hard" or "This thing is soft" depend upon an actual
verification by means of a test. That contradicts the view which he always upheld that the characteristics of the real are independent of
whether they are actually known by human beings. Peirce seems here
to have abandoned meaning-critical Realism, and especially the realist
view of universals implicit in it, in favor of a sensualistic Positivism.
All of these theses fit with Chauncey Wright's proto-Pragmatism and
William James's later popular Pragmatism, but they completely nullify
the basic starting point of Peirce's own philosophy. Are we faced here,
as one might be inclined to think, with just a careless formulation?
This guess is nullified by the following passage from the text, in
which Peirce seeks to corroborate his thesis with an example: "Suppose, then, that a diamond could be crystallized in the midst of a
cushion of soft cotton, and should remain there until it was finally
burned up. Would it be false to say that that diamond was soft?"
Peirce continues by making this question more precise: ". . . what
prevents us from saying that all hard bodies remain perfectly soft until they are touched, when their hardness increases with the pressure
until they are scratched." One might expect that Peirce would now
mobilize his realist theory of universals in order to explain what prevents us from adopting such a use of language. However, he instead
answers: ". . . there would be no *falsity* in such modes of speech.
They would involve a modification of our present usage of speech
with regard to the words hard and soft, but not of their meanings. For
they represent no fact to be different from what it is; . . . the question of what would occur under circumstances which do not actually

arise is not a question of fact, but only of the most perspicuous arrangement of them [in language]" (5.403).

Here Peirce unequivocally adopts Nominalism and in doing so anticipates that form of Nominalism which Rudolf Carnap developed in the twentieth century. For Carnap, for example, the question whether the world consists of sense data or of material things is to be replaced by the question whether a sensualistic or a physicalistic manner of speaking is more helpful in science. Peirce would later confirm that he regressed here to the form of Nominalism that I have just described.[51] The question arises, however, how such a lapse into Nominalism could occur after the 1871 Berkeley review. We can arrive at a better understanding of this situation by referring to the "Logic of 1873," where Peirce had already discussed the diamond example at length.

Here Peirce correctly asserts that when we say, "The inkstand upon the table is heavy," then "we only mean, that if its support be removed it will fall to the ground. This may perhaps never happen to it at all—and yet we say that it is really heavy all the time" (7.341). But he wonders about this use of language and sees a paradox in it which he explicates by means of the diamond example in the following way: "But though the hardness is entirely constituted by the fact of another stone rubbing against the diamond yet we do not conceive of it as beginning to be hard when the other stone is rubbed against it" (7.340).

The difficulty that Peirce meets with here, seen in the light of his own philosophy, obviously rests on the following category mistake contained in his formulation of the supposed paradox. The diamond's hardness is not constituted by some kind of "actual" test, but rather by a real "law" according to which certain "sensible effects" *would* appear in all tests that followed a certain procedure. In regard to these real possible tests, the diamond's hardness is a real possibility in things that is merely made present in these tests. But Peirce would not be able to give a basis to this solution explicitly until 1900, in the context of his later modal logical version of his realist theory of universals.[52]

The context in which Peirce presents the diamond example in the "Logic of 1873" betrays a difficulty lying still deeper, however, in his conception of his system or, rather, in the reflective consciousness of this system that he has obtained up to this point. Peirce attempts in the following general way to provide a solution to the "paradox" which confronts him here: "The object of the belief exists, it is true, only because the belief exists; but this is not the same as to say that it begins to exist first when the belief begins to exist" (7.340).

This formulation is obviously not a solution to the paradox, and the reason is that Peirce has evidently not yet completely overcome the Berkeleyian form of Idealism, which is also an Empiricism, that he had criticized in 1871. The object of a belief does not itself in any way exist because any kind of belief exists, not even because we must postulate the existence of a "final opinion" in which it would be known; rather, its existence must be assumed in every belief, as Peirce had correctly recognized in 1868. What does depend upon the beliefs of thinking beings is simply, in a certain sense, the possible meaning of the real, that is, its reality as an object for us.[53] But according to Peirce's definition of reality this is also dependent not upon actually existing beliefs, but only upon the normative, ideal, final opinion towards which the meaning of reality, as a universal meaning, directs us human beings whenever we attempt to give a meaning-critical definition of it.

In order to clarify this problematic situation Peirce had to work out his doctrine of categories, which he did after 1885, going back to his preliminary conception of the categories from 1867. In doing so he was led to clearly distinguish "reality," insofar as it falls under the category of Thirdness (along with "Law," "Thought," "Mediation," "Continuity," and "Universality"), from the "existence" of the real which cannot be known, that is, proven in thought, but can only be experienced as a resistance to our will and can only be indicated in language through "indices," which are dependent upon situations. Under the category of Secondness falls "Existence," the experience of resistance to our will, the indicative function of language—in contrast to "symbolic representation"—and everything that confronts us as an event or confronts us without presupposing any "mediation" through meaning.[54]

As the difficulties I have just now pointed out indicate, Peirce's Pragmatism arose from the fruitful tension between his meaning-critical Realism (which was primarily a transformed Kantianism and secondarily a very modern Scotism) and the Anglo-Saxon tradition, under the constant influence of his empirically and nominalistically oriented friends, which reached its high point at the time of the Metaphysical Club.[55] Under these conditions it cannot surprise us that those friends, especially William James, understood Pragmatism wrongly, if it is viewed against the background of Peirce's systematic conception. But perhaps it will also be clear from the interpretation and documentation that I have presented that the later Peirce remained an inexhaustible source of fruitful misunderstandings, not just for James, but also for the generation of scholars with minute knowledge of Peirce's innumerable *opuscula* that has emerged recently in the United States.

II

Peirce's Development
from Pragmatism to Pragmaticism

The Later Peirce: The Last Two
Periods in the Development
of His Thought

In the spring of 1884, when he was forty-five years old, Peirce was discharged from his position as a faculty member at Johns Hopkins University without a public statement of the reasons for his dismissal. He had held this position since 1879. As we know today, the dismissal took place on the basis of a meeting of the executive committee of the university about certain "information" concerning Mr. Peirce.[1] With this, the very promising academic career of the most original American philosopher came to an end.[2] Despite his illustrious family relationships, as son of the famous Harvard mathematician Benjamin Peirce (1809–80) and brother of the dean of Harvard College, James Peirce (1834–1906), Charles Sanders Peirce was never again given a university position. After he built a house in 1887 in Milford, Pennsylvania, with the help of a small inheritance, he resided there "in almost total isolation."[3] Nevertheless, there is a reason to distinguish between two periods in Peirce's later work, even from the standpoint of his life history. For the lonely thinker was again brought into the spotlight of public opinion near the end of the century, and this final, psychologically important, turn in the outer events of his life led to a new epoch in his philosophy.[4]

After Peirce had worked out his metaphysics of evolution, from about 1890, while isolated in Milford, and after he had tried without success to publish an encompassing system of philosophy, he was in 1898 suddenly made famous as the founder of Pragmatism by William James's "California Address," entitled "Philosophical Conceptions and Practical Results."[5] This new role forced Peirce to return to an approach that he himself had always regarded as a maxim in the larger context of the logic of inquiry, not as the positive foundation

and *ratio sufficiens* of a philosophy or even of a world view. Peirce's
initial reactions to the Pragmatism discussion clearly show how foreign to him in certain regards had become the points that he made in
his essays of 1877 and 1878, essays that James termed the "birth certificates" of Pragmatism.[6] And even Peirce's great Pragmatism lectures—arranged for him by James at Harvard in 1903—are so inter-
twined with Peirce's late systematic program that James was unable to
recognize Pragmatism in them, and in the face of their incomprehensi-
bility urgently advised against their publication.[7] Not until the series
of three essays in *The Monist* in 1905 did Peirce reply in a way ap-
proaching those specific questions that the public associated with the
concept of Pragmatism since James's publications. Here he found it
necessary to differentiate his answer to these questions from that of
the other Pragmatists. He offered his reply expressly as the authentic
interpretation of his own works of 1877–78 and sought to set it apart
by means of the consciously ugly new title "Pragmaticism," in order
to protect it from further "kidnappers."[8]

In an introductory study of Peirce's Pragmatism such as this one, utilizing a limited number of texts, it is tempting to go directly from the
classical period of the birth of Pragmatism in the 1870s to the "Pragmaticism" essays from 1905–6, leaving out the essays on metaphysics
and the ambitious, systematic programs that the lonely thinker from
Milford had written in the intervening period. In a certain sense,
which popularly might be termed "pragmatic," such a procedure
would make the work of this introduction much easier.[9] However, I
placed special value in Part One on exposing the "philosophical background" of Peirce's Pragmatism in particular and in sufficiently distinguishing it from the conceptions of Pragmatism that were widespread in Germany at the beginning of the century. Hence, I attempted
to make Peirce's Pragmatism of the 1870s more understandable by
referring to his efforts of the late 1860s to overcome modern Nominalism through his meaning-critical Realism, without underestimating
the important stimulation that he received from the nominalistic
proto-Pragmatists in the Metaphysical Club, Nicholas St. John Green
and Chauncey Wright.[10] In the same way I want now to try to make
the Pragmaticism of the fourth and final period of Peirce's development much more understandable than would otherwise be possible
by considering it against the background of the systematic conception
that he had developed in the years prior to 1903.

It is advisable in any case to consider the period between the
Pragmatism essays and those on Pragmaticism because the metaphysics of evolution that Peirce worked out in the third period attempted

to explicate and give a cosmological foundation to the relationship between the first and second periods, the "theory of cognition and reality" from 1868 on and the "theory of inquiry" from 1871 and after.[11] Nonetheless, an interpretation of the metaphysics of evolution that Peirce published in the *Monist* series from 1891–93 is not at all sufficient to make understandable the important lectures on Pragmatism from 1903, which document Peirce's return to the topic of the logic of inquiry. Peirce himself evidently did not find it possible, from the standpoint of the metaphysical position he attained in 1898, to take an immediate position on the topic of Pragmatism as it was exposited by William James. For that he needed to reorganize his "architectonic" conception of his system, which was derived from Kant, and this amounted to giving a new foundation to his logic of inquiry in the framework of a comprehensive hierarchy of the sciences.

Before turning to the chronological interpretation of the texts in question I want first to sketch in a preliminary way the problems Peirce dealt with in the final conception of his system, which he completed in about 1903. The final conception of his system probably represents the most difficult problem in the interpretation of Peirce.[12] We proceed here on the belief that this systematic conception from 1903 provides the key to the later Peirce because it places the metaphysics of the third period in its proper systematic context and makes visible the presuppositions for the "Pragmaticism" of the fourth period.

6
Peirce's Late Conception
of His System

Among the fundamental presuppositions of Peirce's philosophy that he took over from Kant is the principle of "architectonic."[1] According to this principle, Peirce could hold neither "logic" nor the individual empirical sciences to be metaphysically neutral, as his teacher Chauncey Wright recommended and as is widely practiced today among followers of a practical Positivism or a conventional Pragmatism. Rather, like Kant, Peirce had to maintain that "formal logic" presents us with the basis for a "metaphysical deduction" of the categories which provides the conditions of the possibility of all empirical science. In place of a "transcendental deduction" of the categories from Kant's "highest point," the "transcendental synthesis of apperception," Peirce began, as I tried to show earlier, with the "logic of inquiry."[2] The task was then to deduce the objective validity of synthetic inference (induction and abduction) in experimental science from the meaning-critical postulate and "regulative principle" of the necessary consensus of an "unlimited community of investigators."

The results of the third period, coupled with James's renewal of the question of Pragmatism, forced Peirce to make a twofold distinction within the architectonic sketched out above. It was necessary, on the one hand, to redefine the relationship between pragmatic logic in the widest sense as the logic of inquiry and semiotic (which now inherited the role of Kant's transcendental logic) and the metaphysics of evolution. This metaphysics, in turn, permitted refining the relationship between pragmatic logic and the individual sciences, especially psychology. On the other hand, the problem of a metaphysical deduction of the categories from formal logic had to be much more clearly distinguished from the problem of a transcendental logic of cognition than it was for Kant. This was to be accomplished by putting it on a different basis, located in the pre-philosophical, newly founded mathe-matical logic of relations. But in order to reestablish the relationship between mathematical logic and the quasi-transcendental logic of in-quiry in the light of the three fundamental categories, Peirce felt com-pelled to introduce between these two disciplines yet another new philosophical field of study: "Phenomenology" or "Phaneroscopy."[3] In it the formal categories of the logic of relations were not yet proven to be empirically valid, but rather were presented schematically in the sense of possible material meaning.

As far as the first question, the place of pragmatic logic in Peirce's architectonic, is concerned, he became aware about 1900 of the neces-sity of stressing the normative character of the logic of inquiry. This was necessary as a countermove to the largely anthropological, psy-chological treatment he gave it in the 1877–78 Pragmatism essays made famous by James. Moreover, it was in opposition to the cosmo-logical and evolutionistic foundation that he worked in the 1890s for the anthropological function of logic.[4] It was necessary here to recon-cile an empirical-genetic perspective, whose absolutization would amount to a "naturalistic fallacy,"[5] with the normative perspective taken over at the outset from Kant (the meaning-critical postulates and regulative principles as well as—not least important—the prag-matic maxim itself). Peirce succeeded in doing this essentially by dif-ferentiating between unconscious, and hence uncontrollable and un-criticizable, inferential processes, which we must presuppose, on the one hand, and controllable, methodologically guiding, inferential pro-cesses, on the other.[6] Regarded in a different way, this is the difference between practically indubitable, common-sense judgments which come about through unconscious inferences in the course of evolutionary adaptation (including constitutionally conditioned perceptual judg-ments and so-called a priori truths in the sense of the *lumen naturale*) and hypotheses in science, to be formulated and tested according to the rules of a logic of inquiry.

This distinction enabled Peirce, on my view, to reconcile the Kantian heritage of his logic of inquiry with the "objective logic" of evolution which, following in the tracks of Hegel, Schelling, Darwin, and Lamarck, he implicitly postulated as early as 1868 and worked out explicitly after 1890. If we take into account that Peirce's meta-physics of evolution was itself naturalistic and Darwinian in inspira-tion, as well as related teleologically to the "admirable" final goal of "evolutionary love," then we can distinctly see that the proclamation of the "normative" logic of the consciously controlled process of in-quiry assumes the function of giving teleological metaphysics a critical foundation in Kant's sense in the form of a regulative principle or normative postulate.

In fact, Peirce's speculative interpretations of self-controlled behavior in terms of "evolutionary love" were in line with the speculative form of the categorical imperative by which Kant defines the universal applicability of the moral law as a possible law of nature and
thereby provides the regulative principle for an interpretation of natural history in the light of its conscious, self-responsible continuation
through human history.[7] Peirce's mediation here among the normative
logic of inquiry, ethics of logic, and metaphysics of evolution had to
go beyond Kant, since Peirce rejected Kant's distinction between phenomena and noumena as meaningless. For Peirce, what we call natural laws could not simply be valid in a mere world of appearances,
because such a world can be conceived of only by presupposing the
bad, nominalistic metaphysics of a world behind the world—that is,
the kind of metaphysics that Kant himself had discredited. Rather,
these laws must, in principle, be metaphysically real, no matter how
provisional or conventional their fixation may be in our knowledge
of them. To this extent they form a continuum with Kant's moral law,
to be embodied through moral and logical self-control in the form of
habits. In this continuum, which Kant could conceive of only in the
form of an "as if" fiction, the critique of meaning permitted Peirce to
see the real possibility of a universe as completed in "concrete reasonableness."

Further problems in the reorganization of Peirce's conception of
his system present themselves, however, in his attempt to give a normative foundation for this vision. These problems required him to
locate the logic of inquiry in context of the foundation of the normative sciences. He was finally forced to transcend hypothetical considerations in the sense of the pragmatic maxim in favor of a speculative
view of the final goal of logically controllable human actions and, to
this end, to take into account two further normative sciences to which
he had paid little attention until then: ethics and aesthetics.

A. The Pragmatic Maxim and the
Foundation of the Normative Sciences

For Peirce the logic of inquiry provides normative guidance to the
conscious continuation of the process of inference that already guides
the evolution of the universe by means of an unconscious "objective
logic." Hence, if the logic of practically relevant inquiry is to provide
a critical foundation for a teleological metaphysics, then it must evidently presuppose the ethics of norms for action. This conclusion was
already present in Peirce's elimination of the Kantian distinction between phenomena and noumena, the constitutive and regulative use

of the understanding, and theoretical and practical reason. Peirce's philosophy began with the view that in the long run the process of inquiry, correctly regulated by norms, would be constitutive not only for the community's true theoretical opinion about the universe, but thereby also for the practical embodiment of reason in the behavioral habits that go with true beliefs. In other words, for Peirce the correct logical regulation of the process of inquiry is a priori morally relevant because it is metaphysically relevant. Moreover, this conclusion resulted in normative logic's presupposing ethics, because the critique of meaning could and must postulate the convergence of all the results of the inquiry process—and therefore, simultaneously, the practical rationalization of the universe—but the actual continuation of the inquiry process begun by human beings on the earth was in no way thereby guaranteed.[8] The process of inquiry therefore demands three things from the members of the "unlimited community of inquirers" that consciously recognize its normative principles and all their implications for moral engagement without a guarantee of success; these are Faith, Hope, and Charity (2.655; cf. 5.357).

Peirce intuitively grasped the point of this ethics of logic as early as the pre-pragmatic period, when he attempted to present the "Grounds of Validity of the Laws of Logic" and formulated this point as the principle of the social nature of logic.[9] In the meantime, however, he had established the principle of Pragmatism. The reason for his choice of the term "Pragmatism," rather than "Practicalism," was, as he later explained, that the explication of the meaning of a scientifically relevant belief always leads to a hypothetical imperative which relates the empirical conditions of a situation to possible practical goals. By the pragmatic maxim, unconditioned imperatives like those which, according to Kant, form the "practical" sphere are excluded *a limine* for the clarification of meaning, as "belonging in a region of thought where no mind of the experimentalist type can ever make sure of solid ground under his feet."[10] But what about the normative logician who happens to see the meaning of his science as residing not in its "nauseating utility" for subjective practical ends, but rather in the furtherance of the rationalization of the universe as an eschatological *summum bonum?*[11] How could he give any meaning at all to his leading belief in the framework of Pragmatism?

Here, doubtless, lies a crucial problem for American Pragmatism as a whole beginning with Peirce. William James often seems to equate the practical, in which he, following Peirce, sees the meaning of all concepts, with the psychological reaction of the one using them, that is, with his behavioral reaction.[12] Moreover, he evidently recognizes only individual utility, including spiritual welfare, as the final goal of all praxis. John Dewey, the consistent "instrumentalist," had

previously adopted Hegel's logic of mediation in response to the im-
potence and "bad infinity" found in absolute expressions of the notion of the "ought." He had consciously sought to avoid the question
of the final goal by always striving to conceive the "intelligent mediation of means and ends" in terms of man's natural needs in each particular intersubjectively binding social situation as the place where
"creative valuation" originates. In spite of this methodological asceti-
cism, Dewey's political and pedagogical engagement and his evolutionary optimism were grounded in the unquestioned presupposition
of the "growth of humanity" or, as Kant would say, the furtherance
of the development of the human race as the absolute moral goal of
nature.[13]

Peirce, the normative logician with a Kantian background and
the eschatologist of the regulative principle of the "indefinite community," could not solve the problem in this way. In blatant contradiction to the position that Dewey would uphold later, Peirce declared
in 1903, "The only moral evil is not to have an ultimate aim" (5.133).
And he explicitly asserted that Pragmatism's validity depends upon
the presupposition of an (in the long run) absolute ethical aim: "In
order to understand pragmatism, therefore, well enough to subject it
to intelligent criticism, it is incumbent upon us to inquire what an
ultimate aim, capable of being pursued in an indefinitely prolonged
course of action, can be" (5.135). Here Peirce obviously overstepped
the region of thought characteristic of the "mind of the experimentalist type," which he had himself delimited in his Pragmatism, in
favor of the "practical" in Kant's sense. On the other hand, the postulate of a final goal that can be pursued in the long run by an unlimited
community obviously corresponds to that ethics of logic which Peirce
envisaged in his first period, prior to founding Pragmatism, when he
thought of equating the regulative principles of the progress of science with moral postulates of practical reason. Peirce now found himself forced to think of this, his oldest philosophy, in conjunction with
the "Pragmatism" that he developed in the 1870s in the Metaphysical
Club. Hence, it is understandable that when he made his first official
appearance as the founder of Pragmatism (in a dictionary article in
1902) he attempted to go beyond the third degree of the clearness of
ideas that he had proposed for his pragmatic maxim in 1878, in contrast to Descartes' and Leibniz's methods of definition.[14] At this point
he proposed a fourth degree of clearness:

The doctrine [from 1878] appears to assume that the end of man is action—
a stoical axiom which, to the present writer at the age of sixty, does not
recommend itself so forcibly as it did at thirty. If it is admitted, on the contrary, that action wants an end, and that end must be something of a general description, then the spirit of the maxim itself, which is that we must

look to the upshot of our concepts in order rightly to apprehend them,
would direct us towards something different from practical facts, namely, to
general ideas, as the true interpreters of our thought. [5.3]

Here it seems as if Peirce wanted to give up the pragmatic maxim
completely in favor of the traditional method of definition in abstract
general concepts. But this is not his intention. Instead, he continues:

He [the author] would venture to suggest that it [the pragmatic maxim]
should always be put into practice with conscientious thoroughness, but
that, when that has been done, and not before, a still higher grade of clearness of thought can be attained by remembering that the only ultimate
good which the practical facts to which it directs attention can subserve is
to further the development of concrete reasonableness; so that the meaning of the concept does not lie in any individual reactions at all, but in
the manner in which those reactions contribute to that development.[15]

Peirce recommends, therefore, that we begin the clarification of
the meaning of concepts by translating the statements that contain
them into conditional statements which, in line with the continuum
of experimental and technical knowledge, are equivalent to hypothetical imperatives. We should then realize that certain goals of action are always presupposed in these hypothetical imperatives. These
goals are themselves supposed to be founded upon the general "manner" in which these actions contribute to the development of "concrete reasonableness" as the highest goal of all actions. It is this new,
second move of our hermeneutic imagination, directed towards the
consequences of thought, that is to constitute the fourth grade of
clearness of thought. This suggestion clearly goes beyond the instrumental framework of Pragmatism in the narrow sense.[16] Nonetheless,
Peirce does not give up the principle of clarifying thought by means
of attention to practical consequences. This is because the "manner"
in which we serve the summum bonum by furthering "concrete reasonableness" does not have the character of an abstract general concept, as it might at first seem to have. Rather, it has the form of a rule
embedded in human behavior, and for Peirce its character is therefore
that of a real universal. As someone familiar with Peirce's early work
will immediately recognize, we are concerned here with a habit in
which the universal concept must be incarnated, in a way, as a rule
for possible behavior if man is not only to understand the meaning
of a statement, but also to believe that this statement is binding
for him.[17]

Peirce does not himself, however, fully realize the extent to which
his conception of habits that contribute to the development of "concrete reasonableness" departs from his instrumentalistic Pragmatism.
He evidently does not reflect on the difference in principle between

rules of behavior that transform knowledge of a law into a technical ability and those dispositions to behave which are supposed to function as the habitual embodiment of the "manner" of our morally relevant choice of goals. As the text reveals throughout, Peirce believes that he has overcome the framework of a "stoic" Pragmatism of utility just by shifting the emphasis of the pragmatic thought experiment from the idea of "individual reactions" to that of a normative, universally valid regulation of behavior. By opposing to James's nominalistic Pragmatism a realist theory of universals and a normative point of view that would "insist upon the reality of the objects of general ideas,"[18] Peirce also believes that he is already dealing with the kinds of habits that serve the embodiment of the final goal and highest good. He succumbs here in the end to the scientistic and technological way of thinking inherent in instrumental Pragmatism that he had called into question. This is the ideology of the social engineer who believes that by implementing the best means to a goal on the basis of his insight into natural laws, he has thereby also grasped that "concrete reasonableness" of goal realization which, in Kantian terms, would be the continuation of natural history through the embodiment of the categorical imperative.

Peirce never realized completely that his attempt to go beyond the 1878 conception of a third grade of clearness of thought to a fourth grade was allied to a corresponding step beyond the belief-doubt theory of 1877. In the context of instrumental Pragmatism, that theory could only be interpreted so that the goal of all inquiry would lie in reestablishing the belief habits that have been disturbed in each case, that is, in reaccommodation of the organism to its surroundings. A human share in the responsibility for the goal of developing nature could not be derived from this interpretation. But that had been Peirce's concern in 1869 when he presented his principle of the ethics of logic and of logical Socialism. It was his explicit concern again, after 1890, in the metaphysics of evolution and in 1902–3 in his foundation of the normative sciences in the framework of his late conception of his system.

This problem, which today also confronts the cybernetically oriented theory of "adaptive systems," can be characterized in the following manner. Since man is distinguished from animals by his work, and hence by his technology, he is less concerned with adapting himself to nature than with adapting nature to his needs. But this, in turn, means that he is concerned with supplementing the laws of nature with habits that are not merely instrumental, but teleologically relevant.

In the early 1890s, however, the problem of defining the final goal of all action had not yet been resolved at all for Peirce by an extension of the pragmatic maxim such as I have sketched here. Although Peirce did not see the difference between technically relevant rules of behavior and the politically and morally relevant rules that he postulated, he did see another difference all the more clearly. He recognized that even those habits which he postulated as the general basis of our selected, particular, individual goals are not immediately identical with the *summum bonum* as the final goal of all actions and of evolution itself. To be more precise, as long as they are seen as specific habits of action they must also be capable of being expressed in such a way that they are applicable to the conditions of a situation. That is, they must be expressible in the form of conditional statements that presuppose the final goal of all action. We are dealing here with the final difference between rules of action, which can be made concrete, and the *summum bonum*, which cannot—a difference that must be recognizable even by the person who—going beyond Peirce—distinguishes between morally relevant and merely instrumentally relevant habits. This latter distinction consists in the fact that habits embodying a morality do not just relate means to ends in the fashion of technical instructions, but rather implicitly relate the final moral goal of all actions to the particular conditions of its realization in a situation, such as do the habits that make up a social style of life.[19]

But this does not eliminate the difference in principle between particular habits and the universally valid, final goal. In reality, it is not possible at all for finite human beings or even finite human societies to embrace within its will a moral law so completely universal that it could be embodied in an attitude and life-style in the way that Pragmatism and Existentialism demand from a genuine belief. A specific difference will always result here, which expresses the law of individuation called for by the philosophy of culture. This difficulty corresponds to the incommensurability in Peirce's logic of inquiry of practically indubitable concrete beliefs and the ideal of truth as the belief of the unlimited community postulated by the critique of meaning. Nevertheless, every finite concretization of reason remains directed to an infinite ideal, insofar as it is reason that is concretized. Peirce never relaxed the tension inherent in this problem, so typical of his thought, as it was usually dealt with in Pragmatism and Existentialism—that is, by treating it in terms of individual concretization.[20] Peirce considered such Finitism, the obstinate insistence upon individuality and abandonment of "evolutionary love," the root of idiosyncrasy and, in moral and religious terms, the source of sin and corruption itself.[21] Here he followed Henry James the elder, who was influenced by Swedenborg, Schelling, and Böhme.

It was therefore all the more urgent for Peirce to answer the question how the *summum bonum* or the final goal of all action in general can be made the object of an idea that is explicable as practically meaningful. Asked differently, how can the vision of a final goal—and Peirce had already expressed such a vision in his metaphysics of evolution—be justified as a *meaningful* hypothesis by means of normative, semiotic logic? After about 1902 this problem became the focal point of Peirce's theorizing about the normative sciences.[22]

If we went back to the meaning-critical theory of reality and truth that Peirce developed as a young man, it would be possible to argue in the following way. Reality cannot be defined otherwise than as the correlate to the consensus of an "unlimited community." This is the only way in which the real's independence from being thought of can be understood as identical with the principle of cognizability of the real, as meaning-critical Realism demands. With this, however, an ethically relevant ideal has been erected for every member of the "community of investigators." Insight into the fundamentally social character of possible knowledge of the real forces the individual investigator into an ethical solidarity with the community, in which the goal of his research can alone be attained. Peirce arrived at this position of logical Socialism in 1869 (5.353 ff.). The Pragmatism of the second period and the metaphysics of the third period provide further content for this ideal by mediating between the process of cognition and the real praxis of life. The realization of the consensus of truth in the unlimited community also means the perfection of the evolution of the real in the form of a final order of modes of behavior that correspond to true beliefs. Therefore, the ethics that lies at the basis of the logic of inquiry could be defined in terms of the following hypothetical rule of behavior: if the goal of cognition (and, hence, also the final goal of action) is to be achieved, then every member of the community of investigators must make it the maxim of his action that he "recognizes the logical necessity of complete self-identification of one's own interests with those of the community" (5.356). Conversely, it would also be the case that if every member of the unlimited community of investigators proceeded in this way, as the maxim of logical Socialism prescribes, then, under the presupposition that the remaining methodological and metaphysical conditions of the postulated real process of inquiry were fulfilled, the goal of cognition and therefore that of action, too, would be achieved in the long run. With this, we would have a conditional formulation showing that the principle of logical Socialism is a meaningful hypothesis in accordance with the conditions of interpretation prescribed by the pragmatic maxim.

Despite this, however, one could ask further, why should the goal of the realization of the consensus of truth and its corresponding final order of rules for action be striven for in the first place? The view that we should take part in the rationalization of the universe in the framework of the "indefinite community" has evidently been presupposed in the foregoing sketch of the foundation of a general ethical maxim and assumed to be itself capable of no further justification. To put it in another way, it has been presupposed as the *summum bonum*, which is attractive in itself.[23] It is due only to this presupposition of a final goal incapable of further justification that it seems possible to establish ethics, the science of right action, on rational maxims, that is, on statements that can be explicated hypothetically. This train of thought, it seems to me, shows in concentrated form the problem of the foundation of the normative sciences that confronted Peirce in about 1902. The answer that he found was just as surprising for Peirce himself as it was for his audience. He suggested it for the first time in a manuscript from 1902–3: "That which renders logic and ethics peculiarly normative is that nothing can be either logically true or morally good without a purpose to be so. For a proposition, and especially the conclusion of an argument, which is only accidently true is not logical" (1.575; cf. 5.131 and 1.173). Here Peirce began—by interpreting the methodological self-control of logical thought pragmatically as being related to a purpose. In this way it was possible for him to treat it as a special case of morally good behavior. But then he continued, "On the other hand, a thing is beautiful or ugly quite irrespective of any purpose to be so" (1.575). He concluded, "Pure ethics, philosophical ethics, is not normative, but pre-normative" (1.577).

Here, with the question of the final goal, which cannot be derived from a further purpose, Peirce found himself driven beyond the sphere of what can be given a normative foundation, to the prenormative. And in the attempt to imagine the prenormative, final justification that is based upon itself, he arrived at the beautiful.

But at this point a fundamental difficulty arose for Peirce, who had described himself as a "logical animal." In his 1868 theory of knowledge he had denied the possibility of immediate intuitive cognition.[24] In 1877, moreover, he accused the "a priori method" of prescientific philosophy of obtaining its ultimate presuppositions from a judgment of taste. Such judgments were not derived from anything further than that the principle in question was "agreeable to reason." At that time Peirce rejected such a foundation for knowledge as a merely subjective authority.[25] Now he was himself forced in that very direction by his attempt to give a normative foundation to his logic of the scientific form of inquiry, which was supposed to overcome the a priori method. In addition, and this point became of primary importance for him after 1903, the question of the prenormative, final reason for the establishment of all goals, which itself cannot be founded rationally, seemed to lead to the agreeable, meaning the satisfaction of sensory needs (see 1.582 and 5.111). But this is the point against which Peirce had struggled with the greatest effort, the so-called satisfaction theory of truth and goodness so typical of vulgar Pragmatism.[26]

On the other hand, Peirce could not avoid concluding that the good in itself, which would be seen to be the final goal of all action, could not be given any further foundation by means of a relation to a purpose. In the terminology of Peirce's doctrine of categories this means that the *summum bonum* must fall under the category of Firstness. That is, it must be a pure kind of being, perceivable in a feeling, free of every relationship to reality. But it was just this category of Firstness that Peirce had usually illustrated through sensory impressions or their qualities. Only in his early years, when he first conceived of the three fundamental categories, did he exemplify Firstness through the pure abstract idea, in the Platonic sense, as the "ground" of the meaning of words.[27] The question of the nature and cognizability of the *summum bonum* led him now to a new illustration of Firstness. It is not a coincidence that he found it in the dimension where Plato, Kant, Schiller, and Schelling had looked for the mediation between the idea and the sensory, in the sphere of the aesthetic. So it happened that in 1903 Peirce presented the following solution to the problem of the normative sciences in, of all places, the lectures on Pragmatism that James had arranged at Harvard:

A logical reasoner is a reasoner who excercises great self-control in his intellectual operations; and therefore the logically good is simply a particular species of the morally good. Ethics . . . is the normative science *par excellence,* because an *end*—the essential object of normative science—is germane to a voluntary act in a primary way in which it is germane to nothing else. . . . On the other hand, an ultimate end of action *deliberately* adopted—that is to say, *reasonably* adopted—must be a state of things that *reasonably recommends itself in itself* aside from any ulterior consideration. It must be an *admirable ideal,* having the only kind of goodness that such an ideal *can* have; namely, esthetic goodness. From this point of view the morally good appears as a particular species of the esthetically good.[28]

The circumstance that makes it possible here for Peirce to accept the feeling quality of beauty as a manifestation of the *summum bonum,* despite his rejection of Hedonism, is his interpretation of this aesthetic quality categorically as the Firstness of Thirdness. That is, he conceives it as the qualitatively unified and therefore intuitively perceivable expression of universality, continuity, and order, or, in other words, of the concrete reasonableness of the future universe. He explains, "I do not succeed in saying exactly *what* it is, but it is a consciousness belonging to the category of Representation [i.e., Thirdness], though representing something in the Category of Quality of Feeling [i.e., Firstness]" (5.113). Later he continues: "In the light of the doctrine of categories I should say that an object, to be esthetically good, must have a multitude of parts so related to one another as to impart a positive simple immediate quality to their totality" (5.132).

Peirce, who again and again emphasizes his incompetence in the sphere of aesthetics (see 5.113, 5.129, and 5.132), arrives here at notions that are thoroughly traditional. The particular significance of his conception of aesthetic consciousness, in the context of his later philosophy, lies in the fact that the idea of an "intuition," which Peirce had so emphatically rejected in the first period of his development because it claimed to have an immediate knowledge of sensory or rational principles of philosophy, appears after 1900 in a completely new light. Earlier, Peirce would have traced every cognition, even seemingly immediate sense perception, to an infinite process of inference which alone had the responsibility of offering a guarantee for the continuity of our knowledge as an approximation to the truth. Now he emphasizes, to the contrary, that we must necessarily have a sensory perception of the real continuity of endless rational mediation. That is, instead of emphasizing the Thirdness of Firstness, he emphasizes the Firstness of Thirdness. Whereas he had earlier traced sensory perception itself to unconscious rationality (see 5.219–23 and 5.291–92), now he founds rational deduction in mathematics and logic upon "diagrammatic" observation (see 2.81, 5.162, 3.363, and 3.556). The following paragraph from the 1903 lectures on Pragmatism is typical of the new way in which he regards the problem: "If you object that there can be no immediate consciousness of generality, I grant that. If you add that one can have no direct experience of the general, I grant that as well" (5.150). After this reconfirmation of his position from 1868, Peirce continues, "Generality, Thirdness, pours in upon us in our very perceptual judgments, and all reasoning, so far as it depends upon necessary reasoning, that is to say, mathematical reasoning, turns upon the perception of generality and continuity at every step" (5.150; cf. 5.157).

The phenomenon that Peirce has in mind here is evidently the one that led Plato to interpret the general validity of the geometrical truths that can be taken from a drawing, which we perceive with the senses, as an indication that the sensory given participates in the ideas. For Plato, however, the sphere of evanescent, sensory appearances and that of the eternal ideas remain separated, despite the former's participation in the latter. This separation is brought about by the fact that Plato regards contemplation of the ideas as ultimately analogous with sense perception and its objects. Peirce, on the other hand, persists in rejecting the notion of the immediate intuition of ideas.

He aims for a philosophy of continuity in which perception and its objects are to be conceived, on the one hand, as the limiting case of rationality (5.181–85), while rationality itself is to be conceived, on the other hand, as an object of sensory perception (5.194, 5.205, 5.209 ff.). Insofar as perception is conceived as the limiting case of rationality, as, so to speak, "mediated immediacy," which was already the case in the first period of Peirce's thought, Leibniz and Hegel emerge for the later Peirce as models for his philosophy of continuity. But insofar as rationality is itself to be perceived, Peirce upholds the primacy of aesthetic consciousness as the Firstness of Thirdness (5.113, 5.119, 5.132, 5.150, 5.157).

The Firstness of Thirdness, the sensory transparence in aesthetic consciousness of the general order of the universe found in the process of its development, cannot be subsumed (aufgehoben) under the Thirdness of the concept for Peirce, as it can be for Hegel, because of what is ultimately a difference in Pragmatism's relationship to time. Although Peirce explicitly equates the three fundamental categories with Hegel's "stages of thought" (5.38, 5.43, 8.213), they are nonetheless also rigidly coordinated with the three dimensions of time (5.458 ff.), and, like these, they are realities that cannot be eliminated (aufgehoben) by thought. Thirdness, the category of infinite continuity and real generality, is for Peirce primarily related to the future, in which it acts as a regulative principle of human action to guarantee the completion of the universe's real lawfulness. We cannot conceive the process of the unending "growth of concrete reasonableness" that is postulated along with Thirdness as past without thereby appearing to reduce it to a fact in the sense of Secondness and so to make it cancel itself out.[29] As a result, faced with an infinite future, human praxis depends upon an aesthetic vision for orientation to some final meaning. Peirce expresses this as follows:

The very being of the General, of Reason, consists in its governing individual events. So, then, the essence of Reason is such that its being never can be completely perfected. It always must be in a state of incipiency, of growth. It is like the character of a man which consists in the ideas that he will conceive and in the efforts that he will make, and which only develops as the occasions actually arise. Yet in all his life long no son of Adam has ever fully manifested what there was in him. So, then, the development of Reason requires as a part of it the occurrence of more individual events than can ever occur. It requires, too, all the coloring of all qualities of feeling, including pleasure in its proper place among the rest. This development of Reason consists, you will observe, in embodiment, that is, in manifestation. The creation of the universe, which did not take place during a certain busy week, in the year 4004 B.C., but is going on today and never will be done, is this very development of Reason. I do not see how one can have a more satisfying ideal of the admirable than the development of Reason so understood. The one thing whose admirableness is not due to an ulterior reason is Reason itself comprehended in all its fullness, so far as we can comprehend it. Under this conception, the ideal of conduct will be to execute our little function in the operation of the creation by giving a hand toward rendering the world more reasonable whenever, as the slang is, it is "up to us" to do so. [1.615]

After offering this aesthetic ideal as the foundation of the normative sciences, Peirce returns once again (in a final 1905 footnote to the 1878 formulation of the pragmatic maxim), via a reflection on the final goal of action, to his attempt to arrive at a fourth degree of clearness of thought expressed in terms of the anticipated consequences of our ideas:

Pragmaticism makes thinking to consist in the living inferential metaboly of symbols whose purport lies in conditional general resolutions to act. As for the ultimate purpose of thought, which must be the purpose of everything, it is beyond human comprehension; but according to the stage of approach which my thought has made to it—with aid from many persons, among whom I may mention Royce (in his *World and Individual*), Schiller (in his *Riddles of the Sphinx*) as well, by the way, as the famous poet [Friedrich Schiller] (in his *Aesthetische Briefe*), Henry James the elder (in his *Substance and Shadow* and in his conversations), together with Swedenborg himself—it is by the indefinite replication of self-control upon self-control that the *vir* is begotten, and by action, through thought, he grows an esthetic ideal, not for the behoof of his own poor noddle merely, but as the share which God permits him to have in the work of creation.

This ideal, by modifying the rules of self-control modifies action, and so experience too—both the man's own and that of others, and this centrifugal movement thus rebounds in a new centripetal movement, and so on; and the whole is a bit of what has been going on, we may presume, for a time in comparison with which the sum of the geological ages is as the surface of an electron in comparison with that of a planet. [5.402 n. 3; cf. 5.3]

This explication of the pragmatic maxim is the culmination of Peirce's attempt to broaden his Pragmatism to encompass his teleological metaphysics of evolution and to overcome what he termed the "stoic" Pragmatism of utility. This attempt was not successful insofar as the step that was supposed to lead beyond the pragmatic maxim of 1878 had to focus upon a meaning that was no longer rationally explicable by Pragmatism. The problem of the rational justification of the quasi-sensory affection of the mind through an "admirable ideal" reveals a parallel between Peirce's aporia and a characteristic difficulty in Kant. For Kant, too, in the *Foundations of the Metaphysics of Morals*, there arose the problem of how reason, in order to become practical, can affect human sensibility, not by a "pathological" interest, but rather by a "pure" one. His statement on this, itself an aporia, reads:

> If we are to will actions for which reason itself prescribes an "ought" to a rational, yet sensuously affected, being, it is admittedly necessary that reason should have a power of *infusing a feeling of pleasure* or satisfaction in the fulfilment of duty, and consequently that it should possess a kind of causality by which it can determine sensibility in accordance with rational principles. It is, however, wholly impossible to comprehend—that is, to make intelligible *a priori*—how a mere thought containing nothing sensible in itself can bring about a sensation of pleasure or displeasure; for there is here a special kind of causality, and—as with all causality—we are totally unable to determine its character a priori: on this we must consult experience alone. . . . Whereas here pure reason by means of mere Ideas (which furnish absolutely no objects for experience) has to be the cause of an effect admittedly found in experience. Hence for us men it is wholly impossible to explain how and why the *universality of a maxim as a law*— and therefore morality—should interest us.[30]

When Kant restricted the use of the categories in his transcendental logic to the sphere of possible appearances in the sense of theoretical natural science, he thereby deprived himself of the possibility of explaining how the mind is affected by the idea of the moral law. Peirce's meaning-critical transformation of transcendental logic had, of course, eliminated the distinction between "appearances" and "things-in-themselves," but in his pragmatic logic of inquiry he, too, limited the possibility of a causal explanation of sensory affection to natural scientific knowledge and the instrumental mediation of theory and praxis. These are areas in which the unconditioned moral law or the "splendid ideal of a universal kingdom of *ends in themselves* (rational beings), to which we can belong as members only if we are scrupulous to live in accordance with maxims of freedom as if they were laws of nature," could not *appear*.[31] Hence, in order to make understandable how the mind was affected by an "admirable ideal," Peirce was forced in 1902–3 to transcend Pragmatism's transcendental logical framework in the direction of an aesthetic foundation for the teleological cosmology that he had developed in the third period as a metaphysical hypothesis. There may be a connection here with the fact that Peirce, who was still attempting in 1903, in his important Harvard lectures on Pragmatism, to integrate all aspects of his philosophy into the proof of the truth of Pragmatism, wrote to James in 1904: "I also want to say that after all pragmatism solves no real problem. It only shows that supposed problems are not real problems. . . . The effect of pragmatism here is simply to open our minds to receiving any evidence, not to furnish evidence" (8.259).

I do not want to dwell longer here on the problem of the normative in Peirce's conception of his system in 1902–3; I wish rather to consider the further consequences that accompany his emphasis on the category of Firstness, attested to by his discovery of aesthetic consciousness. These consequences point towards a rehabilitation of intuitive cognition, as I have already indicated, which in turn leads to a revision of the semiotic basis of the logic of cognition. It was only after establishing this revision that Peirce arrived at what for him was a satisfactory reconciliation of the normative logic of inquiry and the conception of the "objective logic" of evolution that he developed in the third period.

B. The Revision of the Semiotic Foundations of the Logic of Inquiry and Their Incorporation in the Metaphysics of Evolution

Peirce had found it necessary in 1885 to supplement his semiotic theory of the possible "representation" of the real, that is, to add significantly to his meaning-critical theory of the anticipated final result of the methodological process of inquiry. The occasion for this revision was an objection made by the absolute idealist Josiah Royce. Royce objected that it would be impossible to discover mistakes in the way Peirce proposed—by identifying the subjects of false and correct propositions—and so to arrive at an approximate correction of hypotheses, unless we could identify ourselves at the outset with an infinite mind which was able to think of the subject of every proposition and all of its predicates and so offer a present guarantee of eternal truth.[32] Peirce replied to this objection by pointing out that the "indices" of our language, such as demonstrative pronouns, allow us at all times to have real contact with the individual subjects of our sentences. Hence, they provide a kind of noncognitive, temporary identification of the real, a representation of which (by means of general definitions) would be the content of the final opinion of the final community of investigators. "Indices" fulfill, therefore, the function of the category of Secondness within the category of Thirdness, that is, within the triadic function of mediation or representation in language. They do this by establishing a denotative contact with existing facts through a form of language usage that is dependent in principle upon situations. The indices make it possible to direct our attention to similar phenomena and thereby to the inductive confirmation of hypotheses by enumeration of cases that confirm it.[33] With this, the empirical aspect of the logic of inquiry, the possibility of an experience of the real appears, despite the provisional nature of all conceptual representation, to be adequately founded semiotically and, hence, in terms of the analysis of categories as well.

Peirce's work on the final conception of his system, however, brought him to the conclusion that the first category, the category of "quality," also had an indispensable function within the logic of inquiry.[34] The qualitative content of perception and its representation in language could not be exhausted, as Peirce had suggested in the "theory of cognition" in 1868–71, either by the "material quality" of the linguistic sign (5.291), which is something that changes and is readily replaced by other such contents, or by the equally coincidental material of the sense impressions, which is the interchangeable vehicle of "information" for the "communion of minds" (8.13; cf. 5.289 and 5.300).

Two interrelated problems arose in the logic of inquiry, so that an explanation of how the process of inquiry can approximate the truth had to appear unsatisfactory as long as it relied solely upon the postulated validity of synthetic inference in conjunction with a mechanical selection of usable hypotheses through a confrontation with "brute facts."

In the first case, even in the confirmation or falsification of hypotheses, more takes place than can be explained by the mechanical pressure of the successful or unsuccessful confrontation of an existing observer with existing facts. Without a comparison of the predicates in question (relational predicates as well as attributive ones) with the qualitative nature of phenomena, a given existing investigator could not ascertain through his inferences whether the things that he encounters with his senses behave the way his hypotheses lead him to anticipate they will or not. As a result of this reflection, the function of perceptual judgments, which Peirce had interpreted in 1868 as hypothetical results of an unending process of mediation through abductive inferences, seemed to become problematic again. It was not enough to show the compatibility of the endless mediation of perceptual judgments with the possibility of a beginning of cognition in time by turning to certain mathematical considerations.[35] Rather, the point was to explain to what extent precisely those judgments which rest upon sense perceptions have the capacity to express immediately the qualitative nature of reality in their predicates, so that they are able to assume the function of first premises for the inductive confirmation of our theories.[36]

In the second case, the same problem is posed when we consider the ingenious hypotheses which are the basis of theory formation in natural science. That is, how does reality determine the qualitative nature of experience, even prior to any conceptual representation of reality, in such a way that it provides a positive orientation by which we can approximate to the ultimate opinion? These hypotheses, like perceptual judgments, also rest upon abductive inferences. They cannot be explained, according to the later Peirce, simply as arising through the rationalistic principle of coherence and the mechanical selection of usable flashes of wit from those that are just chance notions.[37] For, as Peirce repeatedly asks with astonishment, how is it possible that, from all those insights which are possible according to the law of chance, man relatively quickly and with certainty discovers to be "natural" (in terms of common sense or *lumen naturale*) those which possess a cognitive affinity with reality?[38] The question how hypotheses come about is not to be confused with the quasi-transcendental question of the objective validity of the process of synthetic inference in the long run, which Peirce had answered in 1868–69 by reference to the principle of convergence postulated by the critique of meaning.[39] But it must, as Peirce now recognizes, be answered as well, and it must be answered through the logic of inquiry in conjunction with the metaphysics of evolution, since the "transcendental deduction" of the validity of synthetic inference cannot by itself show how experience in general is possible.[40]

An answer to these central questions of Peirce's logic of inquiry seems possible if we assume that there is a qualitative Firstness in nature, and within the sign function as well, by which nature is represented as something that is not just a coincidental, interchangeable, material vehicle for information,[41] but also a perceptual, imagelike expression of rational structures. The difficulty in categorial analysis that arose here for Peirce was, at bottom, the same one as in the case of the introduction of brute facts into the cognitive process. Such facts were an illustration of Secondness for Peirce; similarly, he also characterized descriptions of sensory qualities as illustrations of Firstness as completely irrational. He thereby divorced them from the actual process of cognition (see 1.420, 1.357, 2.85, and 5.289). The difficulty was overcome in the case of Secondness by finding a linguistic representation of it in the form of "indices." As linguistic symbols, these fall under the category of Thirdness because they are interpreted rationally in the framework of the proposition. At the same time, however, they also represent the Secondness of language's factual connection with the real world in a situation, and their interpretation is dependent upon this relationship to a situation. In this way Peirce could claim that the indexical function of language was the semiotic precondition for the possibility of the identification of individual objects in the context of cognition—for example, in enumerating existing facts in the logic of inquiry for the purpose of inductive corroboration. In a similar way he had now to be on the lookout for a representation of qualitative Firstness in language, and it was an obvious move for him to consider here the iconic function of language which he had postulated in 1867.[42] The breakthrough to this conception was fundamentally equivalent for Peirce to the discovery of aesthetic consciousness.[43]

As early as 1883 and especially after 1891 Peirce had in principle answered in his metaphysics the question of the affinity between human knowledge and nature in terms of an objective Idealism. His answer interpreted the categorical structure of nature as an unconscious preliminary stage and equivalent of the categorial structure of the consciously applied logic of inquiry. Even here, in the theory of Agapasm, Peirce finally regarded as unsatisfactory his attempt to explain successful cognition solely on the basis of chance insights and the mechanical selection of those which are usable. Hence he postulated a sympathetic-divinatory empathy as the final tendency of evolution.[44] However, only after his explicit recourse to aesthetic consciousness in the context of the foundation of the normative sciences was it possible for him to use his semiotic to articulate his categorial conception of a Firstness of Thirdness, that is, quasi-sensory, qualitative perception and the iconic expression of the developing ideal order of the universe. In a paragraph from his 1903 lectures on Pragmatism he summarizes this conception:

Therefore, if you ask me what part Qualities can play in the economy of the universe, I shall reply that the universe is a vast representamen, a great symbol of God's purpose, working out its conclusions in living realities. Now every symbol must have, organically attached to it, its Indices of Reactions [to the actual situation] and its Icons of Qualities; and such part as these reactions and these qualities play in an argument that, they of course, play in the universe—that Universe being precisely an argument. In the little bit that you or I can make out of this huge demonstration, our perceptual judgments are the premises *for us* and these perceptual judgments have icons as their predicates, in which *icons* Qualities are immediately presented. [5.119]

Peirce attempts here to establish the capacity to experience the world through the senses as the semiotic condition for the possibility of a qualitative determination of the cognitive process. Just as the indexical function of language, usually represented in the subject of the sentence, had previously made possible incorporation of pure facticity into the rational process of interpretation, so now the iconic function of language in the predicate of the sentence,[45] that is, as the Firstness of the Thirdness of the proposition's predicative synthesis, is supposed to capture the qualitative expression of the world and embody it in the rational process of interpretation. The cognitive function of Firstness in Thirdness goes further metaphysically, however, than merely embodying facticity. As an illumination of the nature of things, it contributes directly to the intensional structure of concepts (what Peirce terms "depth") and mediates, therefore, between the logic of inquiry and the particular characteristics of nature, just as Peirce had postulated in his metaphysics, in a divinatory and heuristic way. From here it becomes understandable that Peirce tried with the help of the iconic function to articulate the metaphysical analogy between the inference process in nature and the controlled inference process in inquiry:

But what is first for us is not first in nature. The premisses of Nature's own process are all the independent uncaused elements of facts that go to make up the variety of nature which the necessitarian supposes to have been all in existence from the foundation of the world, but which the Tychist supposes are continually receiving new accretions. These premisses of nature, however, though they are not the *perceptual facts* that are premisses to us, nevertheless must resemble them in being premisses. We can only imagine what they are by comparing them with the premisses for us. As premisses they must involve Qualities.

Now as to their function in the economy of the Universe. The Universe as an argument is necessarily a great work of art, a great poem—for every fine argument is a poem and a symphony—just as every true poem is a sound argument. But let us compare it rather with a painting—with an impressionist seashore piece—then every Quality in a Premiss is one of the elementary colored particles of the Painting; they are all meant to go together to make up the intended Quality that belongs to the whole as whole. That total effect [i.e., of the universe] is beyond our ken; but we can appreciate in some measure the resultant Quality of parts of the whole—which Qualities result from the combinations of elementary Qualities that belong to the premisses. [5.119]

In this iconically accentuated vision of the universe as a sign or argument which attains a representation of itself through its conscious continuation in the human activity of science, Peirce's late thought completes his objective, semiotic Idealism. This Idealism was already latent in 1868 in his view of man as sign[46] and was carried out in detail in 1883 in his "theory of probable inference" as the doctrine of unconscious inference in nature (see 2.711–13). There he said:

We usually conceive nature to be perpetually making deductions in *Barbara*. This is our natural and anthropomorphic metaphysics. We conceive that there are Laws of Nature, which are her Rules or major premises. We conceive that Cases arise under these laws; these cases consist in the predication, or occurrence, of *causes*, which are the middle terms of the syllogisms. And, finally, we conceive that the occurrence of these causes, by virtue of the laws of Nature, results in effects which are the conclusions of the syllogisms [made by Nature]. Conceiving of Nature in this way, we naturally

conceive of science as having three tasks—(1) the discovery of Laws, which
is accomplished by induction; (2) the discovery of Causes, which is accomplished by hypothetic inference; and (3) the prediction of Effects, which is
accomplished by deduction. It appears to me to be highly useful to select a
system of logic which shall preserve all these natural conceptions. [2.713]

This "anthropomorphic" understanding of nature was worked
out in the metaphysics of evolution, initially without taking any account of semiotic logic and its relationship to nature.[47] The connection
was made explicit for the first time in the systematic conception that
Peirce developed in 1902–3. There the iconic function of human language and the corresponding "language of nature" which precedes it
have the task of producing the decisive connection between the qualitative features of nature and the predicates of human perceptual judgments as that which is "first for us." It was this iconic contact between
nature and cognition—understood in semiotic terms, between unconscious and conscious "argumentation"—that finally permitted Peirce
to mediate between his normative logic of inquiry and his metaphysics
and to complement the former through this very mediation. The
meaning-critical theory of reality from 1868 seemed to concentrate
the whole process of inquiry into the conceptual representation of the
real by means of rational inferences (Thirdness). The index theory of
1885 took into account only the "denotative" contact with "existing
facts" as found in experimental verification (Secondness). The icon
theory of perceptual predicates for the first time made it possible to
introduce into the framework of conceptual representation the qualitative comparison of knowledge formulated in language and the features of what is real, and, most of all, also made it possible to take
into account the initial perception of these features as a function of
empirical information. Even the "anthropomorphic" understanding of
the world itself, which Peirce refers to again and again as the "affinity of the human soul to the soul of the universe" (5.47; cf. 5.212,
5.536, and 6.477), must, as the heuristic horizon of all scientific hypotheses, be based on the iconic function of cognition conceived in
semiotic terms.

By complementing semiotic in this way Peirce also found it possible to relate the three kinds of inference postulated in 1883 to the
natural occurrences we perceive through the senses. This semiotic
emphasis on Firstness in iconic representation resulted in a new and,
for Peirce, a final outline of the function of abductive inference. In this
outline, deduction has nothing to do with the experience of reality.
For Peirce "the fact that man has a power of Explicating his own
meaning [i.e., the meaning of symbols] renders Deduction valid"
(6.474). "Deduction merely involves the necessary consequences of a
pure hypothesis" (5.171). Induction's contact with reality is in the

"indication" or "denotation" of the facts that we encounter here and now, but that means it does not discover either the qualitative features of some thing or the features of a law, as Peirce had suggested in 1883. Instead, it serves only to "evaluate" hypotheses that already exist, through either confirmation or falsification (5.171; cf. 5.145 and 6.475). Abduction, Peirce says, "is the only logical operation which introduces any new idea" (5.171; cf. 5.145). It does this as an inference that in the limiting case is unconscious and is the basis even of perception and, accordingly, of every scientific "intuition." Abduction expresses the iconic qualities of nature in a hypothesis formulated in language.[48] Abduction is therefore the first stage of all inquiry and, since it is man's spontaneous, divinatory answer to the way his surroundings confront him, it is the human equivalent to animal instinct (see 5.171 ff., 5.181, and 6.475–77).

This analogy between the process of nature and the semiotic process of thought, which underlies the mediation of logic and metaphysics discussed above, might, as Peirce himself noted, "seem very fanciful at first sight" (2.711). It can be seen as a pragmatic philosopher of science's regression to a pretranscendental and, in the American sense of the word, "transcendentalist" metaphysics. And in fact the themes of "nature as language" and of a world-creating "Logos" that "expresses" itself in this language, and in the predicates of the human language by which it is interpreted, were all familiar to Peirce in his earliest years (before 1867).[49] These bear witness to a tradition that reaches from the doctrines of the Logos and the language of nature found from the philosophers of the Renaissance and Baroque (Nicolas of Cusa, Böhme, Leibniz, Berkeley) all the way to Emerson.[50] On the other hand, it cannot be overlooked that, by an internal logic, Peirce was consistently led to this semiotic ontology by his semiotic transformation of the theory of knowledge and by his meaning-critical revision of Kantian transcendental philosophy, which is part of this transformation. The essential steps in the course of his thought can be briefly summarized here.

1. After the critique of meaning exposed the incognizable thing-in-itself as a self-refuting hypothesis and instead defined the real as what is cognizable in the long run by the community of investigators, there was no further way in principle for Peirce to limit the ontological reality of his categories, which he derived from the logic of language, by contrasting them—even tacitly—with the hypothesis of an incognizable world behind the world. Like all scientific hypotheses, they could now be subject to a limitation of their applicability only through the restrictions of Fallibilism, that is, in the sense that all cognition is subject to correction. However, this limitation stems from a critique of knowledge that itself, in principle, presupposes the real

applicability in the long run of the semiotic categories of knowledge. Since the generality of concepts is an indispensable, constitutive element of all knowledge understood semiotically, that is, of all true "representation," it immediately follows that Peirce upheld a realist theory of universals.[51] This is part of Peirce's meaning-critical Realism, while the absurd hypothesis of an incognizable world behind the world is exposed as the πρῶτον ψεῦδος of all Nominalism.

2. For Peirce, the meaning-critical dissolution of the world behind the world went hand in hand with the incorporation of cognition itself into the real world, which can be investigated empirically. Cognition was no longer, as it was for Kant, a limit of the empirical world.[52] It was no longer a function of a transcendental faculty of consciousness conceived to be in contact in a mysterious way with the things-in-themselves that somehow affect it, a problem that forced Kant to use analogy.[53] Now cognition was seen as a historical process manifested in language and society which, from the standpoint of its unconscious foundations, forms a continuum with the evolutionary process of nature, but which, at the other conscious extreme, is subject to "self-control" through normative logic. In place of Kant's distinction between the realm of objects of possible experience and the realm of objects imagined in a transcendental metaphysics, a realm which cannot be separated from the transcendent metaphysics of things-in-themselves, Peirce made a methodological distinction between the questions of empirical science and those of the normative, semiotic logic of inquiry. The former, as a heuristic "overview" (Coenoscopy) that does not itself conduct experimental inquiry (see 6.6 and 1.241), is the metaphysics of the evolution of the universe. It is subdivided into the individual "idioscopic" sciences which subject the heuristic world-view hypotheses of metaphysics to an indirect empirical proof.[54] The latter investigates the conditions for the applicability of consciously practiced methods of inquiry, such as deductive and synthetic inference, including their procedures of experimentation and communication. To this extent it assumes the heritage of Kant's transcendental logic, and Peirce's relationship to post-Kantian philosophy results from this assumption.

3. By eliminating the incognizable thing-in-itself, Peirce also treats the problem of transcendental consciousness as part of the world to be known, namely, as part of the history of this world. In doing so he follows with internal consistency the course taken by post-Kantian idealist philosophy with Shelling and Hegel. Peirce's identification of cognition with the evolutionary process of nature (its unconscious presuppositions) or with the historical process of society (its presuppositions that are subject to control) is different from that of German Idealism, however. Peirce does not reduce the process of

empirical research to the process of consciousness as construed by transcendental philosophy; rather, he conceives all the nontranscendental logical aspects of cognition in terms of empirical hypothesis formation. This is most clearly evident in his treatment of the alternative between Idealism (Spiritualism) and Materialism in his cosmological metaphysics (6.24).

Peirce's decision in the third period to opt for objective Idealism (or perhaps it would be better to say Spiritualism) is an empirical hypothesis in the sense of Peirce's metaphysical Coenoscopy. It is fundamentally dependent upon the position of his meaning-critical Realism as developed in the first and second periods and confirmed in the Pragmaticism of his fourth period. That is, the common-sense assumption that the existence and features of the real are independent from the opinions that limited subjects have about it, which Critical Common-sensism identifies with the cognizability of the real by the unlimited community of thinking beings, itself remains untouched by Peirce's metaphysical hypothesis that matter is rigidified mind (mind as feeling is Firstness) and that natural laws are rigidified habits (mind as a regulatory principle is Thirdness).[55] In fact, Realism's thesis of independence from cognition is reconfirmed by the very fact that even the unconscious foundations of cognition, especially the unconscious abductive inferences that according to Peirce are the basis of perceptual judgments (5.181 ff.), are absolutely uncontrollable through normative logic and so must be considered to belong to a reality that is independent of cognition (5.55, 5.212).

Here, however, we are also confronted with the compatability of the metaphysical hypothesis of objective Idealism with meaning-critical Realism, so that we see beyond the correlative independence of these two Peircean theorems and recognize that they actually support one another. In fact, seen from this perspective, Peirce's 1903 use of speculative semiotic to mediate between metaphysics and the normative logic of cognition seems to me to become quite understandable.

4. Peirce's meaning-critical Realism of 1868 defined the real as the object of conceptual representation met with at the conclusion of an unlimited process of inquiry and communication, but it had to treat the real as it is encountered here and now, existing individually in the outer world and capable only of being indicated by an "index" (as well as those experiential qualities with which the organism reacts in private consciousness to the outer world) as a fundamentally irrational, precognitive aspect of the process of inquiry. On the other hand, these qualities also served as the sources of information that provide the indispensable empirical substratum for synthetic inference operations (induction and abduction). The central aporia which arose

here for Peirce's theory of knowledge resulted from the fact that it had to presuppose something and, furthermore, had to presuppose it as the source of knowledge, even though, as something fundamentally irrational, it cannot even be considered to be real according to meaning-critical Realism. Peirce passed over this aporia in 1868 in his rationalistic "theory of cognition" by believing that he simply had to show that, insofar as experiential qualities or feelings are conceivable in thought, they are always already conceptually interpreted, and insofar as they are immediately given, they cannot be conceived in thought. Hence, to this extent, he believed such qualities to be irrelevant to the meaning-critical theory of knowledge.[56]

But it is clear that Peirce contradicted himself here, because he explicitly conceived such relation-free qualities of experience in terms of the category of Firstness, and in the "logic of inquiry" in 1872–73 he had recognized the indispensable function of the nonrational elements of Firstness and Secondness as the source of information in empirical, experimental cognition (see 7.328). In his speculative semiotic of 1903 Peirce was able to integrate the brute facts we encounter in experience into the representation of the real by conceiving them to be inductively utilizable signals of natural events that are not yet conceptually understood, but are in principle capable of being so understood. Moreover, and more importantly, he was also able to integrate into this representation the qualities of experience. As iconic qualities they enter into the predicates of perceptual judgments as an expression of the affinity between the unconscious inference processes in nature and the inner nature of human beings.

It would be possible to object, of course, that this speculation resolves the central aporia of Peirce's theory of knowledge only if we admit that the elements of Firstness and Secondness, which constitute the empirical foundation of knowledge and the contingent and irrational element in the developing universe, become completely absorbed in the long run by the rational element of Thirdness. In other words, Peirce's solution appears to assume that the irrational elements finally will be *aufgehoben*, to speak in Hegelian terms. This assumption, it could be argued, is implicit in the meaning-critical definition of the real as the cognizable, that is, as the object of the ultimate opinion of an indefinite community of investigators. To put it in another way, Peirce's metaphysics of "objective Idealism" and the meaning-critical Realism in his theory of knowledge would then not just support one another; rather, for true knowledge in the sense of the metaphysical hypothesis, they would amount to the same thing. The irrational confrontations met with in experience and sensory, perceptual qualities would then be only symptoms of what is still unexpected in experience, although such symptoms are able to illuminate themselves. As a result these are merely indications that our conceptual knowledge of the real is not yet adequate.

Numerous strains of thought found in Peirce's later thought seem definitely to point in this direction.[57] We might think that Peirce could all the more easily come to such a conclusion because, in contrast to Hegel, he visualized the absolute point of convergence in his system as residing not in the logos-mystical perfection of reflection, but rather in the infinite future. In addition, the elimination or *Aufhebung* of the irrational elements in cognition was not for Peirce a a task of philosophical speculation, but one of empirical science. Nor was the task of the total rationalization of the universe an affair just of theory; it was also one of praxis mediated by such theory. However, the very circumstances, enumerated above, which appear to remove the odium of the hybrid nature from the Hegelian idea of "total mediation" evidently hindered Peirce from recognizing or accepting the possibility of an *Aufhebung* of Firstness and Secondness in Thirdness. As an epistemologist in the tradition of Kant, Peirce thought in terms of the regulative principles of a normative logic of inquiry and so remained bound to the region [*Ort*] of the historical situation for which the "ecstasies of time" (Heidegger) have transcendental validity.[58] Like Existentialism and Marxism, Pragmatism is not a philosophy of reflection which could conceive itself to be at the end of the real or even just the possible development of the world. For Pragmatism the relationship to the future is constitutive even for meaning (*Sinn*). But as long as there is a relationship to the future and it is constitutive for our understanding of something as something it will remain impossible, at least in empirical science and in our common-sense understanding of the praxis of life, to subsume (*aufheben*) the qualities of experience and the facticity of events under the generality of the concept. On the contrary, generality in law concepts presupposes future confirmation (i.e., the command over facts that is proven therein), and in rules of behavior it presupposes the acts of will that are to be directed, which themselves presuppose qualities of experience (see 5.436 and 5.91). In his mature thought Peirce even conceived the normatively postulated goal of the development of the world, which he takes to be really possible, as only a "would be," and he thereby made the *esse in futuro* of Thirdness dependent upon contingent facts (Secondness) and upon spontaneous freedom (Firstness).[59]

C. Phenomenology as *prima philosophia*

The aspects of Peirce's final conception of his system that I have sketched so far can be understood without too much difficulty as consequences of the basic conceptions already inherent in the first and second periods. In a number of ways they even represent a return by Peirce, now a hermit isolated in Milford from the other members of the Metaphysical Club, to central tendencies of thought he had followed in his earlier days.[60] As I stressed before, this applies to his use of the Kantian approach for developing the normative sciences in his logical Socialism of 1868. It applies even to his metaphysics of evolution and to his speculative semiotic, which was distinctly prefigured in the "New List of Categories" in 1867 and in his semiotic anthropology and doctrine of mind in 1868 (see especially 5.313 ff.). The new emphasis on the category of Firstness, that is, the iconic function of language, the mediated immediacy of perceptual judgments, abduction, and aesthetic consciousness, can be understood in this context as a kind of complementary addition to a philosophical architectonic that was established in 1867 on the basis of the three categories and that, so to speak, attained its integral form in 1903.[61]

With the aspects sketched so far, however, we have only characterized the first or, one might say, the upper half of Peirce's architectonic conception of his system of 1902–3. The metaphysics of evolution and the normative sciences which it presupposes (logic, ethics, aesthetics) stand in various relationships to the real world (including its real possibilities) and, moreover, presuppose two further abstract sciences which are not concerned at all with the real world. Peirce conceives of one of these, which he terms "Phenomenology" or "Phaneroscopy," as a study belonging to philosophy; the second one, the formal logic of relations which Phenomenology itself presupposes, belongs no longer to philosophy, but rather to mathematics. Mathematics thereby assumes the function of being a formal presupposition of philosophy. This part of Peirce's "classification of the sciences" from 1902–3 not only is the least clearly developed of all; it also, without doubt, places the interpreter of Peirce's thought before the greatest difficulties, especially if that interpreter sees Peirce as the founder of Pragmatism.

Whoever is familiar with the history of philosophy will tend, even on the basis of his prejudices, to separate phenomenological and pragmatic thought and place them at opposite poles. These poles could be designated approximately as follows: on the one hand there is an appeal to intuitive evidence, an eidetic theory of meaning, the seeing of essences (*Wesensschau*), and the radical absence of presuppositions; on the other hand there is an appeal to the ability to make or do something, an operational theory of meaning, Constructionism, and the recognition of the presuppositions in the language and situational context of the praxis of life. The two classic models of philosophical Phenomenology, Hegel's *Phenomenology of Spirit* and Husserl's Phenomenology of pure consciousness, do not agree just by chance in excluding willful Actionism, such as Fichte's, from the foundation of philosophy and in holding, instead, that there has to be a revival, through radical reflection, of the Greek idea of pure *theoria* taken as a contemplative submission to things. Moreover, under the conditions for radical reflection in the modern age, it does not seem to be coincidental that both Hegel's and Husserl's Phenomenologies amount to a philosophy of consciousness that reconfirms Descartes' central philosophical theme, and that for Husserl Phenomenology even becomes a kind of Neo-Cartesianism. How is a mediation between Pragmatism and Phenomenology possible under these conditions?

There can be no doubt that Peirce, at least in his first and second periods, developed his logic of inquiry in the spirit of the antiphenomenological Pragmatism I have just described. He rejected Descartes' reliance upon introspective, intuitive evidence as a criterion of truth and meaning. He discredited both the empirical and the eidetic, a priori varieties of intuition philosophy and replaced the classical eidetic-intensional theories of meaning and definition derived from Plato with an operational, experimental view. He conceived cognition as a function of life and termed the radical absence of presuppositions the illusion of "paper doubt." And most importantly he transformed Kant's "theory of knowledge," which is based upon the capacities or functions of transcendental consciousness, into a semiotic logic of inquiry. Carried out radically according to the approach that Peirce developed in 1868 (see 5.289–90 and 5.313 ff., but cf. 5.440–41 and 5.492–93), this theory understands individual human consciousness itself as an iconic sign (a quality of feeling) with which the organism of the man-sign reacts to its environment (Secondness). This iconic sign becomes relevant to cognition only by being integrated into the intersubjective process of synthetic logical inference upon which the intersubjective process of inquiry and interpretation is based (Thirdness). This process leads to the ultimate opinion of the indefinite community of investigators and thereby simultaneously perfects the lawful order of the universe as the habits adopted by human beings (or, more specifically, of beings capable of communication), habits that when perfected are the "ultimate logical interpretants" of all signs.

Despite all this, in 1902 and the years that followed, Peirce developed or, rather, postulated within the framework of his final "classification" of the sciences a program of "Phenomenology" (after 1904 named "Phaneroscopy") as *prima philosophia* which was evidently supposed to meet the following conditions.[62]

1. Its way of knowing is intuitive; that is, it is pure, qualitative vision which describes what is immediately before our eyes, free of all interpretative presuppositions:

What we have to do, as students of phenomenology, is simply to open our mental eyes and look well at the phenomenon and say what are the characteristics that are never wanting in it, whether that phenomenon be something that outward experience forces upon our attention, or whether it be the wildest of dreams, or whether it be the most abstract and general of the conclusions of science. [5.41]

The first and foremost [faculty of the phenomenologist] is that rare faculty, the faculty of seeing what stares one in the face, just as it presents itself, unreplaced by any interpretation. [5.42]

Phenomenology treats of the universal Qualities of Phenomena in their immediate phenomenal character, in themselves as phenomena. It, thus, treats of Phenomena in their Firstness. [5.122]

2. Phenomenology seems to make use of a kind of *Wesensschau*, that is, eidetic generalization, which is independent of the number of individual data involved: "The second faculty we must strive to arm ourselves with is a resolute discrimination which fastens itself like a bulldog upon the particular feature that we are studying. . . . The third faculty we shall need is the generalizing power of the mathematician who produces the abstract formula that comprehends the very essence of the feature under examination purified from all admixture of extraneous and irrelevant accompaniments" (5.42).

3. Phenomenology's insights possess a timeless, intersubjective, universal validity, although they are unmediated by language, and they presuppose a kind of "consciousness in general": "Phaneroscopy is the description of the *phaneron;* and by the *phaneron* I mean the collective total of all that is in any way or in any sense present to the mind, quite regardless of whether it corresponds to any real thing or not. If you ask present *when,* and to *whose* mind, I reply that I leave these questions unanswered, never having entertained a doubt that those features of the phaneron that I have found in my mind are present at all times and to all minds" (1.284).

Whoever compares this characterization of the presupposition-less, intuitive knowledge of "first philosophy" as something which, in particular, is free from language with Peirce's foundation of all other scientific knowledge by the semiotic logic of inferential operations will not be able to avoid concluding that Peirce's late conception of his system contains that very polar opposition of ultimate presuppositions between Phenomenology and Pragmatism which I outlined above. It is likely that William James found Peirce's 1903 lectures on Pragmatism so difficult to understand because Peirce there completely surprised his audience by introducing phenomenological, categorical analysis as the essential presupposition of Pragmatism.[63] Of course, Peirce could object to his friend that his Phenomenology comes very close to what James later called "pure experience" in his "radical Empiricism," but he also had to indicate that this "pure experience" is not experience in the usual sense and has nothing to do with psychology.[64]

As Peirce takes this opportunity to make clear, neither can his conception of Phenomenology be understood as simply a generalization of the doctrine of "perceptual judgment," which is so important to his speculative semiotic of 1903. Yet Peirce evidently wants to remain within the context of his logic of inquiry with this doctrine, even though it so clearly emphasizes the Firstness of qualitative insight, for he understands the perceptual judgment as an unconscious limiting case of abductive inference and the perceived quality or percept as an iconic sign which can enter into experience only by being integrated into the semiotic inference process (see 5.119 and 5.181 ff.). However, he explicitly rejects the attempt to base phenomenological vision upon the semiotic theory of knowledge: "Percepts are signs for psychology; but they are not so for phenomenology" (8.300). This situation results in Peirce's comparison of phenomenological and aesthetic vision. Even though he appeals to the artist's special capacity to know as a requirement both for the speculative (qualitative) view of the universe and for Phenomenology (5.119 and 5.181 ff.), and even though he explicitly includes both Phenomenology and Aesthetics under the heading Firstness,[65] this affinity of phenomenological vision and aesthetic contemplation, like the affinity with perceptual judgment, is not enough to persuade him to consider his semiotic theory of knowledge applicable to such vision. Rather, Peirce insists that Phenomenology's mode of vision is a pure one and as such is not an "experience" at all; therefore, it does not lead to a true proposition about the real world.[66]

How can this conception of a "first philosophy" be reconciled with the architectonic system in Peirce's theory of science? To ask a less demanding question, how can it be understood in the development of Peirce's philosophy?

The immediate occasion demanding the development of Phenomenology as a first philosophy in the framework of Peirce's systematic classification of the sciences evidently arose from his effort to found the semiotic logic of inquiry in the context of the normative sciences. The fact that the dualistic character of all the normative sciences, which must "separate the sheep from the goats" (5.37), and the traditional division within the normative sciences (5.129) already presuppose fundamental categories indicated to Peirce that the logic of inquiry could not itself be equated with the doctrine of categories, but rather presupposed such a doctrine as a more abstract science.[67] Hence, Peirce introduced the term "Phenomenology" as the title for something which for a long time had already had a place in his philosophy, namely, the doctrine of categories (1.280, 5.37, 5.43). Of course the term "Phenomenology" was not introduced simply as a new name, but as the conceptual result of methodological reflection.

This gives us the decisive clue about the connection between Peirce's Phenomenology and his pragmatic logic of inquiry. The need for a phenomenological foundation for the doctrine of categories brought Peirce to consider de facto for the first time that a semiotic logic of experimental "inquiry" that bases such inquiry upon the interaction of the three fundamental categories (i.e., the "experience" of quality and of reaction, with the rational "interpretation" that mediates between them) has in no way thereby provided a foundation for itself as semiotic logic. Here it is necessary for us to return once again to the central problem of architectonic in the development of Peirce's philosophy.[68]

Peirce's doctrine of categories arose together with his semiotic in his 1867 work entitled "New List of Categories," the speculative germ of his whole philosophy.[69] At that time he had derived the three fundamental categories from the representative function of the sign, later termed "semiosis" (1.558–59; cf. 5.283 ff.); in 1885 he derived them in a formalized manner from the logic of relations. His early derivation developed the distinction between the three sign relations, the relationship to an object (*denotatio*), the relationship to an abstract idea as the ground of meaning (*significatio* or *connotatio*), and the relationship to an "interpretant." It also developed the corresponding division of signs into "indices," "icons," and "symbols." This derivation, together with the matching derivation of the three forms of inference and their validity (1.559, 5.318–56) provided Peirce with the long-sought-after analogy to Kant's transcendental deduction of the categories and the objective validity of judgments of experience. This unified, basic approach of Peirce's philosophy was effected in the spirit of a transformation of the transcendental critique of knowledge into a semiotic, meaning-critical logic of inquiry. It had its "highest point" no longer in the "transcendental synthesis of apperception," and hence in the unity of consciousness of objects in general, but rather in the unity of a consistent semiotic representation of the world which, in the final analysis, can be attained only in an unlimited experimenter and communication community.[70]

In the systematic conception of 1902–3 Peirce now seems to take back this whole earlier approach by claiming that semiotic and the doctrine of categories presuppose a way of knowing that itself relies not upon the interpretative mediation of its results in the unlimited process of communication, but solely upon intuition in individual consciousness, which is supposed *eo ipso* to be universally valid. By doing this he seems to give up the program of an architectonic system which he had taken over from Kant, according to which categories are to be derived from logic. Jürgen von Kempski sees this as a confirmation of his thesis that even Peirce's approach to the doctrine of the categories fails to measure up to Kant, because Peirce did not have an adequate understanding of the "transcendental synthesis of apperception." For Kempski, Peirce's introduction of Phenomenology shows only that Peirce had to admit defeat in the face of the task of a transcendental deduction of the categories and so had to fall back upon merely "hunting" for the categories.[71] According to Kempski, therefore, Peirce stands in the epochal context of the "turn to the phenomena" which culminates in Husserl's *Logical Investigations*, a movement that, including even its subjective turn in the later Husserl, becomes understandable only as a result of the failure of nineteenth-century philosophy in reconstructing the *Critique of Pure Reason*.[72]

But Kempski evidently does not take into account that in 1902–3 Peirce has in no way given up facing the Kantian problem of the transition from the logic of inquiry to metaphysics. It is this very problem that he believes he has solved once and for all with his speculative semiotic in 1903.[73] He takes up here a completely new problem which presents itself at a higher level of reflection, namely, how semiotic logic and the speculative doctrine of the categories, which he had worked out since 1867, are themselves possible. Now no matter how one regards the transformation of Kant's transcendental logic in Peirce's semiotic logic of inquiry, certainly nobody can maintain that Kant's transcendental deduction of the categories of "experience" also answers the question how his transcendental philosophy itself is possible. Kempski himself unintentionally confirms that a problem exists here that can lead to Peirce's idea of a phenomenological way of seeing which is not yet an "experience" of the real: "His [Kant's] concern is whether representations [*Vorstellungen*] must be determinable in regard to their objective validity and he shows (or tries to show) that . . . the necessity of the possibility of objective knowledge is identical with the (thinking) ego. That is the *phenomenological* [Kempski's own emphasis] fact that Kant takes as his starting point, which he presupposes, and which he describes, but does not in anyway derive."[74]

In fact, no matter whether we regard the transcendental synthesis of apperception or the unity of the semiotic representation of the world as the "highest point" of a logic of cognition, it is definite that the presupposition of this "highest point," compared with the transcendental deduction, constitutes a new, so to speak, "metatheoretical" problem.[75] Insofar as Peirce reflects at all on the nature of cognition in first philosophy, he does not fall short of Kant, but rather goes fundamentally beyond him, just as does modern Phenomenology and just as Hegel already did with his *Phenomenology of Spirit*. Of course it is another question whether it was at all clear in Peirce's mind that his asking about the kind of knowledge found in first philosophy had the character of reflection and whether his conception of pure phenomenological vision provided an adequate answer to the question of the conditions of the possibility of first philosophy.

That Peirce sharply rejected the possibility of introspection in 1868 and even in 1905 does not seem to me to be necessarily an argument against the reflective character of his thinking about the necessity of a first philosophy, as Spiegelberg thinks it is.[76] This does, however, most certainly determine the difference between Peirce's Phenomenology and Husserl's Act-Phenomenology. The problem of levels of reflection in the philosophy of science ultimately leads by necessity to the problem of methodological self-reflection in philosophy, but in my view this has nothing directly to do with introspection in the psychological sense. This can even be recognized in the often-mentioned insight that psychological introspection cannot make the self into an object, since it always remains something to be anticipated in this act of introspection. For this is itself a valid statement about the self at the level of philosophical reflection, which in turn we can recognize, as we did just now, by considering philosophy's manner of reflection.

Peirce seems to me to have here begun work on the genuine problem of philosophical reflection by discrediting that Augustinian and Cartesian form of self-reflection which is supposed to be private introspection, in the sense of a methodological Solipsism that believes it has succeeded through reflection in removing itself from the sphere of public communication. Moreover, there is evidence which indicates that Peirce did not confront the problem of reflection without some appreciation of its importance. In the passage where he for the first time explains at length the necessity of having a Phenomenology, he does so by appealing to Hegel's *Phenomenology of Spirit* and by pointing out that the three fundamental categories correspond to Hegel's "three stages of thought," an observation that he subsequently repeats again and again.[77] In fact, Peirce here formulates his three fundamental categories with a deliberate allusion to Hegel's dialectical triad as the "immediacy" of the present, the "struggle" or "duality" of the "ego" and "non-ego," and "mediation." He even goes so far as to admit that Thirdness as mediation involves the ideas of Secondness and Firstness and, moreover, that "never will it be possible to find any Secondness or Firstness that is not accompanied by Thirdness" (5.90).

In this passage, however, Peirce rejects the reflective character of

Hegel's *Phenomenology of Spirit*, since he opposes the idea, as I mentioned before, that the third category could subsume (*aufheben*) the first two under itself by transforming the world into a fact that would belong to the past.[78] According to Peirce, as a reflective science of "appearing consciousness" the *Phenomenology* limits its viewpoint to "what *actually* forces itself on the mind," ignores "the distinction between essence and existence," and loses sight of the broad field of possible experience (5.37). Now, since Peirce's Phenomenology does not have this reflective character, it also does not have the character of rational mediation. Instead, it views "mediation," just as it does "immediacy" and "struggle," as irreducible elements of possible experience. But, according to Peirce, such pure vision itself has the character of relation-free Firstness (5.121–24); yet he does not say how such pure seeing could ever *know* that it has this character. Here we can see a parallel with the iconic vision of the development of the universe or of the highest goal of all action, which was discussed earlier. Like this aesthetic mediation of normative science and metaphysics, Peirce's approach to the task of characterizing Phenomenology's mode of knowledge is not Hegelian. It does not conceive Phenomenology in terms of Thirdness, that is, by regarding rational mediation as the final court of appeal for the theory of knowledge and source of definitive reflection upon reality and knowledge. Rather, Peirce's approach is via the Firstness of Thirdness, that is, the givenness of even rational mediation in "pure vision."

This turn towards the Firstness of seeing, however, now brings out clearly the aporia in Peirce's late system. Peirce was able to conceal it in his account of perceptual judgments by understanding such judgments not just as the immediacy of mediation (e.g., seeing the universal as continuity; see: 5.181 and 5.209 ff.), but rather also as "mediated immediacy," as the unconscious limiting case of abductive inferences (5.181 ff.). If Thirdness (generality, law, rule, rationality, continuity, mediation, concept, etc.) can be given qualitatively in perception as Firstness, and, conversely, if this perception, as cognition, can itself also be understood as a case of Thirdness, then we can see this as a triumph of that model or cipher of the "continuum" which, according to the consensus of those most familiar with Peirce's thought, represents the final bracket of his conception of his system.[79] Phenomenology's pure, presuppositionless, interpretation-free mode of vision can hardly be conceived, on Peirce's view, as a kind of mediated immediacy. But whatever is not mediated has no meaning, according to Peirce's semiotic theory of knowledge; that is, it cannot refer or point beyond the present instant. Moreover, that means it cannot be interpreted.[80] Hence, it remains to be seen how Phenomenology could be a science capable of making any meaningful statements. Peirce himself formulated this aporia as follows: "It [phenomenological thought as a 'singular form of thought'] can hardly be said to involve reasoning; for reasoning reaches a conclusion, and asserts it to be true however matters may seem; while in Phenomenology there is no assertion except that there are certain seemings; and even these are not, and cannot be asserted, because they cannot be described. Phenomenology can only tell the reader which way to look and to see what he shall see."[81]

We might see a resolution of this difficulty in the fact that phenomenological vision, in contrast to perception and aesthetic vision, does not actually have to do with the real world, but rather at most considers the character of "reality" to be distinguished from other ontological characters. For this reason we could conclude that Phenomenology is not subject to semiotic logic which measures the meaning of assertions by their interpretability in regard to their possible verification (5.32, 5.543 ff., 5.546 ff.). But how can Phenomenology be considered a universally valid science without having any recourse to true and meaningful propositions? Peirce's characterization of first philosophy comes close to the mystical pronouncement made by the early Wittgenstein about that which only "shows" itself, but cannot be said. The difficulty that both thinkers find themselves in consists evidently in the fact that the very conditions for the possibility of sensory experience and of communicating and reaching an understanding about things in the real world by means of language must themselves be described and stated by philosophy, be it Ontology or transcendental philosophy; for Peirce, these conditions are the three fundamental categories of semiotic logic; for Wittgenstein, they are the "internal relations" that define the logical space of language and the world.

The formal conditions of the possibility of meaningful and true speech do not themselves appear, however, to be conceivable as a topic for meaningful and true speech. On the other hand, a private or "single-minded" observation which cannot be communicated obviously cannot serve as the foundation of a phenomenological science. Peirce, just like Wittgenstein, seems to me to have here uncovered a problem that in fact goes beyond the realm of a logic of the sciences directed to experience. They have shown the problem of the conditions for the possibility of philosophy to be the problem of reflecting by means of language on the conditions for the possibility of experience posed by language.[82] But the aporia in which Peirce's conception of Phenomenology becomes entangled by standing in an unmediated opposition to his semiotic logic of cognition is actually only an amplification of the aporia in which his semiotic logic already became involved when it exposed the irrational (e.g., the thing-in-itself) as inconceivable but then afterwards contested in principle the possibility of subsuming (*aufhebung*) the Firstness of perception and the Second-ness of confrontation with facts under the Thirdness of rational mediation. Hence, for those who still take systematic philosophy seriously, especially if such philosophy is to be able to provide a jus-tification of its own method, this sheds light on the theoretical need for a critically renewed Hegelianism.

D. Mathematical Logic as the Formal Condition for the Possibility of Philosophy

According to Jürgen von Kempski, Peirce produced a counterpart to Kant's "metaphysical deduction" of the categories using his formal logic of relations or, more specifically, by applying this logic of rela-tions to his discovery of "rhemata" (what Russell termed "proposi-tional functions"); but, Kempski thinks, Peirce gave up this deduction of the categories in 1903 in favor of Phenomenology because he was unable in the absence of the guidance provided by the transcendental synthesis of apperception to solve the subordinate problem of a "transcendental deduction" of the categories.[83] Kempski overlooks, however, that by 1903 Peirce is not in any way conceiving Phenome-nology as prior to logic as such; rather, he divides logic in two and inserts Phenomenology between the two parts.[84] In the classification of sciences from 1902–3 Phenomenology is presupposed not by the "formal" logic of relations, but only by the semiotic logic of inquiry, where, on my view, we can find Peirce's counterpart to the "transcen-dental deduction" of the categories.[85] But Phenomenology itself as first philosophy presupposes mathematics, in which Peirce now also includes the formal logic of relations.[86] And it can be conclusively shown that the architectonic of the foundational relationship among metaphysics, the semiotic logic of cognition, Phenomenology, and what Peirce terms the "mathematics of logic" continues to focus in Peirce's late work as a whole upon the problem of the connection be-tween the "metaphysical deduction" of the origin of the categories from the "universal logical functions of thought" and the "transcen-dental deduction" of the objective validity of the categories.[87]

    Peirce explains why philosophy and Phenomenology in particular presuppose the "mathematics of logic":

This science of Phenomenology is in my view the most primal of all the positive sciences. That is, it is not based, as to its principles, upon any other *positive science*. . . . [Phenomenology] nevertheless must, if it is to be properly grounded, be made to depend upon the Conditional or Hypothetical Science of *Pure Mathematics*, whose only aim is to discover not how things actually are, but how they might be supposed to be, if not in our universe, then in some other. A Phenomenology which does not reckon with pure mathematics, a science hardly come to years of discretion when Hegel wrote, will be the same pitiful club-footed affair that Hegel produced. [5.39–40]

Here it becomes more evident than before why Peirce considers the reflective conception of Phenomenology as a science of consciousness' experience of itself to be an unacceptable limitation of first philosophy's field of vision. Peirce not only wants to rescue possible experience as experience of *esse in futuro* from Hegel's standpoint, in which such being is *aufgehoben* at the end of world history; he also wants in his Phenomenology to take account from the beginning of all possible experiences in possible worlds by stepping back from the real world. But for this there evidently must be some guideline for phenomenological insight, and this is to be provided by mathematics as the science of the formal structure of possible worlds. Mathematics is the final formal condition for the possibility of all phenomenological vision because it is concerned solely with "creations of our own minds" (5.166), and thereby also with the conditions of the hypothetical imagination in general. Here Peirce returns again to a Kantian notion and by means of this comes to the old theme of the *mathematicus creator alter deus*, in the spirit of which the modern philosophy of mathematics from Nicolas of Cusa to Leibniz was developed.[88]

But now, with Phenomenology presupposing mathematics as the formal condition for all imagination, we see that Peirce exaggerated when he characterized phenomenological vision as completely without presuppositions and as a completely passive submission to the phenomena.[89] In fact, Peirce offers the following introduction to his Phenomenology in 1905 in "The Basis of Pragmatism":

We find then *a priori* that there are three categories of undecomposable elements to be expected in the phaneron: those which are simply positive totals, those which involve dependence but not combination, those which involve combination.

Now let us turn to the phaneron and see what we find in fact.[90]

Here Peirce declares quite clearly that before Phenomenology can begin as the first positive science to describe phenomena, it must presuppose an a priori derivation of the three fundamental categories. In fact, the presupposition in question is that derivation of Firstness, Secondness, and Thirdness from the logic of relations which Peirce presented in its conclusive form in 1885 and whose use of propositional functions Kempski has characterized as the counterpart of Kant's "metaphysical deduction."[91] The point of this deduction *more mathematico* lies in the fact that exactly three categories are necessary and sufficient. Peirce justifies them as follows: "While it is impossible to form a genuine three by any modification of the pair, without introducing something of a different nature from the unit and the pair, four, five, and every higher number can be formed by mere complications of threes" (1.363; cf. 1.369 ff. and 1.515).

How can Peirce prove this? In 1885 he offers a diagrammatic illustration in the form of this figure:

If the termini of the logic of relations are drawn as roads that turn back on themselves, then "no combination of roads without forks can have more than two termini; but any number of termini can be connected by roads which nowhere have a knot of more than three ways" (1.371).

The conceptual interpretation that Peirce offers in 1890 is more radical: "Indeed, the very idea of a combination involves that of thirdness, for a combination is something which is what it is owing to the parts which it brings into mutual relationship" (1.363; cf. 1.515, from 1896). If we accept this, then the modern logistic reduction of triadic relations to dyadic ones can be readily refuted, because in this case the reduction is possible only in an analysis which leads to elements *and a relation that connects them.*[92] On the other hand, every relation that is greater than triadic can be constructed by combining triads. Peirce exemplifies this deduction of the necessity and completeness of his table of categories by means of, among other things, the examples "A gives B to C" and "A sells C to B for the price D." The first example cannot be reduced to the two dyadic relations "A parts with C" and "B receives C." The second example, however, can be reduced to "A makes with C a certain transaction, which we may name E; and second, that this transaction E is a sale of B for the price of D" (1.363; cf. 1.371).

One could object generally that Peirce's assumption that Thirdness is found here in the form of combination introduces a philosophical interpretation into the method of mathematics and then derives it, dressed as a result, from an analysis of mathematics. Indeed, it is not difficult to recognize that the characteristic point of Peirce's doctrine of categories is brought into play in his concept of "combination": the idea of the triadic nature of all mental operations, which Peirce had first recognized by understanding the cognitive relation in semiotic terms.

The most impressive examples of the irreducibility of Thirdness to Secondness and Firstness that Peirce has to offer are provided, therefore, by his criticisms of the usual "reduction" in naturalistic philosophies of mental phenomena in the broadest sense. For instance, it can be shown in light of Peirce's doctrine of categories that consciousness of something, as a phenomenon of knowledge, cannot be reduced to sense data (Hume's "impression") or to a dyadic subject-object relation (such as the ego's confrontation with the resistance to the will provided by "brute facts") or to a mere coincidence of sensory qualities and an actual meeting with the outer world (see 5.90). The triadic cognitive relation can be established only by the mediation of an object in the outer world by a sign function that defines the object in some way as something for an interpreting consciousness.

Compared to immediate sense experience, be it as a quality of experience or as an encounter here and now with the non-ego, even the mere intention of something, immanent in language as sign mediation, is nevertheless already potential cognition. In order to become actual knowledge, that is, in order to become a true representation, neither "experience" nor even an idea (*Vorstellung*) of the linguistically intended fact in the consciousness of the one possessing this knowledge is required.[93] The knowing "subject" in cognition understood as true representation is, rather, the communication community of inquirers; or, strickly speaking—in terms of Fallibilism—the "unlimited community"; or, practically speaking—in terms of Critical Common-sensism—the community of experts competent in each particular field. Of course, the intersubjective process of inference or interpretation is itself not sufficient to explain how we arrive at a true representation or how such a representation becomes accepted; here Peirce goes beyond the Rationalism of his first period by introducing Secondness and Firstness. To this end qualitative perceptions and enumerable confrontations with facts by individual conscious minds are necessary. Their experiences cannot be *aufgehoben* by rational mediation, according to Peirce, but must rather be taken in a sense from the Firstness and Secondness of pure sensory experience by means of the iconic and indexical functions of language, and introduced into the Thirdness of symbolic representation so as to provide information for abductive and inductive inferences; in this way they contribute to cognition as true sign representation.

Examples like the ones I have just outlined show the fruitfulness of Peirce's categorial analysis, but these illustrations have, of course, overstepped the bounds of a formal or mathematical logic of relations; in the sense of Peirce's classification of the sciences they would have to be counted as belonging to Phenomenology. Nevertheless, it is not inessential, let alone meaningless, that in 1903 Peirce concluded that the formal condition for the possibility of philosophy—as the phenomenological analysis of categories—could be found in the development of the formal, mathematical, logic of relations, a field in which he had himself since 1870 made the most important contributions to the development of modern logic in the narrow sense of the term.[94] This can be elucidated best of all by reference to the chief example of Peirce's Phenomenology, his analysis of the sign function. In 1867 in the "New List of Categories" he had derived the necessity of the three transcendental categories (in a way analogous to Kant's transcendental deduction) from the necessity of sign representation, as the analogue of Kant's transcendental synthesis of apperception. Peirce's later use of the logic of relations to formulate these categories put him in the opposite position of being able to subsume all possible relations, including the sign relation, under the three irreducible classes of relations. The advantages for the phenomenological analysis of the sign function that are provided by the guidelines of the logic of relations can be briefly summarized here (see 5.73–76).

Peirce distinguishes formally between genuine and degenerate dyadic and triadic relations. The former are so constituted that the individual correlates remain subjects of the relation in question only if the existence of the other subjects is presupposed. The latter do not fulfill this condition. A genuine dyad in this sense is therefore, for example, the relation "brother of." An example of a degenerate relation is "as blue as."[95] In this sense, triads can be singly or doubly degenerate, depending upon whether within the triad there are only dyadic relations, which are independent from the existence of the third member, or whether all the individual members retain their characteristics as members of a triadic relation independently of the existence of the other members (1.366–67, 1.370–72). By applying this aspect of the logic of relations to the analysis of the sign function Peirce arrives at certain noteworthy phenomenological results.

The sign relation (representation, signhood, semiosis) as such is fundamentally triadic. That is, crudely stated, it consists of the sign in the narrow sense of the word, the designated object, and the interpretant. Even such a lapidary statement has significant, critical consequences—for example, in regard to the semantic theory developed by logical Positivism, as I will show later. The sign relation is a genuine triad, but only insofar as it is a symbolic one in the strict sense of the term. To this extent, the sign relation in human language is in principle a genuine triad, with limitations that will have to be discussed later. Moreover, there are phenomena outside human language that attain a degenerate sign character when they are introduced into the linguistic interpretation of the world.[96] In this way individual natural phenomena can figure for us as images (icons) or structural models of other, perhaps more complicated, natural phenomena. We can also artificially produce such images or models.[97] These are cases of a doubly degenerate sign function, since these individual images or models retain their character as potential models, independently of the existence of their correlates or of human interpreters. That is, they are potential images or models solely on the basis of their qualitative features or Firstness (see 5.73–74). In addition to such doubly degenerate signs there are also singly degenerate signs outside the sphere of language, that is, in nature and in the technology that man creates as a kind of "second nature." Peirce calls these signs "indices." Their potential sign function is based upon an actual, dynamic, physical relationship to natural processes. But that means they retain their sign character independently of the actual existence of the interpretant as the third member of the sign relation, yet presuppose the actual existence of the correlates of the dyadic relation. Examples of indices outside the sphere of language include smoke as an indication of fire, the weathervane, the beat of our pulse, "symptoms" in the medical sense and in that of the study of expression, and the technically simulatable processes of "information" assumed in cybernetics.[98]

Compared to the examples of the iconic and indexical functions that we have considered, human language is distinguished, as I have already indicated, by the fact that it is based fundamentally upon symbols. These possess a significative function established only by virtue of a conventional interpretation based upon a previous implicit or explicit communicative understanding or agreement about the use of signs in the linguistic community as a "community of interpretation."[99] However, Peirce also shows that if language were to consist only of symbols, then it could not fulfill its function as a means for reaching a communicative understanding [*Verständigungsfunktion*] because it could not be used by human beings.[100] There must also be a kind of presymbolic meaning function, or at least one that is not exclusively conventional, which brings the degenerate iconic and indexical sign functions into play within language or, rather, the use of language. Hence, in order for even simple (monadic) predicates of living language to function in perceptual judgments, they must also have an iconic, picturing, qualitative, expressive character, which also characterizes the aesthetic side of language.[101] Relational predicates function, moreover, as icons in the sense of serving to copy the structure of reality, and they are therefore able to establish language's connection with mathematical diagrams and technical models.[102] In addition, the subject terms of linguistic statements must be able to function directly or indirectly as "indices" which act in a way to attach language, where its usage depends upon the situation, to the sensory reality experienced here and now in concrete individual facts.[103] This latter function is assumed by pronouns (immediately by demonstrative pronouns, mediately by relative pronouns and by logical quantifiers which Peirce calls "selective pronouns"), by adverbial and prepositional expressions of time and space orientation, by proper names, and also, indirectly, by the general names in the subject function.[104]

But even independently of this need for a mediation between language and our experience of situations, which is met by introducing the iconic and indexical functions into the symbolic function, an analysis of the genuine, triadic sign relation in terms of the logic of relations provides us with results that are of the greatest critical relevance for the philosophy of language.

For Peirce, as I have already briefly indicated, in a genuine triad (1) the individual members of the relation cannot function independently of the existence and function of the other members, and (2) a dyadic relation between any arbitrary pair of the relation's members cannot hold independently of the existence and function of the third member of the relation. Applied to the sign relation this means that (1) the three members of semiosis, the sign in the narrow sense (the material vehicle of the sign function), designated objects (*designata* or *denotata*), and interpretants are what they are only by virtue of the nature of semiosis as a unified triadic function; and (2) the three possible dyadic relations within the sign function are founded in each case by the missing third member. That is, the relation between the sign and the designated object is founded by the interpretant, the relation between the interpretant (e.g., human consciousness) and the object is founded by mediation through the sign, and, finally, the relation between the sign and its interpretant is founded by the existence of the object or objects that define the extensional value of the sign.[105]

This analysis must be carried out further in at least one regard. The "interpretant," the characteristic concept of Peirce's semiotic which supports the pragmatic theory of meaning, must itself also be analysed in the light of the three fundamental categories. This results, according to Peirce, in the ability to distinguish among the "emotional" or "immediate" interpretant (the characteristic quality of meaning in the use of language), the "energetic" or "dynamic" interpretant (the individual psychophysical effect of communication), the "normal" or "logical" interpretant (the normatively correct conceptual interpretation), and, finally, the "ultimate logical interpretant" as a behavioral rule or habit.[106]

The critical relevance of this categorial analysis of the sign function using the logic of relations can be shown in a very impressive way, it seems to me, by turning to the so-called logical analysis of language found in Russell's logical Atomism, in Wittgenstein's *Tractatus,* and in the subsequent work of logical Positivism. We should note at the outset that, in the light of Peirce's semiotic, the function of an uninterpreted calculus of signs is equivalent to that of a doubly degenerate sign. To be more precise, it corresponds to the function of an iconic model which could serve to "picture" structures. A simulation of language[107] using such a calculus of signs would be conceivable only if we could formulate a universally valid picturing guide for the relationship between a universal calculus of signs and the world such that every possible indexical and symbolic function of language would be established a priori by the iconic picturing function of the calculus of signs. In other words, if a language system could be founded solely upon the doubly degenerate sign function of the icon— independently, that is, of the indexical function's relation to a situation and the symbolic function's relation to an interpretant—then it would be an unequivocal and universal instrument of signification and could be used as such at any time. This conception is in fact characteristic of the central idea in Leibniz's notion of a *lingua universalis* as a *calculus ratiocinator* and *characteristica universalis,* an idea which Wittgenstein worked out in his *Tractatus* to its final paradoxical conclusion: the impossibility of reflection and, hence, the impossibility of communication about the language that pictures the logical structure of the world. If this hidden metaphysics of the isomorphic relation and the diagrammatic view of the sign form which goes along with it (Leibniz-Peirce) are traced to the iconic function in Peirce's sense, then we see that the calculus of signs constitutes just a partial model of language.[108] It is a model in which the sign vehicle's syntactic relationships picture the logical relations of an axiomatic system and so guarantee the consistency of language. But this is only a partial model because it can be interpreted only with the help of the language that we find already in use.

Concealed in the concept of the interpretation of an icon, however, is an ambiguity which should be analyzed in the light of Peirce's triad of the iconic, indexical, and symbolic function. To begin with, interpretation can mean merely discerning a picturing relationship, which in an extreme case could be isomorphic, between an iconic model and a structured object. But in this case we have a doubly degenerate mode of interpretation, as we see from the fact that it is only on the basis of this relationship that an imaginary object can also function as the model for the interpretation of an icon. The existence of a real model cannot be discerned solely on the basis of the iconic function. For example, in order for a portrait to be interpreted as that of a living human being it is necessary that someone be led through the portrait to a certain person and say something like "That's him." In this case the iconic function of the portrait (Firstness) is integrated into the actual sign function by being conjoined (Thirdness) with the indexical function; this function connects the sign with reality as it exists here and now (Secondness) by means of the interpretative function carried out by the person who is referred by the portrait to the person portrayed in it. The theoretical interpretation of the universal calculus of language that is implicit in the ontology or, more exactly, in the onto-semantics of the *Tratatus logico-philosophicus* seems to me to be equivalent to a doubly degenerate iconic interpretation because it fails to take the indexical function into account. This can be seen, for example, in the fact that the young Wittgenstein simply postulates verification as the criterion of meaning, taking it to be implied by a correct understanding of the "logical form" of language and the world, without ever proving the existence of "elementary propositions" which picture "elementary facts," or even just the existence of "names" which designate elementary "objects."

However, if an interpretation of the sign calculus does take the indexical function of language into account, but conceives its relationship to the picturing function as independent of the interpretative function, then we have what, in Peirce's analysis, would be called simply a degenerate interpretation. Such a view, in fact, seems to me to be tacitly assumed in neopositivistic semantics and to have been a characteristic of that position until Charles Morris drew attention to three-dimensional semiotic. After that, the insufficiency of a purely syntactic analysis of language (regarding language as iconic) was, to be sure, quickly recognized, especially since it contradicted the empiricist ideal of philosophical analysis. But this empiricist ideal itself then enticed positivists into projecting the so-called semantic interpretation as a dyadic relation, in the sense of the sign system's relationship to the facts we can experience with the senses. A sign system interpreted semantically in this way was supposed to be a logically and empirically reliable language of science that would be somehow subsequently adopted and put to use.

The difficulty with such a reduction of interpretation to the conjunction of the iconic and indexical functions had been illustrated earlier in Bertrand Russell's "logical Atomism," in his attempt to understand first proper names and then deictic pronouns as "logical names" that attach to things in a way fundamentally independent of the actual interpretation situation. Together with the depiction of their external relations (of "facts") in the proposition and the syntactically pictured logical form of language, these were to provide a ready-to-use semantic system. This same difficulty recurs in Neopositivism's constructive semantics in the problem of "protocol sentences" which, on the basis of their picturing structure (Firstness) and the introduction of identifying functions (Secondness), are supposed to show that certain real things here and now "are such as these assert."[109]

Faced with the aporetic situation in neopositivistic semantics, which had already been overcome by Karl Popper's calling attention to the fundamental dependence of "basic statements" on conventions, Charles Morris introduced Peirce's analysis of the triadic sign function into his own three-dimensional semiotic.[110] Here the point was that the task of founding abstract, one-dimensional "syntactics" and abstract two-dimensional semantics was assumed by the three-dimensional study of "pragmatics," which is directed to concrete semiosis.[111] The inability to grasp the triadic character of the sign function, which characterized the neopositivistic analysis of language, is still evident in Carnap's reception of Morris's semiotic. The semantic, designating relation is founded upon the pragmatic dimension of signs by the interpretation given to these signs through their use, just as this interpretation itself becomes possible only through the sign's designating function and depends, in the way that an understanding of the world does, upon the mediating function of the sign. For Carnap, however, this dimension is supposed to be an object of empirical study (object language) and is bracketed out of philosophical (metalinguistic) analysis as if the philosopher's attempt to reach an understanding of his own terms (*Selbstverständigung*) when he construes a semantic system has nothing to do with the interpretative use of signs.[112] Even worse, this is as if the communicative exchange (*Verständigung*) with others, which is a necessary part of a thinker's attempt to reach a clear understanding of his language (*Selbstverständigung*) and also a process engaged in by those scientists who utilize and test a reconstructed scientific language, could ever be the object of a purely empirical, behavioristic science.[113]

Like Peirce's theory of inquiry, the modern, neopositivistically inspired logic of science starts with semiotic or linguistic analysis (in contrast with the older psychologistic-empiricist and transcendental "theories of knowledge"), but its failure to recognize fully the triadic nature of the sign function has a significant effect on its basic approach. This can be seen in, for example, attempts that have been made to understand the phenomenon of science using only syntactic or semantic logical theories of systems in association with confirmation theories.[114] In order to avoid the problems of transcendental philosophy, an approach which such theories regard as antiquated, man as the practicing, questioning, and interpreting subject engaged in scientific research is now declared to be an empirical object for scientific research, but we cannot ask about the subject engaged in science as a subject. From Peirce's point of view this means that man no longer carries out the triadic function of interpretation for which he depends upon intersubjective communication in the community, a function whose aim is to transform scientific knowledge into self-controlled behavior or praxis. Instead, man is the object in a dyadic system which seems to presuppose no "interpretant" at all. Among the most serious consequences of such an illegitimate "degeneration" of cognition's triadic structure is, I believe, its elimination of the entire field of intersubjective communicative understanding as a respectable problem in the philosophy of science; it also, of course, eliminates the hermeneutic disciplines—the traditional *Geisteswissenschaften*—which operate within the dimension of intersubjective, communicative understanding.[115]

I do not want to hide the fact that the form in which Charles Morris applied Peirce's triadic semiotic within the unified science program helped to conceal the breadth of implications in the difference between a triadic and a dyadic basis for the analysis of thought. Morris himself believed it possible to understand the triadic function of man's sign-mediated behavior towards real objects, the interpretation of signs through intended objects, and the designative function resulting from the interpretation of man's use of signs, by regarding them all behavioristically, treating them as a topic of empirical observation and description. Yet it is clear that a strictly behavioristic description of interpretation behavior must reduce it to dyadic relations like those which exist between objects of knowledge. We can, for example, observe in the behaviorist sense the stimulus-reaction relation between sign vehicles and what occurs in the actions of human organisms,[116] but we cannot observe the triadic relation in the interpretation of an intention communicated by signs, the relation by which the one receiving the information is directed, as a subject like the one from whom the information was received, by means of the sign to the intended fact. This triadic relation characteristic of all mental acts can be "understood" only on the basis of at least virtual participation in communication. But therefore this triadic relation demands a philosophy of science that does not eliminate the traditional problem of subjectivity, but rather renews it as the problem of the human communication community.

The behavioristic reduction of the pragmatic dimension of semiotic is very closely connected with the fact that Morris does not distinguish, as Peirce does, between the "dynamic interpretant" and the "logical interpretant," but instead reduces the latter to the former.[117] This involves a category mistake or, in Peirce's terms, a reduction of Thirdness, in the form of interpretation that is fundamentally open to the future, to a degenerate mode of interpretation as Secondness. This can be seen best of all by trying as a participant in communication to apply Morris's formula for this reduction to the spoken utterances which we hear and the meaning of which we are to interpret. We can do this through the statement "The meaning of what I hear lies in the behavior that will be observable in me as the effect of these signs." In order to make any use of this definition a participant in communication would have to be able from the start to experience his own act of interpretation as a fact (Secondness), even though it comes about only subsequently by his own attempt to reach an understanding (*Selbstverständigung*) in the general context of intersubjective communicative understanding (*Verständigung*). He must be in a position to stand outside the continuum of intersubjective communicative understanding and praxis and nonetheless be able to understand.

This contradiction only seems to be less severe when it is pointed out that Morris's theory concentrates on the generalized description of the normal meaning of signs, aided by the description of the average behavior of sign users. This is because we cannot discern the rules of sign-mediated behavior simply by external observation and a statistical summary of the characteristics we observe.[118] In positive terms, even an external description of sign-mediated behavior itself presupposes a kind of intersubjective communicative understanding—a kind of deficient mode of communication—between the investigator doing the describing and his "object." This deficient mode of communication in the quasi-objective description of average pragmatic sign interpretation is methodologically important for linguistics, but we must return to intersubjective communicative understanding, which is the basis of interpretation, as soon as we are faced with the hermeneutic task of interpreting certain utterances (e.g., texts from the history of culture). In such cases we are not interested in the average effects of symbols on the behavior of the receiver, which, as in the case of difficult concepts or those burdened by the preconceptions of a world view, might quite easily stem from a collective misunderstanding. Our interest is directed, rather, to the "logical interpretants" normatively involved in symbols. The participant in communication or the person who has to reach an understanding of the meaning of his own thoughts can conceive of these, as Peirce does, as the general rule that should be established—or, in the case of the right understanding, *would* be established—as a habit (the "ultimate logical interpretant" is a habit) through deliberate, self-controlled behavior in each and every interpreter.[119]

The nonreductive conception of interpretation sketched above treats it as the constitutive element in the triadic structure of the sign function or representation, but this implies for Peirce that we must postulate an infinite, open future, because this alone is capable of realizing the universality of meaning in practice (8.208). This is the point in Peirce's late system at which Thirdness calls for a transition from the guidelines of mathematics as the logic of relations to the guidelines of the mathematics of continua.[120] We can characterize this transition as the formal condition for the possibility of that metaphysical conception of Peirce's later system to which he gave the name "Synechism."[121] We will return to this later in the discussion of the metaphysics of evolution,[122] but this reference should be enough to shed light on the place that Peirce's 1902–3 classification of the sciences gave to mathematics as the most abstract science. This brings us back again to architectonic as the central problem connecting Peirce's later conception of his system with Kant's metaphysical or transcendental deduction of the categories.

In 1896 Peirce referred to his use of the logic of relations in his deduction of the fundamental categories as the "logic of mathematics," rather than the "mathematics of logic." The relationship between this formal classification of categories and its use in metaphysics was obviously so conceived that the new science of Phenomenology had to be inserted between formal logic and metaphysics: in this way the "metaphysical deduction" of the origin of the categories a priori from the universal, logical functions of thought could be linked with the "transcendental deduction" of the objective validity of the categories. For this task Kant had introduced the "schematism of pure understanding" as the faculty which introduces concepts into a sensible form.[123] In 1896 Peirce wrote: "The metaphysical categories of quality, fact, and law, being categories of the matter of phenomena, do not precisely correspond with the logical categories of the monad, the dyad, and the polyad or higher set, since these are the categories of the forms of experience" (1.452).

I have attempted in the foregoing to illustrate how Peirce's mathematical derivation of the formal categories of Firstness, Secondness, and Thirdness was applied, with the help of Phenomenology, to semiosis or the function of the sign, which itself is the transcendental condition for the possibility of any kind of empirical knowledge of reality in metaphysics or the various individual sciences. The architectonic of Peirce's system—an idea taken from Kant—was thereby completed for Peirce in 1902 in the form of a hierarchy of sciences built upon the principle that the more abstract sciences are presupposed by the more concrete ones.[124]

However, Peirce only seemed with this principle of classification to have found for his system the noncircular basis that he evidently had in mind.[125] The old, quasi-transcendental, philosophical conception of a derivation of the conditions for the possibility and validity of all knowledge from the "highest point" of semiotic representation remained in unmitigated conflict with the system's linear construction, based solely upon the "metaphysical deduction" (in Kant's sense) of the categories from formal logic, that is, from the mathematics of relations. I have already pointed out the tension that exists in Phenomenology between the need for phenomenological reflection on semiosis and the necessity of justifying phenomenological cognition with the aid of the semiotic logic of cognition. This tension between correlative foundational claims is repeated in a still more complicated way in the relationship between philosophy and mathematics. Peirce explicitly granted that, by virtue of its *logica utens*, mathematics as the "science that draws necessary conclusions" is prior to all philosophy as *logica docens* and therefore cannot be founded by it.[126] But this assertion is itself clearly a *philosophical* justification of the primacy of mathematics. In fact, it merely reinforces Peirce's 1869 insight that the attempt to give a deductive foundation to logic must result in a *petitio principii*, since every deductive foundation of logic must already presuppose logic.[127] But this insight does not hinder Peirce from taking mathematics—as the science that practices the logical thought presupposed by all other sciences and unfolds all of its possibilities—as the topic of philosophical reflection on the conditions for its possibility and validity, just as he did with logic in 1869.

In doing this Peirce not only reflects on the fact that mathematics, as the creative unfolding of *logica utens* in hypothetical imagination, provides the formal conditions for all sciences, including philosophy; he also considers that mathematical cognition, in turn, implies Phenomenology's pure intuition as diagrammatic reasoning (5.148–49, 5.162 ff.) and, finally, that mathematics conducts experiments with the aid of diagrammatic construction and observation in the imaginative sphere of the possible (5.162 ff., 3.363, 3.556). To this extent its hypotheses are subject to the normative logic of inquiry, especially to the pragmatic critique of meaning using operational and verificationist criteria, just as are the assertions of all the other sciences (except, perhaps, those of Phenomenology).[128] Peirce would hardly deny in the end that mathematical knowledge, which can be verified operationally, also contributes to establishing human habits whose final metaphysical significance lies in the progressive rationalization of the universe in line with the fourth grade of the clearness of ideas that he had postulated in 1902.

Here, at last, it becomes evident that the architectonic of Peirce's philosophy as he unfolded it in 1902–3 in his mature conception of his system can only be very superficially and artificially characterized through the Comte-inspired linear scheme of a hierarchy of the sciences. At a deeper level of its *logica utens*, it continues to stand under the influence of the Kantian heritage of tension between the derivation of categories from formal logic (for Peirce, ultimately from mathematics) and their derivation from the theory of knowledge (for

Peirce, from Phenomenology and semiotic). In addition, the heuristic application of the three fundamental categories in Peirce's characterization of the sciences, with whose help the content of the categories is derived or developed, results for Peirce finally in a de facto combination of perspectives which sees everything presupposed in everything else, for example, Firstness in the perception of Thirdness as concrete reasonableness and Thirdness in the rational mediation found in perception. Perhaps one could attempt to interpret this particular feature of Peirce's "system" (it would be better to say Peirce's "systematic" philosophy) as itself also an expression of his idea of the absolute continuum, that is, of his "Synechism," which many Peirce scholars wish to regard as the main idea of his mature thought.[129]

This vague speculation brings us to the end of this exposition of Peirce's late systematic conception. In the following chapters, I interpret selected texts from the last two phases of Peirce's philosophy, taking them in chronological order in the light of that view of the whole which I have established.[130]

The Third Period:
From Pragmatism to the Metaphysics
of Evolution (ca. 1885–98)

A. Overture from 1885: The Defense of Meaning-Critical
Realism against Royce's Absolute Idealism
and Peirce's Program of a Metaphysics of Evolution

Our division of Peirce's development into periods suggests a comparison between his review of Josiah Royce's *Religious Aspect of Philosophy*, which Peirce's editors date 1885, and the important Berkeley review from 1871 which mediates between Peirce's first and second periods and contains the first formulation of the pragmatic maxim. The external difference between these is that the Royce review, which stands at the beginning of the third period, was not accepted for publication, a fact that can shed light upon the reviewer's altered relationship to the academic world after the end of his university career.[1] What is more essential for us, however, is a comparison of the two reviews from the viewpoint of the history of philosophy.

In both cases we are faced with a confrontation between a supporter of a theistic, idealistic metaphysics and Peirce's early meaning-critical Realism, the central approach of which stands as the point of contention. Peirce's, whose stance is based upon a radicalization of Kant's fundamental idea in the transcendental analytic (limitation of the meaningful application of concepts about the real to possible experience), is forced to come to grips in both reviews with idealistic positions that often come disconcertingly close to his own and cannot be overcome in any case without leading meaning-critical Realism itself into a new phase of critical self-reflection that results in each case in a new philosophical program.

The 1871 Berkeley review forced Peirce (1) to clarify the difference between a nominalistic reduction of reality to actual, present experience and a reduction of reality to possible experience by a realist theory of universals, and (2) to suggest a critique of meaning as an alternative to Berkeley's critique of the meaning of concepts that cannot be reduced to sense data. This alternative permits us to explicate differences between general ideas by means of differences in the rules of practical behavior and thereby to lay claim to a real applicability for general ideas (8.33). Herein lay the program of "Pragmatism." However, as Peirce's treatment of the diamond example in the logic of 1873 and in "How to Make Our Ideas Clear" shows, Pragmatism's virtual overcoming of the Berkeleian form of Nominalism and Idealism was not yet sure of itself.[2] In the 1885 Royce review the topic was also, at bottom, that of overcoming Idealism by means of a meaning-critical Realism which reconciles the idea that the concept of reality is limited to the sphere of possible experience with the idea that the reality of the real is independent of its being actually experienced. Peirce's aim here is, of course, to defend his position against the attack made, from the standpoint of absolute Idealism, by Josiah Royce (1855–1916), the former Johns Hopkins student who had advanced in 1882 to the position of Harvard professor.[3]

Royce's absolute Idealism was essentially inspired by his years as a student in Germany and was developed through constant critical discussions with his Harvard colleague William James.[4] Royce's religious, speculative metaphysics became one of the classic positions of American philosophy. Later it came more and more to be the decisive discussion partner for Peirce.[5] Bishop Berkeley, who represented the English variation of Idealism, had significantly influenced Peirce's creation of Pragmatism; but after 1885 it was Royce's thought that was important in provoking the further development of Peirce's philosophy as a religiously influenced metaphysics of evolution intended to absorb the results of the pragmatic approach to the philosophy of science, as well as the results of the empirical sciences themselves, especially biology. After about 1900 Royce, in turn, came increasingly under the influence of Peirce, who encouraged him, with astonishing success, to study modern mathematical logic.[6] Royce's idea of the "community of interpreters," expounded in the second volume of his last work, *The Problem of Christianity* (1913), provided perhaps the most important single contribution to the extension and development in hermeneutic and social philosophical terms of Peirce's semiotic.[7]

Even in his 1885 review Peirce confronted Royce's idealistic dialectics with his logic and semiotic. The problem here was not really the principle of the triadic nature of sign interpretation as mediation. Royce, as a Hegelian, of course implicitly took it into account already, and in 1913 he would explicitly develop a foundation for it, using

Peirce's logic of relations. The problem was, rather, the dyadic, pre-cognitive experience of the "Outward Clash" with the world, the re-sistance of the non-ego to the ego's will, that is, to that for which, according to Peirce, "indices" stand in the triadic interpretative func-tion of language. In 1885 Peirce said that Hegel "almost completely ignores" this principle, that it "enters into all cognition" as a "direct consciousness of hitting and of getting hit" and "serves to make it [cognition] mean something real" (8.41). Peirce pointed out that even Kant, when he noted the necessity of having spatial and temporal in-tuition (*Anschauung*), took into account the principle that the real object or experience here and now cannot be distinguished from other objects merely by means of concepts (8.41). Moreover, "recent studies in formal logic" have also shown that the real subject of the proposi-tion does not have to be designated through general concepts; instead, "besides general terms, two other kinds of signs are perfectly indis-pensable in all reasoning."[8]

Peirce is referring here to the three kinds of signs that he had distinguished from one another as early as 1867: symbols (for gen-eral concepts), indices ("whose relation to their objects consists in a correspondence in fact" (1.558), and icons. As his footnote (8.41 n. 8) indicates, Peirce includes under "recent studies in formal logic" the discovery of quantifiers by his student O. H. Mitchell in 1883 and his own semiotic application of this discovery in his 1885 "Contribution to the Philosophy of Notation."[9] Peirce appears on this occasion to have recognized for the first time the whole range of the indexical function's applications in relating general concepts of knowledge by means of language to the individuals given in a situation. In his "Con-tribution" from 1885 he writes:

The actual world cannot be distinguished from the world of imagination by any description. Hence the need of pronoun and indices, and the more complicated the subject the greater the need for them. The introduction of indices into the system of algebra of logic is the greatest merit of Mr. Mitchell's system. He writes F_1 to mean that the proposition F is true of every object in the universe, and F_u to mean that the same is true of some object. This distinction can only be made in some such way as this. [3.363]

This observation, that the individual can be identified in a situa-tion as real, but cannot be designated through symbols (i.e., signs for general concepts), yet can be so designated through indices and can in this way be made the subject of a true or a false statement, is a conclusion of the "logical studies" at Johns Hopkins University. It permits Peirce, as I have already indicated, to reject as logically anti-quated Royce's main argument against meaning-critical Realism—his proof from the existence of error of the existence of an absolute, reality-postulating mind.[10]

According to Peirce: "Dr. Royce's main argument . . . is drawn from the existence of error. Namely, the subject of an erroneous proposition could not be identified with the subject of the corresponding true proposition, except by being completely known, and in that knowledge no error would be possible. The truth must, therefore, be present to the actual consciousness of a living being" (8.41). Peirce's reply to this argument is as follows:

If the subject of discourse had to be distinguished from other things, if at all, by a general term, that is, by its peculiar characters, it would be quite true that its complete segregation would require a full knowledge of its characters and would preclude ignorance. But the index, which in point of fact alone can designate the subject of a proposition, designates it without implying any characters at all. A blinding flash of lightning forces my attention and directs it to a certain moment of time with an emphatic "Now!" Directly following it, I may judge that there will be a terrific peal of thunder, and if it does not come I acknowledge an error. [8.41]

Here Peirce obviously uses the index "now" in the sense of "here-now-this" as the designation for an individual, real object or subject of a sentence. He does not simply assume that space and time are *principium individuationis*, because he knows that "one instant of time is, in itself, exactly like any other instant, one point of space like any other point" (8.41). The individuation expressed in the use of indices is dependent upon situations and emerges for Peirce only from an actual collision of the ego's will with the non-ego. For this very reason he is not of the opinion, as Russell was later, that "indices" can function independently of the context of speech as "logical proper names" of unequivocally signified elements of reality in such theoretical atomic statements as "This here next to that there." Peirce's pragmatic semiotic distinguishes itself from such logical Atomism primarily by overcoming its methodological Solipsism. This is something that it has in common with Wittgenstein's theory of language games.

From the standpoint of methodological Solipsism, which Russell upheld in his "principle of acquaintance," an index can by all means be regarded as a univocal designation of a certain particular object, and to this extent it can be regarded as a logical name in the sense of a private language. According to Peirce an index "like a pointing finger exercises a real physiological *force* over the attention, like the power of a mesmerizer, and directs it to a particular object of sense" (8.41). But Peirce knew before Wittgenstein did that a private language is unthinkable because thoughts are not "in me"; rather, I am "in thought" (5.289 n). He knew that a conception of the world and the self established through language, while it necessarily relies upon the deictic identification of experienceable objects in the sense of the category of Secondness, must also be mediated through intersubjectively valid interpretation in the sense of the category of Thirdness.[11] Hence, if the index is to transmit the communicable understanding we have of individual things, then it may not merely express the collision of the ego with the non-ego as a natural event, such as through a scream of pain.[12] Moreover, it may not be isolated as a dyadic relationship in experience as it is conceived in solipsistic Empiricism. Rather, it must be used within the context of the descriptive symbolic function as an example of the way Secondness is included in Thirdness (see 5.448).

Against this background, which Peirce only later considered fully, we can understand his answer to a question he himself proposed, that of *"how* two different men can know they are speaking of the same thing" (8.42). As Aristotle already discerned, the description of characteristic features by means of general concepts must be conducted in this case without thereby replacing the identification of the primarily intended, real subject with the preconceptual deictic function. Peirce writes: "One [of the two communication partners] would say, 'I mean that very brilliant flash which was preceded by three slight flashes, you know'" (8.42). Here we have a way of speaking that is fundamentally enmeshed in situations and not some kind of universally valid definition of individual things capable of grasping everything. Nicolas of Cusa and Leibniz claimed this for God, just as Hegel, Royce, and Bradley claimed it for conceptual knowledge in general. In this way they had to presuppose absolute knowledge for a designation of the real subject of a sentence.

Following such a defense against absolute Idealism, the question naturally arises whether presupposing that cognition is always embedded in a situation and mediated through a precognitive, deictic function permits us still to regard the central postulate of meaning-critical Realism as meaningful at all. This defines the real as that which is cognizable, or, more exactly, as the object of the final opinion of the unlimited communication community of inquirers which would not be bound to a situation.[13] Kant avoided this question by means of his distinction between the thing-in-itself and the world of appearance, but he did this at the price of the paradoxical assumption that the actual object of knowledge is incognizable. Peirce sought to eliminate this nonsensical assumption by means of the meaning-critical distinction between the cognizable and that which is actually known at one time or another (see 5.257). But what meaning does the cognizability of the real have when that which can in fact actually be known at one time or another must be characterized as fundamentally embedded in a situation, owing to the indispensability of the deictic function, and so, to this extent, must be considered not to be a generally valid representation of the real?

What meaning does the concept of possible experience or cognition have in this context? Is it or the concept of the real that it defines ambiguous, depending upon whether we are to think of the real as that which is experienceable here and now or as that which can be known conceptually?

These questions do not yet arise in this urgent form for Peirce in 1885, but after his first rebuttal to Royce's criticisms Peirce addresses them as his most urgent task (8.43 ff.). He wants to show Royce that their two philosophies finally converge, since each maintains "as a theorem that which the other adopts as a definition" (8.41). In fact, Royce asserts as a fact that which Peirce merely assumes in a "would be" definition to be the meaning of the concept of reality, the perfect and complete concept of the real in absolute knowledge. Moreover, Peirce takes as the object of his theory of the possible process of empirical research what Royce assumes as the definition of cognition in the sense of Hegel's "speculative proposition," its principle relationship to the absolutely real. Peirce's comments here are worth noting since they can lead us to a basic distinction between two problems that have been confused by many Peirce scholars.[14] I am referring to the question of a meaning-critical definition of the real in "would be" statements and the question of the theoretically demonstrable existence of the presuppositions of knowledge which are postulated as real, for example, the unlimited community of investigators or unlimited process of inquiry. On my view, after Peirce proves that every attempt to deny the existence of the real world is meaningless,[15] he does not need to make the validity of his definition of the real dependent upon the existence of the unlimited real community of investigators or upon its actually achieving the true opinion.

In the "Logic of 1873" Peirce actually makes this mistake, a reductive fallacy, and becomes involved in a paradoxical interpretation of the diamond example.[16] Later, with the help of his doctrine of categories, he distinguishes between the existence of the real, which can only be factually experienced, and its reality, which can only be interpreted as meaning. He also distinguishes between that which will occur with greater or lesser probability and that which must be postulated in the sense of a "would be" if the meaning of reality or even just a real characteristic of a certain real object is to be defined through possible experience. However, this distinction itself raises the problem of what significance the meaning-critically appropriate definition of the real has for the logic of empirical research. Expressed in a different way, this is the problem of which theoretical hypotheses can be proposed about the possibility or probability of attaining the ideal goal of knowledge of the real.

Keeping these considerations in mind, I believe that Peirce's reconstruction of his theory of reality and cognition in his review of Royce makes it possible for us to give an immanent, critical interpretation of his thought. For the first time, Peirce seems here prima facie to see the problem of the definition of the real as a problem of a "would be" formulation. His reply to Royce's calling into question of a merely possible judge of true and false "who *would* see the error, *if* he were there" (8.41) shows, however, that Peirce has not yet attained complete clarity about the logical relationship between a definition of reality and a theory of the actually possible process of cognition. In accordance with the distinction between a definition and a theory, Peirce distinguishes next between the final opinion "which would be sure to result from sufficient investigation" (8.43) and the empirically conditioned circumstance that the final opinion "may possibly, in reference to a given question, never be actually attained, owing to a final extinction of intellectual life or for some other reason" (8.43).

But if we conclude from this that Peirce will now continue to distinguish clearly the definition of reality, in the sense of this "would be" postulate, from the question of the actual attainment of this postulated goal, the following passage proves disappointing. Peirce begins by stressing, against Royce, that the concept of possible knowledge that he uses for the definition of reality is not to be confused with the concept of merely logical possibility. He then ventures everything upon showing, with the help of inductive logic—and that means showing "with the highest degree of empirical confidence"—that questions which are meaningful in the sense of the pragmatic maxim "are susceptible of receiving final solutions" (8.43). Peirce believes that the assumption of the continued existence of a real community of investigators may be regarded as "most certain," independently of the continuation of the human race, insofar as "intellectual life in the universe will never finally cease" (8.43). But then a mathematical consideration, the comparison of the growth rate of the number of questions posed in regard to the capacity to answer them, forces him to the conclusion that an infinitesimal proportion of questions will, in fact, never be answered. And now Peirce believes that he must make a concession: "In that case . . . that conception was rather a faulty one, for while there is a real so far as a question that will get settled goes, there is none for a question that will never be settled; for an unknowable reality is nonsense" (8.43). Faced with this difficulty, Peirce seems to want to call into question even his meaning-critical argumentation against Kant, for he adds: "The non-idealistic reader will start at this last assertion [with his criticisms?]" (8.43).

As a matter of fact, if Peirce's self-interpretation quoted just now were correct, it would presuppose a nominalistic, idealistic definition of reality that reduced the reality of the real, as Berkeley does, to its actually being known.[17] In this case a realist would rightfully reject as insufficient Peirce's definition of reality as possible knowledge. Faced with this state of affairs, the realist would have to feel that Kant's assumption of something real, but fundamentally incognizable, is the more plausible position.[18] But I believe that the actual point of Peirce's "theory of reality" from 1868, the point of his meaning-critical realism, would be missed if we were to accept this alternative. We are not concerned here either with being able to reduce the real to that which is actually known at some time or with having to conceive of a reality that is incognizable in principle. Rather, the point is first to distinguish the normative justification for the definition of the reality of the real, in the sense of a possible counterfactual if-then proposition, from the empirical question, answered hypothetically, of the chances of actually knowing the real. Only after this has been done can we relate these two points of view to one another.

On my view, the goal of the pragmatic attempt to determine the meaning of reality is not to reduce facts to future facts, just as in the diamond example the aim is not to reduce the meaning of hardness as a fact to future facts. The aim, rather, is to determine and precisely state the correct understanding of the meaning of the real as it exists here and now, something that is always already presupposed in a vague form. This is accomplished by means of a thought experiment in which we imagine that the actual process of knowing reality has been carried to an ideal state of completion, just as is called for by the vaguely understood meaning of reality.[19] In other words, the object is to distinguish and mediate between a normative, pragmatic logic for the clarification of meaning and a hypothetical, inductive metaphysics of evolution in which the postulates derived from the normative critique of meaning serve as regulative principles.

Peirce first arrived at the distinction we proposed just now in his classification of the sciences in 1902–3, but it was not until 1905 that he utilized the diamond example, in a way consistent with meaning-critical Realism, to clarify the relationship between the "would be" definition of reality and the facticity of those operations and experiences postulated within it.[20] In his review of Royce in 1885 Peirce was satisfied to point out in terms of common-sense Pragmatism that on the basis of our practical experience we "have to proceed as if all [meaningful questions] were answerable."[21] This in fact amounts to admitting the definition of the real as an object of absolute knowledge, "as a regulative but not a speculative conception."[22]

However, this pragmatic turn is not Peirce's actual answer to Royce's absolute Idealism. Instead, Peirce refers to a theory which, he says, "I intend to take an early opportunity of putting into print" (8.44); in it he proposes to apply the regulative principle mentioned before. In this theory traditional idealistic metaphysics, for which the reality of the world consists in its actually being thought of by God, is to be opposed by the idea that "the existence of God . . . consists in this, that a tendency towards ends is [a] necessary . . . constituent of the universe," and "that God's omniscience, humanly conceived, consists in the fact that knowledge in its development leaves no questions unanswered" (8.44). The circumstance that this "fact" of the all-knowing God has yet to emerge through the process of the world and, especially, through the human process of cognition, and so is not yet a fact but rather is subject to "the scepticism just spoken of," further increases for Peirce its religious fruitfulness (8.44). We must therefore engage ourselves for this end through "faith, love, and hope."[23]

B. The Metaphysics of Evolution (1891 and after)

In 1885 Peirce announced the publication of his theory of the self-developing universe, but it did not actually appear until the 1890s, when it was presented in the form of a series of essays in *The Monist*.[24] They were preceded by an unfinished attempt at a book, "A Guess at the Riddle" (ca. 1890; see 1.354–68, 1.373–75, and 1.379–416), and followed by three other ambitious publication projects in 1893, all of which failed: (1) the "Grand Logic," completed as a book, but never published; (2) the book "Search for a Method," also unpublished, in which older essays on logic were to be brought together with revisions from 1893; and (3) the idea for a work to consist of twelve volumes, "The Principles of Philosophy or Logic, Physics, and Psychics, Considered as a Unity, in the Light of the Nineteenth Century."[25] Like the two earlier series, those of 1868–69 and 1877–78, the papers in the *Monist* series became an enduring document of a period in the course of Peirce's philosophical development. Compared with the earlier series these essays are, to be sure, far less widely known; in fact, they contain the strangest part of Peirce's philosophy, his cosmological metaphysics.[26]

Even the mere fact that the founder of meaning-critical Pragmatism, who long before Wittgenstein or the neopositivists had expressed the suspicion that the propositions of traditional philosophy were meaningless, himself *expressis verbis* proposed a metaphysics has been enough to scandalize many of his modern readers. Peirce, of course, was never of the opinion that his pragmatic maxim would be able to eliminate completely the problems of metaphysics, even though it could show that propositions from "ontological metaphysics," such as "Energy is an entity," are meaningless (8.43, 5.423). On the contrary, Peirce believed that the attempt to get along without metaphysics led only to a poorer metaphysics, since it would be an unreflective one.[27] For him the flight of speculative imagination should never be restricted, and observing the pragmatic maxim would lead to a purified metaphysics (5.423). Moreover, Peirce recognized that the fruitful development of the sciences, especially the human sciences, depends upon an adequate metaphysical basis (see 5.423 and 6.2 and 6.4 from 1898). At first glance, Comte's criticism of metaphysical hypotheses as having no experimental importance might be regarded as an anticipation of meaning-critical Pragmatism. Peirce gave a more precise statement of it which is fully in line with the philosophy of linguistic analysis: "A metaphysical proposition in Comte's sense would, therefore, be a grammatical arrangement of words simulating a proposition, but in fact, not a proposition, because destitute of meaning" (7.203). But instead of then drawing consequences in the manner of Wittgenstein or Carnap, Peirce continues, "Comte's use of the word metaphysical, in a sense which makes it synonymous with nonsense, simply marks the nominalistic tendency of Comte's time" (7.203).

The key to Peirce's positive assessment of metaphysics is, on the one hand, his realist view of universals and, on the other, his unique conception of metaphysics as a science subject to empirical validation, a conception he definitively set forth in his 1902–3 classification of the sciences, discussed earlier. In 1871 Peirce's realist view of universals permitted him to conceive of the pragmatic maxim as an alternative to Berkeley's nominalistic critique of meaning. As a result Peirce saw that general concepts could not in fact be reduced to sense data. Instead, their meaning could be explicated by regarding them as "habits," and that meant as a real embodiment of generality understood as a continual regulation of praxis (8.33). Even in this, Peirce's earliest conception of Pragmatism, there is an approach to metaphysics which permits us to see human habits as analogous to, and a continuation of, natural laws. The metaphysics of evolution (1891 and after) brought this implication to full, explicit development. Peirce's classification of metaphysics as an empirical science, on the other hand, merely drew the final conclusion implicit in the fact that metaphysics does not, as does the normative logic of inquiry, offer the pragmatic maxim as a rule; it instead takes as the object of inquiry the reality of the concepts postulated as habits by the pragmatic maxim. Thus metaphysics becomes an investigation of the real process of inquiry, which was for Peirce the conscious continuation of natural history and so had to be, for him, a science; hence, it had to presuppose abductive hypotheses which can be made subject to inductive testing by deducing their consequences. To this extent, its propositions were subject a priori to the possible pragmatic clarification of meaning and thus were distinguished *per definitionem* from meaningless propositions.[28]

Peirce's conception of metaphysics was demanded by the critique of meaning itself, and it provides a kind of test or control in terms of the final reality that it always presupposes. The only alternative to it, on my view, would be a philosophy which was able to distinguish between metaphysical and nonmetaphysical propositions on the basis of a criterion of meaning, without thereby making any metaphysical presuppositions. In the twentieth century, the philosophy of linguistic analysis has undertaken this attempt, but I believe that its critique of meaning has proven to presuppose a metaphysics which it is not itself able to accept (as in the case of Wittgenstein's *Tractatus* or early logical Positivism), or to take refuge in arbitrarily proposed criteria of meaningful sentences (as in the case of later Neopositivism's constructive semantics), or to have to renounce every theoretical claim, which, strictly speaking, also implies renouncing the criticism of metaphysics.[29] This amounts in practice to an ideological glorification of the "common use" of "ordinary language" and the social forms of life that go along with it (as in the case of Wittgenstein's late philosophy and the British philosophy it inspired).[30]

On the other hand, it is precisely the later phase of analytic philosophy (including Karl Popper's school) that appears to lead to positions that make plausible Peirce's conception of metaphysics as a cosmological, macro-empirical study whose vague, but heuristically indispensable, global hypotheses are borne out or falsified by theory formation in the individual sciences. Such positions include the opinion prevalent among philosophers of science that it is not individual concepts or even propositions which must be capable of empirical testing, but rather whole theories, which can readily contain very speculative central concepts. If we separate this insight from the context of the formal, abstract analysis of theories and recall the historical dimension of the "growth of science," as Peirce so often demanded, then we can see, among other things, that falsifications do not serve to take a scientific theory out of circulation without further ado. Instead, they more often result in a reconsideration of the "paradigmatic" presuppositions of the language games from which the theory grew. These presuppositions, regarding such things as the nature of space, time, and causality, lead us either to reconstruct the problematic theory or else to call into question the "paradigmatic" presuppositions of "normal science" themselves, resulting in a so-called foundational crisis.[31]

These paradigmatic presuppositions would be identical with what in Peirce's logic of inquiry are the "instinctive" human beliefs that are appealed to by common sense or *lumen naturale*. They are the metaphysical background of all the ingenious hypotheses and theories found in science and are the subject matter of the metaphysics of evolution, itself a hypothetical science (6.12–13). Insofar as metaphysics is concerned with these practically indubitable common-sense presuppositions of the observations made by the different individual sciences, it is, according to Peirce, an observational science in the sense of Coenoscopy, because it "rests upon phenomena which so pervade everybody's experience that no-one usually pays any attention to them" (6.3; see also 1.241).

Of course, according to the architectonic of the transcendental system that Peirce took over from Kant,[32] metaphysics presupposes logic. For Peirce, in line with the differentiated view of the transcendental architectonic he takes in his classification of the sciences, it therefore presupposes the normative logic of inquiry, Phenomenology, and mathematical logic. Metaphysics takes from these nonempirical sciences two sorts of principles which it must presuppose from a heuristic standpoint and which it, at the same time, reconfirms in the course of using the process of evolution to explain our final, common-sense concepts. These principles are (1) the "regulative principles" of the normative logic of inquiry and (2) the three fundamental categories which, just like metaphysics itself, are constituted, from the standpoint of their intuitional (*anschaulichen*) content, in coenoscopic Phenomenology and, from the standpoint of their formal presuppositions, in the mathematical logic of relations. Several comments should be made about this matter with regard to Peirce's conception of metaphysics.

The regulative principles of metaphysics are centered around what Peirce himself often referred to as the "social theory of reality" (see 6.10; cf. 2.220 and 2.654). I have shown how Peirce's defense of this theory against Royce's absolute Idealism pointed the way to the program of a metaphysics of evolution. The most important thing in the present context is to explain how Peirce's "metaphysical" use of "regulative concepts" relates to Kant's use of such concepts. When Peirce designates the idea of realizing an adequate concept of reality in the unlimited process of inquiry as "a regulative but not a speculative conception" (8.44; cf. 1.405), one could assume that he is simply taking over Kant's distinction between these two concepts. Peirce himself seems to confirm this in 1890 when, in speaking of the meaning-critical principle that the real is fundamentally cognizable or explicable, he says, "This is what Kant calls a regulative principle, that is to say, an intellectual hope" (1.405). However, the fact that Peirce differs from Kant precisely because of the meaning-critical principle of the fundamental cognizability of the real indicates that his "metaphysical use" of regulative principles must also differ from Kant's. As a matter of fact, Peirce's distinction between speculative and regulative principles completely lacks the foundation provided by Kant's distinction between phenomena and noumena.[33] Since Peirce rejects this distinction as nominalistic, his regulative concepts must—in this regard—be at the same time speculative.[34] Although Peirce takes over Kant's distinction despite this, he does so not because it is possible to recognize a priori that our knowledge is limited to mere appearances, but rather because we cannot know a priori if the knowing process will attain its goal. Nor do we know, at a deeper level, whether the evolutionary process of the real will come to its real possible end through the process of knowing and the praxis that is led by it.[35] For this reason the pragmatic turn, which Peirce sometimes uses—that is, the view that we ought to proceed practically as if every meaningful question will be answered in the long run (8.43)—lacks that specifically fictionalistic point which Vaihinger takes from Kant and Nietzsche and which underlies his *Philosophy of "As If."* Instead, Peirce subsumes the practical side of Kant's conception of "regulative ideas" under his "principle of hope."[36]

In Peirce's later writings he found a compelling reason to return to the genuine Kantian conception of regulative ideas, despite his rejection of incognizable things-in-themselves. Since a "regulative principle" falls under the category of Thirdness, which is illustrated by cognition as rational mediation or by the infinite continuity of *esse in futuro* (whereas every actual cognition falls under the category of Secondness), a regulative principle is therefore something to which, as Kant said, "nothing empirical can correspond," and which is completely independent of our uncertainty about the future. Reality, as that which would be known in an unlimited, continuous process of inquiry, is therefore inconceivable as something actually known.[37] Here, evidently, the paradoxes of Kant's thing-in-itself have returned for Peirce in the form of paradoxes of the infinite.

In discussing these points previously, I brought in the final presuppositions of the architectonic of Peirce's system, the doctrine of the three fundamental categories. As I have already mentioned, Peirce returns to these presuppositions in his metaphysics of evolution as well. In fact, it can be maintained that his metaphysics ultimately owes its strange character to the doctrine of categories and, in any case, cannot be understood without presupposing them. Murray Murphey believes that the metaphysics of the 1890s, taken as an empirical verification of the doctrine of categories, is supposed in fact to replace the transcendental deduction of the universality and necessity of the three fundamental categories which Peirce bases on the original phenomenon of the representation of the real in signs (Peirce's transformation of Kant's "transcendental synthesis of apperception").[38] Murphey is of the opinion that Peirce failed at this task and abandoned it in favor of his metaphysics of evolution.

This view does not seem convincing to me, either as an interpretation of Peirce or as a view of the problems themselves. Peirce never took back his transcendental-semiotic deduction of the three fundamental categories given in the "New List of Categories" in 1867, neither in founding his metaphysics nor later in founding his Phenomenology. In my view, moreover, there is no reason for him to have done so. According to the semiotic view of knowledge, whatever topic we consider must be experienced in an actual confrontation between the ego and the non-ego as something qualitative and must be symbolically represented in an intersubjectively valid expression. The derivation of the three categories from this semiotic understanding of the original phenomenon of knowledge seems to me to be completely plausible as an alternative to Kant's derivation.[39] At the same time, this derivation is able to base the three logical forms of judgment on the three forms of logical inference. And as I explained earlier,[40] a metaphysics of evolution which seeks to grasp this semiotic process of cognition and inference, and thereby to understand its own insights and their confirmation in practice, as the product and controllable continuation of something that is at first an unconscious, natural process, does not seem to me to be contradictory to a transcendental philosophy that understands knowledge itself and its transcendental object (the thing-in-itself) as limiting concepts in the sense of the cognizable, rather than as something transcendent and incognizable. The metaphysics of evolution seems to me to this extent, in the context of Peirce's architectonic, to be more a test requiring empirical confirmation by means of the individual sciences than an alternative to the transcendental-semiotic derivation of the validity of the three fundamental categories. Starting from these heuristic considerations, which, admittedly, go beyond Peirce's 1890 level of understanding of his method, I want to attempt to give a more exact interpretation of the architectonic introduction of this series of essays.

As the plan and the remaining parts of the unfinished book "A Guess at the Riddle" show, Peirce wanted to construct his whole philosophy in strictly architectonic terms, that is, from the presupposition of the doctrine of categories and in accordance with the hierarchy of sciences which he had already developed, except for Phenomenology. The derivation of the categories by means of the logic of relations in "One, Two, Three" is followed by a presentation of the categories in the framework of the semiotic logic of inquiry entitled "The Triad in Reasoning." This is followed by sections which are supposed to treat the triad in metaphysics, psychology, physiology, biology, physics, sociology or "pneumatology," and, finally, theology (see 1.354–416). In the introduction to his series of essays Peirce speaks only in an unsystematic, consciously popular way about the architectonic outline of his philosophy (6.9). The categories, which during Peirce's lifetime and long afterwards tended to seem like strange curiosities to his audience, are not explained in terms of their function as a foundation, but are just brought out in the closing paragraphs (6.32 ff.) as a kind of astounding organization for the theses and points of view that were illustrated before. He arrives at these by inductive means with reference to an overview of the problem of founding several individual sciences (6.9).

His first main thesis is supposed to establish the necessity of a metaphysics of evolution by considering the philosophy of science. It results from reflecting on the development of the fundamental hypotheses about physical laws from the time of Galileo up to the crisis of mechanical principles at the end of the nineteenth century, a development which Peirce followed with great expertise.

First, Peirce explains the most basic thesis of his theory of evolution, a thesis he would later often repeat, by referring to the discovery of the basic laws of mechanics, which, like the axioms of Euclidean geometry they presuppose, arise not so much from experiment as from an appeal to common sense and to what Galileo called *il lume naturale* (6.10). The basic ideas of modern science are obtained neither inductively (i.e., on the basis of a Darwinian selection from all the possible theoretical constructions) nor simply on the basis of a general logical, mathematical, a priori form of possible theory constructions. Rather, they stem from an earlier, instinctlike accommodation of the human mind to the environment it seeks to know:

The straight line appears to us simple, because, as Euclid says, it lies evenly between its extremities; that is, because viewed endwise it appears as a point. That is, again, because light moves in straight lines. Now, light moves in straight lines because of the part which the straight line plays in the laws of dynamics. Thus it is that, our minds having been formed under the influence of phenomena governed by the laws of mechanics, certain conceptions entering into those laws become implanted in our minds, so that we readily guess at what the laws are. Without such a natural prompting, having to search blindfolded for a law which would suit the phenomena, our chance of finding it would be as one to infinity.[41]

But what holds for the simple, beginning notions of mechanics no longer holds on Peirce's view for the development of physics in the theory of light, electrodynamics, the kinetic theory of gas, and the correlative study of the structure of molecules and atoms, all of which move further and further away from "phenomena which have directly influenced the growth of the mind" (6.10). With this entry into a sphere unknown to human beings, we must expect that we will no longer find the laws that govern them to be " 'simple,' that is, composed of a few conceptions natural to our minds" (6.10). Hence, for Peirce, "There is room for serious doubt whether the fundamental laws of mechanics hold good for single atoms, and it seems quite likely that they are capable of motion in more than three dimensions" (6.12; cf. 6.575).

These critical reflections about the paradigmatic principles of mechanics anticipate, as we see today, a number of the characteristic ideas in the twentieth-century discussion of the relationship between classical physics and the theory of relativity, on the one hand, and quantum theory, on the other. For example, Peirce anticipates the agreement sought by Hugo Dingler and the Copenhagen school, concerning an anthropological a priori for classical principles (including Euclidean geometry) in the field of experimental physics which nonetheless would recognize the inapplicability of these principles in the theoretical representation of the microcosmic and macrocosmic.[42]

These thoughts about the history of science constitute only the starting point for Peirce's first main thesis about the theory of evolution. In the perspective of the present discussion it seems, in part, familiar and plausible, but also, in part, extremely odd. From the confrontation of these two theses about the origin of classical mechanics, on the one hand, and the problem of the foundation of molecular and atomic physics, on the other, Peirce draws the conclusion that the almost instinctive metaphysics of common sense or *lumen naturale*, which provides physics with its first fundamental hypotheses about laws, is insufficient in the present age. The function of this naive metaphysics must now be taken over by a historical metaphysics of metaphysics which reflects on the natural historical conditions for the construction of scientific hypotheses. This metaphysics of evolution is supposed to explain natural laws themselves historically and show us what kind of laws to expect (6.12).

This call for reflection on the historical conditions for the discovery of natural laws seems reasonable to us today, and so does Peirce's demand for an explanation of laws which are capable of being apprehended by the mind and yet have no reason for their special forms (6.12). But difficulties arise for us from the fact that Peirce seems to identify these two tasks. Normally, we would "explain" a natural law by its derivation from a more general law, while we would expect reflection upon historical conditions to give us, primarily, a hermeneutical understanding of the discovery of natural laws in the context of the history of ideas or social history. Beyond that, we might also, like Peirce, take it as including an evolutionary conception of the epistemological and anthropological universals contained in that context.[43]

For a unification, in the sense of a final "explanation," to be conceivable here, this explanation could at most consist, according to Peirce's and other modern logics of science, in a derivation of all historical occurrences from a law which is itself not derivable, and from the underivable original conditions of all occurrences. In fact, a number of the characteristic features of Peirce's cosmology can be understood as this sort of quasi-natural scientific explanation of the development of the world. As such it offers a kind of historical, genetic explanation which emphasizes that an explanation requires not only laws, but also original conditions to which the laws can be applied, or, more exactly, to which we can conceive them to be related. Peirce's chief intention, however, is evidently more radical. He aims not to offer an explanation by presupposing laws, but rather to use the original conditions of world history as a basis for offering a historical-genetic explanation of all laws and, indeed, of lawfulness itself. In short, his aim is not a "cosmology," but a "cosmogony" (6.33). Peirce writes: "Now the only possible way of accounting for the laws of nature and for *uniformity in general* [emphasis added] is to suppose them results of evolution. This supposes them not to be absolute, not to be obeyed precisely. It makes an element of indeterminacy, spontaneity, or absolute chance in nature" (6.13).

As far as the indeterminism thesis that Peirce arrives at here is concerned, it has become particularly important in the twentieth century in connection with the relativization of classical mechanics which has now become the limiting case of statistical quantum theory. This too must be viewed, however, in the context of the attempt to find an explanation of laws by means of more comprehensive (more general) laws. (We must here, of course, assume particular marginal conditions for inferring the limiting case.) Peirce himself refers again and again to a new type of statistical theory construction that has to presuppose even chance as a requirement for making explanations.[44] But his introduction of chance or spontaneity serves not so much to infer strictly deterministic laws as limiting cases from statistical laws, in some systematic field where there is free play, as to explain lawfulness historically and genetically from chance. For Peirce, it seems that it is not a law valid *sub specie aeternitatis* which has the last word, but a "natural history of laws."[45]

Peirce goes on in his architectonic outline of the history of physics to consider nineteenth-century theories of evolution. He had occupied himself intensively with these since the time of the Metaphysical Club, if not earlier—since Darwin's *On the Origin of Species* appeared in 1859.[46] In 1877 he had already compared Darwin's theory, as an application in biology of statistical method, to Clausius and Maxwell's theory of gases (5.364). He tried again and again to generalize Darwin's theory with the help of the mathematical theory of probability developed since the work of Fermat and Pascal, using the example of games of chance (6.15). But Peirce was not content to view statistical theories in the way that Maxwell or Darwin himself did, as a substitute—possibly temporary—for a deterministic explanation of individual events, an explanation which cannot be given at the moment, owing to a lack of knowledge. In the same way Peirce also dismissed Spencer's attempt to trace evolution to mechanical principles of necessity (6.14). For Peirce, Darwin's assumption of "chance variation" (sporting, arbitrary heterogeneity) contains a reference to a principle of absolute, creative spontaneity or possibility in an active sense, without which phenomena like variety, heterogeneity, differentiation, specification, and growth cannot be explained.[47] Peirce conceived even natural laws themselves as phenomena of chance specification in which the original continuum of creative potentialities became more and more limited. Hence, it was possible for him to "generalize" Darwin's theory of evolution in this way: "Whenever there are large numbers of objects having a tendency to retain certain characters unaltered, this tendency, however, not being absolute but giving room for chance variations, then, if the amount of variation is absolutely limited in certain directions by the destruction of everything which reaches those limits, there will be a gradual tendency to change in directions of departure from them" (6.15).

This generalization of the formation of different genuses and species of living things (or, in the sphere of human history, of institutions and habits of behavior) as the product of chance variation and selection was evidently Peirce's model of the rise of natural laws in general.

Peirce summarizes his reasons for rejecting mechanistic, deterministic ("necessitarian" or "anancastic") explanations of evolution in four arguments (see 6.14 and 6.613): (1) the principle of evolution, meaning the creative principle of chance variation referred to here, needs no explanation when it is understood as a principle of growth, since it "requires no extraneous cause," but only the tendency to growth which "can be supposed itself to have grown from an infinitesimal germ accidentally started" (6.14); (2) laws, more than anything else, must be explained as the result of evolution; (3) the variety (heterogeneity, specification) of the universe cannot be exactly explained as the necessary result of homogeneity, but is rather in its essence chance variation; (4) all processes that are subject to the laws of mechanics are reversible.[48] For this reason, Peirce says, "growth is not explicable by those laws, even if they be not violated in the process of growth" (6.14).

The first, third, and fourth arguments do not, I think, seem unplausible, especially if they are seen in the light of the philosophies worked out at the beginning of the twentieth century, that is, Bergson's *évolution créatrice* and the "emergent evolutionism" of C. Lloyd Morgan and S. Alexander. The conceptions implicit in the second argument, however, continue to cause problems in the context of Peirce's logic of science, since this argument supposes that natural laws are to be explained by a theory of evolution without thereby referring to any law.[49] It becomes necessary here to introduce the three fundamental categories as the actual presuppositions of a "cosmogonic explanation" in Peirce's sense, categories that his book outline from 1890 indicate to be the final heuristic aspect of his metaphysics. Seen in their light, the principle of evolution referred to in the first argument (chance variation, spontaneity, and, later, the undifferentiated continuum of possibilities, qualities, or feelings) becomes recognizable as an illustration of the category of Firstness; the second, Darwinian, principle of the selection of what is usable by eliminating what is less well adapted in the "struggle for life" proves to be an illustration of the category of Secondness (action-reaction, collision, struggle, facticity, confrontation with the real as something existing here and now, the actualization of the possible, or, in theological terms, the will of God which calls the real universe into being from the continuum of his ideas of the possible or, as Böhme and Schelling conceive God, his Divine Agony of "contracting" himself and his laws from possibility to emerge as the existence of the real).[50] But from the outset Peirce presupposes a third principle in this process, which is inherent in the undifferentiated continuum of possibilities in the sense of Firstness. By means of this principle, coherence in the form of similarity is maintained in chance variation qua differentiation and growth. It insures that even the (divine will's) introduction of facticity in the form of individuation does not dissolve coherence in the universe, but merely makes the original continuum of possible being specific as a differentiated continuum of natural laws or behavioral habits.

In his metaphysics, Peirce characterizes this principle of rational mediation, which we are already familiar with as the category of Thirdness, as temporally real generality or "continuity." As the "law of habit" it functions as the tacitly presupposed fundamental law of evolution and permits Peirce to "explain" all particular natural laws in a way that also accords with the rules of rational inquiry and praxis.[51]

From the standpoint of the doctrine of categories, it is understandable that Peirce's metaphysics of evolution does not treat just of Darwin's theory, in which the "nominalistic and materialistic" aspects of the categories, such as chance as blind coincidence and selection as brutal force, stand in the forefront, but also of two other theories of evolution: Clarence King's catastrophe theory and, especially, Lamarck's theory of teleological accommodation and the inheritance of accommodation capacities.[52] Catastrophe theory evidently interests Peirce as a theory of stimulation or challenge (Secondness) and, hence, as an analogy of his own theory of the disturbance of habits by doubt, which he presented in "The Fixation of Belief." He therefore attributes special significance to it for the evolution of institutions and ideas (6.17). Lamarck's theory, on the other hand, provides Peirce with an analogy to his positive theory of the acquisition of habits by means of goal-directed efforts. In this way it makes possible an understanding of evolution in terms of the category of Thirdness, since it conceives evolution from within in the manner of objective Idealism and the realist theory of universals (6.16). While Peirce generalizes the principle of Darwinism as "Tychism" and defends it in a special essay against mechanistic "Necessitarianism" (6.35 ff.), Lamarck's principle provides the transition to the psychological observation of the principle of continuity which Peirce generalizes in his essay "The Law of Mind" as the principle of "Synechism."[53]

Just as the category of Thirdness is illustrated in the logic of inquiry by the mediation of spontaneity in qualitative insights (Firstness) and the selective confirmation or falsification of insights by "brute facts" (Secondness) in the pursuit of truth, it is found in a similar way in biological evolution in the mediation of chance variation and selection by habit-taking in the sense of biological adaptation. In this sense Lamarck's principle is an objective, idealistic one. It is supposed finally to make possible a synthesis in Peirce's theory of evolution between Darwin's (and King's and Hegel's) tychastic and ananchastic principles, in the form of the sympathetic empathy in "creative love," or what Peirce calls "Agapasm."[54] According to Peirce: "The agapastic development of thought is the adoption of certain mental tendencies, not altogether heedlessly, as in tychasm, nor quite blindly by the mere force of circumstances or of logic, as in anancasm, but by an immediate attraction for the idea itself, whose nature is divined before the mind possesses it, by the power of sympathy, that is, by virtue of the continuity of mind."[55]

The heuristic function of the three fundamental categories in

Peirce's architectonic becomes more evident when we consider the transition to psychology (6.18 ff.; cf. 5.290). The nonrelational category of Firstness is illustrated here by the precognitive feeling we have of something. The category of Secondness is illustrated by the feelings of action and reaction. These are experienced actively as effort and resistance, passively as the surprising intrusion of the outer world, of "brute facts" or fate, or even just as a change in our inner state or in the relation between thoughts, insofar as this is not yet a true cognition of something as something. Finally, the category of Thirdness is illustrated by the general concept which is constituted by "consciousness of . . . a habit" (6.21). Peirce's reference to "the one primary and fundamental law of mental action" (6.21) is interesting in the present context. It consists, he says, in "a tendency to generalization" (6.21). Ever since 1868 Peirce had interpreted all forms of the association of ideas as Thirdness in the sense of rational mediation by synthetic inferences, including induction as habit-taking (see especially 5.297, 5.367 ff., and 5.397-401). In 1891 he turned this interpretation of association into a cosmological theory in order to make the gradual rise of the cosmos from chaos understandable from the viewpoint of the continuity of mind.[56]

To this end, however, it was requisite to conceive the Firstness substratum of the "Law of Mind," the continuum of feelings, as a substratum of chance variation in the sense of a cosmogony. In other words, it was necessary to trace an aspect of matter back to the substratum of Firstness. Peirce was able to borrow from Aristotle's concept of matter something that was a cosmogonically helpful aspect of Firstness: matter as pure possibility. It could be understood as the element from which the world begins and which cannot be explained, since every explanation presupposes it. This element, which Peirce had sought to discover, could in fact be conceived as the absolute nothing from which creation begins.[57] Here he could even establish a non-required, but desired, connection with religious tradition (6.216, 6.490, 6.553, 6.613). As a thinker schooled in natural science he could not, of course, overlook actual existence or determination by laws as aspects in the modern concept of matter. It was precisely these which permitted him to interpret the complete phenomenon of matter, so to speak, from within, in terms of his three fundamental categories. Hence, he visualized the inside of the continuum of matter's possibilities in terms of Firstness as spontaneity, freedom, and, at one with this, as intense feeling or "quali-consciousness."[58] He understood matter's brutal, resistant existence internally, in terms of Secondness, as will or the "contraction" of the vague.[59] Finally, he understood lawfulness from within in terms of Thirdness as rigidified habits. This rigidity is an indication that for Peirce the limiting case of the mechanistic aspect of matter is mind's internal and spontaneous nature: "The one intelligible theory of the universe is that of objective idealism, that matter is effete mind, inveterate habits becoming physical laws."[60] Later Peirce writes: "We must . . . regard matter as mind whose habits have become fixed so as to lose the powers of forming them and losing them, while mind [in the narrow sense] is to be regarded as a chemical genus of extreme complexity and instability. It has acquired in a remarkable degree a habit of taking and laying aside habits" (6.101; cf. 6.23, 6.148).

This formulation also includes an indication of how Peirce tried to comprehend the difference between natural laws and human habits of behavior and the effects of evolution on this difference. He drew upon the evolution of feeling in order to clarify this difference in the following passage from the fourth article of the 1892 *Monist* series:

But once grant that the phenomena of matter are but the result of the sensibly complete sway of habits upon the mind, and it only remains to explain why in the protoplasm these habits are to some slight extent broken up, so that, according to the law of mind, in that special clause of it sometimes called the principle of accommodation, feeling becomes intensified. Now the manner in which habits generally broken up is this. Reactions usually terminate in the removal of a stimulus; for the excitation continues as long as the stimulus is present. Accordingly, habits are general ways of behavior which are associated with the removal of stimuli. But when the expected removal of the stimulus fails to occur, the excitation continues and increases, and non-habitual reactions take place; and these tend to weaken the habit. If, then, we suppose that matter never does obey its ideal laws with absolute precision, but that there are almost insensible fortuitous departures from regularity, these will produce, in general, equally minute effects. But protoplasm is in an excessively unstable condition; and it is the characteristic of unstable equilibrium that near that point excessively minute causes may produce startlingly large effects. Here, then, the usual departures from regularity will be followed by others that are very great; and the large fortuitous departures from law so produced will tend still further to break up the laws, supposing that these are of the nature of habits. Now, this breaking up of habit and renewed fortuitous spontaneity will, according to the law of mind, be accompanied by an intensification of feeling. The nerve-protoplasm is, without doubt, in the most unstable condition of any kind of matter; and consequently there the resulting feeling is the most manifest. [6.264]

One could get the impression after this description of evolution that there is a steady development from rigid, unfeeling, inorganic nature towards ever greater flexibility, instability, and nervous differentiation of feeling. But that impression appears to be contradicted by that other conception, often noted before, that evolution as habit-taking (6.132, 6.191 ff.) essentially has the character of a limitation on the original continuum of possibilities. According to this conception it is precisely in the original "quale-consciousness" that the intensity and breadth of feeling are greatest.[61] Peirce actually upholds both of these theses and thereby anticipates a model of thought which has since become commonplace in biology. According to this view, all evolution is to be understood, on the one hand, as specialization and, hence, as an increase in rigidity in creative life; on the other hand, it is also recognized as a higher development which breaks through to a more original, nonspecialized potency.[62] Heidegger worked out this model in the history of ideas to the extent of maintaining that radical thought about the possible future must, at the same time, be a "step backwards" to the overlooked and unthought of possibilities that lie at the beginning of our conceptual history. This is what makes it possible for us to transcend what may be called the habits of Western thought.

It seems to me that Peirce is able in this way to uphold simultaneously, without becoming involved in a contradiction, a theory of creative life's "emancipation from law" (e.g., 6.266) and a theory of the rationalization and even personalization of the universe by habit-taking (6.268 ff.).[63] At the conclusion of his architectonic introduction to metaphysics he offers a sketch:

A Cosmogonic Philosophy . . . would suppose that in the beginning—infinitely remote—there was a chaos of unpersonalized feeling, which being without connection or regularity would properly be without existence. This feeling, sporting here and there in pure arbitrariness, would have started the germ of a generalizing tendency. Its other sportings would be evanescent, but this would have a growing virtue. Thus, the tendency to habit would be started; and from this, with the other principles of evolution, all the regularities of the universe would be evolved. At any time, however, an element of pure chance survives and will remain until the world becomes an absolutely perfect, rational, and symmetrical system, in which mind is at last crystallized in the infinitely distant future. [6.33]

In the face of such speculative daring, as well as ambiguity and obscurity, all of which is hardly second to that found in Schelling or Hegel, it is easy to understand the alarm and disappointment of many neopositivists, who would have liked to celebrate the founder of Pragmatism as their forerunner. The temptation is in fact great to regard Peirce, the more we know of his intentions, as a carry-over from the Concord Transcendentalists, rather than as a precursor of modern critical philosophy.[64] In the last analysis, however, this judgment seems to me false, even as far as the metaphysics of the 1890s is concerned. There are several essential characteristics that distinguish Peirce's speculations from the style of the older metaphysics, particularly that of German Idealism. I have already mentioned that the metaphysics of evolution does not constitute "the" philosophy of Peirce. Rather, it assumes his critical and normative logic, which give him the right to engage in unburdened speculation in the form of final, empirically unverifiable hypotheses. This is the reason why we nowhere in Peirce's writings find that strained pathos of the dogmatic thinker who wants to immunize his system against possible criticisms of it as a universally binding world view. Instead, the reader is more likely to be irritated by the carefree way in which Peirce again and again calls his presuppositions and his terminology into question in order to try them on the material offered by the sciences, which he, as one of the last encyclopedic minds, knew in detail.[65] In a fragment from about 1897, Peirce gives a very good description of the methodological attitude he takes as a metaphysician:

My philosophy may be described as the attempt of a physicist to make such conjecture as to the constitution of the universe as the methods of science may permit, with the aid of all that has been done by previous philosophers. I shall support my propositions by such arguments as I can. Demonstrative proof is not to be thought of. The demonstrations of the metaphysicians are all moonshine. The best that can be done is to supply a hypothesis, not devoid of all likelihood, in the general line of growth of scientific ideas, and capable of being verified or refuted by future observers. [1.7]

It is conceivable that in an age in which the principles of the critique of meaning, logical Socialism, an open society of critics, and Fallibilism, all of which Peirce had upheld in his normative logic, had all become generally accepted in philosophy, metaphysics would not die. In such a case it would be conducted as conscious speculation in Peirce's style of hypothetical experimentation—so to speak, as the reflective art of metascientific heuristic.

The Fourth Period:
From Pragmatism to Pragmaticism
(ca. 1898–1914)

A. The Occasion and Motives for the Reexamination
of Pragmatism (1898–1903)

In 1897 William James published his collection of essays *The Will to Believe* and dedicated it to Peirce.[1] This and, more importantly, James's 1898 lecture entitled "Philosophical Conceptions and Practical Results"[2] placed Peirce in a new situation. I have referred to this change several times in preceding chapters.[3] Peirce now found himself being quoted as the founder of "Pragmatism," taken as a new philosophy or world view (5.13 n. 1). At this time he was himself engrossed in working out a theoretical, cosmological metaphysics which had taken him far away from the subjective, praxis-oriented interpretation of his 1870s ideas that James was now presenting. The tension between his position and that of James is best illustrated by the documents that remain from the 1898 Cambridge lectures.[4]

In lecture three, "Detached Ideas on Vitally Important Topics," Peirce presents the following distinction between "science" and the praxis of life. It obviously represents his answer to the existentialist Pragmatism in James's essay "The Will to Believe":

The value of *Facts* to *it* [science], lies only in this, that they belong to Nature; and Nature is something great, and beautiful, and sacred, and eternal, and real—the object of its worship and its aspiration. It therein takes an entirely different attitude toward facts from that which Practice takes. For Practice, facts are the arbitrary forces with which it has to reckon and to wrestle. Science, when it comes to understand itself, regards facts as merely the vehicle of eternal truth, while for Practice they remain the obstacles which it has to turn, the enemy of which it is determined to get the better.

Science feeling that there is an arbitrary element in its theories, still continues its studies, confident that so it will gradually become more and more purified from the dross of subjectivity; but practice requires something to go upon, and it will be no consolation to it to know that it is on the path to objective truth—the actual truth it must have, or when it cannot attain certainty must at least have high probability, that is, must know that, though a few of its ventures may fail, the bulk of them will succeed. Hence the hypothesis which answers the purpose of theory may be perfectly worthless for art. After a while, as Science progresses, it comes upon more solid ground. It is now entitled to reflect: this ground has held a long time without showing signs of yielding. I may hope that it will continue to hold for a great while longer. This reflection, however, is quite aside from the purpose of science. It does not modify its procedure in the least degree. It is extra-scientific. For Practice, however, it is vitally important, quite altering the situation. As Practice apprehends it, the conclusion no longer rests upon mere retroduction, it is inductively supported. . . . In other words there is now reason [for Practice] to believe in the theory, for belief is the willingness to risk a great deal upon a proposition. But this belief is no concern of science, which has nothing at stake on any temporal venture but is in pursuit of eternal verities (not semblances to truth) and looks upon this pursuit, not as the work of one man's life, but as that of generation after generation, indefinitely.[5]

If we disregard the pathos in this antithesis between theory and praxis, it recalls to the modern reader the distinction, common in logical Empiricism,[6] between aspects of knowledge that are relevant for the logic of science and aspects that are *only* pragmatically relevant, such as the distinction between "X explains y" (that is, in general and independently of any real subject) and "X explains y for z" (that is, in the psychological situation of z). Peirce seems prima facie to treat the pragmatic dimension in just this way. But such an interpretation would stand in contradiction to his entire systematic approach.[7] But at least this much remains true, that Peirce rejected all finitistic, situation-oriented forms of Pragmatism, whether psychological, existential, or sociological in nature. He regarded the neopositivistic logic of science and its concept of Pragmatism, which was oriented to situations, as irrelevant to the philosophy of science.[8] Unlike the neopositivists, Peirce could not reduce the logic of science to the syntactic and semantic functions of formalized languages. Even in 1898 he aimed not at a complete exclusion of the pragmatic dimension from the logic of science, but rather at understanding this dimension in terms of the unlimited community of scientists. His task was to develop an alternative to James's subjectivistic Pragmatism by emphasizing the growth of intersubjectivity in this dimension.

Peirce's answer to this situation can be seen in that forced development of the system of classification which I sketched at the beginning of this book. His inclusion of the pragmatic maxim in the context of the three normative sciences[9] was obviously intended in particular to do justice to James's accentuation of the relationship between theoretical thought and the praxis of life in a way that can be reconciled with science's teleological relationship to truth and the evolution of the *summum bonum*, which is to be realized by the progress of science. While James and, soon after him, F. C. S. Schiller generalized Pragmatism into a subjectivistic, humanistic philosophy or world view, Peirce sought to limit it to the status of a maxim in the logic of science that could receive its appropriate place in a comprehensive, systematic philosophy (8.255, 8.259).

Even around the turn of the century, however, after Peirce had worked out a new system of coordinates which offered a place and a foundation for Pragmatism, he remained at first very critical of his own essays from 1877–78, those upon which James had relied. This is evident in all the texts from 1902–3, in which Peirce presents himself to the public for the first time as the founder of Pragmatism.[10] Hence, in his article "Pragmatic and Pragmaticism" in Baldwin's *Dictionary of Philosophy and Psychology*, he allows James's interpretation of the 1878 pragmatic maxim to stand and then proceeds to divorce himself not only from James's exaggerated position, but also from his own "stoic axiom" that "the end of man is action."[11] Whereas the pragmatic maxim is reconfirmed as a useful principle for the clarification of our thoughts, its value is made relative by reference to another, more far-reaching principle.[12] Even in the large and important "Pragmatism" lecture of 1903 Peirce admits right at the beginning that "objections to this way of thinking [i.e., the pragmatic way] have forced themselves upon me" (5.15). Thereafter he emphasizes again and again that it is not enough to exhibit the humanistic significance of Pragmatism—that, rather, its application as a "maxim of logic" has to be proven by evaluating its pros and cons (5.15, 5.27, 8.258).

Why did Peirce continue to have critical reservations in 1902–3 about the validity of the pragmatic maxim? First, as already noted, he objected to the way the pragmatic maxim had been raised to a teleological, metaphysical, and ethical, normative principle; additionally, his reexamination of his Pragmatism raised for him the question whether the meaning of "theoretical beliefs," that is, statements in science, in fact consists entirely in the "expectation" of praxis-related experiences (see 5.538–45 and 5.32). Peirce's reasons for this question are suggested in a passage from his 1902 lexicon article: "The writer saw that the principle might easily be misapplied, so as to sweep away the whole doctrine of incommensurables, and, in fact, the whole Weierstrassian way of regarding the calculus" (5.3; cf. 5.539, 5.541, 5.32–33, and 8.325).

Peirce is faced here with the fundamental problem of how to apply the pragmatic maxim and its critique of meaning to mathematical concepts and theory construction. This is not its first occurrence: Peirce had based his introduction of the pragmatic maxim in 1871 on the observation that Berkeley's empiricist criterion of meaning, which the pragmatic maxim was to replace, simplified science so greatly that "everything about negative quantities, the square root of *minus*, and infinitesimals, had been excluded from the subject on the ground that we can form no idea of such things" (8.33). In the meantime this matter appears, however, to have become a problem for Peirce, so that he wondered whether Pragmatism itself was capable of explaining such mathematical concepts as these.

We should remember that in the 1880s the mathematician L. K. Kronecker had already expressed meaning-critical doubts about the use of irrational numbers and nondecidable definitions.[13] Shortly after 1900, in his "intuitionistic set theory," L. E. J. Brouwer radicalized this critique of meaning, which requires that mathematical definitions be verified by a decision procedure, in order to establish construction as the sole means of definition and the basis of every proof of existence.[14] The close relationship between the intuitionistic-constructionistic approach and the pragmatic critique of meaning (and Bridgeman's Operationalism as well) cannot be overlooked.[15] Naturally, we must also take into consideration that in 1871 and again in his controversy with James's Pragmatism, Peirce emphasized that we cannot reduce the meaning of concepts to current praxis or its correlates from experience, but rather only to habits. As embodiments of Thirdness, nothing empirical, no embodiment of Secondness, can correspond to them. But these habits must at least in principle be capable of being illustrated by actions. And Peirce, like Brouwer, in several places defined mathematics as a kind of constructive activity which, as logical activity, is prior to logic as a reflection of action (see especially 2.191, 1.245 ff., and 1.417).

As Murray Murphey has shown, even after Peirce founded Pragmatism, his philosophy of mathematics, quite unlike his logic of natural science, in fact retained the Platonic-Leibnizian presupposition of a world of ideas existing in themselves that Peirce had taken over from his father.[16] His theory of transfinite sets, which he worked out in the third period, generally follows Georg Cantor, even though particular features, such as the distinction among "enumerated, enumerable and nonenumerable collections," remind us of Brouwer.[17] The essential thing, however, is that Peirce continues to hold to the pre-existence of a totality of possibilities and thereby also to the principle of the excluded middle.[18] Peirce's suggestion that we understand mathematical structures as creatively constructed is not finitistic in the modern sense, but is conceived as an *explicatio mentis dei instar* in a fashion similar to that of the Christian Platonists, Nicholas of Cusa, and Leibniz.

Peirce's reexamination of the pragmatic maxim after the turn of the century, especially in regard to mathematics, should be evaluated against this background. In a fragment from 1902 he not only holds, following Riemann, that he can explicate the meaning of the geometrical predicates "finite" and "infinite" according to the pragmatic maxim with regard to possible measurements, but also asserts that "a quadratic equation which has no real root has two different imaginary roots" (5.541) and that "the diagonal of a square is incommensurable with its side" (5.539). This last statement, Peirce says, expresses "what is expectable for a person dealing with fractions" (5.541), namely, that it is "useless" to try to find the exact expression of the diagonal as a rational fraction of the side (5.539).

The Pragmatism lecture of 1903, in contrast, states that "it seems quite absurd to say that there is any objective practical difference between commensurable and incommensurable" (5.32). The difference in possible operations for computing fractions or their results, to which Peirce gave attention in 1902, now seems to him to be just a difference "in one's conduct about words and modes of expression" (5.33). But since the pragmatic maxim is supposed to serve to expose mere verbal differences as perhaps meaningless, Peirce has evidently come to believe that he can no longer admit a difference between operations with mathematical symbols and their results as something of practical or experimental relevance (see 5.33).

In a letter to F. C. S. Schiller dated September 10, 1906, Peirce seems once again to want to admit "the conduct of the arithmetician as such" (8.323) as the pragmatic criterion of meaning. But even now he has misgivings about "abnumerable multitudes," which can be described only in general concepts and which represent the greatest difficulty for the principle of Pragmatism (see 8.325).

If we compare Peirce's ambivalent attempts to apply the pragmatic maxim to mathematics with the critique of meaning found in intuitionism-constructionism (he was apparently unaware of these), then it must strike us that Peirce skipped over the starting point of that critique. On the one hand, he seems for the present inclined not to admit any differences among mathematical symbol operations as criteria. To do so would obviously "simplify" this science too much, as Peirce would have said in 1871.[19] On the other hand, he evidently does not consider proposing specific prescriptions or prohibitions for meaning-critically acceptable, symbolic decision procedures in arithmetic that might then seriously limit set theory's sphere of applicability. As a Platonist in mathematics he does not, basically, doubt the meaningfulness and validity of concepts of transfinite sets (see 8.325), and in 1898, without misgivings, he had applied the operations of classical logic, including the principle of the excluded middle, to such concepts (see 6.185–86). Indeed, Peirce believes that the metaphysical concept of the reality of generality so central to his late system itself presupposes, qua continuity, the mathematical existence of transfinite sets (5.67, 5.103).

Another difficulty with which Peirce confronts Pragmatism in 1902 is the question of historical judgments of fact (5.541–42, 5.461). Here too, as in the mathematical examples mentioned above, Peirce is concerned with demonstrating that every meaningful, theoretical belief includes an expectation about the future. In the case of historical judgments, the answer arises de facto from the distinction between the extensional meaning of sentences in regard to objects ("reference," in more modern terminology) and their meaning in the sense of what Peirce was later to call the "logical interpretant," which must meet the pragmatic maxim's criterion of meaning.[20] In this way, to take an example, the traditional belief "that Aristotle was unable to pronounce the letter R," to which Diogenes Laertius, Suidas, and Plutarch bear witness, is related to the past as far as its reference to objects is concerned. But its pragmatically relevant meaning must be sought in the expectation that this traditional belief will be confirmed or falsified in some way in the future, be it through some further historical sources or on the basis of some possible discovery that the sound waves of Aristotle's voice "have somehow recorded themselves."[21]

Peirce bases his thesis that all meaningful statements have a relationship to the future on the interesting observation, made in 1902, that whoever asserts or claims that a proposition is true thereby assumes responsibility for it, that is, for the conditioned predictions it entails (5.543). Peirce further develops this point of view by means of linguistic analysis, first in his 1903 lecture on Pragmatism (5.29 ff.) and then, most of all, in a fragment from 1908 (5.546–47). Ceremonious statements that explicitly take responsibility for their content, such as an oath before a court, merely make visible, as through a magnifying glass, the willful, morally relevant, active aspect that is inherent in every assertion of the truth of a proposition. For Peirce there is therefore a continuum between "performative" and "constative" utterances, which in modern linguistic analysis, following Austin, are sharply distinguished.[22] Not just the oath as a legal act, but every assertion that implicitly claims truth is an action by which the one making the assertion enters into reality in a causal, dynamic way and becomes engaged morally in the communication community. The "performative utterance" shows, as the self-expressive speech act, that even the constative statement—in contrast to the pragmatically uninterpreted proposition of a formalized language—implies the effective self-reflection of living, "ordinary" language that makes it the medium of intersubjective communication.[23]

B. The Lectures on Pragmatism (1903): The Three "Cotary Propositions"

The Harvard Pragmatism lectures of 1903 provide us with the concluding document of that reorganizing phase in Peirce's philosophy which began in 1898. Moreover, it is the most comprehensive attempt to build Pragmatism into the system of philosophy Peirce called Synechism. That James found these lectures obscure and nearly unintelligible seems, even today, justified, especially if we take into consideration that the audience, including James, knew practically nothing about the theoretical presuppositions that the lonely thinker from Milford took for granted, in particular the doctrine of categories.[24] At the beginning of this book I tried to reconstruct the architectonic background to which the structure of these lectures was supposed to correspond, namely, Peirce's classification of the sciences, which itself was primarily conditioned heuristically by the three fundamental categories. As I indicated, the pragmatic maxim belongs in the first of the three normative sciences which, as a group, themselves constitute the middle element in a group of three philosophical sciences, being situated between Phenomenology and Metaphysics.

The following interpretation concentrates upon the final part of the lectures (lecture seven), in which Peirce focuses within normative logic especially on the logic of abduction as the theme of the pragmatic maxim and attempts to found its function in the context of the three "cotary propositions" which are supposed "to put the edge on the maxim of pragmatism" (5.180).

With the three cotary propositions Peirce attempts to answer the question how information from the uncontrollable part of the mind—and that means from nature, inside and outside man—can enter into logical argumentation, that is, how knowledge as *experience* is possible at all. It is the very question he had treated in 1869 as the key question of philosophy skipped over by Kant (5.348), but Peirce judged that he himself had failed to answer it sufficiently in his "theory of cognition" in 1868–69. He was convinced even then that abductive inference should take the place of Kant's synthesis of perceptual data in judgments of experience and that the transcendental foundation of judgments of experience as categorically a priori valid should be replaced by the foundation of the validity of the process of induction in the long run (which would itself still be transcendental in the sense of the "highest principle of synthetic judgments").[25] But it later became clear that these two presuppositions were not enough to answer the question how the qualitative, material content of experience is in fact possible.[26]

Granted, abductive inference is capable, as a synthetic inference, of expressing the structure of conjecture which underlies every judgment of experience as a judgment that amplifies our knowledge (5.181). This is the logically mediated character of all the seeming immediateness in cognition which Peirce valued so highly in 1868 (see 5.213–317). But as an inference, abduction is incapable of explaining the practical immediateness of cognition's starting point in a situation. Nor can it explain the circumstance that all inference must rely upon the empirical content of premises which, even though they may themselves be logically mediated, can nevertheless not be criticized in the sense of normative logic as the result of inferences (5.194).

On the other hand, the inductive process is no longer completely intelligible for the later Peirce as a procedure for confirming things experimentally, if it is understood only in terms of Darwinian selection as a successful confrontation between human beings, acting on the basis of their beliefs, and facts in the outer world. In this conception of induction he finds no account of the qualitative confrontation of individual things *hic et nunc* with the general law that is supposed to be confirmed by the facts (5.205). More precisely, he does not see how it is possible to *experience* the confirmation of the general law through a comparison of the predictions inferred from law hypotheses with the qualitative character of facts.[27]

In light of the doctrine of categories Peirce's task here must be to show how the qualitative character of experience (Firstness), which is free of relations, arises in cognition as a process of logical mediation (Thirdness) and can function in a process of experimental confirmation through confrontation with surprising facts (Secondness) as an itself uncriticizable starting material and criterion of evidence (see 5.212). Now since deduction, as purely logical mediation, applies only Thirdness and since induction, as a quantitative evaluation of the degree of confirmation provided by a successful confrontation with the facts, primarily is an expression of Secondness, the Firstness of experience must therefore be brought out primarily through a new interpretation of abduction.[28] This is because "it is the only logical operation which introduces any new idea" (5.171). Abduction was postulated in 1868 as an infinite process of logical mediation in which all first experiences were taken only to seem to be "intuitions." Now, in 1903, it is so conceived that the notion of an underivable first experience of a qualitative kind, a beginning of cognition in time, is not only demonstrated to be a consistent notion, something Peirce already tried to show in 1868 (see 5.263), but also considered to be a necessary presupposition of all arguments containing empirical content and so capable of being substantiated by facts.

This is what the three cotary propositions are supposed to accomplish. They are to be understood against the background of the metaphysics of evolution, in which the process of human inquiry is conceived as a consciously controlled continuation of nature's unconscious, inferential information process.[29] This distinction between a conscious and an unconscious part of the nonetheless continuous process of reality is the means by which Peirce's metaphysics of reality is put in relationship to the normative logic of a possible cognition of reality.[30] It is this distinction that is also supposed to make understandable the extent to which cognition can have a beginning in time and a basis in qualitative evidence without prejudicing its fundamental character as Thirdness or mediation. The solution would go something like this. Nature's unconscious inferential process ends in human perception, and the conscious and controllable process of inference, with which normative logic is concerned, begins in the perceptual judgment. But there is an abductive inference mediating between the percept and the perceptual judgment, and this inference is itself a limiting case of unconscious inference. It is supposed to provide the uncriticizable and yet extremely fallible basis of our arguments (see 5.181; cf. 5.115 ff. and 5.142). This results, however, in a fundamental difficulty or ambiguity in Peirce's conception, as I will show later. But let us first examine these three cotary propositions more closely.

The first two cotary propositions give a new accent to Peirce's 1903 version of his theory of knowledge, and they do so in a way which seems prima facie to be provocative. In the first thesis Peirce adopts the scholastic proposition, which derives from Aristotle, that "nihil est in intellectu quod non prius fuerit in sensu" (5.181). In the second thesis he claims that "perceptual judgments contain general elements, so that universal propositions are deducible from them" (5.181). This seems to amount to an Empiricism that completely ignores the Kantian element in Peirce's early theory of knowledge, passing over the abductive inference (which is also linguistic interpretation) that mediates something as something and that cannot be derived from the sensory data of experience. However, Peirce points out at the same time that he does not wish to return to prelinguistic sense perception as psychologically oriented sensationalists do. Instead, in his genetic reduction of the meaning of concepts, he wants to go back only—in compliance with his semiotic theory—to perceptual judgments that can be formulated in sentences (5.181). This is confirmed by the second cotary proposition, which does not seem provocative at all when it is seen in the correct light, since all perceptual judgments that can be formulated in language must in fact contain in their predicates some general meaning that can itself be explicated in conditional statements, the way the pragmatic maxim indicates for possible experiments.[31]

The reason for the second cotary proposition's indication that our perceptual judgments already contain certain general elements (5.186) is provided by the third cotary proposition, which states that "abductive inference shades into perceptual judgment without any sharp line of demarkation between them" (5.181). Peirce indicates that, through the third thesis, the first thesis, that "all general elements are given in perception . . . loses most of its significance. For if a general element were given otherwise than in the perceptual judgment, it could only first appear in an abductive suggestion, and that is now seen to amount substantially to the same thing" (5.186). In fact, if the perceptual judgment is a limiting case of abductive inference or, metaphysically interpreted, the result of nature's unconscious "inferential process" (5.181), then the Aristotelian, quasi-empirical formulation of the first cotary proposition can be supplemented in the sense of Leibnizian Rationalism: "nisi intellectus ipse" (i.e., in the continuous process of inference).

As a proof of the inferential character of perceptual judgments, Peirce calls here, just as in 1868 (5.216), upon the "interpretativeness of the perceptual judgment" (5.186), which he says is "familiar, especially to every psychological student" (5.185). But he also emphasizes the difference between abductive inferences and perceptual judgments as their limiting case, a difference which consists in the fact that we cannot in the slightest conceive of what it would mean to contest a perceptual judgment (see 5.186; cf. 5.181). If this difference did not exist, then it would not be possible to explain, as Peirce himself did in 1868, why knowledge can begin in time at all or why every argument relevant to cognition can have a basis in evidence. But how are we to understand that we can reflect upon perceptual judgments as interpretations, on the one hand, and so it seems also criticize them, while as perceptual judgments, on the other hand, they are supposed to be uncriticizable?[32]

First off, we might think that this problem stems from an equivocation in Peirce's concept of perceptual judgment. In the case of interpretative perceptual judgments, which as such contain general conceptual elements, Peirce also has in mind at least those whose predicates are understood with the help of the logic of relations as dispositional concepts. To this extent they can be interpreted with the aid of the pragmatic maxim as conditional predictions; for example, "This is a diamond," but also "This is hard" (see 5.544). In the case of uncriticizable perceptual judgments, however, Peirce evidently has in mind primarily those with predicates that express only sensory qualities in the sense of Firstness, such as "This is red" (see 5.186). In 1906 he was to say of these qualities that they have "no intrinsic signification beyond themselves" and that they therefore, unlike "intellectual concepts," cannot be interpreted with the help of the pragmatic maxim.[33]

It seems obvious to assume that this reason alone is enough to exclude the perceptual judgments of the second type, and only these, from any criticism. But then, from Peirce's point of view, there would result too sharp a distinction between genuine perceptual judgments and abductive inferences. The former could then no longer be shown to be an interpretation of reality, and to this extent, they could also no longer be regarded as the limiting case of abductive inferences.

These conclusions show, I believe, that this proposed distinction between two types of perceptual judgments, which is supported by Peirce's distinction between two types of predicates (see 5.467 from 1906), is insufficient to explain that perceptual judgments are uncriticizable.

In fact, the examples that Peirce gives for the interpretative character of perceptual judgments show that uncriticizable sense impressions also receive an interpretive function insofar as they are employed in the predicates of perceptual judgments, even though this may be only to fix an aspect of reality selectively, such as in judging a perceptual content *as* something (see 5.186 and 5.184). Yet Peirce insists on the uncriticizable nature not just of sensations, but of their evaluation through a perceptual judgment as well: "But that any man should have a percept similar to mine and should ask himself the question whether this percept be *red*, which would imply that he had already judged *some* percept to be red, and that he should, upon careful attention to this percept, pronounce it to be decidedly and clearly *not* red, when I judge it to be predominantly red, *that* I cannot comprehend at all. An abductive suggestion, however, is something whose truth *can* be questioned or even denied" (5.186).

I think that this thought experiment betrays the reason for Peirce's difficulties here. The uncriticizable nature of perceptual judgments evidently refers only to that subsumption of sensory data under a concept which linguistic interpretation of perceptual contents *as* something does not itself bring about, but rather presupposes. This presupposition is also in no way irrelevant in cases of judgments about sense data. Hence, it is by no means self-evident that the quality of colors can be interpreted in a way that permits us to subsume them under abstract color concepts. That this subsumption was not possible for the Greeks of Homer's time, for example, does not prove that they were color blind; rather, their inability was conditioned by the semantic structure of their language.[34] The proposition "This is red" therefore presupposes an unambiguous interpretation of the meaning of the world, if it is to be a logically uncontrollable judgment of a perceptual content. On the other hand, the presupposition of unequivocal interpretations of meaning, as Peirce himself showed, can also be attained for "intellectual concepts," to a large extent, with the aid of the pragmatic maxim. Using this maxim we can and must also determine the truth or falsity of such perceptual judgments as "This is hard" or even "This is a diamond" by means of a transformation of perceptual contents into perceptual judgments, a transformation which is itself not subject to criticism.[35]

It is therefore decisive for Peirce's evaluation of the function of perceptual judgments to distinguish not between two types of perceptual judgments according to their predicates, but rather between interpretations of meaning, on the one hand, and a mere comparison of the contents of perceptual judgments with the possible predicates in judgments of fact, on the other hand. But since perceptual judgments like "This is red" fulfill both functions (since we can take this proposition as a statement of fact presupposing the interpretation of sensory qualities in the sense of abstract color concepts or as an interpretation of reality), Peirce can understand them both as uncriticizable and as limiting cases of highly fallible and, to this extent, also criticizable abductive inferences (suppositions about reality). Only if we could assume control of the largely unconscious interpretative function of perceptual judgments would they cease to be both practically uncriticizable and quite fallible. In that case their fundamentally unconscious, uncriticizable function of transforming perceptual contents into the predicates of propositions would simply constitute the anthropologically and biologically conditioned genetic threshold and self-evidential basis of all cognitively relevant argumentation.[36] Logically controllable and uncontrollable functions in human cognition would then be clearly distinguished but related to each other as conditions. This conception of cognition establishes the regulative principle for the use of the pragmatic maxim in the sense of the three cotary propositions. This maxim is supposed, according to Peirce, to clarify the meaning of abductive hypotheses to the extent that logical argumentation can finally be anchored in irrefutable perceptual judgments.

But here we are confronted with a further ambiguity adhering to the concept of abductive inference and the transition to perceptual judgments. According to Peirce, abductive inference not only is explicable by means of the pragmatic maxim as an interpretation of meaning, but also can be verified as a synthetic inference, as an explanatory hypothesis in regard to factual truth. The transition that Peirce postulates between abductive inference and uncriticizable perceptual judgments applies now, so it seems, to both the unambiguous nature of its meaning and the certainty of its truth. These two are not the same, however, each being correlatively mediated by the other. The clarification of meaning depends upon the idea of the possible experimental experience that would prove the hypothesis true, while the clarification of meaning is itself presupposed in the inductive test of the truth of the hypothesis. Peirce conceives inductive verification as an unlimited process of approximation to the truth of law hypotheses as confirmed by uncriticizable perceptual judgments. On the other hand, he regards the pragmatic clarification of meaning as an unlimited semiotic process of interpretation, which, as a metascientific thought experiment, is related from the outset to possible experimental experience, that is, to the inductive verification of law hypotheses. Does this sufficiently clarify the relationship between meaning interpretation and the processes of logical inference?

I do not want to raise here the question whether the metascientific orientation in the clarification of meaning is also appropriate to interpretations of the world as history. Unlike nature, which is already subject to laws, the world conceived as history has yet to receive its form according to maxims. These are therefore verifiable not by essentially repeatable experiments, but rather by the irreversible and risk-laden process of human interaction.[37] But we should ask whether the interpretation of the world, something which Peirce held to be implicit in all symbols, can be reduced solely to abductive inferences in perceptual judgments. According to Peirce these inferences are trans-individual and hence a priori intersubjectively valid. Such inferences even take place unconsciously in nature, according to Peirce, and need only to come to consciousness, so to speak, in order to provide each individual person with a situation or world interpreted *as* something. But this is also obviously contrary to a point raised by semantic Pragmatism itself, that is, that human beings must reach an agreement about the meaning of the symbols they use, even to the extent that natural interpretations are expressed in them. This means that there must be another, third factor in the constitution of the meaning of human perceptual judgments, besides trans-individual inference processes and sense data, which, as Peirce often intimates, are the same for all human beings (see 5.118). This factor is present because human experience, unlike that of animals, which are without language, is always already mediated by signs, so that human experiences of situations are mediated by the experiences of their partners in communication, including those of past peoples. As a result, experience is something present to individual consciousness and also virtually public.

In 1868 Peirce had in fact not drawn all the conclusions that follow from the postulate of the "community" upon which he based his semiotic theory of knowledge and which thereby took the place of the Kantian notion of "consciousness in general." He had neglected both the communicative function of sign interpretation and the way our interpretation of the world is conditioned by society and language. Moreover, in 1903 the idea of the community, especially its quasi-transcendental philosophical function, was pushed into the background by the cosmological-metaphysical interpretation of information or inference processes, so that one almost gets the impression that Peirce wanted to reduce the meaning content of all concepts in his cotary propositions to a logically mediated exchange of information between each individual person and nature.[38] By contrast, the late work of Royce, as I mentioned earlier, set on his idea of the "community of interpretation" a new accent which did justice to the third factor in the constitution of meaning just now postulated.[39] For this Royce took Peirce's early writings as his starting point.

Josiah Royce consciously opposed the traditional theory of knowledge when he recognized that human conceptions do not owe their meaning content just to the flow of information back and forth between man and nature as found in perceptions, but rather also to an exchange of information between human beings by means of sign interpretation. Taking issue with William James's interpretation of the pragmatic maxim, Royce emphasized that it is not just the "credit value" of concepts that must be explicated with regard to the possible redemption of their "cash value" in experimental verification. Rather, as this very explication shows, the redemption of "cash value" by perceptual verification presupposes establishing the "credit value" by interpretation.[40] But such an interpretation is not established just by an explicit clarification, definition, or explication of concepts, that is, metascientific reflection. It is instead implicitly present where inherited forms of language are used interpretatively on the occasion of perceptual experience. This is already an instance of that interpretative exchange of information between human beings which is explicitly thematized in communicative understanding between contemporaries and in the historical and philological transmission of tradition. Peirce's suggestion of clarifying concepts with regard to possible experimental experience can be considered only the metascientific limiting case of communicative understanding through the interpretation of signs. I will come back later to this conception, which supplements Peirce's evolutionist view of the controlled continuation of the cosmic information and inference process.[41]

As I have already suggested, Peirce introduced the cotary propositions in order to prove that abduction is the logic of experience, that is, the logic by which new ideas are introduced into argumentation.

The function of Pragmatism therefore lies, according to Peirce, in deciding about the acceptability of hypotheses on the basis of this insight into the logic of abduction (see 5.196). This requires an answer to the question what is to be understood as a good abduction (5.197). This answer, in turn, implies answering the question what is to be understood as an inductively verifiable abductive hypothesis (5.197). In order to provide this answer, Peirce in the last part of the lecture once again directs his attention to the logic of induction (5.198 ff.). The extraordinarily concise observations that he presents here are based upon the presuppositions of his mathematics of the continuum and his doctrine of the categories. They are particularly interesting insofar as they go beyond his earlier positions, including his view of the problem of induction, and bring out the importance of the principle by Synechism (in epistemological terms, the perception of the general or of rational mediation as continuity).[42]

Peirce distinguishes among five different positions on the topic of inductive logic. The first one corresponds to the strict Positivism of Comte and John Stuart Mill, which admits only those hypotheses which can be reduced to sense data (see 5.198). This position's principle is itself inconsistent, since it is self-refuting (5.198). But it also leads to contradictions because it can recognize no general law as real, least of all the law of the regularity of nature upon which Mill based his theory of the validity of induction (see 5.210 and 5.342 ff.).

The second position is the one which Peirce himself previously held, that the truth of hypotheses can be approximated by inductive confirmation "in the long run" (5.199; cf. 5.170 ff.). This position includes assuming vagueness or the unlimited capacity to improve all factual hypotheses.[43]

The third position's logical structure appears to amount to what Karl Popper would later put forth as the falsification theory. Peirce believes, however, that the basic principle of induction which is already presupposed in the second position, and which Popper denies, "entitles us to hold a theory [which cannot be verified by 'positive experimental evidence'], provided it be such that if it involve any falsity, experiment must some day detect that falsity" (5.200).

The fourth and fifth positions deal with a problem that, according to Peirce, cannot be solved by the theories of induction already mentioned. Here he feels compelled, as he himself indicates (5.201), to anticipate the results of his mathematics of the continuum.[44]

According to Peirce, the third position has the advantage over the second position (the idea of a verification in the long run) that, by dispensing with positive experimental evidence, it is enabled to assume that completely general hypotheses or theories can be checked.[45] But, on the other hand, it has the disadvantage of providing a foundation for checking through falsification only by means of existential propositions about discrete events in space and time (or at least in time). Peirce expresses this in terms of his mathematics of the continuum by contending that the third approach to the foundation of induction, in contrast to the second, implies that "we can infer [in an abductive inference] a proposition implying the reality of the infinite multitude itself, while their mode of justifying induction [that of the logicians of the third group] would exclude every infinite multitude except the lowest grade, that of the multitude of all integer numbers" (5.203).

But this limiting of induction's criterion of evidence to a discrete court of appeal gives rise, according to Peirce, to a fundamental difficulty for all hypotheses, affirmative or negative, that apply to the continuum of space and time. He takes as an example the hypothesis that Achilles overtakes the tortoise, whereby we must assume that "our only knowledge was derived inductively from observations of the relative positions of Achilles and the tortoise at those stages of the progress that the sophism supposes, and . . . that Achilles really moves twice as fast as the tortoise" (5.202).

Those who uphold the third position recognize hypotheses of the form "X never occurs" insofar as the event in question is only of the kind that "could not occur without being detected" (5.200). And since this position can admit as discoverable no distance between Achilles and the tortoise that would be smaller than can be measured, it can therefore admit as meaningful the sophistic hypothesis that Achilles can never overtake the turtle, since this hypothesis foresees only discoverable refutations. Yet it can find meaning in the common-sense hypothesis that Achilles overtakes the tortoise only on the impossible presupposition that Achilles could reduce his measurable distance from the tortoise to zero by dividing it in half (5.202). That is, on their presuppositions, those who uphold the third position cannot admit an experienceable continuum of movement for which metrical division is external.[46]

Peirce compares the aporia of this third position with that of the fourth position, which is very widespread among mathematicians, but seems to lead beyond the third one only in regard to the theory of induction.[47] According to this position, any incommensurable quantity of a continuum (e.g., the length of a circle in comparison to that of a polygon, the length of a square's diagonal in comparison to its sides, or the length of a line in comparison to a series of discrete points) can be admitted as an "irrational, real quantity." But at the same time it is assumed that when the distance between two points is smaller than any signifiable quantity, that is, smaller than any finite quantity, then there is no distance at all between them.[48] This position thereby evidently becomes entangled, according to Peirce, in the same contradiction as does the falsification theory sketched before, which, on the one hand, does admit statements about a continuum to be meaningful, but which does this, on the other hand, by presupposing that their falsity can be proven by measurements or by existential assertions about discrete occurrences in space and time. The inner contradiction in both positions lies in their claim to be able to grasp in a rational way something that, according to their presuppositions, is irrational.

The solution to the problem of induction, when it is posed in this way, constitutes a fifth position, which, Peirce explains, complies with the cotary propositions. It admits as meaningful statements about a genuine continuum, especially about a time continuum, under the presupposition that "such continuity is given in perception" (5.205). This presupposition implies for Peirce in particular that "we seem to perceive a genuine flow of time, such that instants melt into one another without separate individuality."[49]

This is where the particular point of the 1903 Pragmatism lectures and, hence, Peirce's late synechistic philosophy becomes apparent. Its implications become visible when we consider that Peirce in his theory of knowledge in 1868 and 1878 argued against the very possibility of "intuition," that is, immediate perception, and, in particular, regarded Berkeley's notion of space and time as the result of inferential processes (5.223, 6.416). The gradual change in his conception which had developed since 1893 (see 6.110–11, 7.451–57, and especially 8.123, from 1902) could have been influenced by his reading of James's *Principles of Psychology*.[50] Logically, this change was based on Peirce's consideration that unconscious inferential processes are not subject to rational control by a normative logic and therefore do not exclude immediate perception as the starting point of conscious, controlled inference but, in fact, require it (5.181). On this Peirce writes:

The man who . . . accepts the cotary propositions will hold, with firmest of grasps, to the recognition that logical criticism is limited to what we can control. . . . But the sum of it all is that our logically controlled thoughts compose a small part of the mind, the mere blossom of a vast complexus, which we may call the instinctive mind, in which this man will not say that he has *faith*, because that implies the conceivability of distrust, but upon which he builds as the very fact to which it is the whole business of his logic to be true.[51]

However, establishing the possibility or, rather, necessity of a perception of continuity by means of the cotary propositions implies yet a further idea that provides an essential correction to both Peirce's Pragmatism and his theory of reality. In the cotary propositions generality and continuity are equated as aspects of the category of Thirdness.[52] From this it follows that, for Peirce, the perception of continuity (especially of time) is the perceivable aspect of generality, because it is the unconscious and uncontrollable aspect of the rational mediation in the inference process.[53] According to Peirce, "Just as Achilles does not have to make the series of distinct endeavors which he is represented as making, so this process of forming the perceptual judgment, because it is subconscious and not so amenable to logical criticism, does not have to make separate acts of inference, but performs its act in one continuous process" (5.181).

But this results in a new consequence for Peirce's realist theory of universals. This position, which he had upheld since 1868, is no longer based merely upon the meaning-critical consideration that general statements (or statements with general predicates) can in principle be true (or objectively valid) if arguments are to be meaningful at all.[54] Rather, they are to be based, in addition, upon the postulate that genuine, empirical, general statements, that is, law hypotheses, must be confirmable by perceiving the general as continuity if they are to be admitted as meaningful hypotheses.

In order to clarify this problematic situation, Peirce at the close of his lecture distinguishes once again among three possible philosophical positions (see 5.209). The first of these is Nominalism, against which he struggled throughout his life. The second one amounts to the view that "thirdness is experimentally verifiable [in the long run], that is, is inferable by induction, although it cannot be directly perceived" (5.209). The third position is that of the cotary propositions. The second position's theory of reality, according to which "the only reality, there could be, would be conformity to the ultimate result of inquiry" (5.211), is very close to Peirce's own view of 1868. Or, perhaps more accurately, it is like that idealistic shortcut approach to meaning-critical Realism from which Peirce could in fact never completely extricate himself.[55] Of course, he had already gone beyond this theory in 1871 and transcended it completely in 1885 by calling for the inductive verification and correction (falsification) of beliefs on the basis of the deictic fixability of the real's existence here and now. But in 1903 this is no longer satisfactory to him, for his chief complaint about the second position is that it has no answer to the question "why perception should be allowed such authority in regard to what is real" (5.211).

Peirce now finds a mediation missing between individual brute facts here and now and the generality of theory, a mediation by means of the experience of the qualitative nature of facts which collide here and now with the ego, but do not confront it *as* something.[56] For this mediation to be possible, we must be able to experience general laws in the qualitative nature of facts that obey these laws. That is, there must be not only a feeling or sensation of this qualitative nature of facts in the sense of Firstness, but also a perception of the general in the particular (Firstness of Thirdness), at least as the vague anticipation of a real possibility.[57] This problem had already led Peirce to postulate a cognitively relevant iconic function of sentence predicates and is here identified with the problem of the experienceability of the continuum.[58] Without such an experience we could not, according to Peirce, verify even "a determinate order of sequence among . . . states" as real (5.211). We could merely postulate it as more easily grasped than another one in the sense of a nominalistic (idealistic) Pragmatism. Then, however, there would be no empirical orientation for the course of the process of inquiry, and this orientation was supposed to lead to the consensus of all investigators in the sense of Peirce's regulative principle, which he continued to recognize (see 5.211).

Peirce ended his 1903 lectures with this connection between Pragmatism and the realist theory of universals, behind which stood his phenomenological doctrine of categories and his mathematics and metaphysics of the continuum. For his contemporaries at least it was a surprise and met with little understanding. It laid the preliminary foundations for the critical confrontation with the contemporary, more or less nominalistic, versions of Pragmatism.

C. The Pragmatism Essays (1905 and after)

On March 7, 1904, Peirce wrote to William James:

> I want to thank you for your kind reference to me in your piece about Schiller's *Humanism*. . . . The humanistic element of pragmatism is very true and important and impressive; but I do not think that the doctrine can be *proved* in that way. The present generation likes to skip proofs. I am tempted to write a little book of 150 pages about pragmatism, just outlining my views of the matter, and appending to it some of my old pieces with critical notes. You and Schiller carry pragmatism too far for me. [8.258]

This excerpt designates very precisely the problematic situation that Peirce found himself in after James advised him against publishing his "incomprehensible" Harvard lectures from 1903.[59] The plan of the small book was realized as a series of essays in *The Monist* in 1905–6. This fourth and final set of representative journal publications to appear in Peirce's lifetime formulated the standpoint of the fourth period of his philosophy under the title "Pragmaticism." Compared with the 1903 Pragmatism lectures, these essays not only are more popular, but also concentrate from the beginning to a greater degree on a critical confrontation between Peirce's own and other contemporary forms of Pragmatism. The background of Peirce's system, into which he tried to integrate his Pragmatism in 1903, appears only in isolated sections of this essay series, but to a greater extent in the unpublished outlines for the continuation of the series.[60]

The introductory essay, "What Pragmatism Is," is clearly conceived as a retrospective or review of the two birth certificates of Peirce's own Pragmatism ("The Fixation of Belief" and "How to Make Our Ideas Clear"). After a general introduction on the "spirit of the laboratory," which distinguishes his own position as "Pragmaticism" in the name of the "ethics of terminology" from the broader concept of James's and Schiller's humanistic Pragmatism (5.411–15), there follows a recapitulation of the belief-doubt theory (5.416–21) and a clarification of misunderstandings about the pragmatic maxim, presented in the form of a "catechism dialogue" (5.422–35). Finally, there is a supplement about Thirdness and Pragmatism in which the topics of the doctrine of categories and synechistic metaphysics come up (5.436), followed by a postscript calling for the reader to submit criticisms (5.437).

Peirce here returns so exactly to the spirit of his 1877 belief-doubt theory that he reproduces to a large extent the psychologism of the theory of truth he had criticized in 1903.[61] More specifically, we must say that he even reproduces that naturalistic psychology which limits the possibilities of reflection to the doubts that are forced upon us from without by new facts. This reduces the history of ideas in an all too simple manner to the mechanism of "trial and error." Hence, the struggle with Descartes that Peirce commenced in 1868 and 1877 cannot as yet be decided by a clear victory in favor of Pragmatism.[62]

Peirce once again makes an impressive case for the view that human thought, including philosophy, cannot begin with a fictitious starting point, be it in the senses or the intellect, but must start from "the very state of mind in which you actually find yourself at the time you do 'set out' " (5.416). Yet even this attempt at a "rehabilitation of prejudices"[63] does not really do justice to the critical attitude of Peirce's own level of reflection or to the possibilities of a critical reconstruction of the history of ideas led by such "formal" doubt, that is, a hermeneutical criticism of tradition including a critique of ideologies. Of course, we will have to grant Peirce that there will always be much that we "do not doubt, in the least" (5.416), that there are factual limits to our ability to doubt—meaning limits for material reflection that are conditioned not just by coincidental circumstances, but by the present state of historical consciousness or even by pre-

suppositions concerning human nature that are determined by evolution.[64] But it does not follow from this that "that which you do not
doubt at all, you must and do regard . . . as absolute truth."[65] Peirce's
own professed adoption of basic Fallibilism cannot, obviously, be resolved with this view.[66] It is also at least amiss to characterize man's
relationship to the final material presuppositions of his thought as
though an individual could say to himself, "I cannot think otherwise."[67] Reflection is incapable of recognizing such a material state of
affairs. On the other hand, it is capable of recognizing the possible
difference between its own belief and *the* truth on the basis of a
philosophical reflection which is possible at all times and derives from
what has been called being "excentrically positioned."[68] On the other
hand, when reflection is effective on the praxis of life and so is bound
to a situation and centristically engaged, it is capable of reaching a
decision on a belief that more or less does justice to one's own possibilities of thought, but it must always break off material reflection by
an act of will.[69] Naturally, the beliefs behind a praxis are not always
applied in such a reflective way, but if they are not we would most
certainly not be able to say that someone must identify that which he
does not doubt with the absolute in the sense of a philosophical definition of absolute truth. Rather, he must only act as if his belief were
the absolute truth.[70] The pragmatist philosopher is able, of course, to
establish this by observing the way people behave, whereby he in fact
presupposes the difference between belief and truth.

As a whole Peirce's text leaves us no doubt that he has as little
interest in 1905 as in 1877 in claiming that the truth is equivalent to
the practically indubitable belief of any human being. His aim is simply to define the truth without assuming metaphysical entities, by instead considering possible praxis and possible human experience. For
this he must rely on the use of the terms "doubt" and "belief."[71]
Truth is then "that to a belief in which belief would tend if it were to
tend indefinitely toward absolute fixity."[72] Peirce has implied here
with the conditional nature of this definition that man is capable of
defining what the truth *would* be, independently of the present standing of his beliefs and as distinguished from them. Man can do this
through a formal and universal reflection, without thereby assuming
any entities that cannot be experienced.[73] However, this "would-be"
definition still lacks a positive description of the alternative criterion
that the individual is to put in the place of metaphysical assumptions,
and against which the finite ego is to compare his firm beliefs. Such a
criterion is necessary if the "would-be" nature of the definition is to
be more than a tautological postulate.

An indication of the way this problem could be solved in Peirce's
fully developed philosophy is given, in part, in the final paragraph of

his recapitulation of his belief-doubt theory (5.421). Following Plato, Peirce points out that all thought is a conversation between the soul and itself in which the soul (and what follows is no longer Plato, but Peirce) brings in society, conceived as a person, as a critical partner, and focuses in this society on the unlimited, ideal community of those engaged in scientific inquiry. In the name of the belief to which the community would attain after completing an unlimited process of inquiry, following all the criteria of the theory of induction, you or any other individual would be able—"but only in the abstract, and in a Pickwickian sense—to distinguish between absolute truth and what you do not doubt."[74] In fact, we must depend upon this abstract distinction if we are to be able to integrate Pragmatism, in the sense of a normative logic of inquiry's ideal criteria of truth, with common-sense Pragmatism's criteria of evidence, as it is available here and now, not just for everyday decisions, but also for those of experts on such matters as basic propositions. A Pragmatism that takes into account this difference between ideal and factual criteria and mediates between them in the situation could be designated, the way Peirce does, as "Critical Common-Sensism."[75]

There follows in the text a clarification of misunderstandings about Pragmatism as it was presented in 1878. This section concentrates on defending Pragmatism against the view that it involves a reduction of the general meaning of concepts to specific actual actions or the data of experience. Peirce counters this view, which for him is a nominalistic, individualistic error, by presenting an analysis of the experiment as it is found in natural science. It presupposes, in the sense of Secondness, "an experimenter of flesh and blood," an "external (or quasi-external) ACT by which he [the experimenter] modifies those objects" to be operated upon, and "the subsequent *reaction* of the world upon the experimenter."[76] To this extent, the meaning of physical concepts is mediated from the beginning by material praxis and its natural limiting conditions.[77] However, the pragmatist's view of experiment considers not disconnected, individual acts or experiences, but repeatable operations that follow rules. It is interested only in intersubjectively reconfirmable "*general kinds* of experimental phenomena" (5.426; cf. 5.425). This brings Peirce to his main concern, a modern, realist theory of universals founded upon the continuum of natural laws and human habits that is expressed in the formulation of conditional predictions and hypothetical imperatives as the possibility of a rationalization of the universe.[78]

The difficulty with this conception lies in the fact that the continual realization of universality which it envisions does not depend just upon human insight into natural laws, but upon a choice of goals as well. This open factor cannot automatically be made rational by translating a knowledge of laws into instrumental reason, if we do not want to assume that the final goal of life is a priori and sufficiently established by means of the organism's need to adapt itself optimally to its milieu. Peirce had recognized this problem, at least in a preliminary way, in his normative logic.[79] Now he attempts to state the "rational meaning of every proposition" in terms of the pragmatic maxim so that the factor of the choice of goals is also taken into consideration and is left open as a continuum of real possibilities for the actualization of habits: "But of myriads of forms into which a proposition may be translated, what is that one which is to be called its very meaning? It is, according to the pragmaticist, that form in which the proposition becomes applicable to human conduct, not in these or those special circumstances, nor when one entertains this or that special design, but that form which is most directly applicable to self-control under every situation, and to every purpose" (5.427).

Peirce himself sees that what he postulates here *in abstracto* cannot be expressed through the form of a proposition. What, for example, is the meaning in the sense just mentioned of a proposition like "This is a diamond" for a physicist or a chemist? Peirce approaches the question a second time and answers that it is "the general description of all the experimental phenomena which the assertion of the proposition virtually predicts" (5.427).

In his semiotic interpretation of Pragmatism in 1907 Peirce goes one step further and defines the "final logical interpretant" of the general meaning of a concept as the normatively implied habit itself, rather than a verbal description: "The concept which is a logical interpretant is only imperfectly so. It somewhat partakes of the nature of a verbal definition, and is as inferior to the habit, and much in the same way, as a verbal definition is inferior to the real definition. The deliberately formed, self-analyzing habit . . . is the living definition, the veritable and final logical interpretant."[80]

This in fact points out *one* dimension of the progressive rationalization of conduct by means of the clarification of meaning, and in 1905 Peirce himself attempts to relate it to the dimension of ethical rationalization:

Now, just as conduct controlled by ethical reason tends toward fixing certain habits of conduct, the nature of which (as to illustrate the meaning, peaceable habits and not quarrelsome habits) does not depend upon any accidental circumstances, and *in that sense* may be said to be *destined*; so, thought, controlled by a rational experimental logic, tends to the fixation of certain opinions, equally destined, the nature of which will be the same in the end, however the perversity of thought of whole generations may cause the postponement of the ultimate fixation." [5.430]

At least in this passage Peirce appears to focus his attention on the bi-dimensionality of human habit formation,[81] taking into account its foundation both in the pragmatic-technological application of knowledge about laws and in the ethical orientation towards the acceptability of a choice of goals. Both of these tendencies towards rationalization reveal their final meaning, according to Peirce, in a fatefully predetermined, eschatological *summum bonum* that is supposed to provide the final measure for the clarification of meaning as it is understood by Pragmaticism.[82] But is there not a difference between the pragmatic clarification of concepts in the sense of a habitual adaptation of behavior to unchanging natural laws and a clarification of concepts (or at least of the meanings of symbols) with regard to the goal-oriented character of a historical, social process? This is not to say that the latter is not possible or even, in fact, necessary; yet it is a process that not only progressively comes to know reality through scientific research, but is also supposed to change and perfect it, as Peirce says, in terms of the great community of love. For example, in regard to the possible habitualization of human behavior, what would be the definition of the concept of justice, a concept that Peirce himself counted among the most "physically efficient" (5.431) ideas in the sense of his realist theory of universals?

Unfortunately, as far as I know Peirce never attempted to give such a definition. However, his comments on the Kantian distinction between "practical" and "pragmatic" seem to indicate that he did not think it could be attained solely through the "experimental attitude" by means of conditional predictions or technical-hypothetical imperatives.[83] Dewey, on the other hand, as a social pedagogue, did not admit this. For him, who of course no longer sought after any general regulative principles for behavior, even value concepts could be explicated pragmatically, that is, through the communicative mediation of needs and the creative evaluations of individual persons and through the "intelligent mediation of means and ends."[84] I believe that Dewey's conception comes as close as possible to the procedure presupposed by a democratic social order for establishing the meaning of value concepts. But one must object to his use of the concept "experimentalism," since here we no longer have repeatable experiments on nature that various freely interchangeable experimenters could undertake under the same isolated starting conditions. Rather, we have experiments in which, strictly speaking, nonrepeatable interactions[85] and communications between individual persons are decisive. In these historical, social quasi-experiments the meaning of value concepts is not explicated, in the end, by reference to experiences that can be predicted in conditional terms. Rather, they are explicated by means of communicative understanding and agreement (*Verständigung*) among all the citizens about the norm of the good life that is to be created, taking all predictable experiences into account.

This communicative understanding and agreement would be, on the one hand, part of a continuum with that hermeneutic transmission of tradition which Josiah Royce had analyzed in 1903 in his philosophy of interpretation, which took Peirce's semiotic as its starting point.[86] On the other hand, it would be practically oriented towards a possible improvement of social interaction and communication *by means of* social interaction and communication. Acting as the "intelligent mediation of means and ends" (Dewey), it must mediate in the historical situation between the process of habitualizing a progressive cognition of reality (Peirce) and the process of habitualizing an ethical orientation towards perfecting and completing reality (Peirce). In all this there lies an element of risk inherent in the one-time-only, irreversible character of the process, an element that also enters into the explication of the meaning of all concepts not of purely scientific and technological relevance. This element of risk is not to be confused with Peirce's recognition of the preliminary and imprecise character of our scientific knowledge of reality, since here the explication of meaning is a priori dependent upon a truth that is not just to be progressively discovered, but—to say it in a provocative way—is to be progressively *made* by practical decisions. Within Pragmatism, William James actually had such a truth in mind in, for example, his famous image of the mountain climber who has to jump over a break in a glacier and whose decision of belief that enters into his jump practically contributes to making the believed truth true.[87] James was inclined to explicate the concept of truth as such according to this model of "veri-fication," something to which Peirce, as a logician of science, had to object.[88] Moreover, James's restriction of this model to the problem of the existential "satisfaction" of the individual person and his particular perspective sometimes seemed to Peirce, as a metaphysician of the community and evolutionary love, to be blatantly immoral.[89] The problem of a truth that has to be created through praxis exists for society as well. This can be made apparent, especially if society is engaged in the "embodiment of concrete reasonableness," as Peirce's ethics and metaphysics of "hope" foresee.[90]

In the end, therefore, it remains doubtful whether "the entire intellectual purport of any symbol consists in the total of all general modes of rational conduct which, conditionally upon all the possible different circumstances and desires, would ensue upon the acceptance of the symbol" (5.438). The question is if a historically conceived ethics or metaphysics such as Peirce's must not contain, in addition to the explication of concepts concerning possible generalizations of behavior, also an explication in terms of a hypothetical totalization of our responsible decisions as they bring about desirable changes in the social situation.[91] In that case the criterion of meaning would be not what can be made at any time by interchangeable experimenters, but what a group of irreplaceable individuals can conceive under certain historically developed conditions as a goal that is both realizable and worthy of realization. There is at least one concept which Peirce had always presupposed for his semiotic logic that can be clarified in this way, the concept explicated by Royce as the unlimited "Community of Interpretation." This concept refers to something that, on the one hand, is already presupposed in all argumentation and yet, on the other hand, must still be produced within society by society.

In the second essay of the 1905 *Monist* series, "Issues of Pragmatism," Peirce seeks to present two doctrines that he had upheld in the first period of his philosophizing (1868–71) as consequences of Pragmatism: Critical Common-sensism and the realist theory of universals.[92] These two topics occur in the first essay of the series as well, but here they are to be considered thematically.

The arguments put forth in Critical Common-sensism go back to Peirce's 1868 criticism of Descartes and to his early meaning critique of Kant's "thing-in-itself" (5.525, 5.451). It takes up the belief-doubt theory, already recapitulated in "What Pragmatism Is," and connects it with the distinction between unconscious ("acritical") and conscious, critically controllable inference processes as it was developed up to 1903 in conjunction with the metaphysics of evolution (in the theory of instinct) and the conception of the "normative sciences." The positive idea that stands behind the comprehensive title "Critical Common-sensism" evidently stems from the confrontation between Thomas Reid's philosophy of common sense and British Empiricism's critical theory of knowledge and, in particular, Kant's critical philosophy (see especially 5.523 ff.). This controversy was widely discussed during Peirce's early years, when, for example, his teacher Chauncey Wright changed sides from Hamilton to John Stuart Mill. Meaning-critical Pragmatism was supposed to provide the perspective from which it would be possible to develop a synthesis of these two directions, such as Hamilton had striven to achieve (5.452). It is unnecessary here to discuss those aspects of Critical Common-sensism which have been dealt with before. However, one of these aspects, namely, that common-sense beliefs are vague and to this extent leave open the possibility of contradictory interpretations, immediately leads to a new aspect discussed in the second essay of the Pragmaticism series, "real vagues" or "real possibilities" (5.453). These give us a new view of the connection between the realist theory of universals and Pragmatism.

Peirce called attention in 1885 in his Royce review to the fact that the meaning-critical definition of the real as the cognizable, or more exactly, as the possible object of the final belief agreed upon by the unlimited community of scientists, makes use of a conception of possibility that is stronger than that of mere logical possibility.[93] He spoke repeatedly about a fateful predetermination or tendency that resides in the teleological process of cognition as postulated in the definition of reality. In addition, he insisted that the question whether the goal will in fact be attained cannot be given a definite answer, and he opposed Royce's and Hegel's absolute Idealism by maintaining that the indefinite factual nature of the future is precisely what provokes our ethical engagement and hope and, hence, constitutes the "religious fruitfulness" of his doctrine.[94] In 1900, in Peirce's second review of Royce, where he again discusses the definition of reality in terms of possible experience (8.101 ff.), the question takes yet another turn with the introduction of the distinction between "would be" and "will be."[95] Peirce places such great value upon this distinction that he would later correct all his formulations of the pragmatic maxim in his early works, putting them into the form of subjunctive, conditional propositions.[96] Now it becomes clear that the indefinite nature of our expectations about the future, as implied by Peirce's definition of reality and by all real predicates according to the pragmatic maxim, is based essentially upon the (as yet) unfulfilled antecedent conditions of all conditioned predictions, whereas the possibility of conditional expectations about the future generally are guaranteed by the reality of general laws.

But this gives rise to another problem for Peirce's realist theory of universals, a problem that had to become important after Peirce developed his metaphysics of continuity in 1900, especially in regard to the continuity of time. The reality of laws must be assumed to be unchanging and actual, but this is not enough to explain that possibility which Pragmatism had always counted upon when it explicated all concepts in terms of possible, that is, predictable, experience. If the real is all that which can be the object of a true proposition, then there must be such a thing as "real vagueness," which corresponds exactly to the vagueness in the conjunctive, conditional propositions utilized by Pragmatism for the purpose of clarifying meaning. This turns out to amount to a widening of the realist theory of universals to include the modalities of being (see 5.453 and 5.454 ff.):

Pragmaticism makes the ultimate intellectual purport of what you please to consist in conceived conditional[97] resolutions, or their substance; and therefore, the conditional propositions, with their hypothetical antecedents, in which such resolutions consist, being of the ultimate nature of meaning, must be capable of being true, that is, of expressing whatever there be which is such as the proposition expresses, independently of being thought to be so in any judgment, or being represented to be so in any other symbol of any man or men. But that amounts to saying that possibility is sometimes of a real kind. [5.453]

This expansion of Peirce's 1868 meaning-critical Realism to include a modal ontology[98] finally gives him the opportunity to separate it consistently from the idealistic-nominalistic model for explicating reality, as he had intended to do in 1871 in his crticism of Berkeley (8.30), and to transform the Kantian model for limiting the validity of concepts to possible experience in a way that accords with Pragmatism, that is, by using real experiments to establish the validity of concepts. The test case for this definitive clarification of Peirce's position is the reinterpretation of the diamond example which had gone afoul in 1872 and 1878 and which Peirce now takes up again.[99]

To begin with, Peirce counters the temptation, to which he repeatedly succumbed, to reduce the meaning of the concept "hard" in "This diamond is hard" to the actual testing of its hardness by confronting such reduction attempts with the logical, grammatical structure of the "would be" *conditionalis* (and, analogously, by confronting the reality of the real with the uncertain fact of its being recognized):

For if the reader will turn to the original maxim of pragmaticism[100] . . . he will see that the question is, not what *did* happen, but whether it would have been well to engage in any line of conduct whose successful issue depended upon whether that diamond *would* resist an attempt to scratch it, or whether all other logical means of determining how it ought to be classed *would* lead to the conclusion which, to quote the very words of that article, would be "the belief which alone could be the result of investigation carried *sufficiently far*." [5.453, self-quotation from 5.408]

It is worth noting that Peirce does not wish, after correcting himself in this way, to take back the 1878 argument according to which the question of the hardness or softness of the diamond is a question of nomenclature. He rejects only the nominalistic, conventionalistic treatment of this question as one of "merely" regulating language, of arbitrary "language use" (5.453; cf. 5.457). His semiotic logic of inquiry anticipates here a characteristic development in the philosophy of linguistic analysis in the twentieth century. Just like the early Carnap, Peirce was temporarily fascinated with the idea of reducing the problems of ontology to mere problems of the logic of language in the formal mode, and of thereby being able to eliminate them.[101] In a way that is similar to the later Carnap of "onto-semantics" and to the language-game theory of the later Wittgenstein, Peirce was to return to the problem of ontology as one to be resolved by the analysis and critique of language.[102]

But wherein lies for Peirce the positive, semiotic, modal ontological resolution of the problem of the hardness of a diamond that is
never actually tested? Peirce seeks the solution by pointing to the
real, lawful order of nature which connects the characteristic that is
predicated of the diamond as hardness with its other experienceable
characteristics and with those of all other diamonds. He asks, "How
can the hardness of all other diamonds fail to bespeak *some* real relation among the diamonds without which a piece of carbon would
not be a diamond?" (5.457). The question wherein the experienceable
hardness of the diamond consists if it is not in fact experienced—in
other words, the question that Berkeley could solve only by introducing a divine *perceptio perennis*—can actually be answered by this
reference to the order of nature. But this will not answer the deeper
question wherein the meaning of hardness, that is, the characteristic
that is predicated *as* hardness, then consists, generally *and* in the case
of its not-yet-verified, but well-founded, predication. The answer to
this question—the question posed by semantic Pragmatism—has already been presupposed when we ask wherein the *experienceable*
hardness of the diamond consists, if it is not actually experienced. Of
what does the ability to experience the hardness of the diamond,
which has been presupposed here, consist? This is actually the question that Peirce poses in 1905 in the farmework of his postulated logic
and ontology of modality. His answer reads:

At the same time [along with considering the real, lawful order of nature],
we must dismiss the idea that the occult state of things (be it a relation
among atoms or something else), which constitutes the reality of a diamond's hardness can possibly consist in anything but in the truth of a
general conditional proposition. For to what does the entire teaching of
chemistry relate except to the "behavior" of different possible kinds of material substance? And in what does that behavior consist except that if a
substance of a certain kind should be exposed to an agency of a certain
kind, a certain kind of sensible result *would* ensue. [5.457]

Interpreted in the context of Peirce's Pragmaticism, I believe that
this answer contains two points. The idea of a transcendental Pragmaticism, developed from Peirce's transformation of Kant by means of
his semiotic and logic of inquiry in 1869 and 1871, is reflected upon
only rarely and in a passing way in 1905.[103] This point about the
framework of Peirce's thought can be expressed in a counterfactual
conditional proposition.[104] If there were no real community of inquirers that acted through logical inference (deduction, induction, and
abduction) and sign interpretation to connect and constitute the correlative foundation between experimental investigation and instrumental action, that is, action led by the "best way" to a goal (*Zweck-*

rationalität), then there could no more be such a thing as the hardness of diamonds than there could be the *reality* of the real. To briefly explain with an example, if nobody could practically test for hardness, then talk about the hardness of a diamond would make no sense. *This* counterfactual conditional proposition at the level of transcendental philosophical reflection indirectly makes visible the a priori horizon of reference or, so to speak, the "paradigm" of the language game found in natural science and technology, including scientistically and technologically stylized social sciences and social technology.[105] But if we accept, with Peirce, that a meaning-critical philosophy implies a realist theory of universals in the sense of granting a fundamental truth to universal statements, then we must recognize that Peirce's reference to the "truth of a general conditional proposition" as that which alone "constitutes the reality of a diamond's hardness" must contain yet a further point regarding modal ontology. This second point is suggested by the counterfactual structure of the explication that follows in the text. It can be brought out by the following consideration.

If we could expect with certainty the experience of the diamond's hardness, or what would be the complete cognition of the reality of the real, so that it could be predicted by an unconditioned prognosis, then the realist theory of universals implied by Pragmatism could be limited to assuming real laws, as Peirce suggests in many places. To be more exact, as laws that have always existed, they would absolutely determine everything that happens. Peirce had already thrown out this assumption in 1891 in his metaphysics of Tychism and had interpreted natural laws themselves as habits that take shape from the continuum of real possibilities.[106] The concept of a real possibility, which was originally postulated in Peirce's metaphysical theory, is reconfirmed in 1905 by the pragmatic logic of inquiry in the analysis of the diamond example. Unconditioned predictions and their equivalent indicative statements are in fact of no help in clarifying the meaning of reality by means of thought experiments. For this purpose only conditional predictions formulated in counterfactual or, rather, subjunctive, conditional statements will serve.[107] The "truth of a general conditional proposition," to which Peirce wants to lay claim, does not in fact imply just the possibility, conditioned by the reality of a law, of deducing the expected experiential result from the antecedent; it implies also the experimenter's ability to provide the antecedent condition by some real praxis. In short, the ability to experience the reality of the real, such as the hardness of a diamond, presupposes real possibility or real vagueness as practical freedom.

The correctness of this interpretation is confirmed by Peirce's excursus on modal logic, in which he contrasts merely subjective possibility, in the sense of a lack of knowledge about a state of affairs, with objective possibility. He illustrates the latter with the statement "I *can* go to the seashore if I like" and with the assumption of absolute chance or, rather, of vagueness in the universe "analogous to the indecision of a person" (5.455).

A further confirmation is offered by the concluding part of the text, which seeks to use the pragmatic maxim to answer the question "What is the intellectual purport of the Past, Present, and Future?" (5.458 ff.). Much like Martin Heidegger in his existential ontology, Peirce investigates time here not as the time of objective dates, as the qualitative or quantitative succession of moments, but in terms of its three aspects (cf. Heidegger's *Ekstasen*), whose different meanings can be explicated *only* through their conceivable bearing upon our conduct (5.460). Nevertheless, Peirce begins his explication of the meaning of time with the presupposition that "time is real" (5.458), and even that "time is a particular variety of objective Modality."[108] Hence, Peirce here too sees it as the task of Pragmaticism to use a description of the practical situation in terms of common sense to make visible the modal ontological implications of the realist theory of universals.[109]

Peirce gives the following characterization of the three aspects of time as they can be conceivably related to our behavior:

1. The past is a mode of time that encompasses everything we can know, that is, existing or completed facts, that which affects us, but which we can no longer affect (see 5.459–60). To this extent it is immediately represented for us by memory. But "that part of the Past that lies beyond memory" has the meaning for us "that we ought to conduct ourselves according to it" (5.461). We can know it and it has an effect on us. That, for Peirce, is the pragmatic theme in historical research, including natural history.

2. The future is a mode of time that cannot affect us as something existing, and to this extent it is not actual. But for Peirce it does not follow from this that the future does not affect us in any way at all or that, on the other hand, we can subject it to unlimited control. Rather, the future affects us "through the idea of it, that is, as a law acts" (5.459). Here once again arises the problem of a real possibility, implied by the structure of counterfactual, conditional propositions. Peirce's answer now reads: ". . . the unsophisticated conception is that everything in the Future is either *destined*, i.e., necessitated already, or is *undecided*" (5.459). This means, as far as its conceivable relationship to our behavior is concerned, "that future facts are the only facts that we can, in a measure, control; and whatever there may be in the Future that is not amenable to control are the things that we

shall be able to infer, or *should* be able to infer under favorable circumstances" (5.461).

3. The present, "this Living Death in which we are born anew" (5.459), is for Peirce the most difficult to explicate rationally. This is evidently because the present is the mode of precognitive experience, both in regard to the pure features of the world (feeling in the sense of relation-free Firstness) and in regard to the non-ego's surprising resistance to our will as an "outer world" independent of the ego (experience in the sense of Secondness) (5.462). There is, according to Peirce, "no time in the Present for any inference at all" (5.462). And that means, therefore, that there is no time for conscious, controllable cognition in the sense of Thirdness, and "least of all" time for an inference of the self. Peirce concludes that as "perception" the present is only a kind of prereflective experience of the object of desire and, hence, also of resistance to the will: "The consciousness of the present is then that of a struggle over what shall be."[110]

The problematic situation that had forced Peirce to postulate a perception in terms of the Firstness of Thirdness arises here again in an aporetic form, for how else could we conceive the possibility of a phenomenological description of the precognitive experience of the present as "the Nascent State of the Actual" between the determinate and the indeterminate (5.462; cf. 5.459)?

The significance of this attempt to explicate time in reference to the practical human situation and the mediation of theory and praxis (as far as I can determine, the first such attempt ever made) becomes evident if we consider a passage in Werner Heisenberg's Gifford lectures on "Physics and Philosophy" in which he introduces Einstein's theory of relativity.[111] Heisenberg first gives a definition of the concepts "past" and "future" which hardly differs from Peirce's. According to Heisenberg, this kind of definition has the advantage of fitting the ordinary use of these words and of not making the content of the future or past depend upon the observer's state of movement or other characteristics.[112] Nonetheless, Heisenberg can make a decisive distinction between classical and relativity theory upon the basis of these presuppositions. This distinction implies that relativity theory differs in its conception of the present from the classical conception and from Peirce's as well. Heisenberg writes:

In classical theory we assume that future and past are separated by an infinitely short time interval which we may call the present moment. In the theory of relativity we have learned that the situation is different: future and past are separated by a finite time interval the length of which depends on the distance from the observer. Any action can only be propagated by a velocity smaller than or equal to the velocity of light. Therefore, an observer can at a given instant neither know of nor influence any event at a distant point which takes place between two characteristic times. The one time is the instant at which a light signal, given by the observer at the instant of the observation, reaches the point of the event. The whole finite time interval between these two instants may be said to belong to the present time for the observer at the instant of observation. Any event taking place between the two characteristic times may be called "simultaneous" with the act of observation.[113]

From this further definition of simultaneity Heisenberg develops the more narrow definition used by Einstein, which begins with the coincidence of two events at the same time at the same point in space. It is decisive for this definition, as well as for the definition of the present instant on which it is based, that time is no longer defined independently from the spatial separation between events and the observer, nor independently from light as the optimal medium of perception and measurement, whose speed is finite. Only because the speed of light can be regarded as infinitely great when it is seen from the standpoint of man's everyday world of measurements could classical physics neglect the space-time continuum (Minkowski-Einstein) and assume that the present is an infinitely small interval in the transition from the future to the past.

Doubtless, Peirce was still subjectively bound to the classical definition of the present instant. But there can also be no doubt that his semantic Pragmatism contains the philosophical prerequisites for explicating and defining every concept relating to physical space and time in terms of the material conditions of the possibility of measurements. At the beginning of his analysis of time, Peirce seems to have already adopted a manner of observation that could have led to the full development of this analysis as Heisenberg presented it. As Peirce points out, "For instance, when a *Nova Stella* bursts out in the heavens, it acts upon one's eyes just as a light struck in the dark by one's own hands would; and yet it is an event which happened before the Pyramids were built" (5.459). He is, of course, interested here in deciding not "whether the distant Past can act upon us *immediately*, but whether it acts upon us just as any Existent does" (5.459). It is precisely this equating of what is past with what exists, which we can know from the standpoint of its "conceivable effects upon our behavior," that opened up the perspective of thought from which the foundational crisis of physics at the beginning of the twentieth century was answered.

9
Conclusion: Peirce and the Future
of the Philosophy of Science

This brings my interpretation of Peirce's individual writings to a kind of end point. The specifically Peircean form of Pragmatism emerged in 1871 as a seminal idea developed under the influence of Peirce's friends in the Metaphysical Club. Out of this developed the further, and I think more original, conception of meaning-critical Realism and the semiotic transformation of Kantianism. This philosophy took its final form in the conception of modality and time that I have just sketched. Peirce himself called it "Pragmaticism," by which he meant the basic conception of a normative, methodological logic of scientific inquiry. As such, he intended Pragmaticism to be narrower and more definitely limited than that "Humanistic world view" into which William James and F. C. S. Schiller had developed Pragmatism after 1897. But Peirce also intended by this metascientific goal and by this limitation of its breadth to make room in Pragmaticism for the primacy of a cosmologically oriented, synechistic metaphysics of evolution, in contrast to the subjectively oriented Pragmatism of James and Schiller. In order to introduce the primacy of this metaphysics, Pragmaticism implied the necessity of upholding both Critical Common-sensism and the realist theory of universals.

To be more precise, Critical Common-sensism had the task, following Kant and Hume, and throughout all of the modern, conventionalistic radicalizations of the critique of knowledge, of making possible a new manner of philosophizing that would be analogous in style with Aristotle's. Obeying the restrictions of Fallibilism and Meliorism, its task was to bring into play through meaning-critical consciousness those proto-ontological truth claims found in common sense and ordinary language which endure quite naïvely in every philosophy, no matter how skeptical or critical it is.[1] It seems to me that Peirce never sufficiently put this, the deepest theme of his philosophy, into conceptual form and that his later attempt to consolidate Critical Common-sensism reflectively as a philosophical position falls short, in part, of the meaning-critical approach he adopted in his early transformation of Kant. To an extent, this also holds for the realist theory of universals which, from the standpoint of Critical Common-sensism, necessarily followed in 1868–71 from Peirce's meaning-critical foundation of Kant's "empirical Realism." Yet, as I have indicated several times, it was not until 1905 that Peirce applied his ingenious meaning-critical approach to the definition of the reality of the real, when he used his modal-logical and modal-ontological conception of the realist theory of universals to criticize all the prejudices of late medieval and modern Nominalism, against which he had struggled his whole life long. Only then was his use of "Mellonization," that is, that interpretation of the meaning of reality in terms of possible future experience which is so typical of Peirce's philosophy, freed from the last remnants of metaphysical Nominalism as it is found in Berkeley or even in Kant. In fact, it seems to me that we must carry out this thought by postulating the possible, real, ontological truth of counterfactual conditional propositions, after we recognize that Berkeley's theological Idealism and Kant's assumption of a world of incognizable things-in-themselves behind the world are bad metaphysics.

If we look back at Peirce's Pragmaticism from the perspective of the present, then we see in it primarily the outline and program of a "logic of science" for the future. It goes without saying that the logic of science that has been developed in the meantime by analytic philosophy, with the aid of mathematical logic, has come much further than Peirce in technicalities. But it seems just as certain to me that the basic, two-dimensional (syntactic-semantic) approach which modern work in the logic of science took over from logical Positivism's anti-metaphysical program is fundamentally inferior to Peirce's three-dimensional semiotic approach. The two-dimensional approach forces philosophers of science to reduce the metaphysical problems of the so-called pragmatic dimension, that is, problems regarding the subject who interprets and engages in science, by making them problems of an empirical science. Moreover, unless all contemporary developments mislead me, we are now already witnessing a restructuring and dissolution of the two-dimensional logic of science. This view, which is ultimately oriented to the ideal of a Platonic metamathematics, has begun now to give way to a three-dimensional, cybernetically oriented, "systems theory" of science which conceives it as a human, social undertaking.

At this juncture, however, where Peirce could today be understood as a forerunner and prophet of a cybernetic, technological Scientism and even of a technocracy, I believe it is important to recall his reflections on the limits of "instrumental reason" and the transcendental, hermeneutic side of the idea of the community of interpreters that he and Royce developed. A systems theory that assumes that it can objectify science's relationship to human praxis, including the communication between the human subjects that are engaged in science, so that these all fit the model of regulation and adaptation processes, must thereby result, in Peirce's view, in a semiotically unacceptable reduction of the community of interpreters as the subject engaged in scientific inquiry. It would constitute a regression to the two-dimensional metatheory. The community of interpreters as the successor in Pragmatism to Kant's "subject in general" has to retain a position of transcendental value. In modern terminology, it must constitute a metadimension to every systems-theoretical objectification of human social undertakings.

Here, moreover, we also have the point at which the philosophical theory of science will have to go beyond Peirce and, hence, beyond the most concealed form of Scientism. If we take to its logical conclusions the idea, which Peirce had already implicitly founded in his logical Socialism, that the world cannot be known or explained merely by its previously fixed, lawful structure, but must rather continue to be developed as a historical, social world of institutions and habits for which we must assume responsibility, then it becomes evident that man confronts mankind with other tasks besides that of objectifying and explaining the world through science or of converting science into efficient behavior, that is, technology in the broadest sense. As members of the community of interpreters, human beings must remain for mankind the subject engaged in science and nonetheless be capable of being made the topic of rational knowledge and praxis.

Peirce and, implicitly, the modern logic of science as well take this situation into account when they consider the metascientific problem of reaching an agreement (*Verständigung*) on the concepts and operations used in science. But we must also recognize that reaching such an agreement represents, as a technical problem, only a limiting case among those communicative tasks, posed by the community of interpreters, which require an intersubjective agreement. It is that particular limiting case in which, in the event of a complete success, the relevant process of reaching an agreement (*Verständigung*) about meaning is virtually settled in a historical situation, among unique and irreplaceable individuals, by means of logical and technical operations that can be repeated by interchangeable experimenters.

But in practice even this requires that we have a genuine, hermeneutic, historically oriented communicative understanding (*Verständigung*) in the community of investigators of the kind that is just now getting under way as the "critique of tradition" in scientific schools.[2] This understanding should be within and among the different schools and finally, as a task that becomes more urgent from day to day, between the esoteric language games practiced by these scientific schools and society at large, which is supposed to organize science responsibly and apply its findings. But arriving at an understanding through scientific communication ultimately constitutes a continuum with the activity of reaching a communicative understanding about politics and morality, which consists in transmitting tradition and establishing a goal orientation in the human community of interpretation generally, as Royce has seen.

In this way the transcendental semiotic foundation of Peirce's philosophy, the a priori of the communication community, itself opens the way for a complementary, nonscientistic interpretation of Peirce.[3] It designates, I believe, the starting point for a new foundation of the human sciences (*Geisteswissenschaften*) and their method of "understanding [*Verstehen*]," by conceiving them as the sciences of communicative understanding (*Verständigung*).[4] From the viewpoint of these sciences of communicative understanding, Peirce's pragmatistic explanation of the dimension of time would also require a further revision. This is because the future cannot be clearly enough defined, either as something determined or as something that can be changed through manipulation, to allow an intersubjective communicative understanding about the horizon of meaning of different possible goals.

The future, insofar as it is represented by human beings, such as through the pedagogical notion of the pupil, cannot in practice be regarded simply as an object for possible manipulation to the extent that it is not already determined. For even to the extent that manipulation is possible, or even desirable from the standpoint of social technology, it presupposes a communicative understanding between those doing the manipulating and those who are supposed to be the subjects of this planned management in the future.[5] The past, too, as the former intersubjective nature of the community of interpreters, is not so constituted that it contains nothing but completed facts to which we must respond as to effective causes. Only matters of fact and documents from so-called real history and those documents which must be evaluated as remainders of this history, or, at most, as "sources" for research into real, historical facts can be adapted to the metascientific explication of the past as Peirce presents it. This is not so, however, with documents in the sense of texts whose meaning can be evaluated as a kind of communicative contribution to the discussion in the community of interpreters. This is where the actual hermeneutic business of the *Geisteswissenschaften* begins and where we are confronted with the peculiar circumstance that the human documents from the past could contain, preserved within them, as yet unrealized possibilities of life for us. Here I am not referring to Peirce's contention that the meaning of such historical documents lies for us in the possible future confirmation or falsification of information about certain facts that are still efficacious. I mean something completely different, something that, according to Peirce, is supposed to have its place in the future. The documents of the past contain themes of meaning which neither have already been nor are now becoming exhausted as causal explanations. Instead, as visions of goals which we are able to understand, they are able to open up goals that are realizable for us as possibilities.[6]

In the problem of communication, which Peirce recognized to be a problem concerning the presuppositions of the modern logic of science, we therefore find the beginnings of a program complementary to the pragmaticistic analysis of the possible mediation of theory and praxis. The concern here is not just to establish a consensus, as Peirce understood it, about the interpretation of scientific findings that would guarantee self-control in human technological habits. The aim is rather a consensus about interpretations of meaning that are to be borne out by the risk-laden, historical interactions between human beings. All relevant interpretations of the *Geisteswissenschaften* and the critical social sciences must in the end rely upon such a consensus. As I have already indicated, this is where James's and Dewey's ideas of a truth to be made by human beings in fact become the center of a humanistic Pragmatism that goes beyond Peirce. These ideas do not deserve for this reason to be evaluated as an expansion of Peirce's Pragmaticism, because that would mean that Peirce's idea of the real as a possible objective truth to be attained in the long run would be an illusion and would have to be abandoned in favor af a subjectivistic, fictionalistic, usefulness conception of truth. That kind of vulgar Pragmatism, which could claim to derive from Nietzsche or James, does not have any chance of standing up in the face of the meaning-critical foundation of possible argumentation as Peirce developed it. The case is different, however, with James's discovery of the problem of the truth of matters of fact that human beings have yet to make on the basis of and as a supplement to existing realities.

This is where science's concept of objectivity, as well as the technical, instrumental rationality that applies to everyone, must be taken into account and, finally, transcended. Here, too, humanistic Pragmatism meets with the other two philosophies of the mediation of theory and praxis that have been developed in contemporary industrial society.[7] In *The Will to Believe* James gave a classical defense of the justifiability of the existential mediation of theory and praxis in "limit situations," according to which every free and conscious human being is an "individual" (as for Kierkegaard) in every conceivable type of social order. This existential perspective serves to establish the pragmatic limits of claims that can be made not only upon the individual as these claims are formulated in Peirce's logical Socialism, but, even more so, upon Marx's much farther reaching theory, no matter how justified the latter might be in calling upon the individual to integrate his existential engagement into that of society. On the other hand, it will hardly be enough in the long run to glorify ideologically the system of complementarity that has become established in the West, in which the public Pragmatism of value-free, scientific-technological rationality relegates all problems relating to ethics to the sphere of private, supposedly existential, decisions. This kind of depoliticizing and the dissolution of "public opinion" that goes along with it will not guarantee freedom. Under the present conditions of modern social technology and manipulation, it will rather act in the long run to eliminate the very political and moral presuppositions that support both value-free science and the individual's existential value decisions.

This, it seems to me, outlines the field and the tasks for a public, emancipatory mediation of theory and praxis in which in the future the leading ideas of Marxism and Pragmatism, as developed by Peirce and Dewey, will carry out their struggle over the essence of democracy. From Marxism, Pragmatism will have to learn one thing, that the structure of the historical mediation of theory and praxis cannot be reduced to experiments that are fundamentally repeatable in the scientific, technical sense. Marxism, on the other hand, will have a chance of being taken seriously as a philosophy of science only if it once and for all gives up its claim to be an objective *science* while it, in contrast to the science that Peirce analyzes, claims to be able to make unconditioned predictions about the course of history.[8] It will have to withdraw from this position to the program of a nonscientific, nonobjectivistic, but emancipatory, engaged, "critical" mediation of theory and praxis. In order really to support this program as the possible emancipation of humanity, it will have to learn from Pragmatism to overcome the spirit of dogmatism in its belief that it possesses man's salvation in the form of knowledge to be administered by a party elite. This will have to be replaced by the spirit of the communication and experimentation community that Peirce and Dewey had in mind.

Notes

Chapter 1

1. It should be emphasized from the outset that I use these concepts here in a way that is in keeping with the right of the constructive historian of philosophy to utilize vague, broad classifications. It is well known that the authors subsumed under such concepts do not want to be classified during their lifetimes, since that would constitute admitting having failed to provide a truly comprehensive philosophy. As soon as the historians of philosophy take them on, systematic thinkers tend to change their labels. Besides the early Sartre, none of the founders of Existentialism wanted to be termed an existentialist. Marx did not want to be a Marxist. James later preferred to be termed a "radical empiricist." Dewey liked rather to be called an "instrumentalist," an "experimentalist," or even a "naturalist." Peirce distanced himself from the term "Pragmatism" after it became well known and adopted the title "Pragmaticism."

    On the key problem of philosophy after Hegel, the mediation of theory and practice, see Jürgen Habermas, *Theory and Practice*, trans. John Viertel (Boston: Beacon Press, 1973). [On the same topic see also Richard J. Bernstein, *Praxis and Action* (Philadelphia: University of Pennsylvania Press, 1971–Trans.]

2. It is unnecessary to illustrate this thesis in terms of the differentiation between the positions taken among countries in Eastern Europe.

3. Karl R. Popper, *The Open Society and Its Enemies*, 2 vols. (London: Routledge and Kegan Paul, 1945).

4. In modern times it has been institutionalized through the separation of church and state.

5. Whenever authors promise to "take seriously" such questions, what often results is a distorted exaggeration that confuses the philosophy of Pragmatism with those opportunistic practices which, without the sober analyses offered by that philosophy, would in fact escape all conscious control and degrade "official" philosophy to a powerless ideology. A symptomatic example of such confusion, which also gives a résumé of provincial German prejudices about the teachings of American Pragmatism, can be found in Wilhelm

Seeberger, *Wahrheit in der Politik: Pragmatismus in Theorie und Praxis,*
Political Series 3 (Stuttgart: J. Fink, 1965).

6. William James, *The Will to Believe* (New York, 1897).

7. The First German Peirce edition is *Charles S. Peirce: Schriften,* 2 vols., ed.
Karl-Otto Apel, trans. G. Wartenberg (Frankfurt am Main: Suhrkamp,
1967–70). The most significant German expositions of Pragmatism do not
take Peirce into account. See Günther Jacoby, *Der Pragmatismus: Neue
Bahnen in der Wissenschaftslehre des Auslands* (Leipzig: Dürr'sche Buch-
handlung, 1909); Max Scheler, "Erkenntnis und Arbeit: Eine Studie über
Wert und Grenzen des pragmatischen Motivs in der Erkenntnis der Welt,"
in *Gesammelte Werke,* ed. Maria Scheler (Bern and Munich: Franke, 1960),
8:191–382; and Eduard Baumgarten, *Die geistigen Grundlagen des amerikanischen Gemeinwesens,* vol. 2, *Der Pragmatismus: R. W. Emerson,
W. James, J. Dewey* (Frankfurt am Main: Vittorio Klostermann, 1938).
Baumgarten consciously omits Peirce. Scheler knows of him only through
the writings of James. Although he traces the "two main theses of Pragmatism" back to Peirce, Scheler misunderstands their implications much as
James does.

The only German book on Peirce up to now is Jürgen von Kempski, *Charles
S. Peirce und der Pragmatismus* (Stuttgart and Cologne: Kohlhammer,
1952). There we also find references to the few informed opinions on Peirce
in older German philosophical literature, such as the important book reviews of the *Collected Papers* by H. Scholz in the *Deutsche Literaturzeitung*
(1934), pp. 392 ff., and (1936), pp. 137 ff.

In his comprehensive bibliography, Max H. Fisch lists two further essays
that have appeared since Kempski's book. See Max H. Fisch, "A Draft of
a Bibliography of Writings about C. S. Peirce," in Edward C. Moore and
Richard S. Robin, *Studies in the Philosophy of Charles Sanders Peirce,* 2d
ser. (Amherst: University of Massachusetts Press, 1964), pp. 486–514. The
essays are Peter Krausser, "Die drei fundamentalen Strukturkategorien bei
Charles S. Peirce," *Philosophia Naturalis* 6 (1960):3–31 [an English translation by Christian J. W. Kloesel, "The Three Fundamental Structural Categories of Charles S. Peirce," has since appeared in the *Transactions of the
Charles S. Peirce Society* 13, no. 3 (1977):189–215—Trans.] and book reviews
by Walter Jung of Manley Thompson's and Jürgen von Kempski's books on
Peirce, in *Philosophische Rundschau* 4 (1956):129–43, 143–58. I owe thanks
to Prof. Klaus Oehler for referring me to the article by Elizabeth Walter,
"Die Begründung der Zeichentheorie bei Charles S. Peirce," in *Grundlagen-
studien aus Kybernetik und Geisteswissenschaften* 3 (1962):33–44. Finally,
two works by Georg Klaus also examine problems in Peirce's and Morris's
semiotic: *Semiotik und Erkenntnistheorie* (Berlin, DDR: Deutscher Verlag
der Wissenschaften, 1963) and *Die Macht des Wortes* (Berlin, DDR: Deutscher Verlag der Wissenschaften, 1964).

8. See Kempski, pp. 84 ff. See also I. M. Bocheński, *A History of Formal Logic,*
trans. Ivo Thomas (Notre Dame, Ind.: Notre Dame University Press, 1961).

9. *Collected Papers of Charles Sanders Peirce,* 8 vols. (Cambridge, Mass.:
Harvard University Press, 1931–58). Cf. the chronology of the books listed
as secondary sources in the bibliography with the publication dates of the
Collected Papers, as well as those of the four editions of selections.

10. For an account of this mysterious chapter in Peirce's life, which initiated the
tragic turn in his illustriously begun university career, see Max H. Fisch
and J. I. Cope, "Peirce at the Johns Hopkins University," in *Studies in the*

Philosophy of Charles S. Peirce, ed. Philip P. Wiener and Frederic Young (Cambridge, Mass.: Harvard University Press, 1952), pp. 277–311. The effects of this turn of events on the development of Peirce's philosophy are examined in Murray G. Murphey's book, *The Development of Peirce's Philosophy* (Cambridge, Mass.: Harvard University Press, 1961), pp. 291 ff.

11. See below, Chap. 5 and Chap. 8, Sec. A.

12. See Peirce's letter to Dewey from June 9, 1904 (*Collected Papers,* 8.239 ff).

13. Bertrand Russell and Alfred North Whitehead, *Principia Mathematica,* 3 vols., 2d ed. (Cambridge: Cambridge University Press, 1950).

14. See Viktor Kraft, *Der Wiener Kreis* (Vienna: Springer, 1950).

15. For a discussion of these aporias see Wolfgang Stegmüller, *Hauptströmungen der Gegenwartsphilosophie,* 2 vols. (Stuttgart: Kröner, 1960), 1:chaps. 9, 10.

16. On Morris's semiotic see Karl-Otto Apel, "Sprache und Wahrheit in der gegenwärtigen Situation der Philosophie," *Philosophische Rundschau* 7 (1959):161–84. See also Ernst Tugendhat, "Tarskis Semantische Definition der Wahrheit und ihre Stellung innerhalb der Geschichte des Wahrheitsproblems im logischen Positivismus," *Philosophische Rundschau* 8 (1960): 131–59. On the relationship between Morris and Peirce see the controversy between Morris and Dewey in the *Journal of Philosophy* 43 (1946):85–95, 196, 280, and 363–64. Cf. my critical introduction to the German translation of Morris's *Signs, Language and Behavior* (New York: George Braziller, 1946): "Charles W. Morris und das Problem einer pragmatisch integrierten Semiotik" in *Zeichen, Sprache und Verhalten* (Düsseldorf: Schwann, 1973), pp. 9–66.

17. See below, Chap. 3, Secs. C.b and C.c, and Chap. 4, Sec. B.b. Peirce's thought is related to Popper's generally by a particular interest in the philosophy and history of science.

18. See Stegmüller, *Hauptströmungen der Gegenwartsphilosophie,* p. 462.

19. Charles Morris explicitly embraces Behaviorism in *Signs, Language and Behavior,* but George Herbert Mead's theory of reciprocal, behavioral expectations, as expressed in his *Mind, Self, and Society: From the Standpoint of a Social Behaviorist* (Chicago: University of Chicago Press, 1934), cannot be counted as a consistent Behaviorism and in many respects is closer to Peirce than is Morris's theory. Peirce's doctrine of categories gave him insight into the "reductive fallacy" inherent in every form of Materialism, Positivism, and Behaviorism, insight that clearly anticipated later developments in philosophy.

20. Cf. below, Chap. 3, Secs. B and C.c. Peirce took up this philosophy of interpretation again in his later years and, emphasizing its importance, explicitly connected it with "Pragmaticism." On this topic see my essay "Scientism or Transcendental Hermeneutics? On the Question of the Subject of the Interpretation of Signs in the Semiotics of Pragmatism," in Karl-Otto Apel, *Towards a Transformation of Philosophy,* trans. Glyn Adey and David Frisby (London, Boston, and Henley: Routledge and Kegan Paul, 1980), pp. 93–135. [This is a translation of selected essays from Apel's two volume *Transformation der Philosophie,* vol. 1, *Sprachanalytik, Semiotik, Hermeneutic;* vol. 2, *Das A priori der Kommunikationsgemeinschaft* (Frankfurt am Main: Suhrkamp, 1973). Citations of this work refer to the English edition unless the essay in question is available only in the original German work—Trans.]

21. See Karl-Otto Apel, *Analytic Philosophy of Language and the "Geisteswissenschaften,"* Foundations of Language Supplementary Series, vol. 5, trans. Glyn Adey and David Frisby (Dordrecht: Reidel, 1967), and "Witt-

genstein and the Problem of Hermeneutic Understanding," in *Towards a Transformation of Philosophy*, pp. 1–45. On the relationship between Wittgenstein and Peirce see Richard Rorty, "Pragmatism, Categories, and Language," *Philosophical Review* 70 (1961):197–223.

22. The development of "Critical Common-sensism" falls largely into the late period of Pragmaticism. See esp. 5.497 ff. and 5.523 ff.

23. The only book that Peirce published during his lifetime was his *Photometric Researches*, vol. 9 of the Annals of the Astronomical Observatory of Harvard College (Leipzig, 1878). The connection between Peirce's scientific works and his philosophy has been given greater attention recently. See Victor F. Lenzen, "Charles S. Peirce as Astronomer," in Moore and Robin, pp. 33–50. Cf. *Collected Papers*, 7.1–36.

24. I take the designation "semantically consistent system" of physics from oral comments by Carl Friedrich von Weizsäcker, but for the interpretation sketched here I bear the responsibility myself. On the concept of the "material constraints of the experimental realization of physical concepts" see also Peter Mittelstaedt, *Philosophical Problems of Modern Physics*, Boston Studies in the Philosophy of Science, vol. 18 (Dordrecht and Boston: Reidel, 1976), pp. 14, 32.

25. In his *Logic of Modern Physics* (1927; reprint ed., New York: Macmillan, 1961), P. W. Bridgeman worked out what amounts to a part of Peirce's "Logic of Inquiry," i.e., Peirce's call for the replaceability of the definitions of physical concepts with operative instructions for experimental physics. Bridgeman evidently had no knowledge of Peirce at the time. I also believe that an attempt, like Paul Lorenzen's to understand the operative explication of the meaning of logical connectives in the context of a logical agon between a proponent and an opponent is a consistent development of Peirce's semantic Pragmatism. See Paul Lorenzen, "Logik und Agon," *Atti del XII Congresso Internazionale di Filosofia* (Venice, 1958), and "Ein dialogisches Konstruktivitätskriterium," in *Infinitistic Methods: Proceedings of the Symposium on Foundations of Mathematics*, Warsaw, Sept. 2–9, 1959 (Oxford: Pergamon Press, 1961).

26. It goes without saying that I do not intend to claim here that Peirce, with his fragmentary, ingenious insights, anticipated or even made superfluous this century's detailed clarification of the foundational problems in science, a clarification that, among other things, we owe to the reckless aporias of the neopositivists.

27. William James, *The Works of William James: Pragmatism* (1907; reprint ed., Cambridge, Mass.; Harvard University Press, 1975).

28. Hermann Noack, *Die Philosophie Westeuropas*, 2d ed. (Darmstadt: Wissenschaftliche Buchgesellschaft, 1965), pp. 73–74.

29. Hans Vaihinger, *The Philosophy of "As If,"* trans. from the 6th ed. by C. K. Ogden (New York: Harcourt, Brace and Co., 1925).

30. See Scheler, "Erkenntnis und Arbeit," in *Gesammelte Werke*, 8, 207—Trans.

31. Friedrich Nietzsche, *The Will to Power*, trans. Walter Kaufmann and R. J. Hollingdale (New York: Random House, Vintage, 1967), p. 272.

32. Cf. below, Chap. 3, Sec. B.

33. Cf. below, Chap. 3, Sec. C.e. Many American expositions pay little or no attention to Peirce's Kantianism and arrive in this way, at Peirce's expense, at a unified conception of American Pragmatism. This is especially the case for Edward C. Moore (*American Pragmatism: Peirce, James, Dewey* [New York: Columbia University Press, 1961]), who believes that the "indefinite community of investigators" postulated and hoped for by Peirce, which can

be given real validity only by the "ideal limit" of the "ultimate opinion" postulated in the definition of truth, may be identified with mankind as something finite. This crass simplification destroys, I believe, the dialectic between "Common-sensism" and Infinitism which is so central to Peirce's philosophy.

34. Here and throughout I follow the convention of citing the *Collected Papers* by giving the volume and paragraph numbers separated by a period.

35. In the printed proposal from 1893 of a work ("The Principles of Philosophy") that was to be twelve volumes and was partially completed, Peirce characterizes his position as follows: "The principles supported by Mr. Peirce bear a close affinity with those of Hegel; perhaps are what Hegel's might have been had he been educated in a physical laboratory instead of in a theological seminary. Thus, Mr. Peirce acknowledges an objective logic (though its movement differs from the Hegelian dialectic), and like Hegel endeavors to assimilate truth got from many a looted system" (*Collected Papers* [Bibliography] 8, p. 283). In an 1893 article in *The Monist*, in which he answers the criticisms of the journal's editor, Dr. Carus, who had characterized him as "David Hume Redivivus," Peirce writes: "In the first paper of this series [Peirce is referring here to "The Architecture of Theories," which appeared in *The Monist* in 1891; see 6.7–34], in which I gave a preliminary sketch of such of my ideas as could be so presented, I carefully recorded my opposition to all philosophies which deny the reality of the Absolute, and asserted that 'the one intelligible theory of the universe is that of objective idealism, that matter is effete mind' " (6.605).

36. According to Peirce, the only guard against metaphysics, in the last analysis, is metaphysics itself: "Find a scientific man who proposes to get along without any metaphysics . . . and you have found one whose doctrines are thoroughly vitiated by the crude and uncriticized metaphysics with which they are packed. We must philosophize, said the great naturalist Aristotle— if only to avoid philosophizing" (1.129).

37. On the relationship between Peirce's "Phenomenology" and those of Hegel and Husserl, see Herbert Spiegelberg, "Husserl's and Peirce's Phenomenologies: Coincidence or Interaction," *Philosophy and Phenomenological Research* 17 (1956):164–85. On the relationship of Peirce's doctrine of the categories to Nicolai Hartmann's, see Krausser, "Three Fundamental Structural Categories."

38. Murphey, *Development*, pp. 406 ff.

Chapter 2

1. Justus Buchler developed this conception in his book *Charles Peirce's Empiricism* (New York: Harcourt, Brace and Co., 1939). In his edition of selections from Peirce, however, he also took account of Peirce as a metaphysician. Edward C. Moore undertook a positivistic reduction of Peirce's philosophy in his *American Pragmatism*. On this question see my essay, "From Kant to Peirce: the Semiotical Transformation of Transcendental Logic," in *Towards a Transformation of Philosophy*.

2. This is the view of Kempski, whose analysis was the first to have introduced the consideration of Peirce's Kantian presuppositions as a necessary addition to the topics examined in American expositions. Murphey, who analyzed Peirce's early Kant studies and made them generally accessible, takes largely the same position as Kempski, claiming that Peirce basically

misunderstood Kant. To me, however, both appear to overestimate Kant's position or, rather, to underestimate the meaning-critical arguments which Peirce brings forward against Kant's unexamined, metaphysical Nominalism.

3. This characterization applies to Feibleman, who was the first to have examined Peirce's whole philosophy—in the form which the editors of the *Collected Papers* gave to it—as a system.

4. See Wiener and Young, *Studies*, and Moore and Robin, *Studies*, as well as Richard J. Bernstein, ed., *Perspectives on Peirce* (New Haven and London: Yale University Press, 1965).

5. See 5.13 n., 5.18, 5.464, 8.206, and 8.259.

6. The most important principle in Peirce's philosophy, besides Pragmatism, is without doubt his doctrine of categories.

7. See below, Chap. 6, Sec. A, and Chap. 8, Sec. A.

8. See James's 1898 lecture at the University of California, "Philosophical Conceptions and Practical Results," in *Pragmatism*, pp. 257–70.

9. See below, Chap. 6, Sec. A, and Chap. 8, Sec. A.

10. The classic exposition of this conception is Philip P. Wiener, *Evolution and the Founders of Pragmatism* (Cambridge, Mass.: Harvard University Press, 1949). A valuable supplement is provided by Max H. Fisch, "Alexander Bain and the Genealogy of Pragmatism," *Journal of the History of Ideas* 15 (1954):413–44. Peirce's relationship to the Metaphysical Club is minutely explained in Max H. Fisch, "Was There a Metaphysical Club in Cambridge?" in Moore and Robin, *Studies*, pp. 3–32.

11. See Murphey, *Development*, pp. 106–50.

12. See ibid., pp. 358 ff.

13. See Paul Weiss, "Biography of Charles S. Peirce" in Bernstein, *Perspectives*, pp. 1–12.

14. See above, n. 10 to Chap. 1. Whether Peirce's dismissal was connected with his divorce in 1883 from his first wife, Harriet Melusina Fay, granddaughter of Bishop John Henry Hopkins, or with his marriage in the same year to Julliette Froissy of Nancy, France, remains unknown to this day.

15. See above, n. 23 to Chap. 1.

16. Charles S. Peirce, ed., *Studies in Logic, by Members of the Johns Hopkins University* (Boston, 1883). Murphey (*Development*, p. 297) terms this "the most important single volume on logic written in America in the nineteenth century."

17. Weiss, "Biography," p. 11.

Chapter 3

1. See, e.g., 5.413 and 5.502. For the study of the history of terminology, which has now gained so much currency, Peirce's work represents a major find, especially on the subject of the history of logical terms.

2. Peirce's evaluation of Prantl's *Geschichte der Logik im Abendlande*, 4 vols. (Leipzig, 1855–85) is comparable in many ways to that of I. M. Bocheński, *History of Formal Logic*, although Peirce's primary interest was definitely not formal logic in the narrow sense of the term.

3. See his characterization of the Middle Ages, particularly the idea of the *consensus catholicus*, in the 1871 Berkeley review and in the doctrine of the four methods of the fixation of belief, 8.11, 8.12, and 5.379 ff.

4. See 3.613, 6.318, and 6.330. Cf. also n. 103 to Chap. 6 and n. 59 to Chap. 7, below.

5. See Murphey, *Development*, pp. 90 ff.

6. I therefore believe it conceivable that until 1867 Peirce, as a "semiotic phenomenalist" and Kantian, considered himself a "nominalist." Recent investigations by Max Fisch, which were made available to me in manuscript form, also tend to corroborate this theory.

7. In "One, Two, Three: Fundamental Categories of Thought and Nature," from ca. 1885 (1.369–72, 1.376–78). Cf. Murphey, *Development*, pp. 303 ff., and Krausser, "Three Fundamental Structural Categories," passim.

8. I must admit that I have here explicated the extremely complicated and not always internally consistent movement of Peirce's thought in the first period (between 1860 and 1871) along the main lines of its development, lines which can be recognized only *ex post*. Moreover, on several points, such as the question of the categories and the closely related question of the mediated immediacy of experience of the outer world, I have anticipated Peirce's later solutions to the problems that here pose themselves.

9. Here and elsewhere, unless otherwise noted, the interpolations are Apel's— Trans.

10. 6.619–28. In a lecture in 1898 (4.2) Peirce mentions that he owed his early knowledge of Hegel to a book by Augusto Vera, *Introduction à la Philosophie de Hegel* (Paris, 1855).

11. See, e.g., 8.41, 6.436, and 5.90 ff.

12. For Peirce, therefore, Hegel is not a realist as regards universals, but rather a "Nominalist of realistic yearnings" (1.19).

13. See *Collected Papers*, 8, p. 292: "Nominalism, up to that of Hegel, looks at reality retrospectively. What all modern Philosophy does is to deny that there is any *esse in futuro*."

14. In the fragment headed "Principles" (1861), where he criticizes Kant, Peirce characterizes the nominalistic framework of modern theories of knowledge as follows:

"The common, and as I think, erroneous view of the relation of the thing known to the person knowing is as follows:—First, there is the Subject, the *Ego*. The Thing Known, is known by an *affection* of the consciousness, consequently only by its effect. Therefore, a distinction is drawn between (2) the *neumenon* or thing as it exists–which is entirely unknown (except, according to some philosophies, by reason) and (3) the Object or *thing* as *thought*. (4) There is the affection of the consciousness or Phenomenon and (5) There is the relation of Causality between the Object and the Phenomenon. . . . I [on the contrary] represent the relationship as follows:—(1) There is the soul (2) There is the field of consciousness in which we know the soul (3) There is the thing *thought of* (4) There is the power it exerts on the soul (5) There is the Idea or impression it makes on the soul (6) There is the *thought* or the idea as it appears in consciousness" ["Principles," MS dated Aug. 21, 1861, I B 2, Box 8, Peirce manuscripts, Houghton Library, Harvard University, Cambridge, Mass., as quoted in Murphey, *Development*, pp. 23–24].

It is worth noting that in this early sketch Peirce has already clearly distinguished knowledge itself, "thought" in (6), from the conditions of the causal mechanism under which it comes about. With this, he has already overcome in principle the assumptions on which rest the Cartesian problem of knowledge of the "external world" and, tacitly, the Kantian presupposition of things-in-themselves. The thing itself, even though it is not yet known in the predicate of a sentence "as something," is nonetheless, according to Peirce, posited in the subject of the sentence as that which is "thought of" (3). This "hypothesis," he believes, vouchsafes the identity of both the object of knowledge and the external thing.

15. Kempski, I believe, has overlooked this fact, so central to Peirce's early interpretation of Kant. Of course, this oversight is probably attributable to the fact that Kempski was unaware of the relevant writings from Peirce's early work on Kant, which Murphey has made generally accessible. See below, Sec. C.b in this chapter.

16. The decisive nuance of Peirce's early Kant interpretation is largely concealed by the fact that Kant's term *Vorstellung* is translated into English as "representation," even by orthodox Kantians. For Peirce, however, standing behind this term, which designates the earliest and characteristic illustration of "Thirdness," there is the whole semiotic transformation of the modern concept of knowledge and, hence, the possibility of advancing from the critique of knowledge to the critique of meaning.

17. This line of argument remained implicit in Peirce, but it was repeated in an explicit way in the twentieth century by Moritz Schlick. Schlick was then able to bring in the fact that in modern physics knowledge is formulated in mathematical sign systems and so oversteps the bounds of an intuitively schematizable world view. This he took to be an argument for the semiotic transformation of the concept of knowledge that Wittgenstein and Schlick himself each initiated. See Moritz Schlick, "Erleben, Erkennen, Metaphysik," *Kantstudien* 31 (1926):146–58.

18. On the decisive motives for this distinction see the end of this section.

19. For a discussion of this problem in the philosophical anthropology of Max Scheler, Helmut Plessner, Arnold Gehlen, and Erich Rothacker, see the article "Anthropologie" by Jürgen Habermas in *Das Fischer Lexikon: Philosophie* (Frankfurt am Main: Fischer, 1958), pp. 18–35.

20. We could compare this with the corresponding doctrines in Maine de Biran and Dilthey.

21. 5.311. The unclarity that leaves the reader asking whether the real object is actually attained "sooner or later" as the final result of cognition, or whether the actual attainment of a "final opinion" presupposes an infinite process of cognition, is eliminated in 1890 in Peirce's review of Josiah Royce's *The World and the Individual*. There Peirce states: ". . . the ultimate opinion . . . will, as we hope, actually be attained concerning any given question (though not in any finite time concerning *all* questions)" (8.113). See below, Sec. C.e in this chapter, on the "principle of hope," which deals, however, not with the correctness of the definition, but with the question whether the "final opinion" can in fact be achieved.

22. See 5.354 ff. (1869), 8.12 (1871), and 5.405 ff. (1878).

23. 5.311. Cf. n. 21 to this chapter.

24. Peirce plays here on the idea of "one universal church," which, without doubt, was a model for his "community of investigators." See the last sentence in 8.12. Cf. also, however, n. 3 to this chapter.

25. According to Peirce, it is essential that we always uphold the normative character of an "ideal limit" in defining truth or reality by means of the "ultimate opinion." All other, merely empirical, definitions would amount for Peirce to what today is called a "category mistake," i.e., to a reductive fallacy.

26. The requirement that the community must be real can be compared to the similar move made by the Young Hegelians, who replaced Hegel's "absolute spirit" with the community of reasoning egos (Bruno Bauer), real mankind

(David Friedrich Strauss), the natural-sensory community (Feuerbach), and, finally, the "class of mankind" (Karl Marx). All of these were taken to serve as the guarantee of final truth and the validity of values.

27. See above, n. 24 to Chap. 1.

28. I am unable to see how this presupposition has anything to do with arguing in a circle, of which Murphey evidently believes it guilty (see Murphey, *Development*, pp. 141–42). In his "theory of reality" Peirce is not concerned in any way at all with a proof of existence, but rather with the clarification of meaning, just as in his later work "How to Make Our Ideas Clear." In 1869 (5.352) and again in 1878 (5.384) he does, however, reduce to absurdity doubt about the existence of reality in general, a doubt which Peirce indicates is meaningless in practice since we already assume the existence of the real world in every possible question or doubt about the reality of a phenomenon, just as we presuppose the validity of logic when we ask about the "foundations of the validity of logic." This kind of argumentation is, on my view, also a preliminary stage of Peirce's later "Critical Commonsensism" and is typical of his meaning-critical approach to philosophy. See Sec. C.e in this chapter.

We "experience" the existence of the world, however, as Peirce emphasizes against Royce in 1885, in the resistance to our will that we meet within the "outward clash." This experience enters *hic et nunc* into the experimental verification of belief as a necessary criterion of evidence. But when Peirce later takes up this experience of the existence of the real (for the first time probably in the concept of "sensation" or "observation" in 1873, 7.326 ff.) as a criterion in the definition of the appropriate "method of research," he does not thereby bring in a proof of the existence of the world. This is because the "experience" of a resistance to our will *hic et nunc*, as a case of "Secondness," is not a cognition ("Thirdness"); rather, it can enter into cognition only through the formation of a meaningful opinion (Thirdness). It must therefore be possible to define the meaning of reality without first giving a proof of the existence of the real, because the mere experience of the existence of the real has meaning "as something" only in the context of possible experience of the real. From this it follows, on my view, that the existence of the world that can be experienced only *hic et nunc* cannot be proven at all, nor need it be. What can be proven is that every attempt to prove the existence of the real world or to doubt it already assumes this existence.

29. Kant suggested in the preface to the *Critique of Pure Reason* that it was possible for reason, by engaging in the praxis of natural science, to utilize "principles of judgment based upon fixed laws, constraining nature to give answers to questions of reason's own determining." *Immanuel Kant's Critique of Pure Reason*, trans. Norman Kemp Smith (New York: St. Martin's Press, 1965), p. 20, B xiii. (In citations to this work, "A" refers to the first edition, 1781, and "B" to the second edition, 1787.) To this end, reason must not only develop conceptual or mathematical models a priori, but also apply them to nature through spherical weights, inclined planes, water vessels, etc. That is, it must embody them in the medium of nature itself in order to let nature reply to nature as "made" by man. In later years, in his *Opus Postumum*, Kant once again took up this problem of the conditions of the possibility of "experimental natural science" and attempted to solve it by means of the concept of the "self-affection of the ego" in the intervention of the bodily ego into nature. On this see the excellent recent work by

Hansgeorg Hoppe, "Die Objektivität der besonderen Naturerkenntnis" (diss., University of Kiel, West Germany, 1966). It seems to me, however, that this is the very point where the aporia of Kant's transcendental philosophy of consciousness makes itself felt. It is unable to recognize as preconditions for the possibility of experience those presuppositions which do not pertain to consciousness, but which transcendental philosophy always already assumed—such as the assumption of an "affection" of "sensibility" through the "thing-in-itself"—and which it absolutely had to assume in the attempt to give a foundation to the possibility of experimental science.

30. See Erich Heintel, *Die Beiden Labyrinthe der Philosophie* (Vienna and Munich: R. Oldenbourg, 1968), vol. 1.

31. It is, of course, true that the real community will itself be recognized by the "ultimate opinion" only in a way that fully accords with the meaning of its reality, but that does not reduce the real community to the "ultimate opinion" qua idea. Peirce is sometimes unclear about this matter, however: see the discussion later on in this section.

32. 5.311. In 1885 Peirce would criticize Royce's Hegelianism by emphasizing that before we achieve a conceptual knowledge of individual things, which is possible only with the ideal perfection of knowledge in the ultimate opinion, we experience them as a resistance to our will. As such, we point them out and identify them as existing things by means of "indices" in language (such as "this here"), even though we do not thereby "know" them. See 8.41–42. Cf. Sec. C.e in this chapter.

33. 8.16. Peirce is probably in debt to Kant for this overcoming of the primacy of so-called inner experience—namely, to the comparison of the first and second editions of the *Critique of Pure Reason*. In his reading of the second edition's added "Refutation of Idealism" (pp. 244–47 [B 274 ff.]), Peirce drew conclusions that went beyond Kant in the direction of meaning-critical Realism. Peirce appears to verify this in a 1903 assessment of Kant's thought, where he distinguishes among three dialectical *Momente* of the unfolding of the problem of Idealism vs. Realism. First, there is the Kantian position which restricts the validity of all concepts to possible experience. Second, we have the idealistic conclusion that, in this case, only our ideas (*Vorstellungen*) exist. Finally, Peirce says, we have "the third moment of Kant's thought, which was only made prominent in the second edition. . . . It is really a most luminous and central element in Kant's thought. I may say that it is the very sun round which all the rest revolves. This third moment consists in the flat denial that the metaphysical conceptions do not apply to things in themselves. Kant *never* said that. What he said is that these conceptions do not apply beyond the limits of possible experience. But we have *direct experience of things in themselves*" (6.95).

34. This should be compared not only to Wittgenstein's criticism of *metaphorischer Schein* in the *Philosophical Investigations*, trans. G. E. M. Anscombe (New York: The Macmillan Co., 1953), which further extends the meaning-critical approach as such, but also to the following passage in Martin Heidegger, *Being and Time*, trans. John Macquarrie and Edward Robinson (New York: Harper and Row, 1962), p. 89: "When Dasein directs itself towards something and grasps it, it does not somehow first get out of an inner sphere in which it has been proximally encapsulated, but its primary kind of Being is such that it is always 'outside' alongside entities which it encounters and which belong to a world already discovered. Nor is any inner sphere abandoned when Dasein dwells alongside the entity to be known, and determines its character; but even in this 'Being-outside' along-

side the object, Dasein is still 'inside', if we understand this in the correct sense; that is to say, it is itself 'inside' as a Being-in-the-world which knows. And furthermore, the perceiving of what is known is not a process of returning with one's booty to the 'cabinet' of consciousness after one has gone out and grasped it; even in perceiving, retaining, and preserving, the Dasein which knows *remains outside*, and it does so *as Dasein*." Here and in the context of Heidegger's discussion of "Being-in-the-world in General as the Basic State of Dasein" (pp. 78 ff.) that goes along with this passage, we find the phenomenological-hermeneutical equivalent of a "critique of knowledge," which is in line with the "critique of meaning" of Peirce and Wittgenstein.

35. Peirce is referring here to a publication from 1892, "The Critic of Arguments," 3.417 ff.

36. 6.610. This is a passage from Peirce's critical rejoinder to the editor of *The Monist*, Dr. Carus, to which Peirce gave the title "Reply to the Necessitarians."

37. 5.407. Cf. also the following important passage from the "Logic of 1873": ". . . the object of the final opinion which we have seen to be independent of what any particular person thinks, may very well be external to the mind. And there is no objection to saying that this external reality causes the sensation and through the sensation has caused all that line of thought which has finally led to the belief" (7.339).

38. 8.129. This, again, is from the 1890 review of Royce's *The World and the Individual*.

39. Peirce was first to develop this thought in 1898 (see 5.313 ff.); he worked it out in more detail in his metaphysics of evolution from 1892 and after.

40. See, e.g., 5.433. Cf. the footnotes that Peirce added in his later years to "How to Make Our Ideas Clear," 5.402 n.

41. For a complete discussion of this problem see the perceptive, aporetic commentaries by Manley Thompson ("The Paradox of Peirce's Realism," in Wiener and Young, *Studies*, pp. 133–42) and John E. Smith ("Community and Reality," in Bernstein, *Perspectives*, pp. 92–119).

42. In the present context we can ignore that the choice between the correct use of linguistic means, on the one hand, and being misled by the *metaphorischer Schein* of language, on the other, does not do justice to the problem of creative thought, which allows itself to be led by the preconceptual, revelatory character of metaphors without succumbing to their *Schein*. Even for someone who, like Heidegger, understands metaphors as "simultaneously serving to uncover and conceal," the critique of meaning is a *conditio sine qua non* of modern philosophy.

43. The second main motive is to rescue freedom, or rather the moral world of the "ego language game," in the face of the mechanical necessity of the contemporary natural scientific "language game."

44. The complicated hierarchy of philosophical disciplines from 1901 and after, according to which the normative logic of science presupposes the Phenomenology of the categories, does not necessarily contradict this, since "Phenomenology" itself presupposes the formal logic of relations, which is part of mathematics, wherein the categories are already deduced as possibilities for thought. In 1898 Peirce wrote about his first attempts at the deduction of the categories, which led to the "New List": "In the early sixties I was a passionate devotee of Kant, at least as regarded the transcendental Analytic in the *Critic of Pure Reason*. I believed more implicitly in the two tables of the Functions of Judgment and the Categories than if they had been brought from Sinai" (4.2). About 1905 Peirce wrote

about the further development in a footnote to the "New List": "The first question . . . was whether or not the fundamental categories of thought really have that sort of dependence upon formal logic that Kant asserted. I became thoroughly convinced that such a relation really did and must exist. After a series of inquiries, I came to see that Kant ought not to have confined himself to divisions of propositions, or "judgments," as the Germans confuse the subject by calling them, but ought to have taken account of all elementary and significant differences of form among signs of all sorts, and that, above all, he ought not to have left out of account fundamental forms of reasonings. At last after the hardest two years' mental work that I have ever done in my life, I found myself with but a single assured result of any positive importance. This was that there are but three elementary forms of predication or signification, which as I originally named them . . . were *qualities* (of feeling), (dyadic) *relations*, and (predications of) *representations*" [1.561].

45. See above, n. 15 to this chapter.
46. This view is shared by Murphey (*Development*, pp. 23 ff.) and Kempski. In most of the places where Murphey claims that Peirce misunderstands Kant, one can also see a justifiable criticism of Kant, if Peirce's position is assumed to be more tenable than Kant's. Peirce probably was not clear about the breadth of the implications of his criticisms of Kant.
47. But it is not that "middle way" of a system of the preformation of pure reason which Kant briefly describes in the *Critique of Pure Reason* (B 167). At the beginning of his study of philosophy Peirce shared that view with his father, Benjamin Peirce, who was a mathematician oriented toward Leibniz, but the younger Peirce abandoned this view after 1862. See Murphey, *Development*, p. 41.
48. My exposition here is oriented to Peirce's more advanced interpretation of the relationship between induction and hypothesis. Peirce's logic of synthetic inferences makes it possible to limit once and for all the applicability of the *circulus-vitiosus* postulate to its appropriate place within deductive logic.
49. Here I adopt a term used by Kempski.
50: On this see Gerard Radnitzky, "Ueber emphelenswerte und verwerfliche Spielarten der Skepsis," *Ratio* 7 (1965):109–35.
51. See below, Chap. 4, Sec. B.a.
52. In doing this I am also taking into account those texts from Peirce's early study of Kant which Murphey has made accessible, as well as the published works on logic and the doctrine of categories from 1867.
53. See Murphey, *Development*, p. 21.
54. Peirce, "Principles," as quoted in ibid., p. 26. One could speak here of a psychologistic misunderstanding of Kant that is eradicated by the second edition of the *Critique of Pure Reason*. But the question is whether a really consistent elimination of all "psychological transcendentalism" from the *Critique of Pure Reason* must not lead to the end result that the necessary truth of synthetic judgments a priori is valid only under the assumption that the empirical propositions of science, which presuppose these judgments, are themselves apodictically certain.
55. Peirce, "Principles," as quoted in Murphey, *Development*, pp. 26–27.
56. 5.382 n. I am grateful to Prof. Peter Krausser for kindly pointing out to me the symptomatic meaning of this passage regarding Peirce's orientation to the postulates of practical reason.
57. See above, Sec. A of this chapter. Cf. Murphey, *Development*, pp. 55–94. It seems to me that we have here not only a "metaphysical deduction," in

Kant's sense, but also a "transcendental deduction," since attaining a consistent opinion about the real is for Peirce the "highest point" to which *his* transcendental is bound. In a draft of the "New List of Categories" Peirce criticizes Kant's method of deducing the categories by reference to the table of judgments because it "does not display that direct reference to the unity of consistency which alone gives validity to the categories" (Peirce, "Draft 2 of the 'New List of Categories,'" printed in the appendix of Murphey, *Development*, p. 412. Cf. also Murphey's discussion of this draft, p. 65). Peirce hopes that the "New List" has established just such a direct reference in its analysis of the concepts contained in the representation of the real by signs (1.550). In the transcendental deduction of the validity of synthetic inferences, which Peirce presented in 1868 and again in 1878, the "ultimate opinion" of the community to be attained "in the long run" functions as the "highest point" (see below, Sec. C.e of this chapter). This concretization of the "highest point" of transcendental philosophy was already present in Peirce's semiotic transformation of the concept of knowledge and is characteristic of the general transition from a philosophy of "consciousness in general" to Pragmatism as meaning-critical Realism. In contemporary philosophy this problem is discussed under the heading "language and consciousness" or, more specifically, "society, language, and consciousness."

58. In an 1898 autobiographical sketch Peirce was to write: "This [i.e., the interpretation of the relation between subject and predicate as a sign relation] led me to see that the relation between subject and predicate, or antecedent and consequent, is essentially the same as that between premiss and conclusion" (4.3).

59. See Murphey, *Development*, p. 56.

60. Peirce, "Logic: 1865–1867," MS dated Dec. 13, 1865, I B 2, Box 8, Peirce manuscripts, Houghton Library, Harvard University, Cambridge, Mass., as quoted in Murphey, *Development*, p. 56.

61. On Peirce's interpretation of natural processes as unconscious inferences see 2.711–13.

62. Peirce, "Lowell Lectures," 1903, Vol. 1, No. 8, pp. 12–16, I B, Box 4, Peirce manuscripts, Houghton Library, Harvard University, Cambridge, Mass., as quoted in Murphey, *Development*, p. 60. In 1868, in his "Memoranda concerning the Aristotelian Syllogism" (2.792–807) Peirce shows that, contrary to Kant's view in "Die falsche Spitzfindigkeit der vier syllogistischen Figuren" of 1762, each of the three syllogistic figures involves an independent principle of inference, or, more precisely, "that every figure involves the principle of the first figure, but the second and third figures contain other principles, besides" (2.807). Cf. Murphey, *Development*, pp. 57–63.

63. I cannot enter here into the modifications that resulted in Peirce's conception of deduction because of his later development of the logic of relations.

64. In modern theories of the logic of science, "explanation" is interpreted as the deduction of an explanandum on the basis of general laws and antecedent conditions. Hence, there is no logical difference between an explanation and a prediction. This view is expressed in, for example, Carl Hempel and Paul Oppenheim, *Readings in the Philosophy of Science* (New York, 1953). But in this case too the assumption of antecedent conditions which would permit the deduction of the explanandum under the presupposition of a general law is itself possible only with a greater or lesser degree of probability. This assumption, which makes possible an "explanation" (as Hempel and Oppenheim use the term), is what Peirce calls an explanation of phe-

nomena by means of a "hypothesis." This shift in accent in the direction of an *ars inveniendi* or "logic of discovery," which the Neopositivists regarded as psychological, is very relevant for the philosophy of science. For example, it is relevant whenever, as in the case of historical explanation, everything depends upon finding the antecedent conditions, and where more general premises can be presupposed only in such a vague form that a deduction of occurrences such as Hempel and Oppenheim describe is not possible in principle. On this see William Dray, *Laws and Explanation in History* (Oxford: Oxford University Press, 1964). Cf. also 1.272.

65. On this see Erich Heintel's introduction to Johann Gottfried Herder, *Sprachphilosophische Schriften*, 2d ed. (Hamburg: Felix Meiner, 1964), pp. xv–lvii. The problem which Peirce is concerned with here could be expressed in Weisgerber's phrase, the "Wortung der Welt" in language. See Leo Weisgerber, "Das Worten der Welt als sprachliche Aufgabe der Menschheit," *Sprachforum* 1 (1955): 10–19.

66. Peirce, "Draft 2 of the 'New List of Categories,' " in Murphey, *Development*, p. 413. Cf. ibid., pp. 67–68.

67. In his semiotic, which is inspired by the medieval logic of language ("Tractatus de proprietatibus terminorum"), Peirce distinguishes *denotatio*, the designation of things that fall under a concept extensionally, from *connotatio*, the designation of the features that belong to the intensional meaning of a symbol. Peirce conceives these two traditional dimensions of meaning of "speculative grammar" as illustrations of either Secondness (*denotatio* as the relation of a sign to the outer object in a situation) or Firstness (*connotatio* as the designation of the qualitative characteristics that express a kind of being). In addition to this there is, as a theme of what Peirce called "speculative rhetoric," the relation of a sign to human beings' understanding consciousness in the form of the "Interpretant." This dimension of Thirdness ("mediation" qua "interpretation") is, in addition, the dimension in which the clarification of the meaning of concepts or statements by means of the pragmatic maxim has its semiotic locus. Charles Morris, whose reception of Peirce's semiotic amounts to a behavioristic reduction, speaks here of the "pragmatic dimension" of signs as an equivalent to traditional "rhetoric." See below, Chap. 6, Sec. B, and Chap. 8, Secs. B and C.

68. Peirce, "Appendix. No. 2," n.d., I B 2, Box 8, pp. 3–4, Peirce manuscripts, Houghton Library, Harvard University, Cambridge, Mass., as quoted in Murphey, *Development*, pp. 69 ff.

69. We are concerned here, according to Peirce's later terminology, with an "interpreting symbol," which must be distinguished categorically from a merely "indexical" proper name.

70. See Murphey, *Development*, p. 70.

71. See above, n. 48 to this chapter.

72. See Joachim Wach, *Das Verstehen*, 3 vols. (Tübingen: J. C. B. Mohr [Paul Siebeck], 1926–33).

73. Peirce, "Appendix. No. 2," pp. 7–8.

74. Peirce, "Draft 4 of the 'The New List of Categories,' " in Murphey, *Development*, p. 415. Cf. ibid., p. 71.

75. Recent research on language has shown that the cognitive function of language plays a role in ordering and disclosing even the perception of color. See H. Gipper, "Ueber Aufgabe und Leistung der Sprache beim Umgang mit Farben," *Die Farbe* 6 (1957): 23–48.

76. See Murphey, *Development*, p. 71.

77. See below, Chap. 6, Sec. B, and Chap. 8, Sec. B.

78. Attention to this architectonic is as important to interpreting Peirce here as is constant attention in his later works to the categories Firstness, Secondness, and Thirdness.

79. See below, Chap. 4, Sec. B.a.

80. 5.235. This idea was probably influenced by the Swedenborgian philosophy found in Henry James the elder's *Substance and Shadow* (Boston, 1863). Peirce was to reconfirm this idea explicitly in his later metaphysics (see Murphey, *Development*, pp. 350 ff.). The close ties with Böhme and Schelling, which stand out particularly in the third period of Peirce's development, were also probably mediated by the "Transcendentalism" of Henry James the elder.

81. "Embodying" or "incarnation" is the central concept in the metaphysics of Henry James the elder. See Murphey, *Development*, pp. 350 ff.

82. 5.251. This passage recalls in a striking way Hegel's definition of language as "self-consciousness existing *for others*; it is self-consciousness which as such is there immediately present, and which in its individuality is universal" (G. W. F. Hegel, *Phenomenology of Mind*, trans. J. B. Baillie [New York: Harper and Row, 1967], p. 660). Marx's corresponding definition of language characterizes it as "unmittelbare Wirklichkeit des Gedankens, das praktische, auch für andere Menschen existierende, also auch für mich selbst erst existierende wirkliche Bewusstsein" (Karl Marx, "Die Deutsche Ideologie," in *Marx Engels Werke*, 39 vols. [Berlin, DDR: Dietz Verlag, 1953], 3:473). The individual's identity with the other or, rather, with society, which is already established in language, is expressed in Peirce's conception of the "community," which becomes the intersecting point of his whole philosophy. On Peirce's principle of "hope" see below, Sec. C.e of this chapter.

83. In a footnote to the previous text (5.289 n) Peirce remarks: "Accordingly, just as we say that a body is in motion, and not that motion is in a body we ought to say that we are in thought and not that thoughts are in us." [Apel notes here that a translation into German of Peirce's statement readily makes this point and that this kind of philosophical insight, found by considering language, would later be typical of Heidegger—Trans.]

84. 5.315. In contrast to this, an "idiot" in the original, strict sense of the term is a "private person."

85. Cf. above, Sec. B of this chapter.

86. Ibid.

87. Peirce does not really introduce this doctrine until the second 1868 essay and does not utilize it fully for the theory of knowledge until 1903.

88. The problem that concerns us here was once given the following insightful formulation by Heidegger: No matter how close a chair is put to a wall, it can never really meet the wall. Being's "clearing [*Lichtung*]" in the logos can never be reduced to events or relationships within the world.

89. Here Peirce follows Berkeley's "Theory of Vision"; see 5.219. Peirce traces the unification of phenomena, which was later the object of study in Gestalt psychology, to unconscious inferences. About this he writes: "Now, it is a known law of mind, that when phenomena of an extreme complexity are presented, which yet would be reduced to *order* or mediate simplicity by the application of a certain conception, that conception sooner or later arises in application to those phenomena" (2.223).

90. See 5.250, 5.263, 5.157, 5.181, and 5.202.

91. Peirce linked semiotic to the doctrine of categories in the second 1868 essay (5.283–90). He had developed both of these in 1867, in the "New List of

Categories," from a single, basic conception. On the relationship between semiotic and the doctrine of categories, see below, esp. Chap. 6, Secs. B–D.

92. 5.267. Cf. above, Sec. C.b of this chapter.

93. Peirce developed this doctrine for the first time in a general way in his article "On the Natural Classification of Arguments" (1867, 2.461–516). The second such exposition followed in the "logic of science" series (1878, 2.619–44). For a discussion and further, systematic development of this see Kempski, *Peirce*, Chaps. 1, 3, and 4.

94. Peirce knew in 1869 about the beginnings of physiological psychology in Germany, with Fechner and Wundt, as Max Fisch has shown in "A Chronicle of Pragmatism, 1865–1879," *The Monist* 48 (1964):442–66.

95. On this see the comprehensive monograph on the concept of "habit" by Gerhard Funke, *Gewohnheit, Archiv für Begriffsgeschichte*, vol. 3 (Bonn: Bouvier Verlag, 1958). Even here Peirce, the classic thinker on the concept of "habit," appears almost exclusively through the medium of William James.

96. See below, Chap. 4, Secs. A and B.b.

97. Harris was a student and friend of the German founder of the St. Louis Hegelian school, Henry Brockmeyer. He wrote a book about Hegel's logic and, along with Denton J. Snider, founded in 1867 America's first philosophical journal, the *Journal of Speculative Philosophy*. See the amusing description of the rise of an American Hegel school at the edge of the Wild West in Gustav E. Müller, *Amerikanische Philosophie*, 2d ed. (Stuttgart: Frommann, 1950), pp. 110 ff. On Peirce's approach to Harris's question see Fisch, "A Chronicle of Pragmatism," p. 446.

98. 2.692. See Peirce's 1867 review of Venn's book, 8.1–6.

99. English usage does not adequately render the active, physical effort of *machen* that Apel refers to here, i.e., acquiring experience by engaging in some action, doing something—Trans.

100. Peirce is thinking here of a deductive inference of probability in the sense of the mathematical theory of probability, which is by no means to be confused with merely probable, i.e., inductive or abductive, inferences. See 5.346 and 2.620–23.

101. The objective validity of the hypotheses based upon "abduction" can be confirmed only inductively, according to Peirce. That is also the logical structure of the principle of verification implicit in the pragmatic maxim. Hence, the question of the validity of induction acquires for Peirce in every respect the significance that the question of the validity of synthetic judgments a priori had for Kant. That is the objective reason why Peirce, after he had dealt with deduction, could concentrate completely in the third essay from the 1868–69 series on induction. Peirce himself, of course, does not bring this out very clearly in the 1869 essay; he suggests, rather, an analogy between induction and abduction (5.349 and 5.352).

102. Murphey seems to expect a proof of this kind from Peirce. See Sec. B and n. 28 earlier in this chapter.

103. 5.352. At the beginning of the essay Peirce shows in an analogous way that whoever wants to deny or to prove the validity of deductive logic already presupposes it (5.318–19).

104. In this vein Heidegger termed the demand for a proof of the existence of the outer world, which arose after Descartes, a "scandal." Giambattista Vico held that to want to prove the existence of God or the world means to want to be able to make them.

105. Cf. above, Chap. 1.

106. Cf. above, Sec. C.b of this chapter.

107. 5.357. This passage provides a necessary supplement to the characterization of the "community" found in 8.13. Cf. above, Sec. B of this chapter. [Apel's term "logical Socialism" as a designation for an idea in Peirce has been discussed in a book on Peirce by one of Apel's students. See Gerd Wartenberg, *Logischer Sozialismus* (Frankfurt: Suhrkamp, 1971)—Trans.]

108. William James, *The Will to Believe* (New York, 1897). On the "principle of hope" in Peirce see 5.357, 5.402, 5.407–8, 2.652–55, and 8.12–14. Apel's use of the term "principle of hope [*Prinzip Hoffnung*]" refers also to the title of the main work by the contemporary German, Neo-Marxist philosopher Ernst Bloch. See *Das Prinzip Hoffnung* (1953-56), vol. 5 of Ernst Bloch, *Gesamtausgabe*, 16 vols. (Frankfurt am Main: Suhrkamp Verlag, 1959)—Trans.

Chapter 4

1. According to Max H. Fisch, "Alexander Bain."

2. Here Peirce anticipates the problem of so-called theoretical concepts which constituted the limit of Carnap's neopositivistic program of definitions. See Rudolf Carnap, Minnesota Studies in the Philosophy of Science, vol. 1 (Minneapolis: University of Minnesota Press, 1956). Cf. Stegmüller, *Hauptströmungen der Gegenwartsphilosophie*, p. 462.

3. See above, Chap. 3, Sec. C.e.

4. Peirce wrote in 1908 concerning this title that "In 1871, in a Metaphysical Club in Cambridge, Massachusetts, I used to preach this principle as a sort of logical gospel, representing the unformulated method followed by Berkeley, and in conversation about it I called it 'Pragmatism' " (6.482).

Max Fisch ("A Chronicle of Pragmatism," p. 442) found in Peirce's notebook on philosophical terminology numerous entries from 1865 under "practical" and the following one under "pragmatic": "Pragmatic Anthropology Kant VII (b) 4 [Peirce owned the edition of Rosenkranz and Schubert, 1838–42] . . . (horizon) . . . Kant III 206." In 1902 Peirce began a lexicon article on the topic "Pragmatic and Pragmatism" with these two references to Kant (5.1). More important is the reference to Kant in 1905 in "What Pragmatism Is." There Peirce answers the question why he has not named his theory "Practicism" or "Practicalism" by writing: "For one who had learned philosophy out of Kant, as the writer, along with nineteen out of every twenty experimentalists who have turned to philosophy, had done, and who still thought in Kantian terms most readily, *praktisch* and *pragmatisch* were as far apart as the two poles, the former belonging in a region of thought where no mind of the experimentalist type can ever make sure of solid ground under his feet, the latter expressing relation to some definite human purpose. Now quite the most striking feature of the new theory was its recognition of an inseparable connection between rational cognition and rational purpose; and that consideration it was which determined the preference for the name *pragmatism*" (5.412). In his definition of the pragmatic maxim in 1902 Peirce simply comments: "The writer was led to the maxim by reflection upon Kant's *Critique of the Pure Reason*" (5.3). The most important passage in the *Critique of Pure Reason* which could have suggested the pragmatic maxim is the following: "By 'the practical' I mean everything that is possible through freedom. When, however, the conditions of the exercise of our free will are empirical, reason can have no other than a regulative employment in regard to it, and can serve only to effect unity in its empirical laws. . . . In this field, therefore, reason can supply none but *pragmatic* laws of free action, for the attainment of those ends which are commended to us by the senses; it cannot yield us laws that are pure and determined completely *a priori*" (p. 632 [B 828]).

In the second chapter of the *Groundwork of the Metaphysics of Morals* Kant distinguishes between those "hypothetical imperatives" which are suggestions for prudence and are also called "pragmatic" (leading to our well-being) and those mere "technical" imperatives which only state what ways and means are needed to attain a particular goal. [See Immanuel Kant, *Groundwork of the Metaphysics of Morals*, trans. H. J. Paton (New York: Harper and Row, 1964), pp. 83–84. Quotations of this work are from this translation—Trans.] Peirce's pragmatic maxim for the clarification of our ideas is, in fact, best characterized as the first kind of "hypothetical imperative," because in it the particular goal of clarifying certain concepts is presupposed. See Peirce's authoritative definition of the pragmatic maxim in 5.402.

5. 5.12. Cf. "Peirce's Description of the Metaphysical Club in a 1909 Draft of a preface to 'My Pragmatism,'" published as an appendix to Fisch, "Was There a Metaphysical Club?" in Moore and Robin, *Studies*, pp. 24–29.

6. Fisch, "A Chronicle of Pragmatism," p. 444.

7. My characterization follows Edward H. Madden, "Pragmatism, Positivism, and Chauncey Wright," *Philosophy and Phenomenological Research* 15 (1953): 62–71. See also Edward H. Madden, *Chauncey Wright and the Foundations of Pragmatism* (Seattle: University of Washington Press, 1963). Madden's article is based upon the following writings by Chauncey Wright: "The Philosophy of Herbert Spencer," *North American Review* (1865): 423–76; "The Evolution of Self-Consciousness," *North American Review* (1873), and the posthumously published book *Philosophical Discussions* (New York, 1877).

8. Wright, "Herbert Spencer," p. 427.

9. Ibid., p. 431.

10. Ibid.

11. Max Fisch has established this fact in his essay "Alexander Bain," p. 423. My interpretation here follows Fisch's exposition.

12. Bain, *The Emotions and the Will*, 3d ed. (New York, 1875), pp. 505 ff., as quoted by Fisch, "Alexander Bain," p. 423.

13. Bain, *The Emotions and the Will*, pp. 505 ff., as quoted by Fisch, "Alexander Bain," p. 419.

14. Alexander Bain, *Mental and Moral Science* (London, 1872), p. 373, as quoted by Fisch, "Alexander Bain," p. 420.

15. Bain, ibid., p. 100, as quoted by Fisch, ibid., p. 422.

16. Bain, *The Emotions and the Will*, p. 573, as quoted by Fisch, "Alexander Bain," p. 420.

17. Peirce always preferred Whewell's historically conceived philosophy of science to that of his great opponent, John Stuart Mill. See Fisch, "A Chronicle of Pragmatism," p. 450.

18. As Max Fisch has demonstrated (see his "Chronicle of Pragmatism," pp. 465–66), Peirce could not decide whether to publish his Metaphysical Club Pragmatism lecture separately from his planned book on "The Logic of Science." Later he made a compromise by publishing his series of articles

"Illustrations of the Logic of Science" in the *Popular Science Monthly*, a compromise that he still later often regretted.

19. See Fisch, "A Chronicle of Pragmatism," pp. 454 ff., 466.
20. An important example of this attempt is his Harvard lecture entitled "Pragmatism" from 1903 (5.13 ff.).
21. On the diamond example see 5.403. Cf. 7.340–41 (from the "Logic of 1873") and also the later corrections in 5.453–58 and 8.208.
22. Murphey, *Development*, p. 164.
23. See the impressive example of the convergence of the experiences of a blind person and a deaf person which Peirce presents in his Berkeley review (8.12).
24. This naturalistic reduction of truth proceeds according to this schema: "These activities are *nothing but* the satisfaction of such and such needs. I am the only one who sees through all this and recognizes the 'truth' for what it is." The classic representatives of this kind of thought are Schopenhauer and Nietzsche.
25. Peirce himself would often complain later about the psychologism in the Pragmatism essays of 1877–78.
26. Giambattista Vico was the first thinker to criticize Descartes' radical doubt from the standpoint of the historical, substantial presuppositions of the development of knowledge found in the *sensus communis*. Recently, the Cartesian fiction of an absolute freedom from presuppositions has been criticized from a similar viewpoint in the name of the existential, hermeneutical, a priori structure of our preconceptions (*Vorverständnisses*, in Heidegger's terminology). See Hans-Georg Gadamer, *Truth and Method*, trans. and ed. Garrett Barden and John Cumming (New York: Seabury Press, 1975).
27. Cf. above, Chap. 3, Sec. C.c.
28. It is significant that this criticism applies not only to all of Pragmatism, but also to Life-philosophy, Existentialism, and Marxism. The achievements of these philosophies lie in the different ways they work out the forms in which knowledge is engaged in the world. Their limitations lie in their blindness to the highest level of reflection, reflection that thematizes the conditions of the possibility of philosophy and, hence, of undogmatic thinking as such.
29. See below, Chap. 8, Sec. C.
30. See Scheler, "Erkenntnis und Arbeit," in *Gesammelte Werke*, Chap. 2 Wesen und Sinn von Wissen und Erkenntnis.—Trans.
31. Peirce repulsed his audience during his lifetime with his logical precision and the attention to detail which went along with the broad synthetic aims of his system. But this logical rigor is also what laid the groundwork for his growing fame in the twentieth century.
32. This is precisely what has not been accomplished either by the traditional, Aristotelian adequation theory of truth or by what is called its "modern, more precise formulation" in Alfred Tarski's logical semantics. Neopositivism admitted this inadequacy when it (in the persons of Morris and Carnap) separated the task of solving the problem of verification from semantics and transferred it to the behavioristic analysis of the use of language, i.e., to the "pragmatic dimension" of the use of signs, and considered this analysis to be a task for empirical scientists.
33. See also Peirce's ironic, biting criticism of the ideal of being determined to get what one wants, which guides "men of action" (5.386).
34. One might recall here Petrarch's idea of a spiritual discussion or, histori-

cally, the passionate, dialectical discussions of the intellectual elite during the Greek enlightenment.

35. 5.382. At the end of the third period in the development of Peirce's thought, he himself recognized this aesthetic criterion of harmony as the highest principle of his own speculative architectonic. Of course, he demands of metaphysics (which is not itself a normative science, but which presupposes such a science in the form of logic) that it must comply with empirical criteria of verification and falsification, since it is a science of experience, writ large.

36. 5.384. This judgment of Peirce's corresponds quite precisely to Dilthey's complaint that metaphysical systems or world views stand in an irresolvable conflict with one another. Like Dilthey, Peirce thinks that Kant, too, remained within the confines of the a priori method and constructed a metaphysical system motivated by a certain specific world view. Peirce also sees that Hegel wanted, on a fundamentally new level of reflection, to elevate the opposition between different metaphysical points of view to a path leading to the truth. But for Peirce this is only the final confirmation that the a priori method is a method based upon being "agreeable to reason" (5.382 n. 1).

37. Peirce had already discerned in 1871 that "we find our opinions constrained" (8.12). The "external permanency" that he refers to here was probably largely influenced by Berkeley's and John Stuart Mill's definition of outer substances as "permanent possibilities of sensation." On this see Fisch, "A Chronicle of Pragmatism," p. 444.

38. This is confirmed by the confrontation of the principle of convergence in the "method of investigation" with the Hegelian dialectical method of convergence that Peirce used in the "Logic of 1873." While for Hegel all the opposing opinions that we begin with enter into the synthesis and help to define it, in the "method of science" the "final conclusion" in which all must finally agree is predetermined, "without reference to the initial state of belief" (7.319).

39. See Ludwig Wittgenstein, *Tractatus logico-philosophicus*, trans. D. F. Pears and B. F. McGuinness (London: Routledge and Kegan Paul, 1961) proposition 4.024: "To understand a proposition means to know what is the case if it is true. (One can understand it, therefore, without knowing whether it is true.) It is understood by anyone who understands its constituents."

40. Leibniz in fact saw the foundation of his idea of an *ars combinatoria* in the reducibility of the contents of all concepts to final, abstract ideas (*simplices*). This foundation was, moreover, again conceived as the basis of his idea of a *lingua universalis sive philosophica*, which was supposed to rule out once and for all every misunderstanding between philosophers. These ideas were taken up again in a modified form in the logical Atomism of Bertrand Russell and the early Wittgenstein, as well as in Carnap's *Logical Structure of the World*, trans. Rolf A. George (London: Routledge and Kegan Paul, 1967). The further development by Wittgenstein and logical Empiricism of the notion of clarifying meaning or the use of language led in the very direction first suggested by Peirce's pragmatic-operative method. This method attempted not to clarify ideas through ideas or ideas through sense data, but rather to clarify ideas through the possibilities of their application, including possible inferences and the chance of their being borne out by sense data.

41. Later, in about 1900, when Peirce founded his Phenomenology, he once again introduced the notion of self-evidence by rehabilitating it under the

category of Firstness and attempting to reconcile it with the other fundamental categories of Pragmatism, Secondness (e.g., the brute force and impulses offered by outer experience) and Thirdness (rules of behavior, laws).
Cf. below, esp. Chap. 6, Secs. B and C, and also Chap. 8, Sec. B.

42. See Apel, "Wittgenstein and the Problem of Hermeneutic Understanding,"
in *Towards a Transformation of Philosophy*, pp. 1–45.

43. This distinction can be founded on the basis of the Peircean idea of synthetic logic so that it might also appear to be plausible even for those
logicians to whom the well-known "hermeneutical circle" seems unscientific.
Cf. above, Chap. 3, Sec. C.a and n. 48.

44. A closely related form of this type of thought can be found in Heidegger,
for whom in fact every instance in which we understand something "as
something" rests upon the correlative presupposition of an anticipation of
the possibilities of our present existence (our *Entwurf*) and the simultaneous,
determinate character of this anticipation with regard to that which is to be
understood (*Geworfenheit*). Moreover, Marx's mediation of all historical
instances of the giving of meanings through social engagement (taking sides
on future praxis) reveals basically the same structure, or, at least, did so
until Marxian theory became dogmatized. But here, however, as in the case
of "existential engagement," we must choose the explications of a meaning
that in our situation are practically relevant (ethically, politically, and existentially relevant) from the unlimited number of those which are, according
to Peirce, in principle, technically and practically possible. Hence, the possible meaning is ultimately to be determined by a subjective decision which
can, of course, be rationally motivated—for example, the meaning of the
sentence "We have atomic weapons." In the comparison that I have postulated here among three forms of mediating our understanding of meaning
in terms of future praxis, there lies, I think, the key to the problem discussed at the beginning of this book, the distribution of the tasks that are
shared today by Pragmatism, Existentialism, and Marxism.

45. On the metaphysics of evolution that Peirce had in mind here, see below,
Chap. 7, Sec. B.

46. 1.527. This passage comes from a lecture manuscript (1903) on the doctrine
of categories. It came to my attention through Peter Krausser's essay.

47. See the discussion further on in this section.

48. The leading principle in the modern philosophy of science, from Nicolas of
Cusa and Cardanus up to Vico and Kant, is that we can understand only
what we can make; here this principle is given concrete form. In his "Re-
flexionen" (no. 395) Kant added, ". . . if we are given the stuff for this."
An analogy to the pragmatic concretization of making things with some
material stuff can be found in Friedrich Engels's example of synthetic
alizarine: "If we can prove the correctness of our interpretation of a natural
process by making it ourselves, creating it from its preconditions, and make
it serve our own ends, then that is the end of the unknowable Kantian
'thing-in-itself.'" (*Ludwig Feuerbach und der Ausgang der klassischen
deutschen Philosophie*, ed. Hans Hajek [Leipzig: Meiner, 1946], p. 15). It is
hardly necessary to mention that Peirce agreed completely with Engels's
realistic conclusions, although he was not himself a materialist.

49. Here too we have an interesting form of "circle" that is found especially in
Bridgeman's work, although he leaves it unexplained. On this see Karl
Popper's critique of reductive "Operationalism" in *Conjectures and Refuta-
tions* (London: Routledge and Kegan Paul, 1963), p. 62, as well as in his
Logic of Scientific Discovery (London: Hutchinson, 1960), pp. 440–41.

50. Peirce had in fact almost instinctively made use of the "contrary to fact *condicionalis*" (the famous "would be") in his writings, even in the first and second periods of his thought. But only in the final period did he make a principle of it and subsequently replace all indicative formulations of the anticipated consequences of a test with "would be" formulations. On this see editors' comments in the *Collected Papers*.

51. See 5.453–58 and 8.208. Cf. below, Chap. 8, Sec. C.

52. See below, Chap. 8, Sec. C.

53. This distinction, made here in terms of Peirce's doctrine of categories, corresponds to this extent to Heidegger's distinction in the "ontic-ontological difference"; but note the following sentence.

54. See above, n. 4 to Chap. 3.

55. On this see Peirce's description of this situation in his preface to "My Pragmatism" (1909). This was published for the first time as the appendix to Max Fisch's article "Was there a Metaphysical Club in Cambridge?" See Moore and Robin, *Studies*, pp. 24–29.

Chapter 5

1. See Murphey, *Development*, pp. 281–82.

2. Peirce could have realized his ideal of a community of scholars at Johns Hopkins. With a class of students that included Christine Ladd and O. H. Mitchell, the cofounder of logical quantification, he prepared the *Studies in Logic, by Members of the Johns Hopkins University*. As an academic instructor and as the leader of the Metaphysical Club which he founded in 1879, a club modeled after the famous Metaphysical Club of 1871 and subsequent years, in which Pragmatism was born, Peirce could influence an elite of young American researchers, among whom were Thomas Craig, Josiah Royce, John Dewey, and Thorstein Veblen. See Fisch and Cope, "Peirce at the Johns Hopkins University," in Wiener and Young, *Studies*, pp. 277–311.

3. Murphey, *Development*, p. 292.

4. Cf. above, Chap. 2.

5. On Peirce's attempts to publish this system, see above, n. 35 to Chap. 1, and Chap. 2. Concerning Pragmatism Peirce wrote to William James on November 10, 1900: "Who originated the term *pragmatism*, I or you? Where did it first appear in print? What do you understand by it?" (8.253). James answered on a postcard dated November 26, 1900: "You invented 'pragmatism' for which I gave full credit in a lecture entitled 'Philosophical conceptions and practical results' of which I sent you 2 (unacknowledged) copies a couple years ago" (8.253 n. 8). Cf. Peirce's detailed recollections of the Metaphysical Club written in 1907 and 1909 (5.13).

6. The essays in question are "The Fixation of Belief" and "How to Make Our Ideas Clear." How strange some of Peirce's early ideas had since become to him is apparent in "Philosophy and the Conduct of Life" (1.616–77), the popular lecture that James had arranged for him to give in 1898. There the "father of Pragmatism" presented himself to the astonished audience with the words: "I stand before you an Aristotelian and a scientific man, condemning with the whole strength of conviction the Hellenic tendency to mingle philosophy and practice" (1.618). With this he gave vent to his anger that he was not to speak about "objective logic," i.e., the logic of

evolution, as he had suggested, but was rather supposed to talk about "topics of vital importance" (see 1.623). In 1902 Peirce wrote in his contribution to Baldwin's *Dictionary of Philosophy and Psychology*, entitled "Pragmatic and Pragmatism," "The doctrine appears to assume that the end of man is action—a stoical axiom which, to the present writer at the age of sixty, does not recommend itself so forcibly as it did at thirty" (5.3). Cf. below, Chap. 6, Sec. A, and Chap. 8, Sec. A.

7. See Peirce's letter to Mrs. Ladd-Franklin dated Oct. 20, 1904: "In the spring of 1903 I was invited by the influence of James, Royce, and Münsterberg, to give a course of lectures in Harvard University on Pragmatism. I had intended to print them; but James said he could not understand them himself and could not recommend their being printed. I do not myself think there is any difficulty in understanding them, but all modern psychologists are so soaked with sensationalism that they can not understand anything that does not mean that, and mistranslate into the ideas of Wundt whatever one says about logic . . ." As reprinted in Christine Ladd-Franklin, "Charles S. Peirce at the Johns Hopkins," *Journal of Philosophy* 13 [1916]: 719–20). James characterized Peirce's Pragmatism lecture of 1908 as "flashes of brilliant light relieved against Cimmerian darkness" (as quoted by the editors of the *Collected Papers*, vol. 5, p. 11).

8. 5.414. In the following I refer to the texts from the last series of papers from *The Monist* as the "Pragmaticism essays."

9. Apel is referring here to the fact that his book was conceived as the introduction to a German edition of Peirce's writings—Trans.

10. Cf. above, Chap. 4. I have given too little attention to the relationship between the pragmatic theory of meaning as it first appears in the Berkeley review (1871) and the logic of relations, which Peirce worked out in 1869–70, starting from the work of De Morgan. See Murphey, *Development*, pp. 151 ff. Cf. below, Chap. 6, Sec. D.

11. On the separation of Peirce's thought into four distinct periods, see above, Chap. 2.

12. See Murphey, *Development*, chap. 17.

Chapter 6

1. See Kant, *Critique of Pure Reason*, pp. 653–54 (A 832–33, B 860–61). Cf. Peirce, *Collected Papers*, 5.7–12 and 1.176–79. Murphey utilized the principle of architectonic as the underlying heuristic hypothesis of his impressive historical account of the development of Peirce's philosophy.

2. See above, Chap. 3, Sec. C.a.

3. It is important to distinguish sharply between the transcendental problem of the conditions for the possibility of experience as this problem is found in the "logic of inquiry," especially the "transcendental deduction" of the validity of synthetic inferences which Peirce presented in 1869 and 1878, and that "transcendentalism" which Peirce always refused to accept. By the latter he understood the metaphysics of a transcendental subject, its faculties, and its a priori functions, all of which assume the possibility and, indeed, the necessity of synthetic judgments a priori, which are to be explained by means of a distinction between a world of appearances constituted by the subject and a world of incognizable things-in-themselves. In 1859 Peirce said of this metaphysics, "There is no need for Transcendental-

ism." See Murphey, *Development*, p. 39. On the other hand, in 1893 he still used the title "Transcendental Logic" for a section of his completed, but unpublished, "Grand Logic." See *Collected Papers*, 8, p. 279.

4. See the letter to William James dated Nov. 25, 1902 (8.254–57).

5. I do not wish to hide the fact that numerous passages can be found in Peirce's writings, especially from the third period, which amount in the light of his Kantian-oriented "normative logic" to a confusion of the *quaestio iuris* with the *quaestio facti*. More important here, however, is his attempt to mediate between these opposites, an attempt that goes beyond Kant, that can be reconstructed in a way that overcomes this confusion of norms and facts. Moreover, Peirce, after founding his "normative logic," struggled explicitly against the "naturalistic fallacy." An example is his criticism of Dewey's program to replace logic with the "Natural History of Thought." See 8.239–43.

6. This distinction is found for the first time in a manuscript from 1893, "Introduction, Association of Ideas." Murphey (*Development*, pp. 359–60) concludes that Peirce arrived at this distinction through his own work in experimental psychology conducted with Jastrow (see 7.21–35) and, in particular, through William James's *Principles of Psychology*, 2 vols. (New York, 1890). In his manuscript Peirce writes: "All inferences are really performed under the influence of the law of association. But all physical actions divide into two great classes, those which are performed under the *uncontrolled* governance of association and those in which by the 'agency' of consciousness,—whatever that may mean,—the actions come under self-criticism and self-control. The latter class of actions may be pronounced *good* or *bad*; the former could not be otherwise than they were" (7.444). In the following paragraphs he attempts with very interesting illustrations to make understandable the gradual differentiation in the control of consciousness, from the unconscious inferences in animals (association by contiguity), through those partially conscious associations of similarity (inferences by analogy) found only in human beings, which are supposed to play an especially large role in mythical thought, up to logically controlled inferences and their sedimentation in professed habits.

7. See Kant, *Groundwork of the Metaphysic of Morals*: "Since the universality of the law governing the production of effects constitutes what is properly called *nature* in its most general sense (nature as regards its form)—that is, the existence of things so far as determined by universal laws—the universal imperative of duty may also run as follows: '*Act as if the maxim of your action were to become through your will a universal law of nature*'" (p. 89). See also p. 96: "The ground of this principle [i.e., the categorical imperative] is: *Rational nature exists as an end in itself*." See also p. 104: "a complete determination of all maxims by the following formula, namely: 'All maxims as proceeding from our own making of law ought to harmonize with a possible kingdom of ends as a kingdom of nature.'" A footnote to this adds: "Teleology views nature as a kingdom of ends; ethics views a possible kingdom of ends as a kingdom of nature. In the first case the kingdom of ends is a theoretical Idea used to explain what exists. In the second case it is a practical Idea used to bring into existence what does not exist but can be made actual by our conduct—and indeed to bring it into existence in conformity with this Idea."

8. 5.357. It should be remembered that a divergence in the results of research is not possible, according to the pragmatic maxim, because it mediates semantically a priori between the criteria of evidence for coherence among

theories on the one hand and their experimental corroboration on the other. When, for instance, two concurring consistent theories explain exactly the same experimental phenomena in the long run, then they are, according to the pragmatic maxim, identical in their meaning.

9. 5.354 ff., 2.654 ff. Cf. above, Chap. 3, Sec. C.e.

10. 5.412. Cf. above, n. 4 to Chap. 4. In the manuscript "Basis of Pragmatism" (1906), unpublished during his lifetime, Peirce in fact termed ethics, as the theory of the conformity of action to an ideal, "practics." See 1.573.

11. In 1898, the year in which "Pragmatism" was surprisingly remembered, Peirce wrote: "Ethics . . . is as useless a science as can be conceived. But it must be said, in favor of ethical writers, that they are commonly free from the nauseating custom of boasting of the utility of their science" (1.667). Cf. also 1.635, 1.637, 1.653, and 1.672, all passages from 1868. On the idea of the *summum bonum* see 5.3–4 and 5.433; the earliest passage is probably 2.116, which dates from 1900.

12. See Peirce's letters to James from 1897 (esp. 8.251) and 1902 (esp. 8.256).

13. See n. 7 to this chapter.

14. Cf. 5.392 and 5.394. See above, Chap. 4, Sec. B.b.

15. 5.3. The comment on "individual reactions" is directed against William James's interpretation of the pragmatic maxim. See 5.491. Compare this quotation to 5.402, n. 2, which is nearly the same in its basic tone.

16. See the discussion earlier in this section.

17. See above, Chap. 4, Sec. A.

18. 5.3. Cf. 5.430 ff. On this see below, Chap. 8, Sec. C.

19. Using the framework of a relativistic historicism, Erich Rothacker has shown how "cultures as styles of life" are related differently to the *summum bonum*. See esp. his *Probleme der Kulturanthropologie* (Bonn: Bouvier, 1948). John Dewey developed the idea of habitualized "value beliefs," which could probably be best compared with the notion of habits as Peirce conceived them in 1902, i.e., as serving to embody "concrete reasonableness."

20. It can be conclusively shown that all of Peirce's important and logically well-thought-out theorems converge in the paradoxes of the infinite or, as Peirce would say, in the problem of "continuity" or "synechism." See below, Secs. C and D in this chapter and Sec. B in Chap. 7.

21. Cf. above, Chap. 3, Sec. C.e; see also below, n. 36 to Chap. 7.

22. Cf. 1.575–84, 1.585–90, 1.591–615, and 5.121–36.

23. In 1877 in "The Fixation of Belief" Peirce characterized the decision to adopt the method of science as a "choice which is far more than the adoption of any intellectual opinion, which is one of the ruling decisions of his life [that is, any person's life] . . ." (5.387). In 1902 Peirce wrote: "What is good? Now this is hardly a normative question: it is pre-normative. It does not ask for the conditions of fulfillment of a definitely accepted purpose, but asks what is to be sought, *not* for a reason, but back of every reason" (1.577). This could be compared with Karl Popper's calling for us to opt for "Critical Rationalism" on the basis of an "irrational decision," a "moral decision," or an "act of faith." See *The Open Society*, 2:231 ff:

24. 5.213–63. Cf. above, Chap. 3, Sec. C.c.

25. 5.382–83. Cf. above, Chap. 4, Sec. B.a. and esp. n. 35.

26. In a 1906 critique of William James's "Pluralistic Pragmatism" unpublished during Peirce's lifetime, Peirce asks:
    Is the Satisfactory meant to be whatever excites a certain peculiar feeling of satisfaction? In that case, the doctrine is simply hedonism in so far as it affects the field of cognition. For when the hedonists talk of "pleasure,"

they do not mean what is so-called in ordinary speech, but what excites a feeling of satisfaction.

But to say that an action or the result of an action is Satisfactory is simply to say that it is congruous to the aim of that action. Consequently, the aim must be determined before it can be determined, either in thought or in fact, to be satisfactory. An action that had no other aim than to be congruous to its aim would have no aim at all, and would not be a deliberate action. . . .

. . . Now it is *conceivable* that an action should be disconnected from every other in its aim. Such an action, then, according to hedonistic doctrine, can have no other aim than that of satisfying its own aim, which is absurd. [5.559–61]

27. 1.551. Cf. Murphey, *Development*, pp. 74 ff., 88, 129.

28. 5.130. Cf. 5.36, 1.91, 1.612–13, and 2.199. Cf. also the notes from 1906 on the pragmatic maxim (5.402 n. 2). Here and in several other places Peirce refers to Schiller's *Aesthetische Briefe*, the first philosophical work that Peirce ever read (he was fifteen at the time).

29. Such a reduction of the general to an individual fact, even if it be to that of world history, is an instance of Nominalism for Peirce. Hence, in 1902, Peirce writes in notes to his article on "Pragmatic and Pragmatism" for Baldwin's *Dictionary* that "Nominalism, up to that of Hegel, looks at reality retrospectively. What all modern philosophy does is to deny that there is any *esse in futuro*." (*Collected Papers*, 8, p. 292). Cf. also his criticism of Hegelianism as an absolutization of Thirdness (5.90 ff.). For Peirce the absolutization of reason itself amounts to a reduction of its generality to mere factuality.

30. Kant, *Groundwork of the Metaphysic of Morals*, p. 128.

31. Ibid., p. 131. Cf. Jürgen Habermas, *Knowledge and Human Interests* (Boston: Beacon Press, 1971), Chap. 9.

32. See 8.39 ff. For a more detailed interpretation of Peirce's 1885 Royce review, see below, Chap. 7, Sec. A.

33. This interpretation of the index function was developed in 1868, but still lacked the corresponding ontological distinction between the individual "existence" of individual referents and the "reality" representable in general concepts. See 5.287, 5.296, and 5.352.

34. On deducing Firstness from the sign function, cf. above, Chap. 3, Secs. A and C.b.

In 1885 Peirce wrote: "We now find that, besides general terms, two other kinds of signs are perfectly indispensable in all reasoning" (8.41). At that time, however, he seems not yet to have conceived of icons as expressions of the material contents of sentences. Rather, he thought only that they were necessary for the intuitive depiction of the logical form of the sentence in the sense of "diagrammatic observation." This can be seen in his "Contribution to the Philosophy of Notation," where he introduces icons in the following way: "With these two kinds of signs alone [symbols and indices] any proposition can be expressed; but it cannot be reasoned upon, for reasoning consists in the observation that where certain relations subsist certain others are found, and it accordingly requires the exhibition of relations reasoned within an icon" (3.363). If we recall that for Peirce judgments of experience are also synthetic inferences, it then seems obvious for him to postulate here an iconic content to the data of experience which must enter into judgments of experience. Just as the iconic sign function in language provides a "thread of Ariadne" (Leibniz's phrase) to the calculus of logic, there must somehow be an iconic language of nature to offer a starting point for the implicit formation of hypotheses in our judgments of experience. Peirce arrived at this conclusion in 1903. See 5.119.

35. 5.263. Cf. above, Chap. 3, Sec. C.c.

36. Peirce adopted the doctrine of "immediate perception" of the outer world when he rejected the "container" theory of knowledge and its Phenomenalism of immanence in his Berkeley review in 1871 (8.16). He did not explain how this view of perception was to be reconciled with the view he so strongly upheld in 1868, according to which all perceptual judgments are mediated.

As far as induction is concerned, the difficulty for Peirce, as well as later for Neopositivism and for Popper, was that the truth of hypotheses can be *proven* only by statements which are themselves hypotheses, and so on ad infinitum, and not by a comparison of statements with so-called facts. For, as Peirce remarks in a brilliant argument in the sixth Lowell lecture of 1903: ". . . you look at an object and say, 'That is red.' I ask you how you prove that. You tell me you see it. Yes, you see something; but you do not see *that it is red*; because *that it is red* is a proposition." At the same time Peirce also has to show the way perceptual judgments are distinguished in practice as ultimate premises by being based upon perceived images, i.e., so-called percepts that enter as the source of information into the predicates of perceptual judgments.

37. On Peirce's critical views of Darwinism and Lamarckism see below, Chap. 7, Sec. B.

38. See 5.172–73, 5.591, 5.603 ff., 6.10, and 6.474 ff.

39. Cf. above, Chap. 3, Sec. C.a and C.e.

40. See, however, 5.348–52. In 1869 Peirce had identified the question of the conditions for the possibility of experience in Kant's sense with the transcendental logical question of the validity of experience, and this, in turn, with the question of the validity of inference in the long run. Now, however, Peirce separates the question of the origin of hypotheses, i.e., of abductive inferences (which even lie at the base of the perceptual judgments that are presupposed in induction verification), from the question of the validity of experience. That latter question is to be answered by means of the theory of induction.

41. For this reason Peirce in 1903 also called into question the transcendental doctrine of the subjectivity of sensory qualities. See 5.116 ff. Cf. below, Chap. 8, Sec. B.

42. It was first conceived under the name "likeness" in "The New List of Categories," where it was regarded in relation to the category of the First (1.558). Cf. also 5.283.

43. Peirce now conceives as cognitive correlates of the Firstness of Thirdness such different phenomena or *topoi* as aesthetic consciousness, natural "insight," "common sense," *lumen naturale*, and, most of all, animal "instincts." He takes the human ability to "divine" knowledge through qualities to be a transformation of these instincts. The functions involved correspond to abductive inferences in synthetic logic, through which it is alone possible to gain new insights. In contrast, he now understands induction to be only a method for confirming or falsifying something by means of a confrontation with existing facts (Secondness). He associates it with Darwinian selection in evolution. The development of Peirce's theory in line with his three fundamental categories reveals an interesting parallel to Arnold Gehlen's

anthropology. Gehlen first considered adaptation and trial and error in "experimental behavior" solely responsible for the development of culture. Later, however, he developed a theory of aesthetic-noumenal qualities associated with "representational behavior" that he took to distinguish this behavior from the trigger qualities to which animal instincts are directed. See Arnold Gehlen, *Urmensch und Spätkultur* (Bonn: Athenäum Verlag, 1956).

44. See, e.g., 6.307: "The agapastic development of thought is the adoption of certain mental tendencies, not altogether heedlessly, as in tychasm, nor quite blindly by the mere force of circumstances or of logic, as in anancasm, but by an immediate attraction for the idea itself, whose nature is divined before the mind possesses it, by the power of sympathy, that is, by virtue of the continuity of the mind."

45. Here we should think not only of the iconic expressiveness of simple predicates, but also, especially in science, of the reproduction of the structure of reality through complex relational predicates which themselves connect up with the iconic function of technical models and mathematical diagrams. See below, Chap. 6, Sec. B.

46. See 5.313 ff. Here we have a line of theorizing in Peirce that appears to point directly to Norbert Wiener's conception of man as information and the universe as a process of information.

47. See, e.g., 6.189 ff. Cf. below, Chap. 7, Sec. B.

48. Here Peirce is thinking of that limiting case of discursive knowledge, formulated in language, which Croce identified with the equation of *intuitione* and *espressione* in art. Cf. above, n. 43 to this chapter.

49. See Murphey, *Development*, pt. 1.

50. Ralph Waldo Emerson put forth three famous theses: (1) words are signs of natural facts; (2) particular natural facts are symbols of particular spiritual facts; and (3) nature is the symbol of spirit. See his *Nature, Addresses and Lectures* (Boston, 1885), p. 31, as quoted in Murphey, *Development*, p. 51.

51. See 8.14–15. Cf. above, Chap. 3, Sec. B.

52. This transcendental dualism of Kant's undergoes a transformation in Wittgenstein's early *Tractatus* by means of the analysis of language. This transformation is simultaneously a reductio ad absurdum in which the subject, without any possibility of engaging in self-reflection, is at one with the form of language which constitutes the "limits of the world."

53. See Ernst Konrad Specht, "Der Analogiebegriff bei Kant und Hegel," *Kantstudien*, supplementary no. 66 (Cologne: Kölner Universitätsverlag, 1952).

54. Cf. below, Chap. 7, Sec. B.

55. Peirce refers here in particular to Schelling's metaphysics. Cf. below, Chap. 7, Sec. B esp. nn. 50 and 60.

56. See 5.289. Peirce comes very close here to Hegel's interpretation of "sense certainty," which he would later utilize in his semiotic interpretation of "this here" and the "immediate meaning" of perception. Cf. 5.44 and 5.92.

57. See, e.g., 8.103 (1900): "Those blind compulsions, then, can be regarded as actions of the future on the past. From that point of view, it is seen that they can but be brute and blind, and, further, that in the course of time they must be seen to rationalize themselves and fall into place as the cognition develops."

58. On the use of the term *Ort* in Heidegger see *Being and Time*, p. 269, and

cf. pp. 210, 427, 429. On the "ecstasies of time" see ibid., p. 377 (§ 65 passim)—Trans.

59. See his critique of Hegel's "Anancasm" in regard to the metaphysics of evolution, 6.63 and esp. 6.218 ff. and 6.305.

60. Cf. above, Chap. 2.

61. On this see Peirce's approach to a typology of philosophical systems on the basis of the three fundamental categories, 5.77 ff.

62. Peirce introduced Phenomenology for the first time in his "Minute Logic" (1902), 2.120. In 1901 the second volume of Edmund Husserl's *Logische Untersuchungen* appeared, bearing the title *Untersuchungen zur Phänomenologie und Theorie der Erkenntnis*. (trans. into English by J. N. Findlay as *Logical Investigations*, vol. 2, [Atlantic Highlands, N.J.: Humanities Press, 1970]). Despite a number of parallels in the objects of their studies, it is evidently not possible to find a historical connection between these two foundings of Phenomenology. See Herbert Spiegelberg, "Husserl's and Peirce's Phenomenologies: Coincidence or Interaction," *Philosophy and Phenomenological Research* 17 (1956):164–85.

63. See Spiegelberg, "Husserl's and Peirce's Phenomenologies," pp. 168 ff.

64. See 8.295, 8.297, and 8.301. Even Husserl's distinction between Phenomenology and psychology in vol. 2 of the *Logische Untersuchungen* is evidently insufficient for Peirce, because in 1906 he writes: "How many writers of our generation (. . . let it be in this case the distinguished Husserl), after underscored protestations that their discourse shall be of logic exclusively and not by any means of psychology (almost all logicians protest that on file), forthwith become intent upon those elements of the process of thinking which seem to be special to a mind like that of the human race, as we find it, to too great a neglect of those elements which must belong as much to any one as to any other mode of embodying the same thought" (4.7). Cf. Spiegelberg, "Husserl's and Peirce's Phenomenologies," pp. 183–84.

65. 5.122 ff., 5.129. The former is included in the triad "Phenomenology," "Normative Science," and "Metaphysics" and the latter in the triad "Aesthetics," "Ethics," and "Logic."

66. See esp. 2.197: "It can hardly be said to involve reasoning; for reasoning reaches a conclusion, and asserts to be true however matters may seem."

67. See Murphey, *Development*, p. 366.

68. See above, Chap. 6, passim.

69. See Murphey, *Development*, chap. 3.

70. See above, n. 57 to Chap. 3.

71. See Kempski, *Peirce*, pp. 58 ff. Cf. above, n. 2 to Chap. 2.

72. Kempski, *Peirce*, pp. 58 ff.

73. See above, this chapter.

74. Kempski, *Peirce*, p. 63.

75. Walter Jung brought this point out clearly in his review of Kempski's book in *Philosophische Rundschau* 4 (1956):143–58, esp. 148–49. However, he seems to me to have gone too far in calling Peirce's phenomenological position "by far clearer than Kant's." Most of all, Peirce's statement that "we directly perceive the continuity of consciousness" (6.182), which he himself describes as the "highest point" of "Phaneroscopy," does not seem to me to provide an explanation of how Peirce can leave phenomenological knowledge in philosophy without a semiotic foundation (see Jung's review, p. 157). The "continuity of consciousness" may be the highest point of the metaphysical "mediation" between knowledge and reality in the sense of the

Peircean category of Thirdness, but that does not yet free the Phenomenology of Thirdness qua continuity from the task of semiotically founding its own validity by referring to this Thirdness, just as it had previously done in founding the validity of empirical inquiry. See below, this chapter.

76. On Peirce's rejection of introspection see 5.244 ff. and 5.462. Cf., however, 5.71 ff., where Peirce compares self-consciousness with the infinite system of a map which also includes a representation of itself. See also 8.288 ff. on the three categorial aspects of consciousness. For criticisms see Spiegelberg, "Husserl's and Peirce's Phenomenologies," p. 174.

77. See 5.37–38, 5.43 ff., 5.90 ff., 5.436, 8.213, 8.267 ff., 8.297–98, and 8.329.

78. See above.

79. See above, Chap. 6, Secs. A and B. Cf. below, Chap. 7, Secs. A and B.

80. See 5.289, 5.428, 5.467, 5.475–76, 5.501, and 5.541 ff.

81. 2.197. Cf. 1.287: "The student's effort is not to be influenced by any tradition, any authority, any reasons for supposing that such and such ought to be the facts, or any fancies of any kind, and to confine himself to honest, singleminded observation of the appearances. The reader, upon his side, must repeat the author's observation for himself, and decide from his own observations whether the author's account of appearances is correct or not."

82. See Karl-Otto Apel, "Wittgenstein und Heidegger: Die Frage nach dem Sinn von Sein und der Sinnlosigkeitsverdacht gegen alle Metaphysik," in *Transformation der Philosophie*, 1:225–75, and "Sprache als Thema und Medium der transzendentalen Reflexion," in *Transformation der Philosophie*, 2:311–29.

83. For his evaluation of Peirce's "metaphysical deduction" Kempski refers to 3.422 ff. (from 1892); see Kempski, *Peirce*, pp. 56–57.

84. See Murphey, *Development*, p. 368.

85. See above, Chap. 1. Cf. above, Chap. 3, Secs. A, B, and C. and below, this chapter.

86. See "The Simplest Mathematics" (1902), 4.227–323. This is chapter 3 of the unfinished "Minute Logic," where Peirce introduces the term "Phenomenology" for the first time. Cf. above, n. 64 to this chapter. Cf. also 1.247 (1903).

87. Kant, *Critique of Pure Reason*, pp. 169–70 (B 159).

88. See Karl-Otto Apel, *Die Idee der Sprache in der Tradition des Humanismus von Dante bis Vico* (Bonn: Bouvier, 1963), pp. 321 ff.

89. See, e.g., 1.357: "What the world was to Adam on the day he opened his eyes to it, before he had drawn any distinctions, or had become conscious of his own existence . . ."

90. 1.299. Cf. Murphey, *Development*, p. 367.

91. See "One, Two, Three: Fundamental Categories of Thought and of Nature," ca. 1885. Parts of this manuscript are published in the *Collected Papers* as 1.369–72 and 1.376–78. Cf. Murphey, *Development*, pp. 296 ff.

92. On such a reduction see Willard V. O. Quine, *Mathematical Logic* (Cambridge, Mass.: Harvard University Press, 1951), pp. 198 ff. Cf. Murphey, *Development*, pp. 304–5.

93. One could, with Moritz Schlick, go beyond Peirce and even assert that modern theoretical physics can be regarded as a true representation without its being either immediately evident to anybody's consciousness through experience or translatable into an intuitively schematizable idea. Cf. above, Chap. 3, n. 17.

94. Peirce writes: "It must have been in 1866 that Professor De Morgan honored

the unknown beginner in philosophy . . . by sending me a copy of his memoir 'On the Logic of Relations'" (1.562). In 1870 Peirce published his original and more advanced contribution, "Description of a Notation for the Logic of Relatives" (3.45–149), which essentially influenced Schröder's calculus of relations. See C. I. Lewis, *A Survey of Symbolic Logic* (1918; reprint ed., New York: Dover, 1960), pp. 79–117. Cf. Bocheński, *History of Formal Logic*, and Murphey, *Development*, pp. 151 ff.

95. See 1.365 and 1.358. Cf. Murphey, *Development*, p. 304.

96. The following analyses of the iconic and indexical functions outside the sphere of language in the narrow sense could be regarded as providing possible rationalizations for the old *topoi* of "nature's language" in Jacob Böhme or nature's "signature" in Paracelsus, especially if we follow Peirce in making further combinations, such as between the iconic and indexical functions or between these and the symbolic function.

97. We can see here that the semiotic "icon" concept is able to provide a generic concept for the different uses of the term "model" as it applied to theories or technical constructions including diagrams and artificial languages, on the one hand, and to illustrations of these theories and constructions, on the other.

98. According to Peirce, genuine indices are in themselves dual. That is, besides a spatial and temporal connection with their object, they also imply an iconic representation of it through which they provide information. See 5.75. Accordingly, there must be a continuum between "symptoms" in the medical sense, e.g., the pulse, and those found in the study of expression, such as in graphology, where the iconic function appears to be in the forefront for the interpreter. We could expect more complicated combinations of the iconic, indexical, and symbolic functions in hermeneutics—for example, in the interpretation of works of art.

An example of the processes studied in cybernetics would be the information acting as a guiding mechanism in genetics or in the direction of missiles by radar. But the "influence on the behavior of organisms through signs" as it in fact takes place in the framework of communication between human beings is only a degenerate mode of the sign function in the sense of Secondness when seen in the light of Peirce's semiotic. This is because the "logical interpretant," the translation of a sign's meaning into a rule of behavior based upon a correct understanding, is reduced in the cybernetic view to the "dynamic interpretant," the practical, successful completion of communication. For Peirce, it is important to stress the difference between guidance on the basis of signs and a merely causal mechanical process. The difference lets him conclude that the cybernetic simulation of communication processes, as well as of the iconic and indexical functions, can be appreciated only in the context of human communicative understanding, from the standpoint of which such simulations are a degenerate mode of just such communicative understanding. See below, Chap. 6, Sec. D.

99. This idea is clearly implicit in Peirce's concept of "community," but the term itself is found for the first time in the late work of Josiah Royce, who employed it in his efforts to explore the hermeneutic dimension of intersubjectivity, efforts that went beyond those of Peirce. Cf. below, Chap. 7, Sec. A.

100. According to Peirce, pure symbols are only arguments. While they univocally establish a rational interpretation, as do statements and concepts, they do not provide us with definitive information about something *hic et nunc* in the way that genuine indices, such as statements, do, nor do they awaken

such information by association in the way that icons and degenerate indexical images of something, such as concepts, do. On this see 5.76.

101. See above, Chap. 6, Sec. B. Peirce's relationship to Croce or to Gehlen, as I
mentioned in nn. 43 and 48 to this chapter, should be extended to include
Giambattista Vico's idea of the *universale fantastico* and its significance for
the original structure of language. There is also a relationship to Wilhelm
von Humboldt's thesis that words used in ordinary speech always possess
the character of both "signs" and "copies" of things, in contrast to the
scientific use of language, where the copy character of the synthetic structure of signs can be utilized to a greater extent.

102. Here Peirce's semiotic takes up virtually all those tendencies in the history
of the philosophy of language which either strive to reduce the cognitive
function of scientific language to structural picturing and "blind thought,"
using "diagrammatic observation" of the sign form as a thread of Ariadne
(this is the tradition of Leibniz and the early Wittgenstein), or seek to oppose the natural picturing found in drawings and mathematical diagrams to
the falseness of conventional language (this is the tradition of Leonardo da
Vinci and Paul Valéry).

103. Peirce first introduced "indices" in 1867 (1.558). Despite the difference between them and symbols, according to categorial analysis, Peirce still in
1867 regarded indices as concepts of "the present in general" (1.547). Only
in 1885 did he come to conceive them as referring to what is individual in
the sense of Duns Scotus's *haecceitas*, for which, according to Peirce, there
can be no concept. In 1885 in his review of Royce, Peirce observed: "He
[Royce] seems to think that the real subject of a proposition can be de-
noted by a general term of the proposition. . . . Recent studies in formal
logic [see Chap. 7 n. 4 below] have put it in a clearer light. We now find
that, besides general terms, two other kinds of signs are perfectly indispensable in all reasoning. One of these kinds is the *index*" (8.41).

104. In 1903 Peirce wrote: "The pronoun, which may be defined as a part of
speech intended to fulfill the function of an index, is never intelligible taken
by itself apart from the circumstances of its utterance; and the noun, which
may be defined as a part of speech put in place of a pronoun, is always
liable to be equivocal" (5.153). Cf. 2.287 n. on the history of grammar.

The discovery of "quantifiers by Peirce and his student O. H. Mitchell came
about during their work together at Johns Hopkins University. See O. H.
Mitchell, "On a New Algebra of Logic," in Peirce, *Studies in Logic*. Cf.
3.351–54, 3.393 ff., and 3.361 ff. On this see also Murphey, *Development*, pp.
298 ff. In 1879 Gottlob Frege had already anticipated this discovery in his
Begriffsschrift, 2d ed., ed. Ignacio Angelelli (Darmstadt: Wissenschaftliche
Buchgesellschaft, 1964), but without finding any recognition at the time. See
Bocheński, *History of Formal Logic*. For an extensive exposition of these
complicated matters see the *Collected Papers*, 2, bk. 2, entitled "Speculative
Grammar." See also the correspondence with Lady Welby, 8.327–79.

105. For this reason ficticious *designata* without a denotational extension, for example, unicorns, cannot provide the foundation for the triadic sign function. They are in fact only understandable as fictions under the presupposition that there are real *designata* of some kind. If all *designata* were mere
fictions, then the expression "mere fiction" would lose its meaning. This
shows us how the sign function depends upon the existence of the real
world, which can be represented as something.

106. See 5.482, 5.491, and 8.315. Cf. below, Chap. 8, Sec. C.

107. I.e., "natural" languages—Trans.
108. See below, this chapter.
109. See Tarski's scheme of possible definitions of truth.
110. Charles Morris, *Foundations of the Theory of Signs* (Chicago: University of Chicago Press, 1938).
111. This pragmatic point is concealed, however, by the typical schematic representation of the triadic nature of signs. Such representations suggest that the syntactic, semantic, and pragmatic dimensions of signs are equivalent, dyadic relations:

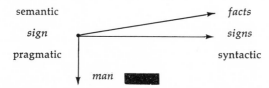

112. See Rudolf Carnap, *An Introduction to Semantics* (Cambridge, Mass.: Harvard University Press, 1942), secs. 5, 39. The fundamental importance of the triadic structure of the sign function seems to me to go unrecognized if we restrict the concept of "the pragmatics of signs" to the actual use of language, i.e., to *parole* as Saussure used the term, while thinking it sufficient to analyze the system of language, Saussure's *langue*, by construing it as a semantic system of dyadic relations. If we consistently pursue such a view, then we are forced to interpret the extensional meanings of signs as designations of matters of fact which exist independently of language, and we must overlook the interpretation of matters of fact "as something" which is given with a system of language as a kind of intensional collective product of its speakers. It seems to me that what is referred to as the "content-directed study of language," associated with Leo Weisgerber and others, undertakes a more appropriate abstraction of *langue* in regard to the triadic sign function when it does not consider man's interpretation of signs and the world they mediate to be something foreign to this system [that of *langue*—Trans.] as such, but rather sees this interpretation as a product that has become fixed within the system so as to form what Wilhelm von Humboldt termed a linguistic "world view."
113. See below, n. 118 to this chapter, on Peter Winch and Chomsky.
114. This does not apply to those cybernetically inspired "systems theories" which take cognizance of man as the pragmatic subject who uses signs in his scientific orientation to the world only after they have previously likened the concept of human *praxis* to that of "adaptive behavior" aimed at survival.
115. An example of legitimate "degeneration" in Peirce's sense of the term would be the case in which we remain conscious of the abstraction involved in analyses of the logic of science (e.g., in the analysis of the problem of "explanation" using a formalized language) and supplement and in some cases even correct it by analyses of the anthropological aspects of cognition in situations in which the meaning of the question "why" is pragmatically constituted. See Gerard Radnitzky, *Contemporary Schools of Metascience*, 2 vols. (Göteburg: Scandinavian University Books, 1968), 1:146 ff. On the subject of the *Geisteswissenschaften* see Karl-Otto Apel, *Analytic Philosophy of Language and the "Geisteswissenschaften,"* Foundations of Language Supplementary Series, vol. 5, trans.

(Dordrecht: Reidel, 1967); and Karl-Otto Apel, "Scientistics, Hermeneutics and the Critique of Ideology: Outline of a Theory of Science from a Cognitive-Anthropological Standpoint" and "Scientism or Transcendental Hermeneutics? On the Question of the Subject of the Interpretation of Signs in the Semiotics of Pragmatism," both in *Towards a Transformation of Philosophy*, pp. 46–76 and pp. 93–135, respectively. See also Karl-Otto Apel, "Zur Idee einer transzendentalen Sprachpragmatik (Die Dreistelligkeit der Zeichenrelation und die 'abstractive fallacy' in den Grundlagen der klassischen Transzendentalphilosophie und der sprachanalytischen Wissenschaftslogik)," in *Aspekte und Probleme der Sprachphilosophie*, ed. Josef Simon (Freiburg: Alber, 1974), pp. 283–326.

116. For strict Behaviorism, therefore, the triadic relation "A gives B to C" must be regarded as reducible to the two dyadic relations "A separates itself from B" (or better, "B leaves A behind") and "C takes possession of B" (or better, "Between B and C there is a coming together").

117. See above, Chap. 6, Sec. D.

118. On this see Peter Winch, *The Idea of a Social Science and Its Relation to Philosophy* (London: Routledge and Kegan Paul, 1970). For the theory of language see esp. Noam Chomsky's critique of Skinner and the Bloomfield in *The Structure of Language*, ed. J. A. Fodor and J. J. Katz (Englewood Cliffs, N.J.: Prentice-Hall, 1964).

119. See 5.403 n. 3, 5.491, and 8.315.

120. On the introduction to mathematics see 1.185 and 1.285. Cf. Murphey, *Development*, chaps. 11–13, 18.

121. In a 1905 letter to F. C. S. Schiller Peirce writes: "Corresponding to *generality* in nonrelative logic is *continuity* in *relative* logic, and the development of the principle of continuity in the light of that logical view and the adoption of it as the central principle of metaphysics is an indication of what I mean by synechism" ("To F. C. S. Schiller," May 12, 1905, Peirce Papers, Houghton Library, Harvard University, Cambridge, Mass., as quoted in Murphey, *Development*, p. 397).

122. See below, Chap. 7, Sec. B.

123. See above, Chap. 6, Sec. A.

124. On architectonic see also "The Architectonic of Theories" (1891), 5.7–12 and 1.176–283. Peirce's principle of classification follows Auguste Comte's *Cours de Philosophie Positive*, 6 vols. (Paris, 1830–42). See 3.428.

125. See Manley Thompson, *The Pragmatic Philosophy of C. S. Peirce* (Chicago: University of Chicago Press, 1953), pp. 156–62. Cf. Murphey, *Development*, p. 368.

126. See 1.245 ff. and 1.417. Peirce took this definition from his father, Benjamin Peirce. See Murphey, *Development*, p. 229.

127. See 5.319. Here again we see that Peirce never recognized the method of reflection on the indispensable conditions of all argumentation (the meaning-critical transformation of the transcendental critique of knowledge) that he himself practiced with such virtuosity, especially in 1869, nor did he take possession of it as the specific method of providing a foundation for his philosophy.

128. Cf. 5.8 and 5.32–33.

129. See above, Chap. 6, Secs. B and C. See below, Chap. 7, Sec. B and Chap. 8, Sec. B. See also Murphey, *Development*, Chap. 18.

130. See above, Chap. 5, and below, Chap. 8, Sec. A.

Chapter 7

1. See Peirce's letter to James dated Oct. 28, 1885, William James Collection, Houghton Library, Harvard University, Cambridge, Mass. There Peirce says that he wrote a review of Royce's book for Youmans, but that he would not accept it. E. L. and W. J. Youmans edited the *Popular Science Monthly* at that time, and Peirce refers to this journal earlier in his letter. The date of the letter and of the publication of Royce's work make it possible to date the review ca. 1885. However, several pages and numerous corrections of the manuscript are in different inks and finer handwriting than others and could, therefore, have been written at different times.
2. See above, Chap. 5.
3. See above, Chap. 5, n. 6.
4. On this see Karl-Theo Humbach, *Das Verhältnis von Einzelperson und Gemeinschaft nach Josiah Royce*, Jahrbuch für Amerika-Studien, supp. 9 (Heidelberg, 1962), introduction.
5. Cf. Peirce's review (1900–1902) of Royce's *The World and the Individual* (8.100–131) and his reference to Royce in the last footnote (1905) to the pragmatic maxim (5.402 n).
6. See Peirce's letter to Royce dated May 27, 1902 (8.117 n. 10) and Royce's "Principles of Logic" in *Enzyclopädie der philosophischen Wissenschaften* (Tübingen, 1912), vol. 1, esp. p. 78, where Royce refers to Peirce as his teacher in logic.
7. See Humbach, *Das Verhältnis von Einzelperson und Gemeinschaft*, pp. 110 ff. Cf. John E. Smith, *Royce's Social Infinite* (New York: Liberal Arts Press, 1950); and Karl-Otto Apel, "Scientism or transcendental hermeneutics?" in *Towards a Transformation of Philosophy*, pp. 93–135.
8. 8.41. Cf. above, n. 103 to Chap. 7.
9. See 3.359–403, and Mitchell, "New Algebra of Logic," pp. 72–106.
10. See above, Chap. 6, Sec. B. Royce's argument is a variation on a proof of God's existence sketched out by Leibniz and developed by Hegel. Its exact opposite is Berkeley's theistic form of Phenomenalism.
11. See above, Chap. 3, Sec. C.c.
12. For Wittgenstein even a scream of pain is a part of a language game and so is an instance of Thirdness, because as pain behavior it is something learned.
13. Modern "situation-oriented" philosophies, including the Pragmatism of James and Dewey, Existentialism, some varieties of Neo-Marxism, and the late Wittgenstein, all avoid Peirce's problem by explicitly regarding theoretical metaphysical questions—like that of absolute truth, the real as an object of knowledge in general, and others—as more or less meaningless.
14. I would also include here such an exceptional Peirce expert as Murray Murphey, when he regards the tenability of Peirce's definition of the real and, hence, his meaning-critical approach as depending upon Peirce's first proving the "existence" of a real world in general, as well as the existence of "other minds" and, finally, even the existence of an unlimited process of inquiry. See Murphey, *Development*, pp. 141, 301 ff. The difficulties that Murphey analyzes cannot be solved in my view by giving up the definition of reality as possible experience. Rather, they can be solved by a further specification of this definition, with the aid of "would be" statements that make it independent of actual attempts to determine the chances for success

of the search for knowledge. Of course, Peirce had to give up the attempt
to *reduce* reality to the "opinion ultimately agreed upon," as Murphey discerned. After 1885 (see below, n. 22, this chapter) Peirce recognized that
the "would be" definition can be valid only as a regulative principle for
evaluating the actual process of cognition. As such the definition of the
real in terms of absolute knowledge allows room for us to establish what
is real by *deixis* or *haecceitas* (Secondness) and by recognizing the general
as the continuity of experience (the Firstness of Thirdness), an insight that
Peirce postulated in 1903. See 5.205 and 5.209–12.

15. I believe that Peirce implicitly provided such a reductio ad absurdum in
his 1868 criticism of Descartes' universal doubt. For an explicit reduction
argument from this period see 5.352 and 5.384.

16. See 7.341–42. Cf. above, Chap. 4, Sec. C.

17. Here Peirce evidently once again entangles himself in the "paradoxes" that
gave him troubles in 1872–73 and in 1878 in his interpretation of the diamond example. See above. He is unable to mobilize the real point of his
meaning-critical Realism against the idealist Royce, just as he was unable
to do against Berkeley. In contrast, however, see below, Chap. 8, Sec. C.

18. In this way Georg Jánoska, for example, regards the attempt to interpret
reality in terms of possible experience, which for him also means in terms
of the criterion of verifiability, as fundamentally idealistic. To that extent
he is correct in regarding it as unsuccessful. See his *Die Sprachlichen
Grundlagen der Philosophie* (Graz: Akademischer Verlag, 1962), pp. 16 ff.
Criticism of Bridgeman's Operationalism has also focused upon the irreducibility of the reality of the real. See A. Cornelius Benjamin, *Operationalism* (Springfield, Ill.: Blackwell Scientific Pub., 1955), pp. 79 ff. It
seems to me, however, that Peirce's approach, when it is consistently interpreted in terms of what I have called "meaning-critical Realism," opens up
a way out of the dilemma between either accepting Idealism or forfeiting
meaning-criticism (of the incognizable object of knowledge). Even the sentence "The planets will continue their revolution even after all consciousness has been extinguished," which Jánoska, following C. I. Lewis, uses to
argue against the verificationist point of view, can be made, I believe, to
refer to possible experience in the sense of a counterfactual "would be"
formulation (a counterfactual conditional). See below, n. 21 to this chapter.

19. We must grant that actually carrying out the operations imagined in the
thought experiment, e.g., those by which the hardness of a diamond is to
be checked, can lead to falsification or correction of our hypothetical interpretation (based upon abductive inferences) of the real "as something,"
i.e., possessing certain characteristics. In practice, of course, we are and
always have been led to such revisions. But this unavoidable and highly
fruitful "hermeneutic" (cf. above), circular structure of deduction, induction, and abduction (hypothesis) only reconfirms the unique normative
nature of the deductive phase in which the practical implications of an
understanding of meaning are to be brought out in the form of "would be"
postulates. In addition to this, the hypothesis "There are real things," whose
meaning Peirce wants finally to explicate in terms of concepts of possible
experience, cannot be either falsified or corrected, since every falsification or
correction of a hypothesis already assumes the existence of a real world.
Herein lies an indirect proof of the existence of a real world. Because this
is a meaning-critical proof, it shows that Murphey's demand that Peirce
provide a verifiable proof of the existence of the external world is, as a
demand, itself meaningless. Cf. above, this chapter, nn. 14, 15.

Jürgen Habermas, in interpreting Peirce in *Knowledge and Human Interests*, criticizes the indirect proof of the existence of the real world, as well as the meaning-critical postulate of the cognizability of this real world in an unlimited process of inquiry. Habermas takes them to be *petitiones principii*, because both the assumptions and the fact that they imply one another correlatively go to make up the *transcendental framework* of Peirce's philosophy, and only to that extent can they not be called into question. (See *Knowledge and Human Interests*, pp. 117–18). I would maintain against such a view that this transcendental framework is not arbitrary, but is rather necessarily presupposed in our speech about what is real. This is clearly evident in Habermas's own attempt to call this framework into question by means of Nietzsche's "perspectival and irrationalistic concept of reality," which proclaims that we can very well conceive of a reality that consists only of a plurality of "fictions related to a standpoint." It seems to me, however, that we cannot hold such a concept of reality. To do so we must either change the meaning of "reality" so that we destroy the point we are trying to make (just as in the sentence "Everything is *only* my dream," where the point of the sentence cancels itself out) or tacitly assume Peirce's concept of reality in our use of the concept "fiction." See below, Chap. 8, Sec. C, n. 105.

20. See below, Chap. 8, Sec. C.

21. 8.43. To my knowledge, Peirce's first reflection on the relationship of "would be" and "will be" can be found in his 1900 review of Royce's *The World and the Individual*, where he writes: "To our apprehension this 'would be' is readily resolved into a hope for a *will be*. For what we mean by saying that any event, B, *would* happen under conditions, A, that are never fulfilled, is that the ultimate opinion which will, as we hope, actually be attained concerning any given question (though not in any finite time concerning *all* questions), will accept certain general laws from which a formal logical consequence will be that conditions, A, in any other world in which they may be fulfilled will, those laws still obtaining, involve the happening of the event, B" (8.113).

Peirce distinguishes here in fact between the natural laws that are ultimately recognized and the contingent, antecedent conditions of possible, predictable causal processes. This distinction is the basis both for the difference between "would be" and "will be" and for the real—not just logical—possibility of eliminating this difference. If Peirce's pragmatic maxim is interpreted along these lines, then in my view it must be possible to take a statement about the temperature of the interior of the sun, whose verification must be considered in our world to be impossible, and nonetheless see it in relationship to possible experience and so as meaningful. Even the sentence "The planets will continue their revolution even after all consciousness has been extinguished" must prove to be meaningful in this way. The belief that the movement of the planets takes place independently of the empirically discernible existence of human consciousness complies with a general natural law which should hold for both our world, where the conditions for its observation are given, and the imagined world without consciousness. See below, Chap. 8, Sec. C.

22. 8.44. Cf. 1.405. But see also below, this chapter, about the different place given to "regulative principles" in Kant and in Peirce.

23. See 5.357, 2.652–55, and the essay "Evolutionary Love" (1893; 6.287 ff.). On this essay see below, this chapter. See also the Royce review from 1900, esp. 8.105.

24. These include (1) "The Architecture of Theories," Jan. 1891 (6.7–34); (2) "The Doctrine of Necessity Examined," Apr. 1892 (6.35–65); (3) "The Law of Mind," July 1892 (6.102–63); (4) "Man's Glassy Essence," Oct. 1892 (6.238–71); and (5) "Evolutionary Love," Jan. 1893 (6.287–317). In addition, there is Peirce's very revealing reply to Carus, the editor of *The Monist*: "Reply to the Necessitarians," July 1893 (6.588–618).

25. See *Collected Papers*, 8, pp. 278–80, for a description of the "Grand Logic"; on the "Search for a Method" see p. 280, and on the "Principles" see pp. 282–86.

26. W. B. Gallie calls it the "white elephant" of Peirce's philosophy. See his *Peirce and Pragmatism* (New York: Dover, 1966). Cf. also Murray Murphey, "On Peirce's Metaphysics," *Transactions of the Charles S. Peirce Society* 1, no. 1 (1965): 12 ff.

27. 1.129; Cf. above, Chap. 1, n. 36.

28. In a fragment from 1903 (6.6) Peirce presents a catalogue of questions that in his opinion metaphysics has to answer. Several of these, e.g., the question whether space and time have a limit, can also be found in the catalogue of supposedly meaningless questions that P. W. Bridgeman, the founder of Operationalism, brought together in his *Logic of Modern Physics*, pp. 30–31.

29. See Karl-Otto Apel, "Heideggers philosophische Radikalisierung der Hermeneutik und die Frage nach dem Sinnkriterium der Sprache," in *Transformation der Philosophie*, 1:276–334.

30. See Herbert Marcuse's critique of "one dimensional philosophy" in his *One Dimensional Man* (Boston: Beacon Press, 1964), Chap. 7. Marcuse's critique does not do justice, however, to the positive significance of Wittgenstein's critique of meaning.

31. On this see Thomas S. Kuhn, *The Structure of Scientific Revolutions*, International Encyclopedia of Unified Science, vol. 2, no. 2 (Chicago: University of Chicago Press, 1962). In addition, see Stephen Toulmin, *Foresight and Understanding* (Cambridge: Cambridge University Press, 1961).

32. See above, Chap. 6, beginning.

33. See above, Chap. 3, Sec. B.

34. Hence, Peirce could write in 1896: "Metaphysics consists in the results of the absolute acceptance of logical principles not merely as regulatively valid, but as truths of being. Accordingly, it is to be assumed that the universe has an explanation, the function of which, like that of every logical explanation, is to unify its observed variety" (1.487).

35. This makes passages like the following one more understandable: "In that way, if we think that some questions are never going to get settled, we ought to admit that our conception of nature as absolutely real is only partially correct" (8.43). In contrast to the passage I criticized above (this section), Peirce's concern here is not so much that reality is conceived as depending upon actually being known, the way it is in nominalistic Idealism, as that we must regard the completion or perfection of the world through knowledge as uncertain.

36. See above, Chap. 4, Sec. A. James arrives in 1896 at the existential Pragmatism of his *Will to Believe*, which follows ideas of Peirce's from 1869, while Peirce transforms his logical Socialism during the third period of his thought into evolutionary "Agapism."

37. Cf. above, Chap. 6, Secs. A, B, and C, on the opposition of Peirce and Hegel.

38. See Murphey, "On Peirce's Metaphysics." Murphey regards Phenomenology—and on this point his view agrees with Kempski's—as an analogous attempt to demonstrate the universal and necessary validity of the cate-

gories inductively, in this case by means of an inductive investigation of all merely possible experience.

39. See Karl-Otto Apel, "From Kant to Peirce," in *Towards a Transformation of Philosophy*, pp. 77–92.

40. See above, Chap. 6, Sec. A and Sec. B.

41. 6.10. Cf. 6.50, 5.47 and 5.173, 5.445 and 5.498, 5.586, 5.591, 5.603, and 1.118.

42. Cf. C. F. von Weizsäcker's formulation: "Mankind is earlier than natural science, but nature is earlier than mankind."

43. This kind of problem is the subject of discussion today, e.g., in the controversy in the philosophy of language between supporters of the relativistic Sapir-Whorff thesis about linguistic world views and those upholding the postulate of syntactic-semantic "universals" in Chomsky's generative grammar.

44. According to Phillip Wiener, Peirce was the first to have analyzed the relationship between the statistical methods used in theory formation in nineteenth-century physics, sociology, and economics on the one hand and Darwin's idea of "chance variations" on the other. In 1909 the aged Peirce wrote: "Anyone who is old enough, as I am, to have been acquainted with the spirit and habits of science before 1860, must admit that . . . the work of elevating the character of science that has been achieved by a simple principle of probability has been truly stupendous" (as quoted in Wiener, *Evolution and the Founders of Pragmatism*, p. 82).

45. 6.12. Like Marx and Engels, Peirce, Schelling, and Darwin went beyond Hegel in the historicization of nature and in this way arrived, along with Peirce's contemporary Croce, at a kind of "absolute Historicism."

46. See Wiener, *Evolution and the Founders of Pragmatism*, pp. 70 ff.

47. See 6.553: "The endless variety in the world has not been created by law. It is not the nature of uniformity to originate variation, nor of law to beget circumstance. When we gaze upon the multifariousness of nature, we are looking straight into the face of a living spontaneity." Cf. 6.47 ff.

48. Peirce falsely identifies these processes with those that are subject to the law of the conservation of energy, and attempts to confront them with irreversible processes, in the sense of the second principle of thermodynamics. See 6.14, 6.69 f, 6.101, 6.213, 6.261, 6.275, 6.298, and 6.316.

49. In his controversy with the editor of *The Monist*, Carus, Peirce himself raises the objection that "from mere nonlaw nothing necessarily follows, and therefore nothing can be explained" (6.606). His answer to this difficulty is: ". . . the *existence* of absolute chance, as well as many of its characters, are not themselves absolute chances, or sporadic events, unsubject to general law. On the contrary, these things *are* general laws. Everybody is familiar with the fact that chance has laws, and that statistical results follow therefrom. . . . I only propose to explain the regularities of nature as consequences of the only uniformity, or general fact, there was in the chaos, namely, the general absence of any determinate law" (6.606). Cf. 6.63.

50. See 6.191 ff. At the beginning of his third *Monist* essay, Peirce comments with irony:
I may mention . . . that I was born and reared in the neighborhood of Concord . . . at that time when Emerson, Hedge, and their friends were disseminating the ideas that they had caught from Shelling, and Shelling from Plotinus, from Boehm, or from God knows what minds stricken with the monstrous mysticism of the East. But the atmosphere of Cambridge held many an antiseptic against Concord transcendentalism; and I am not conscious of having any of that virus. Nevertheless, it is probable that some

cultured bacilli, some benignant form of the disease was implanted in my soul, unawares, and that now, after long incubation, it comes to the surface, modified by mathematical conceptions and by training in physical investigations. [6.102]

Peirce does not mention here his attraction to the speculative religious works of Henry James the elder, which were greatly influenced by Böhme and Swedenborg. See 6.287, 6.507, 5.402 n. 3.

51. See 6.23. Peirce responds in terms of this metalaw to Carus's objection "that absolute chance could not beget order." According to Peirce: ". . . the tendency to take habits, being itself a habit has *eo ipso* a tendency to grow; so that only a slightest germ is needed. A realist, such as I am, can find no difficulty in the production of that first infinitesimal germ of habit-taking by chance, provided that he thinks chance could act at all" (6.612). Cf. 6.259–63. Cf. also below, this section n. 63.

52. Despite all his admiration for the ingenious simplicity of the logical structure of Darwin's theory, Peirce called it the "Gospel of Greed" (6.294). He also offered the following ideological critique: "*The Origin of Species* of Darwin merely extends politico-economic views of progress to the entire realm of animal and vegetable life" (6.293). On the other theories of evolution see 6.16–17, 6.29 ff., 1.103–4, and 1.173–74.

53. 6.102 ff. Cf. 6.21 ff. and above, Chap. 7, Sec. B, n. 24.

54. See the final essay of the *Monist* series from 1893, "Evolutionary Love," esp. 6.296–307.

55. 6.306. This is preceded by Peirce's reference to a learning theory that would have to integrate "tychastic" and "anacastic" development of thought (on the basis of chance spontaneity and conditioning by means of inner and outer forces) in the sense of agapastic insight; cf. 6.301 ff.

56. See esp. "The Law of Mind," 6.103 and 6.152.

57. See 6.215 ff., 6.265, 6.490, and 6.612–13. The interrelationship among cosmogonic aspects of Firstness—such as matter as possibility, freedom, spontaneity, or nothingness as the possibility of being, which characterizes the beginning as well as the open future of the world—makes a point that can be found in Heidegger's late philosophy or, on the other hand, in Ernst Bloch's quasi-materialistic ontology of the "not yet."

58. In "Man's Glassy Essence" (1892) Peirce writes: "Wherever chance—spontaneity is found, there in the same proportion feeling exists. In fact, chance is but the outward aspect of that which within itself is feeling" (6.265). In 1898 he says: ". . . the zero of bare possibility, by evolutionary logic, leapt into the *unit* of some quality" (6.220). Peirce interprets this leap into "quali-consciousness" as nature's first hypothetic inference (6.220–21). The cosmogonic function of this "quale-consciousness," described as being incomparably intensive, recalls Böhme's *Qualen* or *Qualgeister*.

59. 6.196 ff. Peirce is indebted here not only to Böhme and Shelling, but in particular to Duns Scotus, for whom the nature of things, which are universal in the mind, is "contracted" by God's will in the *haecceitas* of the existing particular thing so that they attain individuality. See 8.18 and 8.208.

60. 6.25. Cf. 6.101, 6.158, 6.261, 6.264 ff., and 6.605.

61. See 6.265. In line with this second approach to the theory of evolution, Peirce expresses an idea that Bergson was later to work out in a similar form: "The development of the human mind has practically extinguished all [original] feelings, except a few sporadic kinds, sound, colors, smells, warmth, etc." (6.132; cf. 6.197, 1.312).

62. See, e.g., Julian Huxley, *Evolution in Action* (London: Harper, 1953).

63. The paradoxes of infinity emerge here, of course, as they do in all of Peirce's other visions of the future. The problem here, like that of whether in the long run the number of questions or of answers will increase with greater rapidity, is how "habits" are ever supposed to overtake the emergence of original potential feeling—such as doubt or wonder. Here, evidently, we need to find out which of the two aspects of evolution is to be the "regulative principle" of praxis. But this is not an easy matter for the individual, in his situation, to decide, nor is it easy for society.

64. Murphey is without doubt correct in including him among those nineteenth-century thinkers who wanted to reconcile science and religion. See Murray G. Murphey, "Kant's Children: The Cambridge Pragmatists," *Transactions of the Charles S. Peirce Society* 4 (1968): 3 ff.

65. In the foregoing I have paid little attention to Peirce's excurses into mathematics and the exact sciences; even in his metaphysics, these are never lacking.

Chapter 8

1. See Peirce's reply to James dated Mar. 13, 1897 (8.249–52) and his critical remarks in 5.3.

2. *University of California Chronicle* (1898), reprinted in James, *Pragmatism*, pp. 255–70.

3. Cf. above, Chap. 5.

4. Cf. above, Chap 5.

5. 5.589. Peirce seems to forget here that he himself had once identified truth with belief that could not in practice be doubted. On this see below, Chap. 8, Sec. C.

6. See, e.g., Carl G. Hempel, *Aspects of Scientific Explanation* (New York: Macmillan, 1965). See also Wolfgang Stegmüller, *Probleme und Resulte der Wissenschaftstheorie und Analytischen Philosophie*, 2 vols. (Berlin, Heidelberg, and New York: Springer Verlag, 1969), vol. 1.

7. See esp. above, Chap. 6, Sec. D, about the implications of the triadic sign relation for the philosophy of science.

8. The fact is that a "pragmatically" useful explanation in the context of a school classroom, for example, is one that is relevant to the students' amount of knowledge and their level of problem awareness, but this is irrelevant to the philosophy of science. It is an entirely different question, however, whether the concept of explanation that is relevant to the philosophy of science does not imply a relation to a real subject, such as in the sense of the "community of investigators."

9. See Peirce's letter to James from Nov. 25, 1902, where he refers to this supplemental part of his system, which was still missing in 1898 (8.255). Cf. the introduction to the Pragmatism lecture of 1903 (5.34 ff.).

10. He made this claim only after he had reconfirmed through James that he, Peirce, and not James had first used the term "Pragmatism." See above, Chapter 5, n. 5.

11. But in 1905 Peirce would take back this 1902 criticism that the pragmatic maxim expressed a stoic principle, a criticism he then termed "mistaken" in the direction of James's interpretation. See 5.402, n. 3.

12. 5.3. Cf. above, Chap. 6, Sec. A.

13. See L. K. Kronecker, *Grundzüge einer arithmetischen Theorie der algebra-*

ischen Grössen (Berlin, 1882), sec. 4, and "Ueber den Zahlbegriff," in *Philosophische Aufsätze: Eduard Zeller zu seinem 50 jährigen Doktor-Jubiläum* (Leipzig, 1887).

14. See L. E. J. Brouwer, "On the Foundations of Mathematics" (1907), in *Collected Works*, vol. 1, *Philosophy and Foundations of Mathematics*, ed. A. Heyting (Amsterdam and Oxford: North-American Pub. Co.; New York: American Elsevier Pub. Co., 1975), pp. 13–101.

15. On this see J. Klüver, *Operationalismus* (Stuttgart-Bad Cannstadt: Frommann-Holzboog, 1971).

16. See Murphey, *Development*, chap. 13. In Peirce's 1893 advertisement of his planned twelve-volume work, "Principles of Philosophy," the fourth volume bears the title "Plato's World: An Elucidation of the Ideas of Modern Mathematics." see *Collected Papers*, 7, p. 284.

17. Murphey, *Development*, pp. 286–87.

18. See, however, 5.505 and 5.448, where Peirce defines the general as the objectively indeterminate and, to that extent, as that to which the principle of the excluded middle cannot be applied.

19. In fact, it would also contradict everything that Peirce says about the possibility of mathematical and logical discoveries using diagrammatic observation. See above, Chap. 6, Sec. A and Chap. 6, Sec. D.

20. See below, Chap. 8, Sec. C.

21. 5.542. Cf. 5.461. In 1901 Peirce had combined a corresponding interpretation of the statement "Caesar crosses the Rubicon" with a reference to the fact that the pragmatic explication of meaning by means of possible experience does justice to the meaning-critical definition of reality, if this experience is conceived as temporally unlimited (5.565). Some astonishing illustrations have recently been provided of the ways in which methods of natural science might be used to confirm historical information. For example, the work of the biochemist Margaret Oakley Dayhoff makes it seem possible for us one day to reconstruct the genetic code of prehistoric animals long extinct and, from this, to reconstruct the environment to which they were adapted. See Hoimar v. Ditfurth, "Nichts ist endgültig vorüber," *Die Zeit*, Sept. 12, 1969.

22. See John L. Austin, "Performative-Constative" in *Philosophy and Ordinary Language*, ed. Charles E. Caton (Urbana: University of Illinois Press, 1963), pp. 22–33.

23. Effective self-reflection is, of course, not to be confused with metatheoretical self-objectification, which Peirce, as a logician, declares to be impossible (5.86). Peirce gives as little thought to this difference as has modern logistically oriented semantics. Modern semantics, since Russell's theory of types and Wittgenstein's *Tractatus*, has considered philosophical reflection on language and the subject using language, along with metatheoretical self-objectification, to be taboo as topics. See Karl-Otto Apel, "Sprache und Reflexion," *Akten des XIV. Kongress für Philosophie*, vol. 3, Vienna, 1969, pp. 417 ff.

24. Cf. above, Chap. 5.

25. See above, Chap. 3, Sec. C.e. Cf. 5.170, where Peirce, of course, no longer refers to the transcendental framework of the theory of induction given in 1869 and 1878.

26. See above, Chap. 6, Sec. B.

27. See above, Chap. 6, Sec. B.

28. See 5.170–71. Cf., however, 5.201 ff. On this see also below, Chap. 8, Sec. B.

29. See above, Chap. 6, Sec. A.

30. See above, Chap. 6, Sec. B.
31. Cf. in this regard the neopositivistic aporia of such protocol or basic sentences as "Here is a piece of chalk." With the help of his logic of relations, Peirce goes much further than does the modern theory of dispositional concepts. In 5.157, e.g., he shows that the perceptual report "Event C *appears to be* subsequent to another event A" can be interpreted by means of the conclusion that if A follows B, then C must also follow B. Therefore, the general predicate "to be subsequent" in the particular proposition "C seems to be subsequent to A" can be interpreted by means of the universal proposition "Whatever is subsequent to C is subsequent to anything, A, to which C is subsequent." For the logic of relations even the proposition "Tully is Cicero" contains a general predicate which can be explicated by means of a conditional statement, because "Tully is Cicero" predicates the general relation of identity of Tully and Cicero (see 5.151). Peirce paraphrases the content of the second cotary proposition in terms of this explication of the predicates of perceptual judgments, using the logic of relations, when he says, "Thirdness pours in upon us through every avenue of sense" (5.157; cf. 5.150).
32. Peirce himself recognizes "that we perceive, or seem to perceive, objects differently from how they really are, accommodating them to their manifest intentions" (5.185).
33. 5.467. In 1902, on the other hand, Peirce had attempted with the aid of the pragmatic maxim to interpret the sentence "This wafer looks red." However, in doing so he arrived not at an explication of the concept "red," but only at an operative instruction for future confirmations of this perceptual judgment, which itself cannot be further explicated (5.544).
34. Leo Weisgerber, *Vom Weltbild der deutschen Sprache*, Vol. 2 (Düsseldorf: Schwann, 1950), pp. 140–41.
35. The tacit presupposition in the clarification of meaning seems to me also to constitute the point of the seemingly trivial definition schema which Tarski takes as the basis for his semantic clarification of the concept of truth: "The sentence: 'The facts of the matter are so and so' is true if and only if the facts of the matter are so and so." It follows naturally that the semantic clarification of the concept of truth utilizing formalized languages has always already presupposed a "pragmatic" clarification of the concept of truth as Peirce conceived it. Here Peirce expresses the relationship between the interpretation of meaning and the recognition of truth or falsity by means of uncriticizable perceptual judgments: "A false proposition is a proposition of which some interpretant represents that, on an occasion which it indicates, a percept will have a certain character, while the immediate perceptual judgment on that occasion is that the percept has not that character. A true proposition is a proposition belief in which would never lead to such disappointment so long as the proposition is not understood otherwise than it was intended" (5.569).
36. This theory presupposes, as I have already indicated (Chap. 6, Sec. B), that sensory qualities are not merely subjective, i.e., readily interchangeable vehicles of information, but rather a kind of iconic limiting case of information utilizing the symbolic interpretation of nature. Peirce himself says this in 1903 (see 5.115–19). In 1906, however, Peirce would appear to have fallen back into regarding them as he had done in 1868, taking color qualities to be "mere subjective feelings" whose special character is completely irrelevant to the argumentative process of information (5.467).
37. See below, Chap. 8, Sec. C.

38. On this see also the metaphor at the end of the lecture in which Peirce summarizes the point of the cotary propositions in relation to Pragmatism: "The elements of every concept enter into logical thought at the gate of perception and make their exit at the gate of purposive action; and whatever cannot show its passports at both those two gates is to be arrested as unauthorized by reason" (5.212).

39. On the following see Josiah Royce, *The Problem of Christianity*, vol. 2 (New York: Macmillan, 1918), pp. 146 ff.

40. This aspect of the circular, correlative, conditional nature of interpretation and the experimental testing of hypotheses or theories becomes particularly relevant if a surprising result of the experiments—a falsification of the presupposed interpretation of the hypothesis—demands an innovative abduction combined with a new interpretation of those basic concepts of theories which, according to Peirce, possess a high degree of vagueness because they are "anthropomorphic" and instinctlike. See 5.446 on the vagueness of "common-sense" concepts. This, for Peirce the most interesting function of abduction, leads to new ideas and evidently falls outside the methodological framework of logically controllable inference processes (deduction, induction, abduction)—not because it represents the transition from abduction to uncriticizable, perceptual judgments, but rather because it makes use of the function of *interpretation*, which Peirce mixes together in the concept of abduction with that of *explanation*. On this see Habermas, *Knowledge and Human Interests*, p. 396, n. 30. [The author's view of this question is now available in Karl-Otto Apel, *Die Erklären: Verstehen-Kontroverse* (Frankfurt am Main: Suhrkamp, 1979)—Trans.]

41. See below. Cf. pt. 3 of Apel, "Scientism or Transcendental Hermeneutics?" in *Towards a Transformation of Philosophy*.

42. He also goes beyond the position on induction that he had advocated in earlier lectures (5.170 ff.). Cf. below, this chapter.

43. In 1901 Peirce had attempted in Baldwin's *Dictionary* to define the concept of truth, giving attention to the fundamental Fallibilism of all hypotheses of which we can predicate truth at all. There he wrote: "Truth is the concordance of an abstract statement with the ideal limit towards which endless investigation would tend to bring scientific belief, which concordance the abstract statement may possess by virtue of the confession of its inaccuracy and one-sidedness, and this confession is an essential ingredient of truth" (5.565).

44. See Murphey, *Development*, pp. 282 ff.

45. The third position is evidently without the second position's critical restrictions concerning imprecision as they were expressed in particular in his 1901 definition of truth. Cf. above, n. 43 to this chapter.

46. See 6.121: ". . . the distinction between a continuous and a discontinuous series is manifestly non-metrical." Cf. 1.276: ". . . years do not *constitute* the flow of time, but only *measure* that flow." Cf. also 5.181.

47. Peirce deals with this aporia in what follows as if it arose for every statement of law. Here it would be possible to counter that Popper's falsification theory, which is explicitly conceived not to be an inductive theory, can indeed generally serve to refute statements of law definitively by means of statements of existence. Of course, Peirce evidently no longer thinks of testing by means of falsification; he now concentrates, in a way that is in line with his presuppositions on the theory of induction, on the notion that the reality of a law must clearly show itself in the continuity of lawful behavior. See below, this chapter.

48. 5.204. Cf. 5.32. Comparison of these paragraphs seems to indicate that Peirce had in mind primarily Newcomb "and all mathematicians of his rather antiquated fashion" as representatives of the fourth position. Peirce's theory of the continuum was also directed against Cantor and Dedekind, insofar as they denied that a linear set of points can be a geometrical continuum. See Murphey, *Development*, pp. 281 ff.

49. 5.205. Cf. 5.210 and, for a more exact exposition, 8.123, n. 20. This could be compared to William James's doctrine of the experience of relations, especially the stream of consciousness first presented in his *Principles of Psychology* (1890) and in Henri Bergson's *Essai sur les donnés immediates de la conscience* (Paris, 1898). Corresponding to these philosophies of continuity is a thesis on mathematics that Bernhard Riemann presented in an 1854 paper: "On the Hypotheses Which Lie at the Basis of Geometry," trans. W. K. Clifford, *Nature* 8 (May 1873):14–17, 36–37. According to Riemann, in a continuous manifold, the basis of its measurability must come from outside. Peirce recognized Riemann as *"the* highest authority upon the philosophy of geometry." See Murphey, *Development*, pp. 219 ff., 285. In physics we might think here of Maxwell's theory of continuous fields, which Peirce seems to not have interpreted, even though it corresponded to the spirit of his Synechism. See ibid., p. 391, n. 11.

50. In his 1891 review (8.55–89) of this work, however, Peirce energetically defends against James his thesis that perception is unconscious inference, but he praises James's commentary about the "stream of thought" (8.89).

51. 5.212. Cf. above, Chap. 8, Sec. B.

52. See 5.205. Cf. 5.181, 5.209, and 5.436, where he says: "Continuity is simply what generality becomes in the logic of relatives."

53. This recalls Schelling's dictum: "Nature is visible mind; mind is invisible nature."

54. Cf. 5.312 and 8.14; cf. also above, Chap. 3, Sec. B. Peirce does not drop this meaning-critical theory, but rather advocates it later as the framework in which to argue for a thoroughgoing realist theory of universals. See, e.g., 5.434.

55. See above.

56. On the corresponding ontological "problem of the principle of individuation" see 5.107.

57. In Peirce's modal ontology possibility represents Firstness, actuality Secondness, and necessity Thirdness. But Peirce had already drawn attention in his Royce review (8.43) to the fact that "real possibility" is stronger than mere logical possibility because the former implies a law, i.e., Thirdness. Therefore, real possibility's categorial structure corresponds to that of anticipatory perceptual understanding, no matter whether this is directed to the realization of a natural law or to "the conformity of action to general intentions" (5.212). Cf. 5.107: "Analogy suggests that the laws of nature are ideas or resolutions in the mind of some vast consciousness." On this see below, Chap. 8, Sec. C.

58. See 5.119 and above, Chap. 6, Sec. B on the revision of the semiotic foundations of the logic of inquiry.

59. Peirce comments in a letter to Mrs. Ladd-Franklin dated Oct. 20, 1904 that "In the spring of 1903 I was invited by the influence of James, Royce, and Münsterberg, to give a course of lectures in Harvard University on Pragmatism. I had intended to print them; but James said he could not understand them himself and could not recommend their being printed. I do not myself think there is any difficulty in understanding them, but all modern

psychologists are so soaked with sensationalism that they can not understand anything that does not mean that, and mistranslate into the ideas of Wundt whatever one says about logic." As published in Christine Ladd-Franklin, "Charles S. Peirce at the Johns Hopkins University," *The Journal of Philosophy* 13 (1916):719–20.

60. See 5.464–573 and 5.555–64.
61. See 5.28. In 1898 this theory was evidently so alien to him that he attributed it not to himself, but to William James's *Will to Believe*, while conceiving his own logic of inquiry as a theory of "eternal truths." See above, Chap. 8, Sec. A.
62. On this and what follows see above, Chap. 4, Sec. B.a.
63. See Gadamer, *Truth and Method*, part two, sec. II.
64. Here Peirce's thought meets with R. G. Collingwood's conception of "absolute presuppositions" of thought which must be accepted "without question," and with Heidegger's thesis of thought's "place in the history of being." On this see J. Brühing, "R. G. Collingwood und das Problem des Historismus" (diss., University of Kiel, 1969); and Otto Pöggeler, "Metaphysik und Seinstopik bei Heidegger," *Philosophisches Jahrbuch* 70 (1962):118–37. On the subject of human nature see 5.419.
65. 5.416. In a fragment from the same year Peirce admits that "while holding certain propositions to be each individually perfectly certain, we may and ought to think it likely that some one of them, if not more, is false" (5.498). He bases the possibility of maintaining this critical perspective in regard to one's own beliefs on the fact that such immediate certainty is something vague, and thus is an "instance of the vague's emancipation from the principle of contradiction" (5.498 n).
66. Cf. the definition of truth from 1901 quoted in n. 43 to this chapter.
67. 5.419. Cf. 5.498. There Peirce reminds himself of his 1868 conviction that "man possess[es] no infallible introspective power into the secrets of his own heart, to know just what he believes and what he doubts."
68. See Helmut Plessner, *Die Stufen des Organischen und der Mensch* (Berlin and Leipzig: Walter de Gruyter, 1928), chap. 7.
69. In 1898 Peirce even brought this point from James's *Will to Believe* to bear on the scientist's fallibilistic attitude. See above, Chap. 8, Sec. A.
70. Peirce arrives at a similar distinction when he writes: "Neither the philosophy of Common-Sense nor the man who holds it accepts any belief *on the ground* that it has not been criticized. . . . But it is quite true that the Common-sensist like everybody else, the Criticist included, believes propositions *because* they have not been criticized . . ." (5.523). Cf. 5.563.
71. 5.416–17. Whoever wants to use Pragmatism to clarify the meaning of the predicate "hard" must make thought experiments with scratchable objects. But whoever wants to clarify the meaning of the predicate "true" must make thought experiments with beliefs, beliefs that could be upheld by an individual in his finite existence, by a society in its historical situation, or by the unlimited community of scientists. This distinction reveals three possible types of pragmatic theories of truth, those of James, of Dewey, and of Peirce.
72. 5.416. Cf. the more exacting definition from 1903, 5.375 n. 2, which introduces the possible, practical confirmation of a belief as the criterion of their possible fixation. On this see above, Chap. 4, Sec. B.a.
73. The text shows, however, that where Peirce discusses possible human self-control (5.418), he is able to conceive the problem of reflection as a psychological one only in the sense of endless iteration or in the sense of the

unending movement towards the limit of absolute certainty. That is, he does not think of reflection as the *elevation* of oneself *to a higher level*, where one may see through the "and so on" of iteration and discern a higher level of generality than is present in one's own claim to possess philosophical knowledge. This dialectical point appears, however, to be intelligible now, in the age of metatheory discussion, only to a number of Neo-Hegelians. For a discussion of this idea see Theodor Litt, *Denken und Sein* (Stuttgart: Hirzel, 1948), and *Mensch und Welt*, 2d ed. (Heidelberg: Quelle und Meyer, 1961).

74. 5.421. Cf. the *locus classicus*, 5.311. The text from 1903 reveals that Peirce gave a metaphysical turn to his 1868 idea of logical Socialism by conceiving a growing integration of individuals and different peoples by means of the "continuity of mind" and "agapastic development" as leading to a cosmic, collective person, i.e., God. See 6.271 and 6.307.

75. On this see below.

76. See 5.424. With the very characteristic expression "quasi-external act" Peirce touches upon a problem in so-called Operationalism that has not yet been fully resolved. It has a parallel in Marxism in the equally unresolved problem of subjective and objective praxis. The question is whether the act of observation and measurement is a mental act of cognition, understandable as something intentional, or whether it is itself an observable and measurable natural occurrence, or whether it is both. In the preface to the *Critique of Pure Reason* Kant wrote this somewhat strange sentence: "Reason, holding in one hand its principles . . . and in the other hand the experiment . . . must approach nature . . ." p. 20 (B XIII). Yet Kant's critique of reason investigated only the a priori of reason (cf., however, above, n. 41). It did not provide an examination of the a priori of the body (*Leibapriori*) by means of which reason can approach nature holding its experiment in its *hand*. Modern Operationalism tends, on the other hand, to open up the problem in the other direction by absolutizing the "external" side of the experimenter's action in a behavioristic manner. See above, Chap. 1. [Apel explains his idea of the "a priori of the body" in his paper "Das Leibapriori der Erkenntnis," *Archiv für Philosophie* 12 (1963):152–72—Trans.]

77. See above, Chap. 1.

78. See 5.427 ff. The modernity of this theory is supposed to lie in the fact that it provides an "experimental proof," i.e., support by means of the theory of induction, for assuming the reality of universals (5.430). The pragmatic maxim's task in showing the possibility of such proof is to use the logic of relations to explicate the meaning of universals, utilizing "if . . . then" propositions and, hence, explicating universals in terms of modal ontology.

79. See above.

80. 5.491. Peirce was to formulate this point concerning his semiotic Pragmatism in a clearer way in a letter to James in 1909: "The Final Interpretant does not consist in the way in which any mind does act but in the way in which every mind would act. . . : 'If so and so were to happen to any mind this sign would determine that mind to such and such *conduct*.' By 'conduct' I mean *action* under an intention of self-control. No event that occurs to any mind, no action of any mind can constitute the truth of that conditional proposition" (8.315).

81. See above, Chap. 6, Sec. A. Cf. also 5.431 about the real, physical efficiency of ideas such as justice and truth.

82. See 5.430 and 5.433. Cf. 5.3, 5.133, and 5.402 n. On this see above, Chap. 6, Sec. A.

83. See above, Chap. 6, Sec. B.

84. See the discussion of this model of Pragmatism in Jürgen Habermas, "The Scientization of Politics and Public Opinion," in his *Towards a Rational Society*, trans. Jeremy J. Shapiro (Boston: Beacon Press, 1970), pp. 62–80. Cf. also, Karl-Otto Apel, "Scientism or Transcendental Hermeneutics?" in *Towards a Transformation of Philosophy*.

85. I am referring here not to reciprocal actions between objects, but to that agreement upon rules which is possible in intersubjective communication only in the sense of anticipated actions. George Herbert Mead was the first to have analyzed these in the context of American Pragmatism. See his posthumously published *Mind, Self, and Society*. In social philosophy and the philosophy of science Jürgen Habermas has contrasted the concept of intersubjective communication with that of work or, rather, experimental, technical behavior. See esp. "Arbeit und Interaktion" in Jürgen Habermas. *Technik und Wissenschaft als "Ideologie"* (Frankfurt am Main: Suhrkamp Verlag, 1968). Cf. also Karl-Otto Apel, "Scientism or Transcendental Hermeneutics?" in *Towards a Transformation of Philosophy*.

86. See above, Chap. 8, Sec. B.

87. See James, *The Will to Believe*, and *Pragmatism*, pp. 257 ff.

88. See James, *Pragmatism*, p. 201 and p. 218. Peirce, at the same time, passes over the problems that interest James, for example, when he discusses with irony James's thesis that cognition changes reality (5.555–56), whereby Peirce has in mind the meaning-critical definition of reality, according to which truth is to be obtained in the long run as the ultimate opinion of inquiry. It is correct that those repeatable, experimental interventions into reality which serve the cognition of laws independently of the act of knowing do not, collectively, change the reality that is to be known. This is also true, in my view, even of microphysical laws about the behavior of elementary particles, laws that can only be established statistically. This is the model that Peirce has in mind in his criticism of James. Yet we can also conceive of a completely different model, according to which knowledge that is existentially, historically, and practically relevant is dependent upon non-repeatable interventions into the reality that is to be known. Such an intervention is not subject to correction by statistical means. This is the model that James basically has in mind.

89. Cf. above, Chap. 3, Sec. C.e. and Chap. 6, Sec. A.

90. See above, Chap. 7, Sec. B. Cf. 5.384 n. 1. On this "Principle of Hope" see 5.357, 8.12–14, 5.402, 5.407–8, and 2.652–55. In these passages the concepts "reality," "truth," "unlimited community," "final opinion," "fate," "hope," "logic," and "ethics" form a characteristic interconnected whole. As such they mark out the existential origin and regulative principle of Peirce's philosophy. At the same time the principle of hope provides the guideline for this philosophy's development from a meaning-critical definition of reality in Kant's sense of a regulative principle of possible experience to a teleological metaphysics of evolution without an a priori guarantee.

91. In order to avoid any misunderstandings, let me state that even Karl Popper's philosophy of an "open society" that is to be created progressively is "historical" in the sense in which I use the term here. What is meant by an "open society" that is to be realized by common effort can be explicated as little for Popper as for Peirce by referring to the conditioned predictions, valid for everyone, of the possible results of social engineering. It can be clarified only by means of constantly renewed, open discussion and attempts to reach a communicative understanding concerning an unconditioned interest

in a goal, shared by various different individuals in a concrete historical situation. Popper's work *The Open Society and Its Enemies* is a hermeneutical and ideology-critical contribution to such a communicative understanding. Such a contribution has no place, of course, in the program of Scientism. On such a totalization, see Jean-Paul Sartre, *Search for a Method*, trans. Hazel E. Barnes (New York: Random House, Vintage Books, 1968).

92. On Critical Common-sensism see 5.439–52. This is supplemented by the fragments 5.497–99 and 5.523–25. On the realist theory of universals see 5.453 ff.

93. 8.43. See also above, Chap. 7, Sec. A.

94. See above, Chap. 7, Sec. B.

95. Cf. 8.104 and 8.113 ff., and n. 22 to Chap. 7.

96. See his footnotes to his essays from 1868–78.

97. Peirce translates the conditioned predictions here into hypothetical instructions for action. See 5.571 n, where he distinguishes among categorial resolutions, conditional resolutions, and conditional habits.

98. We should recall here that this modal ontology, seen from Peirce's perspective, is not a regression to pre-Kantian, dogmatic metaphysics, because the critique of meaning founds it on the inescapable presupposition of the possible truth of philosophical statements. This critique of meaning, in the sense of the semiotic transformation of Kant's critique of knowledge, also provided the first foundation of the realist theory of universals in 1868 and subsequent years. Seen from the viewpoint of the phenomenological doctrine of the categories, the real possibility or vagueness presupposed in counterfactual conditional propositions is an example of the Firstness of Thirdness, while the reality of law is seen as the Secondness of Thirdness. Finally, necessity in the sense of the lawful determination of the real is pure Thirdness. The hypothetical metaphysics of the 1890s was an attempt, based upon these presuppositions, to understand the evolution of the world in a synechistic fashion, conceiving it as a continuum reaching from the limiting case of the beginning of possibility as Nothing or chaos to the eschatological limiting case of the cosmos as crystallized. From the standpoint of Peirce's classification of the sciences, such an attempt goes beyond the ontology he founded upon the critique of meaning, yet it is called for by this classification as an attempt or hypothesis.

99. See above, Chap 4, Sec. C.

100. See the reproduction of the pragmatic maxim of 1878 (5.402) at the beginning of the 1905 article (5.438), which calls special attention to the derivations of "conceive" and so clearly shows its character as a thought experiment.

101. See esp. 5.403 and 5.409. Cf. also the prote-positivistic treatment of ontology in 5.411 and 5.423.

102. On the question of the return to ontology in the form of linguistic analysis, see in particular E. K. Specht, "Die sprachphilosophische und ontologische Grundlagen im Spätwerk Ludwig Wittgensteins," *Kantstudien*, supplementary no. 84 (Cologne: Kölner Universitäts Verlag, 1963), and *Sprache und Sein: Zur sprachanalytischen Grundlegung der Ontologie* (Berlin: Walter de Gruyter, 1967). In contrast to Peirce, however, Specht arrives at a nominalistic resolution of the problem of being. For the opposite position see Apel, "Heideggers philosophische Radikalisierung," in *Transformation der Philosophie*, 1:276–334.

103. See above, Chap. 3, Sec. A.

104. Jürgen Habermas has taken this point as the basis of his Peirce interpreta-

tion, conceiving this framework as a transcendental context for instrumental action and experiment. See *Knowledge and Human Interests,* chap. 6.

105. Transcendental Pragmatism's task of establishing meaning horizons can be understood, in terms of the meaning constitution involved, as a limiting case of the temporalization and spatialization of a world through human *Dasein,* in Heidegger's sense, as the locus of an understanding of Being. Unlike Habermas, however, I would not want to regard the Heideggerian "ontic-ontological" difference in an unaltered form as binding for Peirce's philosophy (see Habermas, *Knowledge and Human Interests,* pp. 131 f). To be specific, as I see the matter, there is an equivalent to Heidegger's ontic-ontological difference in Peirce, in the difference between the existing real as something we can experience by finding it resistant to our will and the interpretable reality of the real. But this means that Peirce's meaning-critical definition of reality in reference to possible experimental experience cannot itself be made relative within the framework of the concept of *reality,* but at most within the framework of *Being,* which is not subject just to experimental experience. Stated positively, under "reality" we must always understand the Being of beings insofar as they exist (as a virtual resistance to our will), i.e., as present for objectifying knowledge of how to make use of them. The "transcendental framework" of this Pragmatism is therefore not a horizon that can be made relative whenever we are concerned with the reality of the real. Rather, it is the only one that is meaning-critically acceptable. This is shown by every attempt to deny the existence of a real world or to reduce the reality of the real to fictions (see above, n. 21). For this reason I believe it is important to distinguish sharply between transcendental Pragmatism as meaning-critical Realism and every form of fictionalistic Pragmatism, such as those of Nietzsche or Vaihinger. The horizon of reference in goal-directed rationality does not serve for Peirce as the basis for a "nothing but" psychologistic reduction of truth in natural scientific knowledge. Instead, it is conceived to be an element that is a priori necessary for bringing about the only possible knowledge we can have of the real. Such knowledge must therefore be characterized as genuine knowledge resulting from Aristotelian curiosity and as a priori technologically relevant. This recognition does not in my view hinder Habermas's attempt to distinguish among different "Interests of knowledge." For as soon as we recognize science and its explanation by laws to be *the* true cognition of the real in its reality, we must also recognize that this knowledge presupposes an agreement on meaning, a communicative understanding, between human beings, and that even if this attempt to reach an understanding is conducted scientifically, it nonetheless does not follow the same interest of knowledge as science does. On this "complementarity" thesis see Apel, "Scientistics, Hermeneutics and the Critique of Ideology," in *Towards a Transformation of Philosophy.*

106. See above, Chap. 7, Sec. B.

107. Nor can this clarification be accomplished by "if . . . then" propositions conceived as material implications and capable of verification in the sense of truth-functional logic. The result would be paradoxes like the one that all counterfactual propositions about "conditional dispositions," as Peirce uses the phrase, would have to be regarded as true a priori, since material implications with false antecedents are true. In that case the statements "If the diamond had been tested, then it would have proven to be capable of being scratched" and "If the diamond had been tested, then it would *not* have proven to be capable of being scratched" would both be true, if their

"would-be" character were interpreted in the sense of material implication. From this it appears to follow that only by interpreting "if . . . then" propositions as counterfactual conditionals and assuming that it is possible in principle for their antecedents to be given will it be possible for us to make the point that statements about "conditional dispositions" remain true in cases when the antecedent conditions are missing and yet are nonetheless dependent upon the *real possibility* of their being given. On this aporia in the contemporary discussion of counterfactual conditional propositions see Wolfgang Stegmüller, *Probleme und Resulte der Wissenschaftstheorie*, 1: chap. 5.

108. 5.459. In fact Heidegger cannot avoid presupposing a certain objectivation in the sense of the "vulgar concept of time" in the "occurrence character" of "temporalization" and, later, in the "event [*Ereignis*]." This is tacitly reconfirmed in his later conception of the "history of Being," without his having conceptually mediated between temporality and time, historicity and history.

109. See the polemics against the practical irrelevance of metaphysical determination (5.459). In 1878 (5.403) he had, of course, argued in a similar way, but he had characterized the moral question whether I could "by an effort of the will, have resisted the temptation, and done otherwise" as not a question of fact, but simply a question of the "arrangement of facts," such as by means of language. This very modern-sounding suggestion to resolve the problem of free will by reducing metaphysical antinomies to differences within language games could be upheld by the later Peirce only in the sense that language games are not merely arbitrary verbal arrangements, but ways of conceiving Being and having a world that is possible in practice.

110. 5.462. Cf., however, 5.45 ff., 5.52, 5.57, 5.39, 8.282, and 8.266. In all of these parallel passages Peirce emphasizes the contemporaneous experience of both the ego and the non-ego, if not actual knowledge of them, in a situation of confrontation, surprise, or conflict. According to 8.282 (1904) we experience the difference between the inner and outer world immediately as one of a difference between past and present.

111. See Werner Heisenberg, *Physics and Philosophy* (New York: Harper & Row, 1962), pp. 115–16.

112. Ibid.

113. Ibid.

Chapter 9

1. Peirce's critique of meaning converges here with the justified intention of Herder's and, especially, of Hegel's metacritique of Kant's critique of knowledge.

2. An example of such a critique of tradition is Gerard Radnitzky's *Contemporary Schools of Metascience*.

3. See Apel, "Scientism or Transcendental Hermeneutics?" in *Towards a Transformation of Philosophy*.

4. See Karl-Otto Apel, "Die Erkenntnis-anthropologische Funktion der Kommunikationsgemeinschaft und die Grundlagen der Hermeneutik," in *Information und Kommunikation*, ed. Simon Moser (Munich and Vienna: Oldenberg, 1968), pp. 163–71.

5. For metaphysicians of cybernetics I should add that in the case of a complete simulation of a human being by computers we would have the tasks

of coming to a communicative understanding with the computers about the goals we are to set for praxis, of hermeneutically inquiring into their opinions, and, possibly, of subjecting them to ideological criticism. In this case in particular the program of Scientism would be pursued ad absurdum.

6. This example shows, incidentally, that the scientistic postulate of conceiving all "motives" as "causes," because we would have to assume motives for actions that have not taken place if we were to adopt a teleological interpretation, misses the knowledge interest of the interpretive (*verstehende*) sciences by a hairbreadth.

7. Cf. above, Chap. 1.

8. See also the devastating criticism of this pretension in orthodox Marxism developed in Karl Popper's *The Poverty of Historicism* (London: Routledge and Kegan Paul, 1957).

Selected Bibliography

Primary Sources

The Collected Papers of Charles Sanders Peirce. 8 vols. Vols. 1–6 edited by Charles Hartshorne and Paul Weiss. Vols. 7 and 8 edited by Arthur W. Burks. Cambridge, Mass.: Harvard University Press, 1931–1958.

The New Elements of Mathematics. Edited by Carolyn Eisele. 4 vols. The Hague: Mouton Publishers; Atlantic Highlands: Humanities Press, 1976.

Chance, Love and Logic. Edited by Morris R. Cohen. New York: George Braziller, 1956.

Charles S. Peirce: Über die Klarheit unserer Gedanken. Edited and translated by Klaus Oehler. Frankfurt am Main: Vittorio Klostermann, 1968.

Philosophical Writings of Peirce. Edited by Justus Buchler. 1940. Reprint New York: Dover Publications, 1955.

Schriften. Edited by Karl-Otto Apel. Translated by Gerd Wartenberg. 2 vols. Volume 1: *Zur Entstehung des Pragmatismus.* Volume 2: *Vom Pragmatismus zu Pragmatizismus.* Frankfurt am Main: Suhrkamp Verlag, 1967 and 1970.

Vorlesungen über den Pragmatismus. Edited and translated by Elizabeth Walther. Hamburg: Felix Meiner Verlag, 1973.

Secondary Sources

Apel, Karl-Otto. "Charles S. Peirce's and Jürgen Habermas' Consensus Theory of Truth." *Transactions of the Charles S. Peirce Society,* in press.

———. "Charles S. Peirce and the Post-Tarskian Problem of an Adequate Explication of the Meaning of Truth." *The Monist* 63:3 (1980), in press.

———. "Der semiotische Pragmatismus von C. S. Peirce und die 'Abstractive Fallacy' in den Grundlagen der Kantschen Erkenntnistheorie und der Carnapschen Wissenschaftslogik," in *bewußt sein, Festschrift für G. Funke,* edited by A. J. Bucher, H. Drüe, and Thomas Seebohm, pp. 49–58. Bonn: Bouvier Verlag, 1975.

———. *Transformation of Philosophy.* Trans. by Glyn Adey and David Frisby. London, Boston, and Henley: Routledge and Kegan Paul, 1980.

Bernstein, Richard J., ed. *Perspectives on Peirce*. New Haven and London: Yale University Press, 1965.

Buchler, Justus. *Charles S. Peirce's Empiricism*. New York: Harcourt, Brace & Co., 1939.

A Comprehensive Bibliography and Index of the Published Works of Charles Sanders Peirce, with a Bibliography of Secondary Studies. Greenwich: Johnson Associates, 1977.

Gallie, W. B. *Peirce and Pragmatism*. New York: Dover Publications, 1966.

Habermas, Jürgen. *Knowledge and Human Interests*. Translated by Jeremy J. Shapiro. Boston: Beacon Press, 1971.

Kempski, Jürgen von. *Peirce und der Pragmatismus*. Stuttgart and Cologne: Kohlhammer Verlag, 1952.

Moore, Edward C. *American Pragmatism: Peirce, James, Dewey*. New York: Columbia University Press, 1961.

Moore, Edward C., and Robin, Richard. *Studies in the Philosophy of Charles Sanders Peirce*, second series. Amherst: The University of Massachusetts Press, 1964.

Murphey, Murray G. *The Development of Peirce's Philosophy*. Cambridge, Mass.: Harvard University Press, 1961.

Peirce Studies. Institute for Studies in Pragmaticism. Lubbock: Texas Tech University Press, 1979ff.

Robin, Richard. *Annotated Catalogue of the Papers of Charles Sanders Peirce*. Amherst: University of Massachusetts Press, 1967.

Transactions of the Charles S. Peirce Society. 1965ff.

Wenneberg, Hjalmar. *The Pragmatism of C. S. Peirce: An analytical study*. Lund and Copenhagen, 1962.

Wiener, Philip. *Evolution and the Founders of Pragmatism*. Cambridge, Mass.: Harvard University Press, 1952.

Wiener, Philip, and Young, F. H., eds. *Studies in the Philosophy of Charles Sanders Peirce*. Cambridge: Harvard University Press, 1952.

Name Index

Library of Congress Cataloging in Publication Data
Apel, Karl Otto.
    Charles S. Peirce : from pragmatism to
pragmaticism.
    Translation of Der Denkweg von Charles S. Peirce.
    Bibliography: p.
    Includes index.
    1. Peirce, Charles Sanders, 1839–1914.
2. Pragmatism.   I. Title.
B945.P44A7513   191   81–3337
ISBN 0–87023–177–4   AACR2